the
Incas

Incas

The Peoples of America

General Editors: Alan Kolata and Dean Snow

This series is about the native peoples and civilizations of the Americas, from their origins in ancient times to the present day. Drawing on archaeological, historical, and anthropological evidence, each volume presents a fresh and absorbing account of a group's culture, society, and history.

Accessible and scholarly, and well illustrated with maps and photographs, the volumes of *The Peoples of America* will together provide a comprehensive and vivid picture of the character and variety of the societies of the American past.

Already published:

The Tiwanaku: A Portrait of an Andean Civilization
Alan Kolata

The Timucua
Jerald T. Milanich

The Aztecs (Second Edition)
Michael E. Smith

The Cheyenne
John Moore

The Iroquois
Dean Snow

The Incas
Terence N. D'Altroy

The Nasca
Helaine Silverman and Donald A. Proulx

The Sioux
Guy Gibbon

the

Incas

Terence N. D'Altroy

Blackwell
Publishing

BLACKWELL PUBLISHING
350 Main Street, Malden, MA 02148-5020, USA
9600 Garsington Road, Oxford OX4 2DQ, UK
550 Swanston Street, Carlton, Victoria 3053, Australia

First published 2002 by Blackwell Publishing Ltd
First published in paperback 2003

10 2011

Library of Congress Cataloging-in-Publication Data

D'Altroy, Terence N.
     The Incas / Terence N. D'Altroy.
          p. cm. —(The Peoples of America)
     Includes bibliographical references and index.
     ISBN 978-0-631-17677-0 (alk. paper) — ISBN 978-1-4051-1676-3 (pbk. alk. paper)
     1. Incas—History. 2. Incas—Social life and customs. I. Title.
     II. Series.
     F3429 .D35 2001
     985'.019—dc21   2001025267

A catalogue record for this title is available from the British Library.

Set in 10 on 12 pt Sabon
by Best-set Typesetter Ltd, Hong Kong
Printed and bound by Sheridan Books, Inc. in the USA

For further information on
Blackwell Publishing, visit our website:
www.blackwellpublishing.com

To Mariela and Nicole

Contents

List of Figures

List of Plates

List of Tables

Preface

The Inca empire, called *Tawantinsuyu* ("The Four Parts Together"), was the grandest civilization ever created in the Andes and perhaps in the entire prehispanic Americas. Spanning over 4,000 km of western South America and encompassing more than ten million inhabitants, Tawantinsuyu was a century-long latecomer to Andean civilization, built on more than three millennia of complex societies. It was a land in which the lines were blurred between the past and the present, and between the quick and the dead, where living and mummified rulers vied for authority with one another and with the deities of the landscape and the cosmos. Inca power, as with so many of their predecessors, arose from a blend of genealogy, myth, mutual obligation, and coercion, all legitimized by a cultural vision that was constantly being reinvented, even after the empire had collapsed.

For all practical purposes, resistance by subject groups within the known world had been quashed, yet this most powerful of Andean societies fell to a relatively small brigade of Spanish invaders in 1532–3. How could that have happened? The Europeans certainly had some technological advantages in horses and armaments, but those alone were insufficient to account for the empire's demise. Instead, we need to look for Tawantinsuyu's fragility in its internal makeup, its political history, and the rifts that existed among its royalty and extraordinarily diverse peoples. This book is an exploration of that society, its history, strengths, and divisions, drawn from both historical and archaeological sources compiled over hundreds of years by eyewitnesses, travelers, and scholars.

I was drawn into research on the Incas almost against my will. Having spent a number of years doing archaeology on simpler societies in the United States, Mexico, and Peru, I was not ready to take up study of such a vast empire, especially one that hundreds of scholars had already been studying for well over a century. Even more daunting was the fact that overviews of the Incas and interpretation of particular archaeological remains were based on a large corpus of historical documents, many of them written in sixteenth-century Spanish peppered with Quechua, the native language of the Incas. I was well versed in anthropological archaeology, but not documentary analysis. When I set out to do fieldwork for my doctoral dissertation, I had intended to study the societies of central Peru in the epoch just before the advent of Inca rule, but my doctoral adviser gently pushed me forward in time, largely because we didn't understand the late pre-Inca chronology very well.

My background meant that I came into the field with a different perspective than that which prevailed in Inca studies, but it also meant that I had an enormous amount of catching up to do and came to rely on the goodwill and support of scores of friends and colleagues. I therefore owe an enormous debt of gratitude to the people who assisted by providing information, reading drafts, and preparing illustrations. Although it would be convenient to blame them for the mistakes that are found here, they probably would not let me get away with it. Brian Bauer has been a great help in a variety of ways. He read the entire manuscript and provided a number of the photos and other illustrations found here. His trenchant comments helped me recognize both the wheat and the chaff and persuaded me to remove most of the latter. Elena Phipps, Luis Jaime Castillo, and Tim Earle read sections of the book and convinced me to set aside as many of the professional debates as I could bear to part with. Special mention must go to the late John Hyslop, who was the first scholar to produce comprehensive archaeological overviews of Inca settlements and the road system, based on fieldwork throughout the empire. John first drew my attention to the southern part of the empire and generously shared his information and ideas with me, as he did with all of his colleagues. Similarly, Craig Morris has been more than gracious in sharing ideas and information, and access to the resources of the American Museum of Natural History. My discussions with Ana María Lorandi pointed me in directions with the historical literature and Andean societies that I would never have considered otherwise. Ramiro Matos and Jeff Parsons also deserve particular thanks for having introduced me to the archaeology of the Andes and for having shared their unpublished data on central Peru.

Many people generously provided information, unpublished manuscripts, references, and publications. Among them are Félix Acuto, Juan Albarracín-Jordan, Sonia Alconini, Roberto Bárcena, Monica Barnes, Brian Bauer, Robert Bradley, M. Constanza Ceruti, Ricardo Céspedes Paz, Antonio Coello, Miguel Cornejo, Beatriz Cremonte, Pío Pablo Díaz, Ian Farrington, Antonio Fresco, Alberto Rex González, Pedro Guibovich, Andrés Gyarmati, Frances Hayashida, Lee Hollowell, Flor de

María Huaycochea, Jaime Idrovo, Catherine Julien, Ann Kendall, Miguel León, Ana María Lorandi, Albert Meyers, Eleanora Mulvany de Peñaloza, Patricia Netherly, Axel Nielsen, Susan Ramírez, Glenn Russell, Dan Sandweiss, Juan Schobinger, Katharina Schreiber, Izumi Shimada, Chip Stanish, Rubén Stehberg, Steve Tomka, Debbie Truhan, and Verónica Williams. Christine Flaherty and Sumru Aricanli both assisted with the illustrations, Christine by preparing many of the maps and Sumru by facilitating access to the wonderful collection of images at the American Museum of Natural History. Scott Kremkau helped with a close reading of the text for citations. Thanks also go to the various sources of funding that have supported my research in the Upper Mantaro Valley, Peru and the Calchaquí Valley, Argentina, where I have studied the effects of Inca rule on provincial societies for more than twenty years. Those sources include the National Science Foundation, Columbia University, UCLA, the UCLA Friends of Archaeology, and the H. John Heinz III Charitable Trust. I would also like to extend a special thanks to Ken Provencher of Blackwell, who showed enormous patience and support in seeing this manuscript through a prolonged period of writing and editing. In addition, I am most grateful to Margaret Aherne, who paid close editorial attention to the text and lent wise counsel in bringing the book to its final form.

Finally, I owe a special debt to my family, first to my parents for exciting my initial interest in archaeology through trips to the Egyptian wing of the Metropolitan Museum of Art in New York. And most of all to my wife and daughter, who put up with me patiently while I finished this book.

chapter one
Introduction

On Friday, November 15, 1532, a force of 168 frightened Spaniards walked into the maw of the most powerful empire ever seen in the Americas. Francisco Pizarro's brigade entered the plaza at Cajamarca, an imperial Inca center in the Peruvian highlands, late in the afternoon, dismayed by the military display blanketing the hillside before them. Near the town, in the midst of his 80,000-man army, the Inca prince Atawallpa was just completing a fast at the nearby hot springs of Kónoj and savoring his recent victory in a war over Cuzco's throne. Atawallpa declined an invitation to disrupt his solemn duties and meet his unwanted guests in the city that afternoon, but agreed to receive them after a night's rest. Astonishingly, he was Pizarro's prisoner by the next evening, captured during a surprise strike that was underpinned by equal parts of bravado, armaments, and faith.

Over the next eight months, the Spaniards extracted a ransom fit for a deity on earth in exchange for Atawallpa's freedom. More than $50 million of treasure was melted down from the empire's architectural ornaments, personal jewelry, idols, and service ware hauled off from temples, aristocratic households, and perhaps even from graves. Once the ransom had been paid, Pizarro gave the order for Atawallpa to be tried and executed on July 26, 1533, overriding the grave misgivings voiced by some members of his party. The power that the Inca had wielded over his vast domain even while captive convinced the Spaniard that decapitating the state was his best hope of staying alive and asserting his own control. In light of the divisions that had already riven the empire, his decision touched off the collapse of *Tawantinsuyu*, or "The Four Parts Together," as the Incas called their grand realm.

Fittingly, the Incas already had a word for a cataclysmic change of such enormity. They called it a *pachakuti*, a "turning over of time and space" – a moment when history ended and then began again. In their eyes, it was not the first time that the world had been destroyed, nor would it be the last. Native chroniclers explained that all of creation had been wiped out four times in the ancient past, each time after a cycle of a thousand years (Guaman Poma 1980; see Urton 1999:41). The first age was a time of darkness when the world was inhabited by a race of wild men. In each successive epoch, humans progressed, as they learned to farm, to make crafts, and to organize themselves for war and peace. The fifth "sun" was the age of the Incas. In their self-promoted vision, it was a glorious era during which they brought civilization and enlightened rule to a chaotic world. And under the circumstances, it was only suitable that the man who had created the empire took *Pachakuti* as his title. After all, he was the son of the Sun, a living deity who remade the world.

Less than a century after Pachakuti joined his celestial father, Atawallpa closed the war with his half-brother Waskhar. According to one native account, his victorious generals declared that it was time for another *pachakuti* (Callapiña et al. 1974). To help move the process along, they massacred Waskhar's extensive family and members of several other royal kin groups who had cast their lot with him. They also killed all the historians they could find and destroyed the knot-records called *khipu* (see below, "Literacy and Data Recording") on which the past was recorded, so that the era could begin unburdened by its past. Before he could properly launch the new epoch, however, Atawallpa fell into Spanish hands and a century of rule by gods on earth came to an end.

The Spanish encounter with the Incas, despite its impact, was not a complete surprise to either people. In 1519, Hernán Cortés had overthrown the Aztec empire of central Mexico through a similar attack on the ruler with the aid of allies made in the new land. The descriptions of Mexico's cities and riches that made their way back to Spain fired enthusiasm for more adventures in the Indies. Many of the men who accompanied Pizarro to the Andes had already seen action in Central America and the Caribbean, while others had just come over to seek their fortunes. Pizarro himself had been in the Americas for thirty years and was hungry to make his mark in an uncharted land called *Pirú*. In the 1520s, a few Spaniards or Portuguese had actually penetrated the Inca domain, but left no significant impression on the Andes or reported back to the Europeans. A tangible glimmer of what the Spaniards were to find reached them in 1527, however, when an expedition captured a boat off Ecuador filled with cloth, metal ornaments, and other riches, but they were still not prepared for the grandeur of Peru.

In 1532, Tawantinsuyu was the largest polity ever created in the native Americas. Its ruler was a hereditary king who the Incas claimed had descended in an unbroken string from a creation separate from the rest of humanity. Though a powerful monarch, the *Sapa Inca* ("Unique Inca") did not rule alone. As the invaders soon discovered, he was counseled by mummies of his immortal ancestors who, along with their descendants, also joined him in Cuzco's most solemn ceremonies and drunken revelry. Totally unpersuaded by the Incas' claims of divinity and appalled at their heresies, the Spaniards were still dazzled by the ruling dynasty's riches and achievements. The early writers often drew on familiar referents to convey images of the realm for their countrymen, but some customs defied a search for analogy. Pedro Sancho de la Hoz and Pedro Pizarro, both members of the original expedition, have left us some impressions of the capital:

> There is a very beautiful fortress of earth and stone with big windows that look over the city [of Cuzco] and make it appear more beautiful . . . [The stones] are as big as pieces of mountains or crags . . . The Spaniards who see them say that neither the bridge of Segovia nor other constructions of Hercules or the Romans are as magnificent as this . . . (Sancho de la Hoz 1917:193–4)

> Most of the people [of Cuzco] served the dead, I have heard it said, who they daily brought out to the main square, setting them down in a ring, each one according to his age, and there the male and female attendants ate and drank. The attendants made fires for each of the dead in front of them . . . and lighting [them], burned everything they had put before them, so that the dead should eat of everything that the living ate . . . (P. Pizarro 1986:89–90)

Everywhere they traveled, the invaders saw the imperial imprint, whether it was in Cuzco's grand architecture, the roads that traversed 40,000 km of rugged terrain, thousands of provincial installations, stocks of every supply imaginable, works of artistry in precious metal, stone, and cloth, or the government designed to manage the whole affair. About twenty years after the conquest, the soldier Pedro Cieza de León (1967:213–14; translation from Hyslop 1984:343) expressed his admiration for the entire system:

> In human memory, I believe that there is no account of a road as great as this, running through deep valleys, high mountains, banks of snow, torrents of water, living rock, and wild rivers . . . In all places it was clean and swept free of refuse, with lodgings, storehouses, Sun temples, and posts along the route. Oh! Can anything similar be claimed for Alexander or any of the powerful kings who ruled the world . . . ?

The Incas' feats seemed all the more fabulous when the conquistadores learned that the realm was only about four generations old. As the Incas

Table 1.1 The conventional Inca king list

Name as ruler	Gloss	Given name
1 Manqo Qhapaq	Powerful [Ancestor]	—
2 Zinchi Roq'a	Warlord Roq'a	—
3 Lloq'e Yupanki	Honored Left-handed	—
4 Mayta Qhapaq	Powerful Mayta	—
5 Qhapaq Yupanki	Powerful Honored	—
6 Inka Roq'a	Inca Roq'a	—
7 Yawar Waqaq	He Who Cries Bloody Tears	Inka Yupanki, Mayta Yupanki, Titu Cusi Wallpa
8 Wiraqocha Inka	Creator God Inca	Hatun Thupa Inka
9 Pachakuti Inka Yupanki	Cataclysm Honored Inca	Inka Yupanki, Cusi Yupanki
10 Thupa Inka Yupanki	Royal Honored Inca	—
11 Wayna Qhapaq	Powerful Youth	Titu Cusi Wallpa
12 Waskhar Inka	Golden Chain Ruler	Thupa Cusi Wallpa
13 Atawallpa	—	—

explained it, the empire was launched when Pachakuti usurped the throne from his father Wiraqocha Inka and began to conquer the peoples around Cuzco. His victories and organizational genius were followed only by those of his son Thupa Inka Yupanki and grandson Wayna Qhapaq, and then by the final dynastic war (table 1.1).

For their part, the Incas were taken aback by the Spanish invasion, although they would recall legends that had predicted the return of white, bearded strangers from the sea. Even so, their initial response was less one of awe than of anger and disbelief at the invaders' arrogance. Who were these men who dared to kill the *Sapa Inca*'s subjects and seize the holy women for their carnal pleasures? Rather than wipe them out directly as they so richly deserved, the Incas let their curiosity get the better of them and allowed the interlopers to ascend the Andes to be examined first-hand. To Atawallpa's everlasting regret, the Spanish incursion could not have been more propitiously timed. The prince, contemplating his recent victory and anticipating reunification of the empire, had nothing to fear from a small band of foreigners, as outrageous as their conduct might be. He was wrong.

My goal in this book is to describe the Incas, their emergence as rulers of an empire, and the nature of their society. That sounds straightforward enough, but the Incas have proved to be remarkably malleable in the hands of historians and archaeologists. Depending on the author,

Tawantinsuyu has been held up as an exemplar of almost every form of political society except representative democracy. Garcilaso de la Vega (1966), son of an Inca princess, immortalized Tawantinsuyu as a supremely well-run, homogeneous monarchy ruled by an omnipotent and benevolent king. Although he was writing in 1609 to exalt the glories of his ancestors to a Spanish audience, Garcilaso's vision is still popular today. His efforts aside, other authors have seen the realm in radically different lights – as a type of primitive communism, a feudal society, a despotic Asiatic state, and a territorial empire. Some modern scholars even doubt that an empire existed and instead see a patchwork of ethnic groups that were never truly unified.

How could one polity inspire such contradictory views? Part of the answer lies in the fact that no one who grew up in Tawantinsuyu ever wrote about it. Although they had the tools to record data very precisely, the Incas had no writing system that we have been able to recognize and decipher. Instead, history was kept as oral tradition. In Cuzco, poet-historians called *amautas* and knot-record masters called *khipu kamayuq* recited sagas of the royal past at the bidding of the court. The *khipu* themselves seem to have registered information in ways that had as much to do with cultural visions of power and space as with linear history. Aristocrats also memorized epic poems, some of which they recounted to the Spaniards. Not surprisingly, the descendants of different rulers called up versions of the past that favored their own ancestors, while public recitations by the *amautas* were tailored to please the audience (Rostworowski 1999:vii–ix). Cieza (1967:32) explained things this way:

> . . . and if among the kings one turned out indolent, a coward, given to vices and a homebody without enlarging the domain of his empire, it was ordered that of such [kings] there be little remembrance or almost none at all; and they attended to this so closely that if one [king] was found [in the histories] it was so as not to forget his name and the succession; but in the rest they remained silent, without singing the songs [as they did] of the others who were good and valiant.

Cieza and other Spanish authors thus had to choose among a wide variety of stories in composing their chronicles. Many resolved the problem by favoring the accounts told by their oldest and most aristocratic witnesses and by dismissing reports by common Indians. These circumstances meant that the documentary history of the Incas has been filtered through competing native views, translators, scribes, conflicting mores, and differing notions of the value of the past. Conversion of Andean history into a European-style chronicle is therefore an uncertain task; similar obstacles face us when we try to understand Andean social order, economics, or world views. Fortunately, archaeological research into the Incas has become more active in recent years, so that historical and archaeological study can be viewed as complementary sources of information in a way that was impossible not long ago. Even so, we still have less direct information to work with than scholars who have studied many of the great empires of the Old World. In this introduction, then, I would like to sketch out how we can come to an understanding of the Incas, beginning by outlining how scholars have thought about empires and then by describing the documentary and archaeological information that we have for the Incas themselves.

Investigating Empires

Empires like Tawantinsuyu were the largest and most heterogeneous of the ancient societies, which makes studying them confoundedly difficult. By the term empire, I am referring to an extensive polity – often containing millions of subjects and covering hundreds of thousands of square kilometers – in which a core polity gains control over a range of other societies. The dominion may be political, military, or economic, and it may be remote or immediate, but the essence of an empire is that the core society is able to assert its will over the other peoples brought under its aegis. In the pre-industrial world, there was only a relative handful of such polities. In the Old World, the Qin and Han Chinese and their successors, New Kingdom Egypt, the Macedonians maybe, the Assyrians, Romans, Parthians, Sassanians, Persians, Mongols, Mughals, Mauryas, and Vijayanagara, among others, can fairly be considered to have been empires. In the Americas, the Aztecs, the Incas, and perhaps the Wari qualify, although there is some dispute about the status of each of them. The scale and diversity of these polities make their analysis an enormous challenge. Anyone studying the Romans, for example, might have to consider evidence drawn from more than forty modern countries, written in dozens of languages. Even the Inca empire took in lands that now fall within six countries, whose native inhabitants spoke scores of languages.

Scholars have devised a number of ways in which to reduce the enormous complexity of early empires to manageable concepts that provide a basis for comparison (Sinopoli 1994; Alcock et al. 2001). The most widely used approach divides empires into their *core* and *periphery*. The core is envisioned as the political, economic, and cultural heartland of the empire, while the periphery consists of the societies that are ruled and exploited by the core. Frequently, the relationship between the core and the periphery has been seen in terms of both power and space. The societies of a centrally located core were visualized as having been more complex politically and economically and more sophisticated culturally than the often barbaric peripheral societies. As the power of one core waned, it would be replaced by another center, usually at the margins of the previous heartland. This view owed much to the nature and histories of the Roman and Chinese empires, in which heartland areas were periodically beset by troublesome borderlands peoples.

As historians became more discerning in their analysis of empires as complex systems, they focused less on the layout of empires and more on the relations of inequality between the heartland and surrounding areas. Immanuel Wallerstein's (1974) world-systems model has been widely applied to early empires, even though the scholars who use his concepts often disagree with some of his own notions about pre-modern empires. Wallerstein observed that macro-regions are often organized by economic relations that exceed political boundaries. Labor organization, resource extraction, accrual of wealth, and market relations, for example, result from relationships that integrate vast areas and, frequently, many politically independent states. Archaeologists have adapted this general idea to study relations between the heartlands of ancient states and neighboring regions (e.g., Chase-Dunn and Hall 1991; Algaze 1993).

An alternative conception focuses on strategies of imperial rule according to their intensity and mix of different kinds of power: military, economic, political, and ideological (Mann 1986). At the low end of a continuum of intensity is a *hegemonic* strategy, which produces a fairly loose, indirect kind of imperial rule (Luttwak 1976; Hassig 1985:100–1; D'Altroy 1992:18–24). A hegemonic empire is built on a core state society that comes to dominate a series of client polities through diplomacy or conquest. The goal of a hegemonic approach is to keep the costs of rule low, but a low investment in administration and physical facilities is offset by a relatively low extraction of resources and by limited control over subject peoples. The Aztecs provide a classic case of a hegemonic empire (Hassig 1985; Smith 1996). At the other end of the continuum is a *territorial* strategy, which is an intense, direct approach to ruling subject peoples within an empire. This is a costly approach to governance, since it requires a heavy investment in administration, security against external threats, and the physical infrastructure of imperial rule, such as roads, provincial centers, and frontier defense. The costs may be necessary to ensure the empire's continued existence, however, or to satisfy the demands of the upper classes. Rome of the first century AD and the Han Chinese provide good examples of territorial empires. These two poles grade into each other, of course, and may be applied selectively in different parts of the empire or at different times as the situation changes. Among the factors that may contribute to a particular choice of strategy are the organization of the central polity and the various societies that it annexes, historical relations between the central society and subjects, political negotiation, the distribution of resources, transport technology, and the goals of the imperial leadership.

An approach based on strategies of imperial rule helps us to overcome some problems seen in traditional models (see Stein 2000) and in our analysis of the Incas in particular. One concern is that the division of an empire into a complex, cosmopolitan core and a less developed periphery is simply wrong on empirical grounds in a number of cases. Some imperial societies dominated peoples who surpassed them in urbanization, urbanity, population, social hierarchy, and economic specialization. The Incas are among the most prominent of these counter-examples, which also include the Mongols, Mughals, and Macedonians. A second concern is an unwarranted overemphasis on the power of the core society. Historical records indicate that many empires rose to power through coercive means – often conquest coupled with diplomacy that was backed by not so latent force. Even so, it has become clear that the relations between the imperial elites and peripheral societies were far more negotiated and dynamic than often thought not too long ago. To take just one counter-intuitive example, Barfield (2001) points out that, rather than extracting resources, Chinese emperors paid tribute to the steppe nomads to keep them at bay.

As useful as they are, both the core–periphery and territorial-hegemonic approaches have a major weakness – they focus our attention almost exclusively on the activities of the imperial elite or on interactions between them and subject elites. As research in provincial regions has advanced, especially within local communities, it has become increasingly clear that many important activities in ancient empires occurred without the intervention, interest, or awareness of the central authorities. Historians have long recognized that the grandiose claims of ancient emperors were often exaggerated and that imperial histories, whether inscribed on monumental architecture or written in texts, often attributed all decisions and power to the ruler. In part, that was a literary convention or imperial propaganda, but modern authors still commonly describe the functioning of empires in terms of individual rulers. I feel that this perspective attributes too much power to rulers, who were often at odds with factions made up of their closest associates, and emphasizes a top-down vision that misleads us about household and community life.

Those concerns lead me to the approach taken in this book. My view is that an adequate explanation of an early empire must take into account both the actions and interests of the dominant powers and those of the highly varied mass of subject peoples, if we wish to make sense of life at the grand and small scale. The overarching goal here is to balance and integrate information drawn from historical, anthropological, and archaeological sources. This approach differs from most other overviews of the Incas, which often rely on early documents because they provide a wealth of detail about Inca history, social life, and rationales for behavior that are not available through archaeological sources (J. Rowe 1946; Davies 1995; Rostworowski 1999). When archaeology is brought into overviews, it is often used to illustrate the elegance of Inca architecture or objects or to describe the road system or provincial administrative settlements. The early written record, however, is heavily weighted toward the life and times of the royalty and other elites, especially in and around Cuzco. More troublesome is that vast areas of the empire, especially in the south, are largely blanks in the written record. Conversely, treatments of Inca archaeology are generally descriptive and draw on documents to explain sites' functions or place in the empire's historical development. Some works, especially John Hyslop's (1984, 1990) exceptional studies of the Inca roads and settlement planning, consciously weave the two lines of evidence together. Even so, no overview of the empire that I am familiar with systematically integrates history and archaeology. Because they provide different information and sometimes lead us to incompatible conclusions, I will try to highlight where variations arise and how we might resolve the conflicts.

Readers familiar with non-western polities will probably not be surprised that the chapter categories of this book do not fit very well the way that the members of Inca society thought about their world. The Incas did not distinguish neatly between political and ideological leadership, for example, since the ruler was both a deity and the head of government. Military power arose from a tangled mix of supernatural forces and human endeavor, while economic productivity resulted from the gifts of the earth, labor shared through social ties, and the favor of deities. Priests could be generals and the dead could contribute to political decisions. Any explanation of Inca behavior or organization, therefore, must balance modern western analytical categories with the ways in which the Incas might have viewed any situation and what options may have appeared within their social logic, at least to the degree possible.

The Written Sources

Of the thousands of known documents that contain information on life under the Incas, no more than about fifty contain accounts of Inca history per se. The earliest eyewitness accounts were written by official scribes and soldiers in the heat of a military invasion of an alien land. Their comments were impressions written without time for reflection or understanding of the civilization they were observing. As the Spaniards learned Quechua and began to understand the Andes better, the indigenous peoples found more reason to conceal their activities and beliefs. The situation came to a head in 1559, when the Spaniards were stunned to discover that the Incas around Cuzco were still venerating the mummies of their past kings. In Spanish eyes, the native peoples – far from having assimilated the word of the true church – were still inebriated with their blasphemous beliefs in living ancestors and an animate landscape.

The simultaneous clash and syncretism of cultures, combined with a gradual increase in mutual knowledge, meant that descriptions of the empire are never both immediate and informed. The eyewitnesses who wrote reflectively were very few – Pedro Pizarro stands out among them, and he did not put his quill to parchment until almost forty years had elapsed. They were followed by an assortment of soldiers, administrators, and priests, who prepared their manuscripts as part of their duties or for personal gain through publication. A number of them spoke good Quechua and they were often better informed than the earlier authors, but their reports drew from the memories of informants, rather than from first-hand knowledge of the empire. By the time that the Spaniards took a real interest in the Inca realm, their witnesses provided memories colored by time, political and economic objectives, and wariness of Spanish repression. Some of the authors of the first fifty years conducted or drew from the official inquiries that were periodically undertaken to assess the state of affairs in the Viceroyalty. The questions posed were often slanted by Crown interests in denying Inca legitimacy, rooting out heresies, or discovering effective ways to exploit the rapidly declining population. In contrast, the native peoples did not begin to set down their visions of Tawantinsuyu until the end of the century, a long lifetime after the collapse of Inca power, and they all wrote from the perspective of Christians with a foot in two cultures.

Historians have paid close attention to the lives of these authors, since the context in which the documents were produced heavily affected their content. The first few decades of Spanish rule were a tumultuous era, marked by Inca resistance, Spanish civil wars, and conflicts among clerical, administrative, and private interests, as well as by personal antagonisms. In the practice of the day, authors freely borrowed from one another without citation and could reinforce errors simply by repeating them. For readers interested in more detail on the subject, I recommend a number of works that are devoted to critical examinations of these documents and potential sources of bias and cross-use.[1] What I present here simply highlights some of the major sources of information and how they were composed.

Eyewitness Accounts

Among the earliest writers were Hernando Pizarro, Pedro Sancho de la Hoz, Miguel de Estete, Francisco de Xérez, Cristóbal de Mena, and Juan Ruiz de Arce. All of these men were part of the invading force that captured and killed Atawallpa at Cajamarca and then seized Cuzco. Sancho and Xérez, secretaries to Francisco Pizarro, were charged with keeping official records for the Crown. Their journals provide a virtual day-by-day time line of the initial Spanish experience, without the understanding or revisionism that hindsight can bring. De Mena, on the other hand, was a soldier who returned to Spain and quickly published an account of his experiences in the new land, with the intent of profiting from the work. Pedro Pizarro, younger cousin to the expedition's leader, did not finish his memoirs until 1571. As a result, he could provide a perspective on the Incas that included a feel of immediacy, tempered by knowledge gained and memory lost over decades of life in Peru.

The Sixteenth-Century Spanish Chroniclers

The Spanish authors of the mid-sixteenth century provide our greatest source of information on the Inca empire. Pedro de Cieza de León, a common soldier with an uncommon eye for detail, wrote one of the great early accounts. After spending a number of years in the Indies, he arrived in the northern Andes in April of 1547, at the age of twenty-nine. For the next three years, he traveled through the north half of the realm, making observations and inquiring about climate, constructions, daily life, local customs, myths, and sexual practices. When in Cuzco, Cieza interviewed Inca aristocrats about their past and the nature of their government. He wrote copiously on what he had seen – four volumes of his writings have now been published, but only one appeared in his lifetime (Cieza 1967). Cieza's accounts are filled with admiration for the Inca achievements, blunted by horror at the diabolically inspired religions and sexual customs that he learned about. Many of the best descriptions of Inca rule, the roads, the provincial centers, and Cuzco itself, come from his pen.

Juan de Betanzos's *Narrative of the Incas* (1996) describes Inca history in a form that comes as close as any known source to a version told by a single royal family. Born in Spain, Betanzos lived in Peru during his adult life, becoming the most respected Quechua–Spanish translator in the Viceroyalty. In 1542, he may have served as an interpreter at an inquest held in Cuzco and soon thereafter was commissioned to prepare a bilingual doctrinal volume. He married Doña Angelina Yupanque (i.e., Cuxirimay Ocllo), an Inca princess who experienced a remarkable life. Niece to the emperor Wayna Qhapaq, she was betrothed to his son Atawallpa at one year of age; she married him in 1532 when she was ten, near the end of his war to unseat Waskhar. About 1538, Francisco Pizarro took her as his mistress and she bore him two sons. After Pizarro met his own death in 1541, she married Betanzos, bringing him enormous wealth and status. So adept at the language and so close to a royal family, Betanzos was uniquely suited to write the account of the Incas that Viceroy Mendoza commissioned in 1551 and that was completed in 1557. He apparently drew a great deal of his information from his in-laws, who were members of Pachakuti's descendant kin group (Hamilton 1996:xi). The first part of the account is thus largely a heroic biography of Pachakuti, while the second describes the Colonial era. The Incas' own rationales for proper behavior come through clearly in his narrative, which is only modestly filtered through European eyes. For all its richness, Betanzos's account is notable for its partisanship in favor of Pachakuti and the legitimacy of Atawallpa's cause.

The Licenciado Juan Polo de Ondegardo was probably the best informed of all the administrators of the first fifty years of Colonial rule. He served two terms as the magistrate of Cuzco and one at Potosí. Polo undertook a variety of inquiries in Peru and Bolivia both for the Crown and to satisfy his own curiosity. His concern – as with much of the Spanish attention paid to native institutions – arose from his interest in using existing practices for more effective administration and not from preserving them for their own sake. His view was that the people could best be managed for Spain's interests if its officials understood how indigenous institutions worked. His numerous treatises on Inca religion, economics, politics, social relations, and other elements of native life were used by the Spanish authorities in setting policy, although not as widely as he wished. One of his great successes occurred in 1559, when he discovered the whereabouts of the royal mummies that had been spirited from one hiding place to another around Cuzco since the conquest.

The arrival of the Viceroy Francisco de Toledo in Peru in 1569 irrevocably changed life in the Andes. A controversial figure then as today, Toledo undertook a comprehensive series of reforms that included forced resettlement of natives to communities near Spanish centers, where they could be more easily controlled. He finally defeated the neo-Inca state in

Vilcabamba in 1572 and supervised the execution of its Inca ruler Thupa Amaru over the strenuous objections of many of his compatriots. Three volumes of papers produced by Toledo, which include verbatim interviews with Inca and other elites in 1570–2, as well as petitions brought to his attention, provide useful detail on life in Cuzco and the provinces (Levillier 1940).

Toledo gave one of his assistants, Pedro de Sarmiento, the responsibility of compiling an official history of the Incas, which he completed in 1572. Sarmiento wrote that he had interviewed more than a hundred record-keepers and royal historians in Cuzco and then had the work's veracity confirmed through a public reading before forty-two Inca nobles. Although his work is one of the major sources on the Incas, it is clouded by Toledo's express interest in demonstrating the illegitimacy of Inca rule. Perhaps more than some other chronicles, Sarmiento's treatise was a composite vision that was influenced by the interests of his informants. It is worth noting, for example, that Atawallpa's kin were not represented. Similarly, the descendants of the rulers Thupa Inka Yupanki and Waskhar had been largely wiped out. Despite his efforts to produce a synthesis that suited official interests, Sarmiento's account is salted with examples of unresolved differences among Cuzco's factionalized aristocratic families.

Several important early documents were written by priests either as an official charge or from their own interest.[2] Bartolomé de Segovia (1943), for example, wrote an eyewitness description of the last major Inca solstice ceremony in 1535. Cristóbal de Molina, a hospice priest in Cuzco for most of his life and exceptionally well informed about Inca religion, wrote several manuscripts on the subject. One of his treatises, completed in 1575 (Molina 1988), described Inca rituals in detail. He worked closely with another cleric, Cristóbal de Albornoz (1989), who crusaded against heretical religion from 1568 until 1586. Albornoz helped put down the millenarian Taki Onqoy movement and claimed to have personally demolished over 2,000 native shrines in the Huamanga region. Miguel de Cabello Valboa (1951) wrote a lengthy opus, which probably borrowed from Betanzos and Sarmiento, that interweaves Inca history with a love story. Cabello Valboa is notable for proposing the imperial-era chronology that is most widely used today. Fray Martín de Murúa (1986) also borrowed heavily from earlier authors, but provides quite a few details about Inca life and times that appear to be independently derived.

Among a host of other authors[3] who provide crucial information were the clerics Bartolomé de Las Casas, José de Acosta, Francisco de Avila, and José de Arriaga, who wrote or commissioned important works. Other valuable manuscripts were prepared by Falcón, Santillán, Zárate,

Bibar, Matienzo, Lizárraga, and Valdivia. The last four constitute the few major works that we have by authors who visited the southern Andes in person. Two Quechua lexicons, by Domingo de Santo Tomás and González Holguín, and one in Aymara by Fray Bertonio, are also useful for their clues to social structure and conceptual linkages.

The Native Authors

The earliest native source on Inca royal history may be a disputed account known as the *Quipucamayos de Vaca de Castro* (Callapiña et al. 1974). The document surfaced in 1608, but part of it was ostensibly recorded in an inquest conducted in Cuzco in 1542 by the Licenciado Vaca de Castro. Two of the four witnesses claimed to have been record-keepers (*khipu kamayuq*, or *quipucamayos*) from the descendant kin group of the emperor Wiraqocha Inka (see sidebar on *Literacy*, below). There is little doubt that the 1608 document manipulated mytho-history to sustain a fraudulent royal genealogy, but scholars disagree – despite considerable historical sleuthing – about the authenticity of the 1542 source (Duviols 1979a; Urton 1990; Pease 1995:23). The account emphasized the exploits of Wiraqocha Inka and earlier kings, attributing to them many of the conquests that are usually assigned to the conventional founder of the empire, Pachakuti. The Quipucamayos claimed that Betanzos participated in the inquest but, as just observed, his chronicle closely reproduced the vision of Inca history put forward by Pachakuti's descendants; it conflicted outright with many elements of the Quipucamayos' version.

Both the Quipucamayos and Betanzos differ from another native source, known as the *Probanza de Qhapaq Ayllu* (Rowe 1985b). In 1569, the survivors of a massacre that occurred in Cuzco at the end of the final Inca civil war filed claim to regain their lost estates. The *Probanza* listed the conquests of the emperor Thupa Inka Yupanki, apparently dictated from *khipu* records. It claimed for him alone many of the conquests that are often attributed to his father as monarch, but Thupa Inka Yupanki as general. The conflicted and flexible views of the Inca past seen in these three sources, each told from the perspective of a particular royal kin group, highlight some of the problems in making sense of Inca history in a European framework.

Over the last four centuries, the Inca Garcilaso de la Vega has easily been the most influential Inca chronicler. Son of a Spanish soldier and an Inca princess, Garcilaso lived in Cuzco until 1560, when he turned fifteen and moved permanently to Spain. Late in life, he wrote extensively on the Incas, the most important of his works being the *Royal*

Commentaries of the Incas, which he completed in 1609 (Garcilaso de la Vega 1966). Garcilaso wrote from the perspective of a Christian educated in Spain, with a passion for redeeming his ancestors' reputation. Garcilaso's status as the pre-eminent authority on the Incas stood for centuries and the *Royal Commentaries* are still cited as the earliest literary masterpiece written by a native American. Beginning with Rowe's (1946) critical assessment in 1946, however, the Inca Garcilaso has fallen mightily and he is valued today more for his recollections of Inca customs than for his vision of history. His portrayal of benevolent and omnipresent Inca rule, in a land in which no one ever went hungry, is considered by scholars to be more a rose-colored apology than a portrait of reality, but it remains the dominant image of the Incas in popular publications.

Shortly after Garcilaso completed his great work, Felipe Guaman Poma de Ayala sent a letter of more than a thousand pages to King Carlos V that is a fount of information on life in the Inca realm. A son of mixed ancestry like Garcilaso, Guaman Poma found himself caught between two cultures. Born in Huamanga, he assisted the Colonial administration in a variety of capacities, including efforts to stamp out idolatrous practices. Nonetheless, he was conflicted in his loyalty to things Christian and Spanish and traditional Andean ways of life. In 1613, he completed his epic letter, which included hundreds of drawings of Inca history, religion, and customs, as well as an illustrated litany of Spanish abuses. His drawings are an irreplaceable source of visual detail, while the text – an often incoherent mélange of Spanish and Quechua – contains many useful particulars. Like Garcilaso, Guaman Poma wrote about expansive Inca conquests earlier than most Colonial Spaniards or modern scholars are willing to accept. In recent years, Guaman Poma has excited renewed interest as a resistance author (see Adorno 1986; Pease 1995:261–310).

Literacy and Data Recording: A Problem and its Knotty Solution

Although there was no alphabetic writing system in the Andes that we are aware of, the Incas and earlier societies developed techniques for recording and transmitting information that were remarkably precise and flexible. The best-known tool is a mnemonic device called the *khipu*, or knot-record. Other visual media included painted sticks, designs woven into textiles, and illustrations painted on

continued

wooden boards. The *khipu* is most often associated with Inca accounting, but it was borrowed from well-established Andean traditions that went back almost a thousand years before the Incas. Today, only about 400 *khipu* are known from archaeological deposits, in part because the Spaniards destroyed as many as they could find, distrusting their association with diabolical knowledge. Most that have been found are from coastal sites, where the dry climate aided their preservation (Ascher and Ascher 1981:68).

An individual *khipu* consisted of a longitudinal primary cord or, more rarely, a carved wooden bar to which a multi-colored series of knotted cords were tied. The cords, usually made of cotton and occasionally of wool, were twisted in different directions and a variety of knot forms were employed. They were dyed in hundreds of colors and each shade could have a specific meaning in a particular context. When all the combinations of position, number, order, color, and shape are considered, the possibilities for recording specific information become enormous. Locke (1923) made the first major breakthrough in understanding the *khipu* when he showed that the structure was based on a decimal positional system (see Ascher and Ascher 1981). On a pendant string, the position of the knot group farthest from the primary cord marked units, the next in marked tens, the next hundreds, and so on. A figure-8 knot in a group position marked a unit value; a long knot with the appropriate number of turns marked values from 2 through 9 (figure 1.1). A value of ten was represented with a single "granny" knot and a value of 0 was represented by the lack of a knot in a particular position (Urton 1997:180). The largest decimal position known to have been recorded on a *khipu* is 10,000, although much larger numbers could have easily been registered. Locke also showed that a string superior to the primary cord could represent the sum of several pendant cords.

Using concepts drawn from mathematics and symmetry analysis, other scholars have deciphered a number of other elements of *khipu* structure. Ascher and Ascher (1981) have shown, for instance, that the *khipu* could be organized hierarchically like a branching tree diagram. Within the first level of information, the order of the pendant strings attached to the primary cord signified a ranking of information. By extension, each subsidiary string farther away from the primary cord would record more specific information dependent on the level above. Similarly, various *khipu* could be tied together in a sequence. This format is eminently well suited to data such as census records. For instance, a *khipu* could record the census data

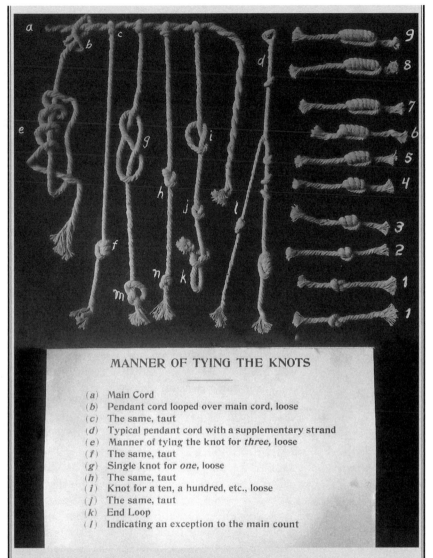

MANNER OF TYING THE KNOTS

(a) Main Cord
(b) Pendant cord looped over main cord, loose
(c) The same, taut
(d) Typical pendant cord with a supplementary strand
(e) Manner of tying the knot for *three*, loose
(f) The same, taut
(g) Single knot for *one*, loose
(h) The same, taut
(i) Knot for a ten, a hundred, etc., loose
(j) The same, taut
(k) End Loop
(l) Indicating an exception to the main count

Figure 1.1 Leland Locke's (1923) illustration of the decimal structure of knot-record accounting. Photo courtesy Dept. of Library Services, American Museum of Natural History; used with permission

for a province; levels of information on pendant and subsidiary cords could include data on decimal subdivisions, males and females, age-grades, marital status, and so on. Scholars have also shown that cords were arrayed in ways that made cross-reference to one another,

continued

and Urton (1995; 1997:30–1, 178–87) has suggested ways that the direction of knot tying was linked to data-recording structures.

Inca *khipu* were used to record a wide range of numerical data, from census records, to warehouse contents, counts of the royal flocks, tax obligations, land measurements, military organization, and calendrical information. They aided in keeping royal genealogies, conquest sequences, and myths, and were even used as aids for literary works, such as poetry. The everyday populace used them to keep track of such things as community herds, a practice that continues today. Each *khipu* was accompanied by an oral account memorized by a knot-record keeper, or *khipu kamayuq*. The position passed down from father to son, along with the oral information that was needed to read each record fully. The Incas made this position into a professional office and ranked the specialists according to the level or kind of information that they were responsible for. Since *khipu*-accounting was common, the Incas probably found it fairly easy to recruit individuals to fill the state offices in many places. Several different forms of tying the *khipu* existed, however, and we do not know if the Incas allowed local techniques to continue or standardized them across the realm. The Spaniards found the accounts to be so reliable that they allowed witnesses to read their data into court records as part of their testimony. The *khipu* was an instrument for recording information, however, and not for doing arithmetic calculations: for that purpose, the Incas used piles of pebbles or grain, or by moving counters about on a tray with rows of compartments (Rowe 1946:326). The amount of oral information needed to read a *khipu* – or conversely the amount of information embedded in a *khipu* that any specialist could read – is still uncertain. Despite the progress that has been made, *khipu* clearly contained a more nuanced code than researchers have been able to crack. The message transmitted by the *chaski* (postal messengers), for example, often consisted of a short verbal message accompanied by a *khipu*. In addition, the way in which the knot-records were used to record narrative verse and other non-numerical information has always been a puzzle.

Some testimony read into Spanish court records helps us to understand the cultural logic embedded in the *khipu*'s structure. For example in 1569, the survivors of Thupa Inka Yupanki's descendant kin group tried to recover the lands that they had lost in the aftermath of the dynastic war and Spanish conquest (Rowe 1985b). In their testimony, they listed the peoples and forts that their ancestor had conquered. The list was organized sequentially from quarter to quarter, starting with the quarter of Chinchaysuyu and running clockwise around to Cuntisuyu. On occasion, the list may have given priority to the status of the conquered people over the chronology of events. This approach to history meant that anyone attempting to create a linear history of the conquest sequence would need additional information in order to intercalate the four parts. Other documents help us understand the cultural values of the labor and goods that the accountants kept track of (see chapter 12).

Over the years, some scholars have suggested ways to link *khipu* to other visual records, such as the geometric designs in some of Guaman Poma's illustrations, or to coded information in other manuscripts (e.g. Laurencich-Minelli 1998), but none has proved really convincing yet. A newly found cache of 32 knot-records from the Chachapoyas area of northeastern Peru, however, holds promise for some advances. Gary Urton's (2001) analysis of the structure of one of those *khipu* provides the first persuasive interpretation of a specific record. While acknowledging that his explanation requires making certain assumptions such as duality in the knot-record's structure, Urton deduces that the *khipu* was a calendrical device that recorded a two-year solar calendar, lunar cycles, and various correlations between solar and lunar periods over several years. He also observes that the total knot count (3,005) on the paired strings on the *khipu* corresponds closely to the number of local taxpayers (~3,000) serving under Inca rule. Linking the two deductions, Urton infers that the *khipu* may have registered a two-year cycle of tribute obligations to the state, kept by a Chachapoya lord named Guaman who provided census information to the Spaniards in 1535.

The Later Spanish Chroniclers

As the seventeenth century moved along, the flurry of manuscripts on the Incas subsided, but some important documents were still produced. The most prominent is the multi-volume work on Inca history, religion, and customs written by the Jesuit priest Bernabé Cobo. Born in Andalusia, Father Cobo traveled widely in his lifetime. He visited Mexico, but spent most of his adult life in Peru, where he completed his great work in 1653 (Cobo 1956; see Rowe 1979b). His writing is lucid and well organized, but Cobo was a naturalist and historian whose descriptions of the Incas were drawn from earlier manuscripts. Since he had access to several manuscripts that are now lost, such as the full account of

Cuzco's shrine system, his work is an invaluable source. Modern authors also rely on Cobo for his descriptions of daily life, even though the Jesuit applied his own observations to the prehispanic past a century after the empire's fall (Rowe 1990a).

Spanish Inspections and Court Records

In the latter half of the twentieth century, historians turned their eyes from the classic chronicles to the Andean and Spanish archives. During the early Colonial era, representatives of the Spanish Crown and the Church produced a blizzard of documents about the people, customs, and resources of their new holdings. Many of those documents were intended to provide information to the Crown that would facilitate administration of the new land and extraction of its wealth. In 1549, for example, the Crown ordered detailed inspections (*visitas*) of its holdings, region by region. The inspectors used a standardized series of questions about life before and under the Incas and recorded information about the natural resources of each region. In part because conditions were changing so rapidly with the decline of the native population and administrative reforms, new inspections were ordered in the 1560s. More inquests were held with Viceroy Toledo's vast restructuring program in 1570–2. Many of the inspections recorded from 1557 through 1585 have been published in the *Relaciones Geográficas de Indias* (1965; hereafter RGI). The Toledan and RGI sources are useful as regional snapshots of the realm that drew from interviews with local native elites.

A final set of archival documents comes from litigation. About two decades after the fall of the Incas, Andean peoples began to use the Spanish courts (*Audiencia Real*) to make claims for services that they had provided the Spaniards and to settle grievances with their neighbors. Many of their complaints arose when local societies tried to regain lands or other resources that had been taken by the Incas and given to colonists resettled by the state. Since several million people moved under Inca rule, the flood of paperwork that fell upon the court system has provided a great deal of useful information on ethnic groups, land tenure and inheritance customs, and land use practices, among many other things. Still other cases stemmed from competition over the inheritance of privileged positions, as local elites learned to make claims based on pre-Inca rights, offices granted by the state, and Spanish laws that favored primogeniture over other traditional customs.

Inca Archaeology

1860–1960

The study of Inca archaeology has a long and often distinguished career, dating back to the nineteenth century. The main figures of the early days were more adventurers than scientists, but some of their contributions to archaeology are still valuable. Among the outstanding figures were Ephraim George Squier, Charles Wiener, and Antonio Raymondi, who traveled throughout the central part of the empire by horse with a pack train, as was typical for the time. They described or mapped many Inca settlements along the main road system and paid special attention to a number of sites in the Urubamba river valley now recognized as royal family estates. The engravings that were featured in their volumes provide indispensable information, even if they were often romanticized, since quite a few of the sites have suffered considerable damage since then.

Just before 1900, a major figure appeared on the Andean archaeological scene – Max Uhle. A remarkably energetic researcher and prolific writer, Uhle set about developing a pan-Andean chronology using the innovative combination of comparisons of ceramic types and analysis of stratigraphic deposits. Uhle took a considerable interest in Inca archaeology, investigating ruins, for example, at the northern Inca capital at Tumipampa (Ecuador), at coastal Pachacamac, in the highland Urubamba valley (Peru), and at Incallacta (Bolivia), thus spanning the coastal desert, the mountains, and the eastern Andean slopes. His studies have proved to be so valuable that some of them are periodically reprinted, not simply out of historical interest, but for the information they contain.

About the same time that Uhle was at work, two other major scholars were advancing our knowledge of what was the southeastern quarter of the Inca empire. Adolph Bandelier, who is also known for his work in the North American Southwest and in Mesoamerica, conducted investigations at a series of Inca sites both on the Peruvian coast and at the sacred islands in Lake Titicaca. In the southernmost part of the empire, Juan de Ambrosetti was working at Inca sites in northwest Argentina. His multi-volume publications from that region describe a variety of sites, notably Puerta de La Paya, where his excavations recovered the most elaborate set of Inca materials yet found in the south Andes.

Inca archaeology did not really catch the public's attention until 1912, however, when Hiram Bingham announced his discovery of Machu Picchu, one of the world's most spectacular archaeological sites. His claim to have found "the lost city of the Incas" in the eastern jungles and the truly breathtaking character of the remains sparked an interest that remains unabated today. Following on Bingham's work was a series of studies in the 1930s and 1940s at the capital of Cuzco and its environs. Most of the work was conducted by Peruvian scholars, notably Luis Valcárcel, Jorge Muelle, and Luis Pardo. These investigators were primarily concerned with monumental sites, such as Saqsawaman, describing material culture, and working out chronological sequences that had not yet been defined. Their studies were complemented by Paul Fejos's work at sites in the Urubamba and by John Rowe's seminal paper on the archaeology of Cuzco.

1960–2000

Starting about 1960, a transformation began to occur in the study of Inca provinces. Throughout the preceding century, archaeologists working in local contexts had been recording Inca sites, but these were consistently interpreted in the context of the written sources and a Cuzco-centric view of the Andes. In an important paper written in 1959, Dorothy Menzel recognized that the Incas had formed a variety of relationships with the societies of the south coast of Peru. She inferred that Inca rule had been adapted to existing local conditions, which was a major step forward in interpreting an empire that had previously been assumed to be essentially homogeneous. The next year saw the initiation of the Huánuco Project in Peru's central highlands. This was the first major project to systematically integrate historical and archaeological research in a regional study. The circumstances for the investigation were exceptional, for the Huánuco region boasted both the most spectacular provincial center in the empire and two Spanish inspections, from 1549 and 1562. The research team, led by John Murra, Donald Thompson, and Craig Morris, took full advantage of the conditions, producing a series of publications that remain the standard against which all provincial research is compared. I will refer to the Huánuco project on numerous occasions throughout this book.

Not until the UNESCO project at Cuzco in 1970 was there a concerted effort to identify, map, and conserve the existing Inca architecture in and around the capital. Until recently, these interests – site mapping, architectural description, ceramic analysis, and culture history – have dominated the archaeology of the Inca heartland. A number of projects have made important contributions in this milieu, for example the work of Ann Kendall and her colleagues on estates in the Cusichaca region (e.g., Kendall et al. 1992, Kendall 1996). Oddly enough, however, no complete survey of the archaeology of the Cuzco region has yet been published, so that we still do not know the full range of Inca sites in the heartland of the empire. That situation has been redressed considerably by study of individual sites, such as the royal estates of Ollantaytambo (e.g., Protzen 1993) and Yucay (Niles 1999), but a reliable archaeological map of the region remains to be published. Other archaeologists have taken a more regional approach to the subject, working from the premise that understanding the formation of the Inca polity and the relationships between the Incas and their surroundings requires study of the sacred landscape (e.g., Bauer 1998; Van de Guchte 1990). Collectively, these studies have moved us much farther ahead in the last decade or so.

These gains have been matched by a proliferation of studies on the Inca provinces by scholars throughout the Andes. Their works are too numerous to mention individually, but their interests take us into topics that were seldom considered before. Most importantly, they are fleshing out how Cuzco interacted with the hundreds of local societies under its dominion and are investigating elements of subject life that were often outside direct state control. Thanks to these studies, we can now recognize stability and change in community life that were beyond our reach until the last decades of the twentieth century. Work on household archaeology now permits scholars to examine how symbols of status, diet, architectural styles, life expectancy, or household labor were impacted (if at all) by the advent of imperial rule. All in all, these advances by hundreds of scholars in the land once encompassed by Tawantinsuyu make this an exciting time to study the Incas.

chapter two
The Land and its People

At first glance, the rugged lands of western South America seem like an improbable place to give birth to grand civilizations. Compressed within a narrow band along the Pacific Ocean lie the highest peaks in the western hemisphere, a coastal desert that may go for years without rain, and dense tropical jungles. As forbidding as the setting seems, a closer look shows that the land contains a mosaic of productive micro-environments and natural resources. The Andes mountains form the continent's most commanding geographic feature. Running 8,000 km along the length of the land mass, they ascend so rapidly that the continental divide lies only 100 km east of the shoreline at Lima, Peru. For a seasoned hiker, the climb up to the high passes takes about a week, but a passenger in a long-distance taxi can reach the divide in just three memorable hours. The descent from the eastern snowcaps to the upper reaches of the Amazon jungle is even more precipitous in some places. To appreciate how geography has condensed the ecology, we may visualize a path across central Peru from the ocean to the forest. In a trip that would cover about 200 km by air, we would pass over 20 of the world's 34 major life zones (Burger 1992:12). In this compact vertical arrangement, which is not duplicated anywhere on the planet, distinct ecological belts may lie less than an hour's walk apart.

The early inhabitants managed to flourish in the demanding conditions, for the Andes contain the richest biota of any zone of its size in the world (Luteyn and Churchill 2000). People first entered the continent at least 15,000 years ago, when hunting and gathering were the way of life everywhere. Over the millennia, they devised a wide variety of foraging, farming, and herding strategies. The marine fisheries of the bone-chilling inshore waters could be exploited with simple technologies, while llama and alpaca herding became both a successful adaptation and a source of wealth for mountain peoples. Although people still foraged for some resources after states appeared about two thousand years ago, all of their staple foods and industrial crops had been domesticated by 3,000 BC. They modified features of the landscape through irrigation, terracing (plate 2.1), and draining wetlands, at the same time that they adjusted the rhythms of their lives to the demands of the climatic cycles. Despite their successes, however, life in the Andes was never easy. Even in some of the most densely occupied highland zones, crops could fail two years out of three (Polo 1965b:71), while earthquakes, floods, erratic rainfall, disease, and a host of other natural forces periodically brought disaster to subsistence systems.

The Inca empire – a latecomer to Andean civilizations – thus built upon millennia of adaptation, tradition, and innovation in carving out their domain. For the most part it was a rural society, as most people lived in small towns and villages and spent their time farming and herding. To set the stage for the rise of Tawantinsuyu, this chapter sketches out the Andean natural environment and the ways that people exploit its resources. That outline is followed by a synopsis of Andean prehistory before the Incas.

The Natural Setting

The Andes

The Andean environment has been molded by a conjunction of geography, geology, and climate. Over the last five million years, the oceanic Nazca plate has been sliding eastward under the South American plate, raising the mountains and creating a deep trench off the coast (Wicander and Monroe 1989:157; Windley 1995:105–12). Two parallel mountain ranges dominate the central Andes – the *Cordillera Oriental* (or *Blanca*) on the east and the *Cordillera Occidental* (or *Negra*) on the west. The peaks of the eastern range are about 1,000 m higher than those of the west; they are also wider and more continuous, but both are effective barriers to the moisture-bearing trade winds. In the north, transverse ranges called *nudos* (knots) break up the landscape into a few large drainages and many small valleys. The highest snowcap in the Americas – Mt. Aconcagua (6,960 m) – lies along the Chile–Argentina border. It was just one of more than fifty peaks that the Incas revered by building a shrine near the summit.

Periodically, the movement of the earth's plates touches off catastrophic earthquakes. In 1970, a temblor centered near Lima claimed about 70,000 lives. In the quake's most dramatic event, a mountain face sheared off in the Callejón de Huaylas, triggering an avalanche that

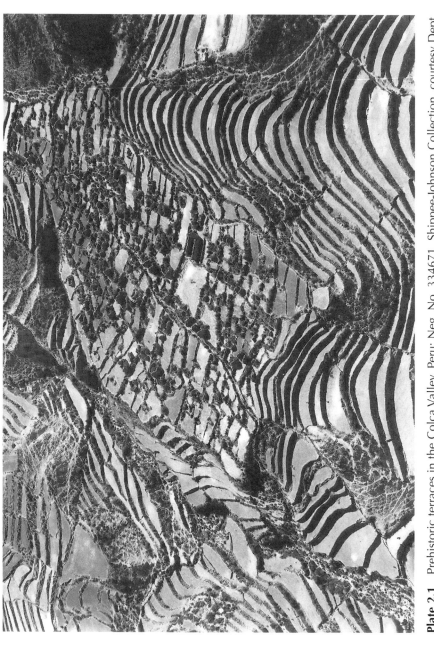

Plate 2.1 Prehistoric terraces in the Colca Valley, Peru; Neg. No. 334671, Shippee-Johnson Collection, courtesy Dept. of Library Services, American Museum of Natural History

wiped out the town of Yungay and most of its 4,000 residents in a few minutes. Plate tectonics have also created three active volcanic zones along the spine of the mountains from central Colombia to central Chile. Even though vulcanism is less of a threat than other natural forces, eruptions can still have a major impact on life. In AD 1600, for instance, the mountain called Huayna Putina (Peru) disappeared in an explosion that killed tens of thousands of people (Moseley 1992:27). Layers of ash in archaeological deposits attest to analogous, though perhaps less catastrophic, events in prehistory.

The Andes abound with mineral deposits, including the volcanic glass called obsidian that was widely used to make cutting tools. Copper-bearing deposits are found along the entire mountain chain, while tin is concentrated in Bolivia and northern Chile. One of the most famous mines of the Colonial era was the silver operation at Potosí, Bolivia, which enriched a few Spaniards at a notable cost in Andean energy and lives. Gold also was found in plenty, much of it along the eastern side of the mountains where it was recovered from veins and placer mining (Berthelot 1986; Windley 1995:111–12).

Climate

The climate has contributed in important ways to Andean life by conditioning the annual round of life for farmers and herders and helping to determine the locations that could support settlements. Broadly speaking, there are two trends in western South America: from the temperate south in Chile to the tropics in Colombia, and from the arid west to the humid east. Those patterns result from the interaction of the ocean currents, mountains, and trade winds. The Chile–Peru trench, which lies just off the shoreline, provides a conduit for the Humboldt Current's frigid waters flowing north from the Antarctic. As the waters well upwards, they bring up nutrients that sustain rich beds of plankton. These tiny plants form the first link in a biotic chain whose fisheries were among the world's most productive until they were over-exploited in the twentieth century. The coastal waters are especially rich in anchovies and sardines, and in larger fish, such as tuna, salmon, and sea bass. Sea lions, seals, and fishing birds such as pelicans and cormorants are sustained in large numbers by the fish. Both the rocky and the sandy littoral zones provide many kinds of shellfish; their remains are piled up to five meters deep in scores of pre-ceramic sites. Even with traditional techniques like the simple nets and reed boats called *caballitos* ("little horses"), the inshore waters have been a bounteous source of food for the last five thousand years.

The climatic cycles produce two wet and dry seasons each year north of Peru, but only one each in the central Andes, the heartland of the Inca empire. From June to November, the prevailing oceanic winds blow in from the southwest. As the air warms up over the land, the relative humidity drops so quickly that rain almost never falls near the coast. Instead, a heavy fog (*garúa*) straddles the shoreline, trapped in place by an upper layer of warmer air. During the rest of the year, when there is no temperature inversion, the air flows up the sharp Andean escarpment and the moisture falls out as rain. Since most precipitation falls above 1,600 m, it can be used for farming only after the water runs back down and is tapped off for irrigation. On the other side of the central Andes, the equatorial easterlies bank up against the mountains, cool, and drop their abundant moisture on the forested mountain faces. All the rain that falls east of the continental divide helps to swell the Amazon, which discharges more water than any other river on the planet – about fifteen times the volume of the Mississippi (Burger 1992:15, 21).

The regular cycles are intermittently disrupted by a phenomenon called *El Niño* (the Child), so named because it normally peaks around Christmas (Diaz and Markgraf 1992). When an event occurs, the trade winds slacken as part of a global weather pattern. Warm equatorial waters flow south along the Peruvian coastline, suppressing the upwelling of cold southern waters. In strong events, like that of 1997–8, the effects are catastrophic. Torrential rains destroy coastal crops and wash away canal systems, roads, and exposed settlements. Fish and birds die in massive numbers or migrate out of the range accessible to traditional methods of capture. Because the environment can take several years to recover fully, some archaeologists suggest that El Niño and other natural forces may have helped trigger social upheavals by disrupting food production (Moseley 1983). At the same time that the coast suffers downpours, the highlands receive less than average rainfall. Since El Niño occurs at intervals of two to eleven years, prehistoric people could not predict its cycle, but could be sure that its damaging effects would recur. Intriguingly, however, potato farmers of the high Andes can anticipate the mountain droughts by gazing at the stars. When the star group called the *qollqa* ("granary," i.e., the Pleiades) is obscured in June by the high clouds that precede an event, the farmers know that dry times are coming and irrigate their crops. Clear skies mean that the rains will come in November and they plan accordingly (Orlove et al. 2000).

Environmental Zones

Over the years, geographers have developed many ways to classify the Andes' natural environments. A widely used scheme, devised by Javier

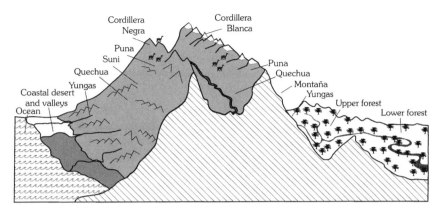

Figure 2.1 Cross-section of the major life zones in the central Andes (source: Burger 1992:21)

Pulgar Vidal (1987), combines native terminology with modern biotic classifications to divide the central Andean environment into eight zones (figure 2.1). From north Peru to central Chile, the entire coast (*chala* or *costa*) is a sere desert, punctuated only by drainages that cut ribbons of green through a pastel landscape of drifting sands and jagged rock formations. Where irrigation is practicable, the valley bottoms are lush croplands, but seepage and evaporation can cost canals as much as 85 percent of their water (Shimada 1994:42). Among the most important indigenous crops are maize, cucurbits (e.g. squash, cucumber), gourd, and cotton; in the twentieth century, sugar cane became a major export crop. Other foods included algarrobo (pods of the carob tree) and fruits such as chirimoya and lúcuma, which is used today to make a popular ice cream flavor that tastes vaguely like caramelized milk. Protein in the coastal diet was enhanced primarily with shellfish and fish. Above the coastal plain lies the warmer *yungas* zone (300–2,300 m). The most important crops here are coca and *ají* (pepper), along with fruits, such as chirimoya, guayabo, avocado, and lúcuma. Together with maize, coca has long been a common element in gifts and sacrifices, and was given in vast quantities to Inca subjects in a kind of obligatory state largess. Another *yungas* band lies on the eastern side of the Andes above the Amazonian jungles; it may have been even more productive than its coastal counterpart.

The temperate *quechua* band (3,100–3,500 m) is the most productive highland ecozone. In the valley bottoms, dry-farming produces maize, beans, garden vegetables, the native grains quinoa and cañihua, a variety of tubers such as potato, ulluco, oca, and mashwa, and the legume called

Plate 2.2 A flock of llamas, the principal beast of burden and source of meat for Andean peoples (slide by author)

talwi. Today the Asian grains of wheat and barley are often sown in place of the native crops. Above these lands lies the *suni* zone (up to 4,000 m), which features cold hills, ridges, and deep valleys. This zone is especially productive for the Andean tubers, quinoa, and talwi. Today, more than 470 varieties of potatoes have been identified, many of which are far tastier than the outsized spuds found in supermarket bins. In prehistory, this was also a prime zone for hunting, especially deer.

Above this land lies the *puna* (up to 5,000 m), an alpine tundra that is the natural habitat for the Andean camelids. The weather is usually cold and damp, with heavy fogs and violent storms that roll over the ground during the wet season. This zone was used for herding llamas and alpacas (plate 2.2) and hunting guanacos, vicuñas, and Virginia and white-tailed deer. Although the puna is marginal for most agriculture, some frost-resistant tubers can be grown, such as bitter potatoes and maca. Even higher is the bone-chilling cold of the *janca* zone, which features permanent snowcaps and glacial lakes, along with abundant mineral wealth. At about 4,700 m, the modern communities near the pass called Ticlio (Peru) are the highest permanently inhabited towns in the world; they are serviced by the world's highest railroad (4,900 m). It is a testament to human resilience that every town has its own football field.

Down the eastern Peruvian slopes lie the upper Amazonian jungles, called the *montaña*, and the lower forest, called the *selva*. The upper edge of the Amazonian forest itself is known as the *ceja de selva* or "eyebrow of the jungle." The steep terraces and valley bottoms of the montaña produce maize, coca, fruit, pepper, and other warm-weather crops. Although this zone was sparsely populated in prehistory, it was still important economically. The verdant Amazonion forest below contains fertile plains where the root crop called manioc is a staple. During Inca times, jungle societies were scattered and simply organized, but the Incas attempted to draw them into the empire, for they coveted the gold, wood, and brilliant feathers that the lowlands yielded.

To the north, Ecuador's coastal mangrove swamps and western woodlands proved inhospitable to the Incas and they never managed to draw them effectively into the empire. The intermontane valleys, in contrast, enjoy such a delightful climate that they were chosen for the northern Inca capital, called Tumipampa. Intermixed in the highlands are the rolling grasslands called the *páramo*, which were suitable for camelid pasturage though generally not part of their natural range. South of Peru, the high cordilleras are bridged by the *altiplano*, a windswept plain that runs through upland Bolivia into northwest Argentina. Potatoes and chenopods are the main cultivars in this cold land, but the great flocks of camelids were more important culturally, for they provided

wool, meat, cargo transport, and wealth for their owners. At its
north end, the plain encloses Lake Titicaca (3,800 m), the world's highest
navigable lake. South of the altiplano on the eastern side of the peaks
lie the dry intermontane valleys (*valliserrana*) of Argentina; to the west
are the Atacama desert and central Chile's temperate uplands. The
southern Andes were less fertile than lands to the north, but they still
supported towns in areas where snow-fed rivers could be tapped for
irrigation.

Such modern classifications only partially mesh with folk categories,
of course. Andean peoples use both their own cultural visions and knowledge amenable to a scientific viewpoint, for they live in a world teem-
ing with all manner of powers. To highland peoples, each land zone
embraces both physical features and symbolic phenomena. The people
in Peru's Ayacucho region, for example, think of the quechua zone as
the land of agriculture and civilized people (Flannery et al. 1989:21–4).
The puna is where the camelids live, farming is insignificant, and the
people are primitive. The snow-capped peaks are home to the *wamanis*
– powerful spirits who control the weather and own the flocks. For many
societies of the late prehistoric Andes, the summits were the origin places
for the ancestors, whose spirits still roam the earth (Reinhard 1985).
In Andean eyes, successful relations with the environment call for an
intimate knowledge of the landscape, a keen eye for weather, and a
congenial relationship with the land's many inhabitants.

Traditional Land Use Today

Farming

Traditional communities in the central Andes are based on a kin group
called the *ayllu*, just as they were in Inca times. Members of this group
believe that they share a common ancestor and place of origin. They hold
their productive resources collectively and allocate them to families
according to their size and status. Whenever possible, an *ayllu* will
include a variety of farmlands and pastures in its holdings. Each household will ideally have access to a full complement of production zones,
so that its members can produce all the basics of life themselves in
concert with their neighbors. *Ayllu* usually contain two or three opposing parts, often called upper (*hanan*) and lower (*hurin*), or left-right-
center (*ichuq-allawqa-chaupi*). *Ayllu* members typically take their
spouses from another division and thus keep resources within the larger
group.

To take advantage of the varied natural environment and achieve self-sufficiency, communities distribute their members across the landscape (Brush 1977). In steep lands like those of the eastern Andes, the main settlement lies at a mid-elevation between maize and tuber lands. Smaller hamlets are placed in the puna for herding or in the lowlands to grow coca, pepper, and fruits. In some cases, the main and offshoot communities lie a week's travel or more apart across the lands of other ethnic groups. This *archipelago* settlement pattern can be employed to exploit resources such as coca, salt, and guano; sometimes members of several different communities share access to the same resources (Murra 1968, 1972; Masuda et al. 1985). Where the gradients are gentler – for example, in the Urubamba Valley where the Inca royalty built estates – the population is spread more evenly across the terrain to take advantage of broader areas of arable land.

William Mitchell's (1980) studies in Quinua, near Cuzco, show how altitude and the local ecology affect agricultural practices. During the most important growing season, crops are planted in November and December. Sowing moves downhill from the highest plots so that the last planting coincides with the first rains. The members of several households may share labor in long-standing relationships of reciprocal assistance. By irrigating crops before the rains arrive, the farmers can move the harvests forward and beat the killing frosts. This approach to land use both increases harvests and reduces risk, because the conditions that cause crops to fail in one zone may produce a bountiful crop elsewhere. The staggered agrarian cycle also uses household labor efficiently, since planting and harvesting are spread out over time.

Several million of Tawantinsuyu's subjects also lived along the Peruvian coast, where the ecological setting, as well as some social and economic features, differed in important ways from the Incas' mountainous heartland. In prehistoric times, the steep terrain and hydrology limited the amount of the major drainage basins that could be farmed to no more than 17 percent (Kroeber 1930; Shimada 1994:42). Even so, the rich bottom lands of entire valleys were irrigated by the beginning of the first millennium AD. The most extensive irrigation systems in the Americas lay along Peru's north coast, where sets of adjacent valleys were linked by canal networks. Once in place, the irrigation networks – and the social systems that depended upon them – could be disrupted by coastal uplift, earthquakes, El Niño events, river channel downcutting, salinization of the aquifers, and wind-blown sands (Moseley et al. 1992). Under the circumstances, building and maintaining canal systems was a continuous challenge.

Herding

Pastoralism has been the indispensable complement to farming in the Andes for millennia. Of the four native camelids, only the llama and alpaca were domesticated, while the guanaco and vicuña remain wild. Llamas are best suited to elevations above 3,000 m, while the alpaca's core range lies above 4,200 m (Gade 1977:116). Archaeological studies indicate that the presence of camelids on the coast or in most of the *páramo* grasslands of northern Peru and Ecuador was a direct result of human intervention (Miller and Gill 1990). Drovers have been taking caravans to the coast for thousands of years and some scholars suggest that herds were tended there in prehistory.

Researchers have taken an intense interest in traditional pastoralists in recent years, because they are one of the few groups who practice lifeways much like those of their pre-Columbian forebears (Flores Ochoa 1977). The alpine tundra contains a patchwork of useful microenvironments, including turf, tallgrass, and moor puna, even if frost falls on the bleak land 9–12 months per year (Flannery et al. 1989:16). Modern herders often live in small, widely scattered units called *kancha*, the Quechua word for "enclosure." In this case, things have changed since prehistory, for Peruvian herding settlements in Inca times housed hundreds of residents (Parsons et al. 1998). Like farmers, the herders maintain a network of group assistance and ritual for herding, shearing, and butchering. They move their small herds of 18–35 animals from pasture to pasture following a seasonal round (Flannery et al. 1989: 50–1). The puna's residents also tend fields in lower reaches to make freeze-dried potatoes, called *chuño*, a delicacy of dubious flavor to a foreign palate. *Chuño* is made by alternating freezing the potatoes and then stamping out their moisture (ibid.:78–81). A similar process of freeze-drying meat produces *ch'arki*, a word that has been adopted into English parlance as "jerky." *Chuño* and *ch'arki* are long-lasting and lightweight foods that are used on trips when travelers carry much of their food. They were staples of the Inca armies on the move.

Both llamas and alpacas produce useful wool, but the light weight and fineness of alpaca wool make it preferable for clothes and other textiles. The wool of vicuñas, prized for its silky warmth, was a royal prerogative under Inca rule; today, vicuñas are a protected species. The llama is used more for meat (100 edible kg for a buck llama) than its smaller relatives and is the only camelid used for cargo. Even though it can tolerate extreme cold and heights and forages for its food, a llama still has its limitations as a beast of burden. A male buck will carry a load of about 30 kg for 20 km per day and it is usually rested one traveling day out of three by carrying no burden (West 1981). Animals break down even with good care and, when tired, will refuse to budge. Their unhurried pace means that a round trip from the altiplano to the coast can take almost two months. Consequently, even though military caravans could contain thousands of llamas, Murra (1980b) judges that human porters carried the bulk of the cargo in late prehistory (chapter 9).

Human Physiology in the Andean Environment

The human occupation of the high Andes is impressive not just because of the challenges of getting adequate food, but because of the physiological stresses the body endures. Today, over ten million people live at elevations between 2,500 m and 5,000 m, while about two-thirds of the Andean population lived above 3,000 m in 1532. At 3,000 m, the partial pressure of oxygen is only about 60–70 percent of the pressure at sea level, which can put severe strains on the human cardio-pulmonary system. Individuals adapted to coastal conditions suffer from shortness of breath, headaches, and nausea at altitudes where highlanders play football or run marathons. In some cases, altitude sickness (called *soroche* or *puna*) can be fatal. Studies of the bioenergetics of modern sierra peoples show that they have a caloric intake much lower than that of most people living in western society. Brooke Thomas's (1973) research in Nuñoa, Peru, shows that an adult male of about 55 kg expends on average 2,094 kcal per day, while an adult female of 50 kg expends 1,610 kcal per day. Those figures are much lower than the 2,500 kcal/day typically recommended for western adults or the 3,500 recommended for US soldiers or estimated for other ancient societies (Van Creveld 1977:21, 24; Engels 1978:123; Hassig 1985:20–1).

Although individuals can adjust to elevation changes and many factors affect stature, some physiological characteristics among native peoples vary genetically. Andean highlanders tend to be shorter and have larger chest capacities than their coastal neighbors. Large lungs especially have been selected for among the highlanders in the 800 or so generations that they have lived in the upper reaches. Intriguingly, some differences also exist between highland groups of Quechua and Aymara ancestry who occupied similar locales in the Titicaca basin. This indicates that choice of mates among ethnic groups also had a hand in creating the biological character of modern Andean peoples.

Predecessors

Archaeologists have made great strides in identifying and explaining the major changes that occurred in Andean prehistory, but readily admit that we still have a long way to go in accounting for the emergence of complex societies. Theories tend to focus on a few key issues in seeking explanations for the rise of the early states. Among the most important are population growth and the concentration of people in more urbanized settlements. As societies expanded and nucleated, their interactions made it harder to maintain social order and obtain adequate food. On the other hand, the close interaction of larger numbers of people provided a setting that fostered intellectual life and creativity. Increases in food production, specialization of labor, and coordination of labor for tasks ranging from erecting monuments to warfare were also crucial. When found together, they indicate that society had centralized leadership and that its members were interdependent for their livelihoods in ways that fed back on one another to produce even more complexity.

Socially, the most important change was the appearance of inherited status differences. This shift signaled differences in access to power and prestige that were ascribed at birth and laid the foundations for class society. Formalized ideologies explained humanity's place in the cosmos and provided rationales for life, but the beliefs also often legitimized social inequality by proposing separate origins for the elite and common members of society. The religions thus simultaneously bonded societies and justified disparities in rank and power. The beliefs were given physical form in monumental architecture, such as pyramids, palaces, and open spaces, in art, and in ceremonies that sometimes venerated the dead as if they were still among the living. In terms of political life, the creation of offices with specific duties allowed a privileged few individuals or kin groups to control the accumulation of information and thus to wield disproportionate power within society. Those individuals gathered and guarded information, set policy, and made day-to-day decisions; all of those actions were advanced by the invention of standardized recording systems.

Each of those features was well established in the Andes more than a thousand years before the rise of Inca power (figures 2.2, 2.3). Until the Incas, however, we only get glimmers of what the people of the time thought about themselves and the forces that surrounded them, and how those views affected the ways that they ordered their lives. Colonial-era documents provide great insights into Andean thought in the sixteenth century, but it is a chancy business to push those ideas too far back into the past. Most of the information came from a few elites with their own

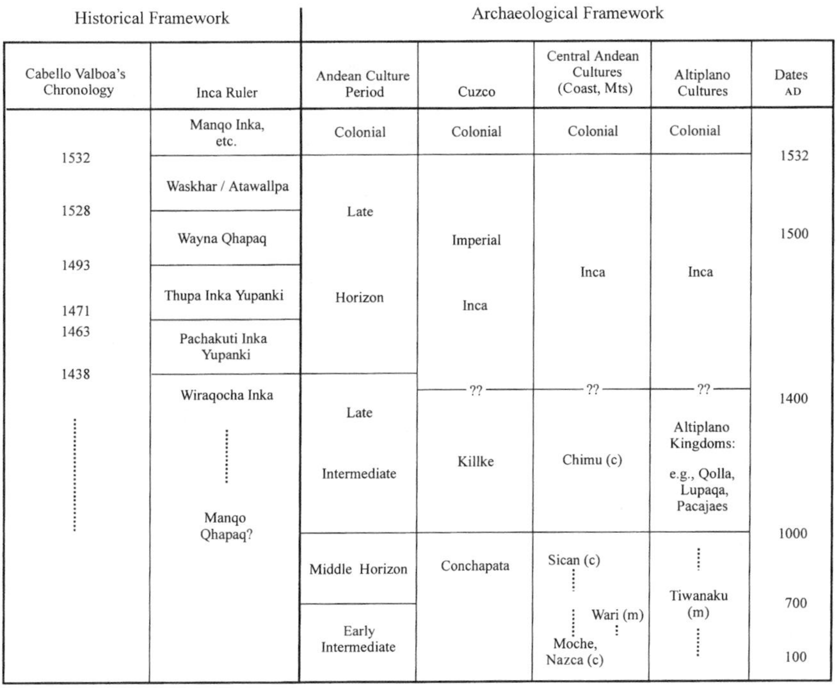

Historical Framework		Archaeological Framework				
Cabello Valboa's Chronology	Inca Ruler	Andean Culture Period	Cuzco	Central Andean Cultures (Coast, Mts)	Altiplano Cultures	Dates AD
1532	Manqo Inka, etc.	Colonial	Colonial	Colonial	Colonial	1532
1528	Waskhar / Atawallpa	Late				
1493	Wayna Qhapaq		Imperial			1500
1471	Thupa Inka Yupanki	Horizon	Inca	Inca	Inca	
1463	Pachakuti Inka Yupanki					
1438						
⋮	Wiraqocha Inka	Late	—??—	—??—	—??—	1400
⋮	⋮		Killke	Chimu (c)	Altiplano Kingdoms: e.g., Qolla, Lupaqa, Pacajaes	
⋮	Manqo Qhapaq?	Intermediate				1000
		Middle Horizon	Conchapata	Sican (c) ⋮	⋮	
				⋮ Wari (m) ⋮	Tiwanaku (m)	700
		Early Intermediate		Moche, Nazca (c)	⋮	100

Figure 2.2 Chronological chart of Andean prehistory

viewpoints and positions to protect. Their ideas were usually filtered through translators, scribes, and administrators whose own convictions were woven into the documents. Because Andean world views are such a rich field, I will just sketch out pre-Inca history here and save an exploration of Andean beliefs for a later point (esp. chapter 7).

Following a long period of slow development, important changes began to occur rapidly by about 2,500 BC in the Cotton Preceramic period. About this time, simple foraging groups began to use crops more frequently and to build the first significant corporate architecture, such as small pyramids (Bird and Hyslop 1985). Soon thereafter (Initial Period: 1800–800 BC), some coastal peoples settled the inland parts of valleys, where they erected spectacular ceremonial complexes and began the irrigation agriculture that provided the foundation for the civilizations to come. Similarities in design among at least 45 ceremonial complexes along the Peruvian coast suggest that the builders shared cosmological notions. The visual imagery of the pyramids was truly imposing. Some had pillared entrances, stairwells, and brilliant friezes,

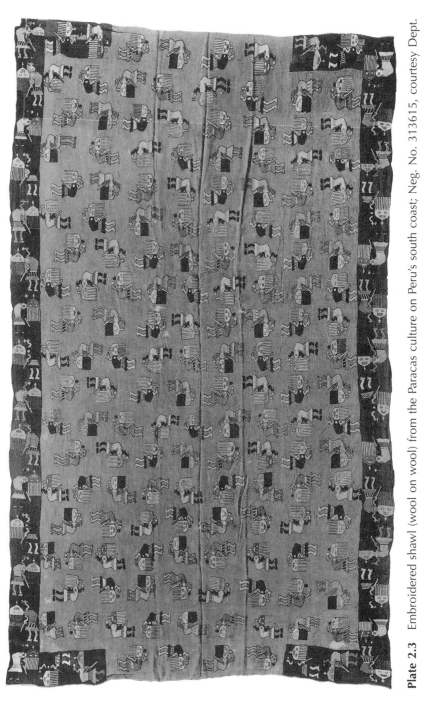

Plate 2.3 Embroidered shawl (wool on wool) from the Paracas culture on Peru's south coast; Neg. No. 313615, courtesy Dept. of Library Services, American Museum of Natural History

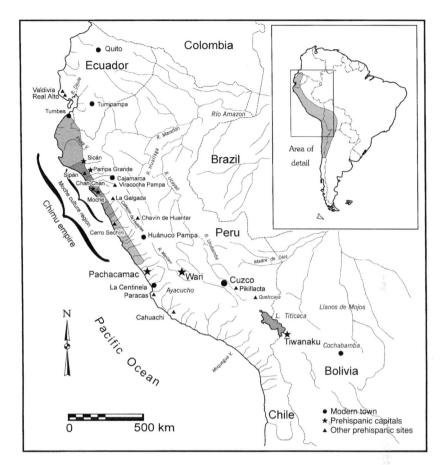

Figure 2.3   Locations of major pre-Inca sites and culture regions described in the text

while a gruesome parade of warriors and dismembered human bodies at Cerro Sechín suggests that human sacrifice or ritualized warfare was important to social power in the area (Donnan 1986; Burger 1992). The first millennium BC is most often associated with the religious iconography of an integrative cult, centered at the highland site called Chavín de Huantar (Burger 1992). The era saw important advances in craft technology. Potters made ornately modeled and incised pieces; metallurgy included soldering, sweat welding, repoussé, and silver-gold alloying; and weaving innovated use of the heddle loom. The most dazzling textiles from the prehistoric Americas date to the end of this period, from cemeteries on the arid Paracas Peninsula (plate 2.3).

Plate 2.4 The Chimu capital city of Chan Chan on the north Peruvian coast; Neg. No. 334897, Shippee-Johnson Collection, courtesy Dept. of Library Services, American Museum of Natural History

From AD 100 to 700, the first state and urban societies in the Andes arose on Peru's north coast. Evidence from burials and iconography suggests that the leaders of Moche society blended sacred, military, political, and social roles without developing the distinct administrative institutions seen in other pristine states, such as Uruk Mesopotamia. The so-called Pyramid of the Sun at Moche, which contained about 143 million bricks, was the largest adobe structure ever raised in the native Americas. Moche crafts, which are coveted on the art market, reflect both artisanry and large-scale manufacturing by specialists who worked for elite patrons and the populace at large. Discoveries at Sipán and other similar sites since 1987 have yielded the most spectacular burials ever excavated professionally in the New World. In modest pyramids, burials of adult men and women dressed as the central figures in a sacrificial ceremony have yielded literally tons of exquisite grave goods (Alva and Donnan 1994; Castillo and Donnan 1994).

About the same time that Moche flourished, two great cities emerged in the highlands. In southern Peru, Wari rose to power in the Ayacucho Basin about AD 500–750 (Schreiber 1992). Its leaders expanded their dominion by erecting far-flung, planned settlements in locations where they could control transport and communications. By this time, knot-records were already in use as a device for precise data recording. Hundreds of years later, the Incas adopted some of the same principles of statecraft and even appropriated Wari's roads. Tiwanaku, which lies just south of Lake Titicaca, became fully urban by about AD 375 and extended ties or founded colonies on the coast, the Bolivian lowlands, and northwest Argentina (Kolata 1993). The capital included temples, a pyramid, and an expansive residential community. Both Tiwanaku and Lake Titicaca were revered in the Inca view of the world, since their origin myths narrated that the Creator God, the sun, the moon, and the stars had all emerged from the lake. The city's Gateway of the Sun and outsized human statues were incorporated into Inca mythology, while the town was recognized as one of two symbolic capitals in a level just below Cuzco.

As Wari and Tiwanaku collapsed, the Peruvian coast resurged as home to the dominant Andean polities. By AD 1400, a group called the Chimu had emerged in the old Moche Valley heartland and united the entire north coast (Rowe 1948; Moseley and Cordy-Collins 1990). The aristocrats who lived in the main city, called Chan Chan, formed the wealthy apex of a highly stratified society (plate 2.4). Sometime in the fifteenth century, the empire of Chimor and its million-plus inhabitants fell to the Inca armies. Minchançaman, the last emperor, was taken to Cuzco, and the empire was dismantled. With him went many of his smiths, renowned as the most skilled in the Andes.

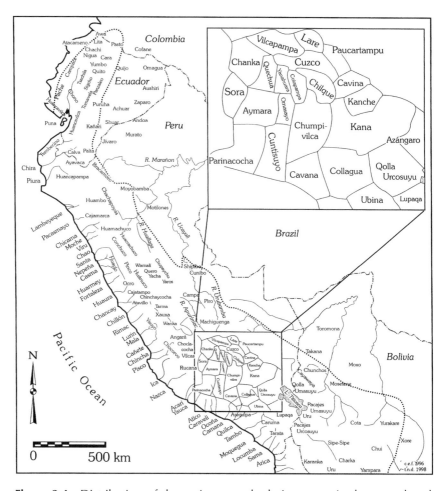

Figure 2.4 Distribution of the major named ethnic groups in the central and north Andes, after Rowe 1946: inset map; Saignes 1985; Fresco, personal communication

The Incas themselves emerged from a highland political environment that was fragmented into hundreds of independent societies by AD 1000. Figures 2.4 and 2.5 illustrate the distribution of many of the major ethnic groups (*etnías*) that were drawn into the Inca empire. The cultural landscape would look different, however, if we changed the scale of our focus. In the pre-Inca era, many ethnic groups had internal social divisions or included several autonomous polities, called *señoríos* by the Spaniards. Although the Inca provinces were usually built on existing

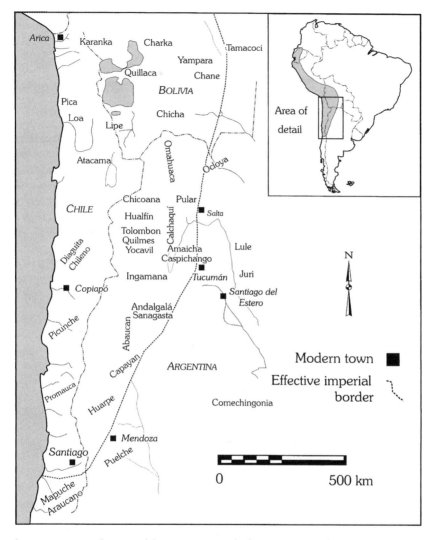

Figure 2.5 Distribution of the major named ethnic groups in the southern Andes, after Berberián and Raffino 1991; Lorandi, personal communication 1998

etnías, groups were often recombined for administrative convenience. These maps therefore provide only an approximation. They follow Rowe's (1946:185–92, inset map) convention of identifying regions along the Peruvian coast by valley name, rather than by the many named groups living there.

Both oral traditions and archaeology suggest that warfare was rife in the sierra from Ecuador to Argentina after AD 1200. Many communities settled on the peaks in protected villages well above the best farmlands. Some of the most powerful societies of the time, including the Lupaqa and Qolla, lived around Lake Titicaca. In the early Colonial era, they called their pre-Inca rulers kings, but they do not seem to have attained a state level of organization. Groups living in the populous Peruvian sierra, such as the Wankas, lived in towns that contained as many as 4,500 densely packed circular houses and may have housed 10,000 or more people. In the south Andes, the largest towns contained a few thousand people, but regional polities still held no more than 20,000. By AD 1200, the Cuzco area itself may have been an oasis of relative tranquility, already integrated under pre-state Inca rule. That development set the stage for the meteoric rise of Tawantinsuyu (chapter 4).

Even this sketch illustrates that complex society had been developing for millennia before Cuzco's ascendancy. The Incas saw things another way, of course, insisting to the Spaniards that they had brought order and civilization to a chaotic world. Conversely, some of their subjects complained that their own cultures had been irrevocably disrupted by barbaric conquerors, Inca and Spaniard alike, but their voices were not so clearly heard.

Languages

The language of the Incas is known today as Southern Peruvian Quechua, but its speakers knew it as *runasimi*, or human speech. The linguist Bruce Mannheim (1991) suggests that the term *Quechua* was probably imposed early in the Colonial period by Spaniards who mistook the word *qheswa* (valley) in the phrase *qheswa simi* (valley speech) for the name of the language. Native peoples then adopted the term back into their own tongue in various forms, including the word for the mountainous ecological zone described earlier. I use the term Quechua here as it is commonly applied, to describe the Incas' language and its close relatives. By 1532, Quechua was entrenched as the *lingua franca* of Tawantinsuyu; it was the language in which all official business was supposed to be conducted. Among the earliest Spanish writers, it was generally known as one of the three principal languages of the land, along with Aymara and the now-defunct Puquina of the Titicaca basin. Scores of other languages also fell into disuse in the Colonial and historical periods. Today there are seven dialects of Quechua, each with its own lexicon and grammar. In Peru, Quechua and Spanish are the two official state languages and the native tongue remains an important or even exclusive language of millions of people. In the Mantaro Valley of Peru's central highlands, where I worked in the 1970s and 1980s, field assistants who had been born by 1945 were fluent in Quechua, but few of those born later spoke it in everyday conversation.

The impact of using Quechua for state business is written today in place names from Ecuador to Argentina, because the Incas renamed mountains and other natural features after sacred locations around Cuzco. For example, the peak named Huanacauri that overlooks modern Cuenca, Ecuador, got its name from a sacred mountain southeast of Cuzco. Similarly, the town in Salta province (Argentina) where I have been working in recent years is named *Cachi* – the Quechua word for salt. A bit farther to the south is a town called Sanogasta – "potter's town" – which combines the Quechua word for clay (*sañu*) with the Kakano word for town (*gasta*; Lorandi 1984). In truth, today's Andes are a memory landscape for the Inca language.

A comment is in order about the spellings used here. Since rules of orthography had not yet been formalized in Spanish in the sixteenth century, the chroniclers used their own discretion in spelling both their own and American languages. In this text, I generally use traditional spellings of place names, but modernize other terminology. In quotations, the names of individuals are kept as in the original. For purposes of broad recognition, I have retained the more traditional spelling of the Inca ethnic group, but otherwise use standardized Quechua orthography for names of important individuals, such as the Inca rulers. A glossary of foreign terms is found at the end of the book.

Time Frames

There is little doubt that the Inca empire was a short-lived phenomenon that lasted about a century. Efforts to assign dates to major events of the Inca past, however, run aground on a host of problems – a lack of indigenous writing, the political uses of history, and the ways that Andean peoples reckoned time. Modern authors usually cite the last part of the chronology outlined in 1586 by the cleric Miguel de Cabello Valboa (1951). He estimated that the imperial era began in AD 1438 when the Incas repelled an attack by the Chankas, an ethnic group that lived to the west of Cuzco. He calculated that the next three successions took place in 1471, 1493, and 1526. In 1944, lacking any means of determining absolute dates, John Rowe (1944:57) judged that this imperial sequence was the most plausible to be found in the chronicles. Rowe made his recommendation cautiously, based on a close analysis of many sources, and considered Cabello's pre-imperial succession dates to be unlikely.

Even though we do not know Cabello's sources, it helped matters that his dates were supported indirectly. Most chroniclers reported that the imperial era lasted through the reigns of Pachakuti Inka Yupanki, Thupa Inka Yupanki, and Wayna Qhapaq, followed by a civil war between two of Wayna Qhapaq's sons. The conquest sequences recounted in Cuzco also often coincided with those recorded in the provinces, albeit with some discrepancies. In addition, members of several ethnic groups living around Cuzco in the 1570s recalled that their ancestors a generation or two back had been brought in by the three emperors named above. Together, those lines of evidence suggest that Cabello may have been pretty close to the mark.

For many scholars, however, use of his chronology has been as much a matter of convention as conviction. The Spanish accounts that drew on Inca narrative history produced at least four date sequences other than Cabello's. Sarmiento's official history, for example, was based on interviews with more than a hundred record-keepers in Cuzco and read publicly before the nobility to assure its veracity. Even so, the process yielded dates that are patently unbelievable, as numerous rulers lived to be well over 100. From the Inca perspective, a specific number of years was incidental. Since eminence and great age went hand in hand, it was only fitting that the rulers had lived well beyond the natural life span of normal human beings.[1] Part of the imprecision can also be traced to the fact that the Incas did not keep close track of the accumulating years, even though they traced annual cycles carefully (Rowe 1946:274). According to Cobo (1979:252–3), "When they are asked about things of the past, if something happened more than four to six years back, what they usually answer is that the incident occurred ñaupapacha, which means 'a long time ago'; and they give the same answer for events of twenty years back as for events of a hundred or a thousand years back, except that when the thing is very ancient, they express this by a certain accent and ponderation of their words."[2] Moreover, as noted in chapter 1, the Spaniards heard many different accounts of the Inca past and the organization of the khipu knot-records. Their history was kept orally by mnemonic specialists, who used the knot-records to assist their memories. Since the khipu were organized partially by hierarchies of power and space as well as by time, some scholars judge that translating the oral sagas into European histories is a futile endeavor.

Archaeologists have therefore turned to radiocarbon and thermo-luminescence dating methods in efforts to pin down the emergence of the empire. Even under the best conditions, however, these techniques contain an intrinsic error term; dates consist of a bracket of calendar years, based on probabilities. They are also subject to a variety of other problems arising, for example, from re-use of materials or misidentified

contexts. The lack of certainty in the dates leaves some scholars skeptical that current radiometric evidence can improve on the historical estimates, while others judge that enough information exists to permit some
tentative statements about the timing of the Inca era. My own view is
that there is enough evidence to suggest that the first major surge of Inca
expansionism occurred early in the fifteenth century, perhaps 40–50
years earlier than the historical chronology estimates (Bauer 1992c;
Adamska and Michczński 1996). A few decades is not a major shift in
calendrical time, but it does imply that we need to be careful in taking
the historical chronologies too literally.

Despite the discrepancies, the chronometric evidence and the historical accounts both suggest that the empire was a late prehistoric phenomenon that lasted somewhere close to a century. Archaeology also
indicates that there was a roughly contemporaneous extension of Inca
material culture across the Andes, as we might expect from a polity that
was rapidly expanding. Beyond those broad conclusions, however, we
cannot refine the chronology any more than to say the empire arose
quickly, probably early in the fifteenth century, and lasted for only a few
generations.

chapter three
The Incas before the Empire

Considering the impact that the Incas had on the Andes, it is remarkable how little we know about their pre-imperial society. We can lay some of our plight at the doorstep of the royal narratives, which were grand epics intended to exalt the heroic and supernatural creation of Inca society. Constantly reshaped in the telling, they flowed smoothly from the mythical origins of mighty ancestors to the lives of people the conquistadores met in the flesh. As for archaeology, the imperial building programs largely wiped out the Killke (pre-imperial) settlements of the Cuzco basin. Even with a recent increase in fieldwork in nearby areas, studies of early Inca occupations are limited. This situation means that explaining what propelled the Incas from their confined homeland to dominate the Andes still calls for a fair amount of informed conjecture.

Following the decline of Wari and Tiwanaku in the late first millennium AD, the Incas were probably just one of several ethnic groups jockeying for power in southern Peru. Sometime around 1400, the Incas began to emerge as the dominant regional polity. The initial pace of change seems to have been gradual, but once the Incas began to expand their realm in earnest, a society of about one hundred thousand people asserted its rule over a population of ten to twelve million in just a few decades. That was an astonishing achievement by any measure, probably best paralleled in antiquity by Alexander the Great's exploits. The signal difference was that Tawantinsuyu did not fracture with the death of its founder.

Although we cannot build a credible early Inca history, it is possible to examine the tales for themes and internal coherence. The politics they describe are consistent with what we know ethnographically about chiefdoms, hierarchical societies in which power tends to coalesce over several generations in the hands of elite lineages. The endemic warfare, marriages between ethnic groups, fragile alliances, and frequent resettlement are also appropriate to societies without centralized rule. The Incas claimed that they emerged from an uneasy regional balance when a young prince named Inka Yupanki defended Cuzco against an aggressive neighbor while his father and most of the residents sought refuge in a nearby redoubt. The prince then pursued wealth, glory, and power in a process that snowballed with each success. There may be some truth in that celebrated account, but a single, overarching cause or an explanation based solely on historical events is almost surely incomplete. It is far more probable that many elements – political and economic conditions, ideology, military strategies, wrangling among kin groups, and maybe even the climate – were linked with historical circumstances. It also seems likely that the forces that led to the first conquests were only partially related to the causes of later expansions. To set the pre-imperial situation, we will take a brief look here at both the legendary and the archaeological information.

Ancient Times

Mythical Origins

Early Inca history consists of genealogies and fables, rooted in primordial time (Urton 1990; Bauer 1991). The annals of the Inca past customarily begin with the deified Manqo Qhapaq and continue through twelve or thirteen rulers (figure 3.1; table 3.1). Like many Andean peoples, the Incas believed that their ancestors had emerged from a natural feature of the landscape. In ancient times, went the main legend, there was a cave called the House of Windows (*Tampu T'oqo*) at the Inn of Dawn (*Pacariqtambo*). The Creator God summoned the four brothers and four sisters who became the Inca ancestors from the central cave called the Rich Window (*Qhapaq T'oqo*) and the Maras and Tambos peoples from two adjoining caves, called *Maras T'oqo* and *Sutiq T'oqo* (Sarmiento 1960:212–14). Either then or soon thereafter, the eight Incas were paired off. In Betanzos's (1996:13–14) version, the richly dressed primordial ancestors emerged as couples, each husband preceding his wife.

Soon thereafter, the Incas decided to seek fertile lands that would make them rich. The principal couple, named Manqo Qhapaq and Mama Oqllu, found a ready ally in the Tambos, whom they grouped into two sets of five *ayllu* (table 3.2). The company then set off, stopping every now and then along the way, but they never found land productive enough to persuade them to settle down. At one resting spot called Tamboquiro, Mama Oqllu gave birth to Zinchi Roq'a, who would become the second Inca ruler. During their sojourn, the travelers' lives were occasionally complicated by the belligerent Inca brother named

Figure 3.1 The Inca royal lineage, as illustrated by the native chronicler Guaman Poma (1936)

Table 3.1 The Inca Ancestors, according to Sarmiento; glosses after Urton (1990:21)

Brothers	Sisters
Ayar Manqo ("first ancestor") also known as Manqo Qhapaq ("first rich [ancestor]")	Mama Oqllu ("shapely [plump] mother")
Ayar Awka ("ancestor enemy")	Mama Waqo ("cheek [jaw] mother"; "grandmother")
Ayar Kachi ("ancestor salt")	Mama Ipakura/Kura ("maternal aunt/daughter-in-law castration mother")
Ayar Uchu ("ancestor chili pepper")	Mama Rawa ("[?] mother")

Table 3.2 The ten *ayllu* formed at Pacariqtambo, according to Sarmiento; spellings after Urton 1990:25

Hanan Cuzco ("Upper Cuzco")	Hurin Cuzco ("Lower Cuzco")
Chawin Cuzco Ayllu	Sutiq-T'oqo Ayllu
Arayraka Ayllu Cuzco-Kallan	Maras Ayllu
Tarpuntay Ayllu	Kuykusa Ayllu
Wakaytqaui Ayllu	Maska Ayllu
Sañuq Ayllu	Oro Ayllu

Ayar Kachi, who fought with people they met along the road and smashed mountains into ravines with stones flung from his mighty sling. So the other siblings tricked him into re-entering the origin cave by claiming that they had forgotten some items inside. When Ayar Kachi fell for the ruse, he was sealed in forever with a large stone.

Their meandering journey eventually led the company to the top of a mountain beyond which they could see a fruitful valley graced by a rainbow – a manifest sign of their long-sought homeland. Before they could descend the slopes, however, brother Ayar Uchu was transformed into a stone. (Both the stone and the mountain became known as Huanacauri and were revered as shrines of surpassing sanctity.) At Matagua, Mama Waqo – some said Manqo Qhapaq – cast two golden rods into the valley. As the first did not stick firmly in the soil, they knew the land was not fertile. When the second plunged deep into the earth at Wanaypata, however, the Incas knew they had found their home. As the company entered Cuzco, Manqo Qhapaq called his brother Ayar Awka to him and said, "Brother! Do you remember that we agreed that you would take possession of the land we would inhabit? Now then, look at that rock! Fly over there (for they said he had been born with wings), sit down on it, and claim the seat where the marker is, because we are going over there to occupy it and live [here]!" (Sarmiento 1960:217). As his brother commanded, Ayar Awka flew to that place and turned himself into a stone pillar that marked the Incas' claim upon the land. To hold the valley, the Incas had to dislodge the people who already lived there. Mama Waqo inflicted terrible cruelties on the Guayllas people especially, tearing one man apart with her bare hands and blowing in his lungs to inflate them. Despite occasional setbacks, the Incas finally expelled the local people and set themselves up as lords of the valley. They divided Cuzco into four parts and built the first house of the Sun at Indicancha. (The myth then continues with the life and times of the early Incas in Cuzco, described below.)

This account illustrates how many elements of Inca social relations and cosmography were woven into their mythology. The Incas, like so many imperial lords, claimed a creation separate from the rest of humanity, even the non-Inca lineages of Cuzco. Bauer (1996) points out that this idea is closely linked to the image of the wandering stranger-king endowed with mystic powers, which is found in many societies around the world (Sahlins 1981). This union of exotic and separate creation allowed the Incas to distinguish their supernaturally blessed line from the rest of the world. Cuzco's social hierarchy also gathered legitimacy from the tale, since the grouping of the non-royal kin into two divisions of five each foreshadowed the social structure that the Spaniards encountered in 1532–3. The sanctification of space – marking the pilgrimage route and the division of Cuzco into four parts – also let the Incas claim specific landmarks as part of their legendary past and started to fashion the sacred geography that defined their relationship with the natural world (chapter 7). Finally, the myth grounded imperial sun worship in primordial times by crediting the first solar temple to the ancestor Manqo Qhapaq. All in all, the Inca myth of their own creation provided a neatly refined tradition that legitimized the sixteenth-century present.

Pacariqtambo

By the end of the imperial era, the Incas had turned their mythical origin place called "The Inn of Dawn," or *Pacariqtambo*, into a shrine. In response to Spanish inquiries, they said that the site was located about 30 km south of Cuzco. Brian Bauer (1991, 1992c) has studied the archaeological remains of the Paruro region, where he located two sites with imperial Inca components that fit elements of the legend. One is a stone outcrop known as *Puma Orqo*, or "Puma Mountain," and the other is a settlement called *Maukallaqta*, or "Old City." At Puma Orqo, several boulders form a cave just as the story of *Tampu T'oqo* recalled. The outcrop's summit was modified by Inca-era carvings of horizontal planes and two puma figures, while Bauer's excavations recovered Wari-era material remains beneath an adjacent Inca building. Maukallaqta, which fronts Puma Orqo, contains more than 200 finely built structures in the imperial style, including some elegant cut-stone walls. Excavations there recovered both Wari-era and imperial Inca materials. Among the latter were a human skeleton, marine shell, a gold llama, a silver *tumi* knife, and two silver *tupu* pins, reminiscent of the kinds of offerings interred in the important *qhapaq ucha* ritual (chapter 7). Bauer infers that the constructions and carvings at this location enshrined the earliest Inca *wak'a* and bonded royal history to the landscape.

The Early Reigns

According to their myths, the Incas often fought their neighbors in their early years in Cuzco. Rostworowski (1999:8–11) points out that some protagonists, such as the Ayarmaca, were named after natural resources, such as quinoa (*ayar*), a tuber crop (*maca*), and salt (*kachi*) (Sarmiento 1960:212–13, 218–19; cf. Cobo 1979:108–12). The Incas thus claimed to have subdued both the peoples of Cuzco and through them the products of the earth. Once conquered, the Ayarmaca largely disappeared from the narratives, although rulers even as late as Pachakuti were said to have vanquished them.

The exploits of Manqo Qhapaq, the Inca ancestor, mainly concerned his divinely inspired origin, the sojourn to Cuzco, and the founding of the first settlements (chapter 7). Most stories about his son and successor, Zinchi Roq'a, said that he was renowned more for his wisdom and generosity than physical valor. His reign featured peaceable relations with the neighbors, which were cemented when he received his wife Mama Kuka from the town of Saño, which lay a few kilometers to the east of Cuzco. Lloq'e Yupanki ("Left-handed"), the third Inca, became ruler even though he had an elder brother. Like his father, Lloq'e Yupanki was usually credited with expanding Inca influence through acumen rather than war. He married the local beauty Mama Kawa late in life, who gave birth to the redoubtable Mayta Qhapaq, the fourth Inca. The legends told that Mayta Qhapaq was an aggressive leader who was repeatedly embroiled in fights – first with other Inca boys and then with nearby peoples. Through marriage with a daughter of the lord of Collaguas, he sired a number of sons, one of whom, Qhapaq Yupanki, eventually succeeded to leadership (Sarmiento 1960:221–4; Cieza 1967:109; Callapiña et al. 1974:30–1; Cobo 1979:115–20; Betanzos 1996:18; Murúa 1986:60–4).

Like most Inca successions, Qhapaq Yupanki's accession may have been indirect. Some narratives said that he was the eldest son, but Sarmiento's (1960:223) witnesses agreed that he had an older brother named Conde Mayta, who was so ugly that he was thought unfit for rule. Another story recalled that Qhapaq Yupanki's brothers hatched a plot to supplant him with another brother named Tarqo Waman, but the ruler was able to forestall the coup attempt with a memorable speech. Intriguingly, the well-informed magistrate of Cuzco, Juan Polo de Ondegardo, reported that Tarqo Waman actually ruled the Incas for some time, but was displaced by Qhapaq Yupanki. Many sources also said that a man named Qhapaq Yupanki had greatly expanded the Inca domain. The issue is complicated by the fact that the ninth ruler

(Pachakuti) had brothers named Qhapaq Yupanki and Inka Roq'a, namesakes of the fifth and sixth monarchs. As a result, the chronicles differed as to whether some conquests should have been attributed to those rulers or to Pachakuti's generals. The ruler Qhapaq Yupanki took as his wife Mama Qori Willpay ("Golden Jewel"), who hailed from the Cuzco area.

Their son Inka Roq'a became the reputed founder of Upper Cuzco (*Hanan Cuzco*). Following his marriage, according to some accounts, he dispatched expeditions into the Vilcanota Valley, where they seized towns as far afield as Quiquijana, about four leagues (~20 km) away (Cieza 1967:115–22; Sarmiento 1960:223–4; Murúa 1986:69). Cobo's (1979:121–5) account added that Inka Roq'a conquered the valley of Andahuaylas, some 34 leagues (~170 km) west of Cuzco. There, they vanquished the Chankas, with mercenary help from the Canas and the Canche, southeast of Cuzco. In a contrasting story, the Pacariqtambo Quipucamayos stated that Inka Roq'a did not expand the domain at all, but devoted himself to pious activities, religious constructions, and improving lands (Callapiña et al. 1974:32).

The royal couple gave birth to four or five sons, the eldest of whom became ruler. In his youth the prince was kidnaped by some neighbors in revenge for Inka Roq'a's marriage to a maid their lord had coveted. The boy was reprieved from a death sentence when he miraculously shed tears of blood. This event later gave rise to the name that he assumed as ruler, Yawar Waqaq ("He who weeps blood") (Cieza 1967:123–7; Sarmiento 1960:224–5; Murúa 1986:71; Cobo 1979:126).[1] Upon his father's death, Yawar Waqaq took vengeance on the enemies of his youth, who had also murdered one of his sons. He followed this triumph by seizing land from many groups (Sarmiento 1960:227); some said that he waged successful battle into the Valley of Pisac and beyond, some 30 km northeast of Cuzco, although others attributed those conquests to Wiraqocha Inka, the next ruler.

Cieza's less flattering version said that Yawar Waqaq was caught unawares by warriors from Condesuyu at a festival he was hosting in Cuzco, in preparation for an expedition against the powerful Qolla of the Lake Titicaca basin. The guests first clubbed the ruler over the head and then killed him in a general slaughter as he tried to flee to the sanctuary of the temple. While the Incas prepared to abandon the city, the skies opened and a mighty storm drove the assailants away. The Inca survivors took advantage of the celestial reprieve to regroup; they recovered their dead and buried Yawar Waqaq without any of the honors conferred on previous royalty. With the leadership in disarray, Cieza wrote (1967:125–7), the third of Yawar Waqaq's sons assumed rule under the name Wiraqocha Inka. He added that a pivotal regional conflict to the west of Cuzco was also being resolved about that time. The Quechuas had been bent on expanding their domain, but saw their designs crushed when they lost a decisive battle to the Chankas. At this point, the tales take on an increasingly imperialist tenor with the exploits attributed to Wiraqocha Inka. This summary will pause here, then, leaving the descriptions of the great conquests to the next chapter.

Scholars generally view the claims of extensive early Inca conquests sketched out above as grandiose legends, told in ways that often cast the Incas in a favorable light, but also peppered with defeats and shameful incidents. It is striking that the chroniclers' accounts vary so widely with respect to the scope of Inca ventures. Some wrote that they stuck fairly close to the Cuzco basin, while others claimed that the Incas ranged over one or two hundred kilometers beyond Cuzco in the pre-imperial era. As Rowe (1946:206–9) and others have inferred, some of those claims may have arisen from confusion over duplicate names or embellishments of history. As the next section describes, the archaeological evidence certainly does not support the idea that the Incas had created an extensive polity before about 1400.

The Archaeological Evidence

Settlement Patterns

The archaeological origins of Inca society are almost as sketchy as the historical record, in part because Cuzco was stripped of its population during the imperial era so that the sacred center of the world could be built from scratch. Archaeological knowledge of the Killke era has therefore been obtained through surveys and a few excavations, most of them conducted many kilometers from the capital.[2] Even so, several hundred Killke sites have been recorded within about 60 km of Cuzco, largely in the Apurimac and Vilcanota-Urubamba drainages (figure 3.2).

Archaeologists generally consider marked differences in size among settlements to be a reliable indicator that a region's population is organized into a social or political hierarchy. In the Cuzco basin, such a settlement hierarchy apparently began to take form between AD 1000 and 1200. Towns covering as much as 60 hectares, such as Choquepuquio, Minas Pata, and Kencha-Kencha, probably housed a few thousand people each. Most of the other settlements that we know about were small villages and hamlets (Rowe 1944:61; Dwyer 1971; Parsons and Hastings 1988:224). Even though it lay in an exposed position, Choquepuquio was occupied continuously from the Middle Horizon (AD 500–750) into the imperial Inca era (Hyslop 1990:20–1). Its position

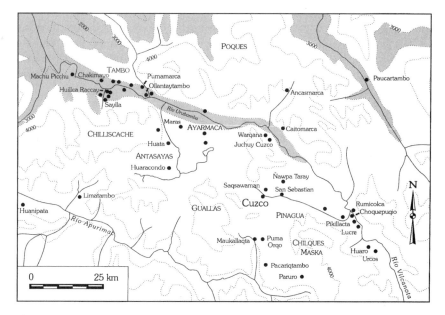

Figure 3.2   Distribution of early Inca (Killke) sites in the Cuzco region (after Kendall 1994, 1996)

indicates that its residents felt fairly secure, which would have been unusual for most of the Andes, but the placement of most known Killke sites in the Cuzco basin suggests that the people were not overly worried about conflict. All sites lie on slight rises above the valley floor, but only two, at Saqsawaman and Old Choqo, were situated defensibly (Dwyer 1971:145). Because only the south side of the valley has been surveyed systematically, it is uncertain if those patterns hold for the whole region.

The nature of pre-imperial Cuzco itself is something of a mystery. Betanzos (1996:70) wrote that the early settlement lay in a swampy area at the foot of Saqsawaman and just above the main part of the town. The native chronicler Guaman Poma (1980:66) wrote that the town's original name had been Acamama before being renamed Cuzco (*qosqo*: "dried-up lake bed"; Hornberger and Hornberger 1983:191), but most of Sarmiento's (1960:216) witnesses agreed that the town's name referred to a stone marker of ownership, called a *cozco*. They also recalled that the founding ancestors had set out four divisions between the Huatanay (Tied River) and Tullumayo (River of the Bone), which formed the capital's core when the Spaniards arrived. The divisions were called

Q'enti Kancha, or Hummingbird Enclosure; *Chumbi Kancha*, or Weaver Enclosure; *Sairi Kancha*, or Tobacco Enclosure; and *Yarambuy Kancha*, a district of mixed ethnicity (Rostworowski 1999:7).

Surface evidence of most pre-imperial architecture in Cuzco has unfortunately been wiped out by human action and natural catastrophe. The imperial building program, Inca efforts to retake the city from the Spaniards in 1536, a devastating earthquake in 1650, and Spanish remodeling have all taken their toll. Excavations under the present-day Hotel Libertador have uncovered early building foundations with orientations like those of nearby imperial masonry. This implies that part of the imperial layout overlay an existing plan (González Corrales 1984; Hyslop 1990:30–4). Killke pottery has also been found *in situ* in a number of places, among them the monastery of Santo Domingo where the style was first distinguished. In 1934, the Peruvian archaeologist Luis Valcárcel recovered abundant ceramics at Saqsawaman, above Cuzco proper. About one-quarter to one-third of the pottery was in the Killke style, on the basis of which Rowe (1944:61) has suggested that a pre-imperial occupation lay on the hilltop.

Outside the Cuzco basin, Killke site patterns parallel the core area in important ways, but differ in scale and hierarchy. Many settlements to the west in Limatambo and to the south in Paruro are unfortified communities. The largest Paruro sites were no more than hamlets (<3.5 ha), one-twentieth the size of the largest Killke sites around Cuzco (Bauer 1992c:94–108). The topographic settings of the Paruro sites are much like those of Cuzco, in that most of the larger sites lie on small knolls or lower valley slopes, near rich bottom lands suitable for maize farming. Other small sites, possibly used temporarily, lay at higher elevations near lands suited to tuber crops or herding. Some sites north of Cuzco lay as low as 2,850 m, where warmer-climate crops could be grown. Sites around Limatambo were about the same size, but most were found on mid-elevation ridges or peaks; only three lay in exposed settings, implying a greater concern with defense (Heffernan 1989:126, 379). Killke settlements north of Cuzco were also small and defensively oriented. Quite a few lie along ridge tops high above the Cusichaca Valley. The villages of Huata and Pantilliclla were protected by surrounding walls, and Huata was extensively burned, implying that worries about defense may have been well founded. Toward the end of the Late Intermediate Period (AD 750–1400), the people used the lower elevations to greater advantage, but still lived in high, fortified locales (Kendall 1976, 1985). Collectively, evidence suggests that people living in the vicinity of the Cuzco basin lived in smaller communities and lacked the hierarchical organization seen in the basin itself. Some of them were also more concerned with defense.

Architecture and Other Material Remains

The architectural evidence suggests that the imperial style of architecture had roots in the Killke era, but it would be modified radically in later years. The best-preserved sites, to the north of Cuzco, contain buildings with both circular and rectangular floor plans, whereas the domestic architecture of the imperial era used mostly rectilinear forms. The preserved masonry of the early era was also of lower quality than that found in fine imperial-era structures. They featured access through ground-level windows, partition walls that divided rectangular buildings into compartments, two-storey structures, and rounded internal corners on rectangular buildings (Kendall 1976; Niles 1980).

Killke artifact styles also hinted at the form of imperial manufactures. The rise of state society often features innovative styles of crafts and architecture, especially in elite, ritual, and administrative contexts. Their creation reveals the elite's interest in controlling the objects that represent the status, perquisites, and tools of power. Imperial Cuzco's tapestry tunics, polychrome pottery, and architectural style are classic examples of that attention to material culture (chapters 6, 12). The varied Killke material assemblage, in contrast, shows no evidence of central management of artisanry. Some of the Killke ceramics do presage imperial Inca motifs (e.g., nested triangles, pendant rows of solid triangles) and vessel shapes, but the varied and sloppy execution contrasts starkly with the standardized and often elegant imperial pottery (Dwyer 1971; Heffernan 1989; Bauer and Stanish 1990). None of the other Killke artifacts, which are only briefly described, hints at large-scale or centrally managed production either. Interestingly, Bauer (1992c) notes that the region in which Killke pottery is found coincides with the area occupied by the ethnic groups who were named honorary Incas, or *Incas de Privilegio*. He suggests that the correspondence signifies that pre-imperial cultural links were being forged among the people of the greater Cuzco region in a relationship that became more formalized later.

Dating the Killke Era

The few radiocarbon dates that have been taken from Killke contexts suggest that the era ran from AD 1000 until about 1400 (Dwyer 1971; Kendall 1985; Bauer 1992c; Adamska and Michczński 1996). The evidence from Pumamarca is especially interesting, because its plan and architecture suggest that the settlement marked the transition from late pre-imperial to imperial times. Carbon dates taken from this architecture end in the fourteenth century (Hollowell 1987). Such early dates for transitional architecture are earlier than we would expect from the historical chronology. Bauer has consequently ventured that some structures usually thought to belong to the imperial era were actually raised during the Killke period (Bauer 1992c:47). Archaeologists are also rethinking the relationship between the Killke and imperial polychrome ceramic styles. Using stratigraphic associations, Kendall suggests that the polychrome style may have appeared well before 1400 as an elite ware that was subsequently transformed into the imperial style (Kendall 1996).

A Sketch of Pre-Imperial Society

The sketchy nature of the information on the Killke era has made scholars justifiably leery of drawing a detailed portrait of early Inca society. Even so – setting aside their fabulous elements – the narratives contain many features compatible with a chiefdom society. One consistent element is the domination of political relations by elite lineages or larger kin groups. Such structures pervaded Andean societies in late prehistory. Even so, there is no reason to infer that the Incas had formed social classes before the great expansions. Whether any story was historically accurate or not, marriage alliances may have also been key to early Inca politics. The theme's repetition suggests that a union between one local lord and the daughter of another may have helped to build political relations among the region's elites and separate them from the remaining populace. If so, their actions would have contrasted with those of the general populace, who conventionally married across divisions within their own *ayllu*.

The marriages were honored with gifts or exchanges of fine textiles and valuables. The exchanges confirmed the lords' generosity at the same time that they created social and economic debts. Inca myths touted their ancestors' largess, because it helped to legitimize their elevated status. Speaking more generally, a chief's position often partly depends on his ability to control labor and its products, without owning the natural resources themselves. Since gift-giving advertises a chief's productive capacity, it can attract new adherents and create public obligations. Among the Incas, ritualized generosity may have helped to mediate political alliances and residential shifts among the Incas and their neighbors. Some authors also think that the manipulation of exchange obligations helped to underwrite the local rise of Inca power because their largess placed the recipients of gifts in an inferior social position (Rostworowski 1999:38–47).

Many accounts also highlighted early military ventures. When the ruler himself did not take the lead, his close kin did, a practice that continued through the entire imperial period. Stories of the era often said that warlords incited their followers by promising them glory and plunder (Sarmiento 1960:218–19, 227; Cobo 1979:130; Betanzos 1996:20). There are few allusions to lands as benefits of war, although Sarmiento surmised that land conflicts underpinned feuds between the newly arrived Incas and the people already living around. Considering the small scope of most highland societies *ca.* AD 1000–1400, few lands may have actually been seized and held until late in the pre-imperial era. Instead, the tales' emphasis on capture of booty and labor may have been closer to the mark. Richard Schaedel (1978) has drawn attention to a slow shift in the motivation and practice of warfare that occurred through the early Inca accounts. The early plundering was augmented by demands for tribute and then replaced by seizure of productive resources. Capture of labor was also important, although it too shifted, from abduction to extorting production. In Sarmiento's (1960:228–9) account, Wiraqocha Inka innovated the practice of occupying the lands of defeated neighbors, rather than just pillaging them. If those trends in the tales approximate the changing goals of war, then the shift to annexing vast territories in the imperial era grew from long developing practices.

An evolving elite ideology may have also underpinned Inca leadership, but it was transformed so much that we cannot be sure when any particular story or claim became part of the canon. The image of the stranger king – seen first in the founding ancestor Manqo Qhapaq – was so potent that some Inca elites told Cieza that Wiraqocha Inka was also an outlander. Other aristocrats, who had their own interests to protect, dismissed the story as puffery. Claims to leadership, though based on genealogy and ability, also gained legitimacy from religious sanction in the royal narratives. Most early kings were imbued with magical qualities granted by the Sun or Creator God. Their deeds exhibited precocious military valor or supernatural assistance, combined with visions of the future. Mayta Qhapaq's life, for instance, was so filled with wondrous feats that the Spaniards used Hercules and Merlin as reference points for their European audiences. He was reputed to have been born with his teeth intact after only a three-month pregnancy, could walk at birth, and had reached the stature of an eight-year-old at just one year (Sarmiento 1960:221). When an Inca ruler took the throne, he also assumed a new, sometimes supernaturally inspired, name. As noted above, Titu Kusi Wallpa received the name "He Who Sheds Bloody Tears" (Yawar Waqaq) for weeping blood, an act that was famously repeated by the "Tired Stone" above Cuzco (chapter 7). We cannot fix when particular narratives became royal doctrine, but the invention of elite dogma was an ongoing process that most likely had some roots in the Killke era.

The question remains as to what triggered the Incas' local successes, rather than a collapse into a simpler polity, as so often happens with chiefdoms. A likely contributing factor was simply the successful pursuit of personal gain by individual leaders in the endemic warfare that pervaded the highlands at the time. By the time the state began to form, the peoples of southern Peru and the northern altiplano had been enmeshed in conflicts and alliances for centuries. The narratives suggest that the political climate put a premium on military leaders who could deliver security and spoils and that the warlords and their adherents benefited especially from predatory warfare. With each success, war may have increasingly concentrated power in the hands of a few families. The Incas and their neighbors may also have seen that it was to their benefit to join forces against the marauding actions ascribed to other neighbors. Finally, it is possible that early Inca ideology contained exhortations for conquest or evangelism. Those features were present in late imperial doctrine, but they sound more like justifications after the fact rather than catalysts for expansion.

Overall, this sketch of pre-imperial society contains some amount of conjecture, but the information is often consistent with a chiefly society moving toward statehood. Archaeology suggests that a potent Inca polity began to take form earlier than has long been thought, but we need to keep in mind that much crucial evidence is missing. Even so, some of the architectural and artifactual elements that led into the imperial styles may have been taking form by the middle of the fourteenth century.

chapter four

The History of the Empire: Narrative Visions

When war is declared, Truth is the first casualty.

Ponsonby

The meteoric rise of Inca power was filled with charismatic leadership, arduous campaigns, spirited opposition, divine aid, heroism, treachery, and wise rule – in short, all the elements of history's grand sweep as told by the victors. About fifty accounts of the Inca past were written down in the early Colonial era, but distilling out an accurate record of the empire's formation may still be impossible today. Even the accounts that drew from *khipu* records could present conspicuously different visions, so that the chroniclers had to choose which stories to preserve for posterity. Modern scholars are split between those who assume that the chronicles captured a core of truth that can be discovered through close comparisons (e.g., Rowe 1946; Pärssinen 1992) and those who judge the chronicles to be too colored by Andean concepts of time and social hierarchy for use as linear narratives (e.g., Zuidema 1982; Urton 1990). My own view is that the accounts are fraught with so many problems that we will probably never come to an authoritative resolution for the earliest stages of the imperial era using the historical sagas alone. On the other hand, it defies credibility that Inca history was invented wholesale in the Colonial era. It appears more likely that different social groups tailored a generally understood past to suit their own political interests, even when describing events that had occurred at the edge of the Colonial era. If we accept this view and keep in mind the limitations of the sources, it is possible to summarize the trajectory of the empire in skeletal form, at least as the Incas chose to remember it. The internal conflicts were so deep and the Inca notions of recording the past so different from European conventions, however, that many of the details of the pre-hispanic era will always be beyond us. What I present in this chapter, then, is a composite account of the imperial expansion as described by the principals' descendants. Rather than dun readers with repeated comments about the legendary tenor of the stories, I simply ask them to keep in mind that this is a synthesis largely composed of Inca sagas filtered through many Andean and Spanish voices.

Expansionist Designs and the Crisis in Cuzco

The reign of Wiraqocha Inka, the eighth ruler on the standard list, usually marks a narrative transition from raiding and alliance to attempted territorial expansion. He is often described as a man bent on amplifying his power through conquest and intrigue during a tumultuous era in the central Andes (Cieza 1967:125–8; Betanzos 1996:19; Sarmiento 1960:227; Cobo 1979:130–1). Soon after ascending the throne, Wiraqocha Inka took his wife from the Anta, who lived a bit to the west of Cuzco, perhaps to cement a local alliance. The Incas were flexing their muscles locally in this era, during which the political stakes were being raised throughout the region. Sarmiento's (1960:228–30) witnesses recalled that several of Wiraqocha Inka's sons accompanied or led expeditions against their neighbors. Among them were the brothers Inka Urqon and Inka Yupanki (later Pachakuti), who would soon feud over the throne. Wiraqocha Inka's ambitions led him to the altiplano, where the powerful societies of the Lake Titicaca basin were locked in a struggle for regional ascendancy (Betanzos 1996:20; Cieza 1967:142–3).[1] As the basin's hostilities escalated, both the Lupaqa and Qolla leaders solicited the Incas' aid. After consulting his oracles and counselors, the Inca ruler chose to favor the Lupaqas but hedged his bets by promising aid to both sides. He then set out for the altiplano with an army, leaving his son Inka Urqon in charge of Cuzco. Before the Incas arrived in the lake region, however, the Lupaqas won a decisive victory. Their lord Qari thus met the Incas from a position of strength and they sealed an alliance by drinking from a golden cup.[2]

The Chanka Wars

Many chroniclers wrote that the repulsion of Chanka assaults on Cuzco late in Wiraqocha Inka's reign propelled the Incas into their imperial phase.[3] In Betanzos's (1996:19–30) history, which is largely a heroic biography of Pachakuti, the Chankas attacked when Wiraqocha Inka arrogantly presumed to take the name of the Creator God as his title. The Chankas assembled a grand army for a three-pronged attack on lands south of Cuzco, into the altiplano, and against Cuzco itself.[4] Wiraqocha Inka fled to a fortified refuge in the face of the attack, along with his heir designate Inka Urqon and most of the aristocracy. The intrepid prince Inka Yupanki spurned retreat, however, and rallied three lords to hold their home. With the battle impending, either the Creator or the Sun appeared in a vision to the prince and promised to send warriors to aid him in defeating the Chankas. At a critical moment in the battle, the vision came to fruition as warriors appeared as if from nowhere and the Incas proved victorious. Several chroniclers reported that the stones from the fields had metamorphosed into warriors, which were later venerated as shrines called *pururaucas* ("hidden thieves"; Polo 1917:46; Pachacuti Yamqui 1993:219; Cobo 1979:128–9; see MacCormack 1991:286–301).

Betanzos continued that Inka Yupanki took the prisoners and spoils of victory to his father, so that Wiraqocha Inka could tread on them in the customary gesture of triumph. The ruler was so perturbed at the prince's newly achieved stature, however, that he orchestrated protocol so that his other son Inka Urqon was treated as if he were already enthroned (see chapter 5). He declared that Inka Urqon must have the first honor with the plunder, but Inka Yupanki refused to let his hard-won victory be defiled and departed for Cuzco. When the irate ruler organized an ambush to kill the defiant prince, it was discovered and thwarted by the young man's loyal captains. Soon thereafter, the two other Chanka contingents attacked Cuzco, but Inka Yupanki emerged victorious once again. Despite the tensions, prince Inka Yupanki implored his father to return to Cuzco. His efforts were in vain, but the elder man was willing to accept an offer of assistance in building a fine estate at his refuge (Caquia Xaquixaguana). For his part, Inka Yupanki kept busy by expanding and organizing the Inca realm; twenty years alone were spent renovating Cuzco (Betanzos 1996:44–55, 69–73). Once the capital was completed, the court persuaded Wiraqocha Inka to travel to Cuzco and place the fringe of rulership on Inka Yupanki's head. The prince himself had refused to visit his father's manor, declaring that he would take the fringe from Inka Urqon only if the head came along with it. So Wiraqocha traveled to Cuzco, where he gave his son the title "Pachacuti Ynga Yupangui Capac Yndichuri, which means 'change of time, King Yupanque, son of the Sun'." The new monarch was not content with this gesture, however, and forced his father to drink *chicha* from a filthy jar while deriding him as a woman. In the end, Pachakuti accepted his father's apologies for past transgressions and invited the aged ex-monarch to participate in Cuzco's festivities, which he did until his death some ten years later (Betanzos 1996:74–9).[5]

Despite the many accounts of the Chanka wars, scholars disagree about their authenticity. Part of the skepticism arises from the discrepancies concerning the succession to the throne and the timing of Inca conflicts with their western neighbors. Cieza (1967:114–15, 125–7, 146–9), for example, understood that Inka Urqon had been truly installed as ruler while Wiraqocha Inka was still alive – an assertion later repeated by the native chronicler Pachacuti Yamqui. Moreover, different sources say the Chankas came under Inca rule during the reigns of the fifth, sixth, eighth, and ninth rulers, or do not mention them at all.[6] Duviols (1980) takes an especially skeptical view, suggesting that the Chankas may have been built up as the consummate but largely mythical foil, used to glorify Pachakuti and to provide a divinely inspired foundation for the empire. With present evidence, it seems plausible that the Chankas were a crucial early enemy, but the sagas of the Chanka wars may still be mostly a glorious epic invoked to burnish the image of the empire's father.

The Major Expansions: Pachakuti and Thupa Inka Yupanki

The sagas tell that Pachakuti began to expand his domain once he had firmly established his power, although they differ on the details. It is striking that they often begin with a litany of battles around Cuzco itself, even some that attributed conquests much farther afield to earlier rulers.[7] From our vantage point, it is hard to say if the Incas really had to reassert local control with every succession or if the chronicling of local triumphs was a narrative device used to ascribe the empire's creation to Pachakuti. If the latter were true, the conquests may have been fictitious or merely symbolic. To help readers follow the subsequent expansions from a historical perspective, figure 4.1 presents Pärssinen's (1992) reconstruction, based on review of a wide array of provincial documents.

Expeditions Southward

We often think of the Inca empire in association with the Peruvian mountains, but the earliest rich targets for Cuzco's expeditions lay in the altiplano. Most chroniclers agreed that the Incas had established a presence in the Titicaca basin during Wiraqocha Inka's reign, either through their alliance with the Lupaqa or through conquest (e.g., Sarmiento 1960:241; Betanzos 1996:92–6). The Qolla remained a potent force in the basin, despite their reported defeat at the hands of the Lupaqa. One version of Pachakuti's exploits told how the ruler himself defeated the Qolla and

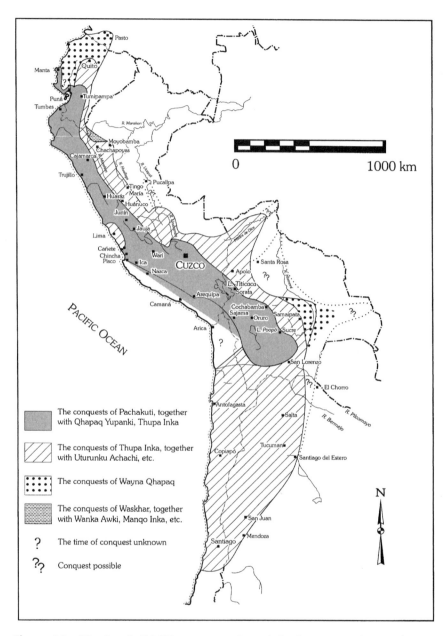

Figure 4.1 Pärssinen's (1992) reconstruction of the Inca expansion, redrawn from the original

their allies by taking a fort in which he then installed an Inca garrison. The Qolla ruler was taken to Cuzco where he was beheaded in a public triumph. In contrast, Cieza (1967:55–6, 160–1, 177–84) wrote that Pachakuti dispatched two Chanka lords at the head of their own soldiers to subdue the Qolla. Although a series of victories advanced Inca interests in the basin, the region had not been fully secured before Chanka forces deserted a parallel Inca campaign in the central Peruvian sierra. As a precaution, Pachakuti recalled the Chanka forces from the altiplano and discharged them. Only after the end of the sierra campaign and expeditions into the montaña did Pachakuti himself venture into the basin to subdue the Qollas and Ayaviris. A number of other sources reported that Pachakuti eventually conquered through south Bolivia before turning his eyes northward (e.g., Callapiña 1974:39; Betanzos 1996:112–14).

The Peruvian Sierra and Coast

Many chroniclers reported that an early campaign into central Peru started to bring the agricultural heartland of the realm into Inca hands, but engaged Cuzco with unintended and dangerous foes. The expedition's mixed success also prompted a crisis in Cuzco typical of the political animosities that erupted periodically. There are three versions of the story, but the gist is as follows (see Rowe 1946:206). At some point, Pachakuti dispatched forces northward, supported by Chanka soldiers pressed into service. They advanced through several hundred kilometers of difficult territory, subduing many redoubtable *etnías* through intimidation, pitched battle, and siege. The Incas and Chankas fell out along the way, apparently because the Incas were embarrassed by the Chankas' superior valor in taking a fort. Before the Inca commander could recoup his honor by punishing the Chankas, they escaped northward. The Incas advanced to Cajamarca in their pursuit, where they defeated the local lord and his coastal allies, the Chimu. After leaving a garrison in Cajamarca, the army turned back to Cuzco laden with booty.

On the return trip, the army took a route through the lower slopes of the western Andes. That venture was the first or second of four or five separate descents described for Inca armies until the entire coast was finally taken (see below). Whether the privileged Chincha valley and its neighbor, Pisco, were taken at that time is unclear. Cieza wrote that Pachakuti sent an army under his brother Qhapaq Yupanki to secure Chincha, but the foray was rebuffed. Chincha's own residents told the Spaniards that the fifth ruler, also named Qhapaq Yupanki, peacefully secured vows of allegiance with gifts of fine cloth and golden beads

(Castro and Ortega Morejón 1974:94–103). Their relationship was later solidified by Thupa Inka Yupanki and Wayna Qhapaq (Rostworowski 1999:71).

When the returning army approached Cuzco, Pachakuti had its generals executed at Limatambo (Cabello Valboa 1951:317–18; Murúa 1986:80; Polo 1917:115). He used the Chanka desertion as a rationale, but his motivation is sometimes conceived as fear that the soldiers could use their triumph as leverage to unseat him. Cabello Valboa (1951:318) wrote that the remaining commanders organized another expedition north as a way to flee Pachakuti's awful presence. The prince Thupa Inka Yupanki, too callow to take command, accompanied his more experienced relatives as a symbolic general and military apprentice. Betanzos typically did not mention any such murders by the hero of his saga. Instead, he wrote that another general named Yamque Yupanki led a pair of expeditions north to relieve Cajamarca. On the first trip, he served as military mentor to his underage brother Qhapaq Yupanki and then to the youthful Thupa Inka Yupanki on the second.

One of these northern expeditions turned toward the north coast, descending through Huamachuco toward Pacasmayo. It is uncertain if the first invasion brought down the Chimu empire or if that formidable foe fell to a later campaign heading south from Ecuador. Rowe (1948:44) has suggested that a first engagement broke Chimor's power and that a later invasion solidified Inca control of the coast. Cabello (1951:320–1; see Rostworowski 1999:78) wrote that Thupa Inka Yupanki used the stratagem of threatening to cut off the coastal water supply to render the coastal populace helpless. At the end of the expedition, the Chimu paramount Minchançaman was taken to Cuzco as a hostage.

Advances into Ecuador

Fairly early in the imperial era, an Inca expedition reportedly pressed into Ecuador in a grand sweep of the north Andes. The achievement of Inca dominion there required numerous campaigns spread over a half century or more. More than a few operations ended in crashing defeats – at least from the Incas' point of view – and even in 1532, many areas bordering the central valleys lay beyond Inca control. In most accounts, while Pachakuti was still ruler, expeditions under Thupa Inka Yupanki's titular leadership worked their way into central Ecuador. The northern limit of the initial push was apparently reached in the southern Quito basin. The advance was a halting, arduous affair, as the forces returned to Cajamarca to reform and supply themselves between expeditions (Betanzos 1996:116–21; Cieza 1967:187–9; Sarmiento 1960:249–50;

Cabello Valboa 1951:320–1; Murúa 1986:81; RGI II:265, 275, 279; Cobo 1979:143).

The sequence of ventures to the Ecuadorian coast is confusing, since campaigns are described for Pachakuti's, Thupa Inka Yupanki's, and Wayna Qhapaq's reigns (Cabello Valboa 1951:320–30, 392–3; Sarmiento 1960:251; Cieza 1967:156, 217–22, 1984:157; Cobo 1979:150; Murúa 1986:82, 92; Rowe 1985b:224, 1946:207; Pärssinen 1992:91–4). At one point, however, Inca forces reportedly descended into the coastal tropics in the Manta region and crossed to the Isla Puná. During that endeavor, one of the more fabled events of Inca history is said to have taken place – a voyage by Thupa Inka Yupanki to the Pacific islands of Anachumbi and Niñachumbi. Sarmiento wrote that some 20,000 soldiers sailed with him on balsa rafts. When the voyage stretched out for close to a year, the commander of the land troops mistakenly presumed that the leader had been lost. His premature celebration cost him his life when Thupa Inka Yupanki returned. Despite the Incas' efforts, coastal Ecuador was never well integrated into the empire, perhaps because it was viewed as unhealthy by the highlanders (McEwan and Silva 1989).

More Ventures onto the Peruvian Coast

The timing of conquests along the coast from Nazca to Mala is hard to pin down even as reconstructed narrative occurrences (Callapiña et al. 1974:32; Rowe 1985b:224; Cobo 1979:139; Cieza 1984:217, 1967: 199–202; Polo 1917; Sarmiento 1960:255; Cabello Valboa 1951: 331, 338–9; see also Rowe 1946:207; see Rostworowski 1999: 73–6; Pärssinen 1992:87–9; Rowe 1946:207 for further discussion). One version suggests that a third coastal campaign occurred before Thupa Inka Yupanki's montaña ventures, described below. Another put the conquest of the south and central coasts after the conquest of the south Andes. Whatever the sequence, the campaigns reportedly took years and constituted one of the most noteworthy Inca achievements. In a familiar pattern, the sources differed over the balance between peaceful submission and stiff resistance by the residents of individual valleys. There was general agreement, however, that the Incas met a resolute foe in the Lunahuaná and Mara peoples of the Cañete valley. After an abortive first campaign, the Incas withdrew to the highlands to escape the summer heat and attendant illness among the soldiers. Cobo (1979:138–9) wrote that the armies alternated contingents of 30,000 soldiers between the coast and highlands, because the coastal lands were so unhealthy for the people of the sierra. Some coastal forces who had been pressed into service took the failure as a sign of Inca weakness and defected. An angered Thupa Inka Yupanki then mounted campaigns for three years from the settlement of Inkawasi, which was built expressly for that purpose (Hyslop 1985). The town was called the "New Cuzco," with streets and districts named after those of the capital. The facility sustained the army on its annual campaign and housed a garrison to maintain pressure on the locals.

According to one story, after all assaults failed to take the local fortress of Ungará, the Incas duped the residents into leaving their redoubt by feigning withdrawal and leaving sacrifices by the sea. The besieged forces foolishly left their strongholds to celebrate, only to be butchered on the beach and in the water. The local people were thereafter called the Guarco – a name derived from the Quechua word for "hang,"[8] since many unfortunates were hanged from the fort's walls (Cabello Valboa 1951:339). At the end of the campaign, Thupa Inka Yupanki ordered another settlement built, probably the site now known as Cerro Azul (Hyslop 1985:12), and installed a governor and colonists. The valley's inhabitants were deported and more compliant peoples from the neighboring Chincha and Coayllo valleys were brought in to occupy their lands (Rostworowski 1990:455–6).

Further Ventures into the Eastern Lowlands

The narratives describe several ventures into the Peruvian and Bolivian jungles and plains late in Pachakuti's reign and again at the beginning of Thupa Inka Yupanki's (Cieza 1967:173–5, 205; Rowe 1985b:225; Sarmiento 1960:238–40, 254; Cabello Valboa 1951:334–5; Murúa 1986:87–8; Cobo 1979:135–7, 143; see Saignes 1985; Pärssinen 1992: 107–19). The *selva* proved a recurrent nightmare, as the highland armies were ill-suited to jungle warfare. Thupa Inka Yupanki reportedly led at least two expeditions, one as Pachakuti's general on a mission of conquest and one as emperor to subdue an uprising following his father's death. In Betanzos's narrative, the first expedition was only modestly productive, yielding gold, feathers, honey, and exotic animals. Shortly thereafter, Pachakuti died and Thupa Inka Yupanki spent a year in mourning, followed by a major campaign back to the jungles. Leaving Yamque Yupanki in Cuzco as governor, the new ruler took two brothers along as military leaders. In countering the expedition, the Incas' opponents made a fatal tactical error by massing their forces, instead of harassing the highland troops and fading into the forest, a method that caused the Incas all kinds of distress on other campaigns. Despite his reported military successes, Thupa Inka Yupanki found little of value and opted to turn back to Cuzco.

In an alternative version, Sarmiento's witnesses explained that the emperor Thupa Inka Yupanki had initially called the warlords of the montaña to Cuzco to pay homage. Once there, the guests took offense when they were required to deliver soil from their lands for the service of the Sun Temple and turned homeward. Thupa Inka Yupanki then assembled a large army divided into three parts, but the Incas found the eastern lands a den of horrors. Many of the men in Thupa Inka Yupanki's contingent perished from hunger and disease as they wandered about lost, until Uturunku Achachi's ("Tiger Ancestor") men found and led them out. How far into the lowlands the Incas penetrated is uncertain. The Chunchos and Mojos peoples east of Lake Titicaca are often mentioned, but the *llanos de Mojos* cover an immense territory. Some sources even mention places down the Madre de Dios river as far east as the border between Bolivia and Brazil (chapter 9; see Pärssinen 1992:107–19).

Rebellion in the Altiplano

Most early accounts agreed that the Qolla and Lupaqa lords of Hatunqolla, Chucuito, and Azángaro led a major uprising in the altiplano during one of the Incas' eastern campaigns (Betanzos 1996:143–7; Cieza 1967:53, 174–84, 204; Rowe 1985b:225–6; Sarmiento 1960: 255; Cabello Valboa 1951:335–6; Cobo 1979:143; Murúa 1986:88–9). Although the chroniclers differed as to whether the rebellion occurred under Pachakuti's or Thupa Inka Yupanki's rule, they agreed that the latter led the punitive force. The altiplano uprising was a serious matter, but was only one of several that periodically threatened Inca hegemony. The Aymará-speaking societies were split in the war, with the Cana and Canche siding with the Inca forces (Rowe 1946:207; Cieza 1967:175–9). In a commonly reported version, a Qolla soldier named Coaquiri deserted the forces in the montaña and fled to the altiplano, where his report that the paramount was lost touched off a rebellion. Such periods of succession or uncertain leadership were often unsettled, as many subjects saw a chance to reassert their independence, which they initiated by killing the resident Inca authorities. Once Thupa Inka Yupanki had been extricated from the jungles, he left Uturunku Achachi as governor and headed directly toward the altiplano to deal with the situation.

Because the Incas did not have standing armies, a major mobilization was required. Betanzos (1996:143–53), who wrote the most detailed account of the events, noted that the situation was complicated by the untimely death of Yamque Yupanki. Determined to take no chances with security elsewhere, the Incas reportedly detached 20,000 men from Antisuyu, along with 20,000 Canas and Canches from Kollasuyu, to help maintain order in Chinchaysuyu. Ten thousand men from Antisuyu, Canas, Quivios, and Canches, were allocated to Cuntisuyu. Betanzos wrote that for his campaign Thupa Inka Yupanki took 100,000 soldiers from Chinchaysuyu, and a personal guard of 5,000 from the Cuzco area. Even if those figures were largely symbolic fiction, the reassertion of Cuzco's dominion over the altiplano societies was a major undertaking that required years of campaigns, at least as recounted in the royal sagas. Over time, the Incas invested and overran a series of fortified settlements sequentially occupied by the retreating Qolla and their allies. The Inca forces ultimately prevailed at the Desaguadero river, which flows out of the south side of Lake Titicaca. They took memorable retribution by flaying the defeated altiplano lords, impaling their heads on poles, and fashioning their skins into drums.

Advances into Argentina and Chile

Most sources ascribed the annexation of the southern Andes to Thupa Inka Yupanki, although those expeditions formed the most schematic slices of the Inca histories (Callapiña et al. 1974:40; Betanzos 1996:148–52; Cieza 1967:204; Polo 1917:116; Rowe 1985b:226; Sarmiento 1960:255; Cabello Valboa 1951:336–7; Murúa 1986:90–1; Guaman Poma 1980:89; Cobo 1979:146–7; see Lorandi and Boixadós 1987–8; Pärssinen 1992:120–36). Because the Spaniards met fierce resistance in that sparsely occupied part of the Andes, they were slow to assimilate it and take down accounts of local history that could be compared to the chronicles. Some areas resisted Spanish rule for 130 years, by which time local peoples had been free of Inca rule for much longer than they had been subjects. In most accounts, once the Inca armies had secured the Lake Titicaca basin, they pressed south through the altiplano into northwest Argentina and Chile. According to Betanzos, the sequence of southern conquests began with the occupation of Guasco and Coquimbo territory and the establishment of a fort and garrison at Coquimbo. The Inca expedition then engaged the Chiriguanos (Guaraníes) and Zuries, east of the Andes, along what would become the troublesome southeastern frontier. Betanzos explained that the army found the rough eastern terrain impassable, especially the Río de la Plata out on the plain. So they shifted back to the high country and crossed over to Chile in pursuit of gold and mineral wealth at Porco, Tarapacá, and Carabaya.

The force then reportedly headed still further south, with a vanguard pressing forward beyond the Río Maule, near Santiago. Betanzos (1996:148–9) wrote that rapacious Thupa Inka Yupanki asked the populace ten days' journey north of the river where they had procured their gold. The natives described a watercourse and the dense human and small camelid populations, six days beyond. The army pressed southward for 15–20 leagues (~70–90 km) and a contingent was sent forward to scout the river. At that point, Thupa Inka Yupanki decided that he had been away from Cuzco for quite a while and had seen enough. In contrast, Cobo (1979:146–7) explained that the allied forces of the bellicose Mapuche and Araucanian societies who lived beyond the river repelled the invasion, killing the Inca commander and most of his soldiers. That setback provided the Incas sufficient motive to turn back north.

In Betanzos's (1996:150–2) account, after settling garrisons in Chile, Thupa Inka Yupanki's forces set course back to Cuzco, divided into four parts. One took the coastal plain to Arequipa; one marched into the central highlands through the lands of the Carangas and Aullagas; and the last went to the east through the lands of the Chichas. Thupa Inka Yupanki himself headed the fourth contingent, following an eastern route. The troops reportedly suffered enormously crossing the desert and endured grave losses in battle en route north. Before arriving in Chucuito, Thupa Inka Yupanki's soldiers established dominion in the province of Ilipa and in Chuquisaca, home to the Charcas, a province that his father had already reportedly conquered. In that march, his forces founded the *tampu* of Paria, above Cochabamba, and compelled tribute of great quantities of gold from the residents of Chuquiabo (La Paz). The easternmost army meanwhile lost about one-third of its personnel in its campaign to secure Chicha territory, in the south Bolivian altiplano. In that endeavor, the Inca army also passed through the modern province of Santa Cruz, establishing fortified settlements at Pocona, Samaipata, and Cuzcotuiro, along a hardened eastern perimeter (Rowe 1985b:226). The ultimate extension of Inca authority or activity in that region probably fell 100 km or more beyond the string of forts (see chapters 9, 10).

According to a number of sources, Pachakuti died during Thupa Inka Yupanki's campaigns in the south Andes, although Sarmiento's account can be read as though the father died before his son's first venture into the montaña. The campaign south may have been Thupa Inka Yupanki's last military venture. However, both the *khipu kamayuq* of Pacariqtambo and Sarmiento report that much of the empire had rebelled during the southern conquests, so the Inca had to return north to resecure those rebellious lands (Callapiña et al. 1974:40; Sarmiento 1960:255).

Sarmiento specifically mentioned the defiant Chachapoyas in that regard. The consensus, however, is that Wayna Qhapaq was the protagonist in the Incas' efforts to finally pacify that troublesome people.

Consolidation of the Empire: Wayna Qhapaq

The transition from Thupa Inka Yupanki to Wayna Qhapaq was reportedly just as turbulent as earlier successions, involving both intrigue and murder among royal kin groups (see chapter 5). Once his kin were in control, Wayna Qhapaq was said to have balanced his reign between military and administrative affairs (Callapiña et al. 1974:42; Betanzos 1996:165–85; Cieza 1984:157, 229, 1967:211–29; Polo 1917:114; Rowe 1985b:224–6; Sarmiento 1960:260–4; Murúa 1986:107–31; Cobo 1979:152–6; Cabello Valboa 1951:361–405). The major expansions were already completed, so his campaigns involved securing perimeter territories and dominating the far north. With his brother Awki Thupa Inka installed as co-ruler, Wayna Qhapaq spent two years in Cuzco before setting out on his first military venture against the Chachapoyas. Using Cajamarca as a base of operations, Wayna Qhapaq's forces ultimately spent years subduing the peoples of that land.

Sometime early in his reign, Wayna Qhapaq inspected his domain, for new rulers had to re-establish their supremacy physically and symbolically. He set off to the south, having entrusted his uncle Waman Achachi ("Hawk Ancestor") with the northern half of the empire. During the tour, the emperor passed through Cochabamba, in eastern Bolivia, where a vast set of state farms was created at his behest (chapter 11). He also ordered the eastern frontier at Pocona hardened against a threat of invasion from the east, by renovating a fort built during Pachakuti's reign. The Incas also mounted an expedition onto the plains of northwest Argentina through Tucuman, but like many marches into the eastern lowlands, the venture ended with the army retreating ingloriously to the mountains. The Incas nonetheless formed an alliance with the natives of Tucuman, who served as internal colonists and as a frontier buffer against depredations from the east in return for Inca protection (Lorandi and Boixadós 1987–8; Lorandi 1988).

After an organizational respite in Cuzco, Wayna Qhapaq set off for new conquests in the north. Cieza (1967:214) placed the total number of soldiers at an improbable 200,000, not counting servants. The forces were sent out in contingents to ease the logistical problems involved in moving so many men and their camp followings. The sovereign's journey was a suitably prolonged affair, as he often paused along the way to tend to affairs of state. In the Mantaro Valley, Cieza (1967:215) heard that the ruler had settled a long-simmering quarrel among the Wanka and Xauxa over the borders of their lands, while Cobo (1979:154) referred to Wayna Qhapaq's settling of a dispute over grazing lands in Kollasuyu. Wayna Qhapaq took quite a few Xauxa along with him to the Ecuadorian campaigns, an episode that their relatives were still complaining about half a century later, since many had never returned. The sojourn also solidified control over fractious *etnías*, including the perennially unruly Chachapoyas, who reportedly succumbed only after three new operations (see Cobo 1979:153).

Wayna Qhapaq's forces reportedly conducted as many as six to eight arduous campaigns over two decades in Ecuador, but his efforts enjoyed only mixed success (see Niles 1999:95–105 for a discussion of his military exploits). They established a base of operations at Tumipampa and, in especially trying regions, such as the Pasto territory at the north end of the empire, they built or took over existing forts as forward bases. There as elsewhere, where the Incas could establish a clear field of battle against a massed opponent or could invest a stronghold, they stood an excellent chance of success over time. Where the enemy proved elusive or held difficult terrain, especially in forested country, Inca military efforts often miscarried. The Brazamoros proved insuperable, sending the Incas packing back to their base camps. Cieza (1967:188, 217–18) wrote that another force was routed even before arriving at the targeted forts, and two others also retreated in the face of native resistance. One of the latter expeditions was led by Atawallpa, whose precipitous flight greatly shamed his father. Only after even more failed efforts led by other officers did Wayna Qhapaq himself take personal command in the field, according to Cabello (Cabello Valboa 1951:368; see also Betanzos 1996:182–3).

The campaigns against the Otavalo and Caranqui included some of the most celebrated battles of late Inca history (Sarmiento 1960:261–3; Cabello Valboa 1951:369–70; see also Murúa 1986:119–20). In one conflict, the Incas met concerted resistance in efforts to take a citadel and Wayna Qhapaq was unseated in an unexpected counterattack. He was saved only by the heroic action of his personal guard composed of *orejones* (literally "long-ears," so named for their pendulous ear lobes in which they inserted large earspools), Cuzqueñans who formed the army's elite. In the aftermath of the battle, the ruler and *orejones* quarreled when he chastened them for letting him fall into mortal danger. The humiliated warriors organized to return home, and were only dissuaded from doing so by personal entreaties from the image of the emperor's mother, sweetened with gifts. Ultimately, the Incas prevailed only by feigning withdrawal and catching the hapless defenders as they poured out of the fort. Most of the defenders were pinned against a lake, where they mistook Inca efforts to capture them as a continued attack. When they resisted, they were slaughtered in the water, thus giving the lake its name – *Yaguarcocha*, or Lake of Blood. Wayna Qhapaq then retired to Tumipampa, but the Incas were continually plagued by a warlord named Pinta, who had escaped with a "thousand" Kañari and raided for some time from a fort at Chillo. When the defiant Pinta refused pardon after he was finally captured, his skin was made into a drum that was played as a gesture of respect in festivals in Cuzco honoring the Sun (Cabello Valboa 1951:382).

Wayna Qhapaq received news about that time that the southeastern frontier at Cuzcotuiro, Bolivia, had been invaded. He dispatched the commander Yasca to assemble a force to counter the incursion of Guaraníes (Chiriguanos), accompanied by the Portuguese adventurer Alejo García. The general headed south, beginning to gather his army in Cajamarca and picking up soldiers along the way. Although Yasca's forces met noteworthy resistance, they ultimately re-established the frontier, rebuilt the forts, and installed garrisons (Cabello Valboa 1951:383–4; Sarmiento 1960:263–4; Murúa 1986:130–1).

In the meantime, Wayna Qhapaq's forces pressed northward into the lands of the Pasto and Quillacinga. They placed the empire's northernmost territorial markers at the Río Angasmayo or a little farther north, near the border of modern Ecuador and Colombia. A vanguard was sent further, but returned with tales of an impoverished land populated by naked cannibals, a description sometimes applied to areas where the Incas could not establish control (Cabello Valboa 1951:384; see RGI 1965:210, 279; see Salomon 1986). At that point, Wayna Qhapaq descended to the coast himself. The Incas advanced only under great hardships, fighting debilitating battles along the way. How far his army traveled is a matter of some dispute, but most sources report an advance no farther than southern Ecuador (Cieza 1967:221–2; Sarmiento 1960:264; Cabello Valboa 1951:392–3). While in the lowlands, Wayna Qhapaq heard of an epidemic that was killing many of his relatives – probably hemorrhagic smallpox (Cook 1981:62) – and quickly headed back to the mountains. Early in 1528, while in Quito or Tumipampa, he was fatally stricken himself. The death of his heir designate Ninan Cuyuchi of the same pestilence soon precipitated a conflict over succession.

Dynastic War: Waskhar and Atawallpa

The succession to Wayna Qhapaq's throne suffered the conflicting claims, fratricide, and pitched battle that often attended the transfer of imperial power, in part because of Ninan Cuyuchi's untimely death (e.g., Callapiña et al. 1974:47; Betanzos 1996:182–5; Cabello Valboa 1951:394; Murúa 1986:140; Cobo 1979:160–1; Sarmiento 1960:264). Waskhar and Atawallpa, two royal sons by different mothers, fought a savage war that ended just as the Spaniards arrived in 1532. In fact, Pizarro's men captured Atawallpa in Cajamarca just as the disgraced Waskhar was being ferried north. Three Spaniards actually had an audience with the fallen emperor shortly before he was murdered along the road, in which he vainly pleaded to be released. The dynastic war split the Andean peoples, providing a wedge that the conquistadores quickly recognized and exploited.

Most accounts agree that Waskhar was enthroned in Cuzco with the assent of the royalty. This view was unsurprisingly countered by Betanzos (1996:183–4), who was married to Atawallpa's sister/wife. In Betanzos's version, Wayna Qhapaq successively named Ninan Cuyuchi, Atawallpa, and Waskhar as the next paramount, while in his deathbed fever. Only because Atawallpa rejected the throne was the fringe to be passed on to Waskhar. Shortly thereafter, his half-brother Atawallpa challenged his authority from a base of power in Ecuador, where the Incas' most seasoned army was stationed. It is uncertain if Atawallpa intended to claim the northern part of the empire at first, or if he did so only after Waskhar's murderous behavior (described in chapter 5) led him to fear for his life. In the context of the narratives, Waskhar's lethal actions toward his immediate male kin would have given any survivors cause for fear. It bears remembering, however, that most of Waskhar's adherents were eliminated at the end of the war, so that he left few supporters to tell his side of the story.

Cabello (1951:394–474; see also Sarmiento 1960:265–71; Betanzos 1996:184) wrote that word of the deaths of Wayna Qhapaq and the prince was sent ahead to Cuzco, while the funeral cortege was mounted. The emperor's organs were removed and the body cured in the sun and air. His attendants then dressed him in precious robes and placed him on a fine litter adorned with feathers and gold to be transported back to Cuzco. Guaman Poma (1980:93; see Rostworowski 1999:90) wrote that the embalmed body was treated as if Wayna Qhapaq were still alive in an effort to allow insiders a chance to install a successor before opposition could be raised. Cabello reported that some members of the funeral party hatched a plot to kill the newly selected Waskhar and enthrone his brother Cusi Atachi, but the plot was foiled when the chief conspirator approached an uncle who remained loyal to Waskhar (Cabello Valboa 1951:396–7; see also Murúa 1986:143; Guaman Poma 1980:93).

Waskhar ordered the funeral train to stop outside Cuzco, according to Cabello (1951:398) and Murúa (1986:144–5), since it had already come within 20 leagues of the city. Perhaps mindful of the recent conspiracy to supplant him, Waskhar commanded the four executors of Wayna Qhapaq's legacy to enter Cuzco one at a time. He demanded to know why Atawallpa had remained in Ecuador, but even under torture, they simply said that Atawallpa did not want to affront the aristocracy with his wretched appearance. To everyone's horror, Waskhar ordered the executors killed, even though they were esteemed relatives from Upper Cuzco (i.e., Hanan Cuzco, the more prestigious half of Cuzco's aristocracy: see chapter 5). Many members of the funeral cortege fled immediately. Some carried the fearsome news to Atawallpa, while Waskhar symbolically divorced himself from Upper Cuzco in a fury (Sarmiento 1960:266). Despite the tumult, Wayna Qhapaq's funeral was a prolonged, elaborate affair, with great pomp and copious drinking. Sometime thereafter, Waskhar took his sister Mama Chukuy Juypa as wife, but reportedly only after embarrassing entreaties and with the grudging acquiescence of her mother.

The chroniclers differed over Atawallpa's intentions in the early stages of Waskhar's rule, although most observed that he initially declared obeisance to his brother. His pledges were ill-received in Cuzco, however, for various messengers were maimed, tortured, or slain (Betanzos 1996: 193; Cabello Valboa 1951:413–14; Sarmiento 1960:266). As word of Waskhar's suspicions of treason got back to him, Atawallpa reportedly set about erecting palaces in Tumipampa and dressed in his father's vestments to visit Quito. The Inca governor of the Kañari reported those actions to an irate Waskhar, who perhaps rightly believed that Atawallpa was staking a claim of legitimacy to the throne (Cabello Valboa 1951:423). Rejecting counsel for restoring amicable relations, Waskhar decided on military action.

The first battles of the dynastic war were remembered in many ways (figure 4.2). Cieza (1967:239–44) commented that he heard so many different versions that he would just go with the majority. He wrote that Waskhar sent Atoq ("Fox") north to assemble a local force of Kañari. Some reports said that Atawallpa was captured either by Atoq in battle or during an appeal to the Kañari for assistance. He was held prisoner in Tumipampa, from where he escaped with the aid of a silver lever or by transmogrifying into a serpent. In Cabello's account, Atoq's local army engaged Atawallpa's forces near Tumipampa. The Cuzco side prevailed, so Atawallpa's men retreated to the Río Ambato, south of Quito, which they had previously secured for such an eventuality. Atawallpa himself remained in Quito, rallying his troops (Cabello Valboa 1951:429–31; see also Murúa 1986:170; Betanzos 1996:200; Cobo 1979:164–5; Sarmiento 1960:266).

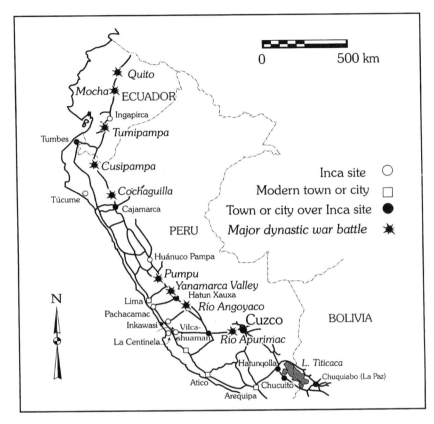

Figure 4.2   The major battles of the dynastic war between Waskhar and Atawallpa

Other chroniclers did not report an initial victory by Cuzco's forces. Betanzos (1996:195–6) – ever the apologist for Pachakuti's kin, including Atawallpa – wrote that the southern generals had mobilized an army of 6,000 in Cuzco and picked up an additional 4,000 along the way. They provisioned the army at state centers along highland roads built for just that purpose. They were reinforced by Kañari forces at Tumipampa, while Atawallpa gathered his own forces in Quito. The two armies met on the fields of Mochacaxa or Riopampa, where the Ecuadorian forces under Atawallpa's personal direction won a resounding victory. One of Waskhar's two commanders was killed, but Cusi Yupanki was taken prisoner and converted to Atawallpa's cause. Cieza (1967:

241–3) estimated that 15,000–16,000 men died in the conflict, a judgment partially based on viewing the battlefield over a decade later.
Cabello (1951:428–32) wrote that Atoq and the governor of the Kañari
were taken prisoner in that battle. They were subsequently executed with
darts and arrows, the former after being tortured for information about
Cuzco's intentions. Atoq's skull was then fashioned into a gilded drinking cup (Sarmiento 1960:266) that the Spanish soldier Ruiz de Arce
saw Atawallpa drinking from in Cajamarca. At that point Wanka Awki
assumed command of Waskhar's forces, supported by *orejones* from
Cuzco and soldiers enlisted from many parts of the empire (Cieza
1967:245–7; Betanzos 1996:206–8; Cabello Valboa 1951:433–4; Murúa
1986:172–5).

There were numerous diplomatic overtures along the way among
Waskhar, Wanka Awki, and Atawallpa, but they ultimately miscarried,
not least because Waskhar feared that Wanka Awki would defect.
Cabello wrote that the great armies soon engaged each other in a second
battle at a bridge controlling access to Tumipampa, where Cuzco's forces
prevailed in a Pyrrhic victory. Atawallpa's men took refuge on a hill slope
for the night, but sallied forth the next morning and forced Wanka
Awki's men to retreat to Tumipampa. Finding that Atawallpa's soldiers
were advancing toward him, Wanka Awki dispatched an army to engage
them, but it was routed at a substantial loss of manpower (Cabello
Valboa 1951:433–5; see also Sarmiento 1960:266–7). He then retreated
to Cusipampa, where he set about constructing a fort.

Even during the war's early stages, the Quiteñan and Cuzqueñan sides
were not always engaged with each other, as some ancillary campaigns
reportedly followed the first conflicts (Betanzos 1996:203–4; Cabello
Valboa 1951:433–8; Cieza 1967:246–7). Part of the rationale may have
arisen from their desire to secure their base territories before engaging
one another. Cabello explained the forays of both sides as training exercises and as a means of keeping the massed forces occupied. Atawallpa
reportedly worked hard to firm up military control and to expand his
domain to the east. He exacted ghastly revenge from the Kañari for their
allegiance to Waskhar, killing many, resettling some in Guambo, and
transporting about 15,000 south for intended resettlement near Cuzco.
Sarmiento (1960:266) and Cabello (1951:437–41; see also Murúa
1986:176–9) also reported that armies under Wanka Awki undertook
similar ventures with mixed results. According to Cabello, Wanka Awki's
defeat on the eastern slopes was rewarded with a derisive present of
women's clothes from Waskhar, which goaded him into taking on
Atawallpa's men in an effort to regain lost prestige. However, he was
defeated again at Cusipampa because his army was so drained after its
ill-fated campaigns to the east.

Those defeats inaugurated a calamitous series of battles commanded by Wanka Awki as he retreated along the Andes. Modern analysts concur with Cobo's (1979:165–6) assessment that the hastily mobilized southern forces, though immense, were no match for Atawallpa's seasoned troops, who had been honing their skills during twenty years of warfare. The continued losses by Wanka Awki both weakened his forces and reduced morale. Following the loss of southern Ecuador, his remaining army retreated to Cajamarca, in north-central Peru. There he was reinforced by an army of 30,000 fresh troops, whose core consisted of 10,000 of the redoubtable Chachapoyas (Betanzos 1996:206–7; Sarmiento 1960:267; Cabello Valboa 1951:436–46; Murúa 1986:183). Those men set out against the advancing forces of Quizquiz, one of Atawallpa's two principal generals, to do battle at Cochaguilla, in northern Peru, between Guancabamba and Guambos. According to Cabello, Quizquiz astutely recognized that the Chachapoyas were key to the battle and concentrated his forces on breaking them. Once the Chachapoyas were put to flight, the remaining southern army quit the field and many men crossed over to the opposition. Reinforced with those soldiers and others forcibly pressed along route, Quizquiz continued south with an army vastly larger than the one he had commanded when departing Quito.

At Pumpu, an important provincial center in the central Peruvian puna, Quizquiz prevailed once more; the southern forces fled to Hatun Xauxa, about 150 km to the south. The ill-fated Wanka Awki was then stripped of command by Mayca Yupanki, who led a considerable array of reinforcements (Sarmiento 1960:267; Murúa 1986:184; Cabello Valboa 1951:448–9). The two contingents soon joined battle in the Yanamarca Valley, just north of Hatun Xauxa. According to Cabello (1951:449–50), Mayca Yupanki's inexperienced soldiers initially held the field, but at such great cost that they retreated to the pass over the Angoyaco (Mantaro River), about 70 km south of Hatun Xauxa. In the aftermath, thousands of corpses were said to have been strewn across the battlefield, their remains still visible to the Spaniards in March 1533 (Herrera 1952:323). Following the victory in the Yanamarca Valley, Quizquiz's forces took a recuperative break at Hatun Xauxa, after which they pushed on to the Angoyaco bridgehead. The constricted topography favored the defenders, but the northern forces ultimately took the pass either through a flanking maneuver or a massed attack.

Waskhar then determined to set out at the head of his own force. After the customary consultation of oracles, fasting, and sacrifices, his armies mobilized to entrap Quizquiz's men. The consensus among the chroniclers is that Waskhar divided his forces into three parts (Betanzos 1996:223; Sarmiento 1960:267–9; Cabello Valboa 1951:453–9; Murúa

1986:188). Cabello and Sarmiento wrote that the two forces on the eastern flank met before the major battle. In the conflict between the forces of the center, Waskhar's troops held the field but failed to press their advantage. They drove the northern forces onto grassy slopes to which they set fire, after which they retired to a state installation to rest. The northern commanders, in contrast, rallied their men during the night. Determined to finish things the next day, Waskhar divided his forces to trap his opponents. However, Sarmiento wrote, Challcochima, Atawallpa's other principal general, successfully employed a similar pincers tactic and routed one of the Cuzqueñan forces.

In a now familiar pattern, the histories differed on how Waskhar fell to Quizquiz's and Challcochima's men. In Cabello's (1951:457–9; see also Murúa 1986:192) account, the emperor's litter was overthrown in a great battle. Seeing their ruler captured, his demoralized men took flight. Betanzos (1996:225–7) and Sarmiento (1960:269) wrote that Waskhar was drawn into an ambush with only a guard of 5,000. Tellingly, that guard was apparently composed of warriors from Hurin Cuzco, since Waskhar did not trust the upper half of Cuzco's royalty, whom he saw as being allied with Atawallpa. A small contingent of northerners placed themselves in his path, feigning sleep and then a disorderly retreat. As Waskhar pursued his apparent advantage, lateral forces closed the trap and took him prisoner. Challcochima then dressed a number of his men in Waskhar's clothes and ordered them to take up the fallen emperor's litter in a march toward the main Cuzqueñan army. When they approached Waskhar's forces, Challcochima's men revealed themselves as the victorious northern army, which so dismayed the Cuzqueñans that they surrendered.

However it occurred, that battle effectively ended the dynastic war. Challcochima and Quizquiz entered Cuzco, where they held Waskhar, his mother, and his wife prisoner. There is confusion over the sequence of events afterward, but the generals may have initially granted a general pardon. Some time later, Cusi Yupanki, Atawallpa's highest-ranking military officer and High Priest of the Sun, arrived in Cuzco. Under his supervision, Waskhar's wives and children were executed one after another in the most ghastly fashion as the lamenting ruler was forced to watch. The carnage was so thorough that only a handful of close relatives were spared or escaped. Cusi Yupanki also supervised the burning of Thupa Inka Yupanki's mummy and the virtual eradication of his descendant kin (see chapter 5 for a political explanation of this episode). Among the lucky few who escaped the carnage were Wayna Qhapaq's sons Manqo Inka, who would lay siege to Cuzco in 1536, and Paullu Inka, who collaborated with Spanish rule (Betanzos 1996:243–4; Sarmiento 1960:271–2; Cobo 1979:168–9).

While the definitive battles were waged outside Cuzco, Atawallpa was slowly wending his way south from Tumipampa. He was in Cajamarca when word arrived that a contingent of strange, bearded men had arrived on the coast at Tumbes, where they were making a general nuisance of themselves by pillaging and killing. Atawallpa dispatched Rumiñawi ("Stone Eye") at the head of a force said to include 20,000 men to meet the Spaniards, who had begun to ascend the Andes by that point. The emperor himself elected to wait in Cajamarca for both his uninvited visitors and the defeated Waskhar. Confident in his victory, Atawallpa could not have foreseen that the arrival of the Spaniards spelled death for him and the end of his hard-won empire.

Explaining the Inca Expansion

Some important factors – especially political history and ideology – remain to be explored, but this is probably a good point to reflect on the causes of the great expansion. Although a prince's ambitions may have fanned the Incas' ardor, the rise of the empire cannot be assigned to that factor alone. Keeping in mind the poetic license of the narratives, we need to think in terms of the dynamics of chiefdoms, not states, for the early stages. Both settlement patterns and the legendary accounts suggest that the conflict endemic to Late Intermediate highland societies set the conditions for Inca expansion. Intriguingly, there are hints of pressure on productive lands in the last century or two before the first Inca expansion. The layers of ice in the Quelccaya glacier testify to a prolonged drought in the south Peruvian Andes *ca.* AD 1245–1310 (Ortloff and Kolata 1993; see also Seltzer and Hastorf 1990). That situation may have threatened highland subsistence and put a premium on leaders who could defend or expand resources. The prospect of aggression by powerful neighbors to the south and west may have also genuinely threatened Cuzco's security, as the narratives recounted. Certainly the immense, walled settlements in the Titicaca basin suggest that the powers developing there were enmeshed in warfare. It thus seems plausible that the Incas' initial expansionist moves combined predation and self-defense. Rowe (1946:206) has also plausibly suggested that the early Inca successes may have also committed them to hostile relations with powerful societies that they had not considered engaging, notably Chimor. Militarism may have played another, more indirect role, as military competence was conspicuously mentioned in the selection of Inca leadership (chapters 5, 9). In the Late Intermediate period, the endemic conflict selected for warlords who could provide security and opportunities for plunder. This ethic carried over into the imperial era. Though the conquistadores' own careers as soldiers colored their views of Inca history, the image of rulers as great warriors pervaded the Incas' own descriptions. The succession process was intended to produce vigorous leaders, and the dynastic histories gave short shrift to rulers who failed to enlarge their domain.

There is no reason to doubt the Incas' own explanation that a quest for wealth also drove their expansion. A change from plunder to annexation of productive resources may have been crucial in the emergence of the expansionist state (Schaedel 1978; see also Rostworowski 1999). The gains realized from seizing resources likely benefited most Incas, but the methods may have concentrated power in a few elite lineages who needed to keep the flow of spoils in motion to maintain power. Booty was a prime motivator for the officers and rank and file soldiers throughout the Inca era, but some regions were most likely targeted for natural resources that could be intensified. The highlands of Peru were attractive for farming and pastoral production, whereas the altiplano was coveted for the wealth of its flocks. Cochabamba, Bolivia, was developed for its productive farmlands (Wachtel 1982). The Incas also sought raw materials that could be used to sustain the elites' privileged position – minerals from the south Andes, gold and feathers from the jungles, and Spondylus shell from tropical waters (chapter 11).

As for politics, the interplay between militarism and genealogy in Inca successions also contributed to the expansion (see also chapter 5). There is fragile balance in a practice of succession that selects for dynamic leadership while providing for continuity of rule. Perhaps recognizing the problems inherent in political instability, the later emperors adopted co-regency as a policy to smooth the transition across generations of leadership. As a consequence, royal successions set aristocratic kin groups against one another, in the names of potential heirs too young to assert their own claims. The transitions to Thupa Inka Yupanki, Wayna Qhapaq, and Waskhar/Atawallpa emphasize that the bloody politics of succession were played out by kin groups. While the paramount was reaching maturity, however, it remained for him to demonstrate competence through effective military leadership. Some late Inca campaigns, especially Wayna Qhapaq's grand tour and his campaigns in Ecuador, are therefore at least partly understandable as a play to royal politics.

Ideological motives often appeared in accounts of the expansion, but their role is complicated because the Incas continually reinvented their grand tradition. Charismatic leadership was almost certainly vital in both strategic and tactical command and the narratives certainly show that the Incas were aware of the utility of promoting a cult of the great leader. The narratives emphasized the importance of the *Sapa Inca* in decisive battles, even though many key expeditions were directed by other kin.

The Incas also generated heroic and supernatural tales about the emperors even after the Spanish invasion. Nonetheless, the infighting among Cuzco's aristocracy should make us chary of crediting the emperor with too much power in describing how Inca rule actually worked. There is also some suggestion that the Incas drew inspiration from an evangelistic creed. Imperial ideology, as told to the Spaniards, contained an edict to civilize the world and we have every reason to believe that the Incas had faith in their gods and ancestors (chapter 7). Because we do not know how much of the imperial ideology was formulated late in the game, however, the degree to which evangelism actually drove the major expansions remains uncertain.

Some scholars have also inferred that the Andean practice called split inheritance drove the expansion (Conrad and Demarest 1984). In that custom, the individual who succeeded to the throne inherited the office and control over state resources. The deceased Inca's personal resources were kept by his kin group to venerate him in perpetuity. This proposition suggests that each new emperor had to expand the empire to feed the capital and build his own wealth, because the resources near Cuzco were soon exhausted. I find the argument unpersuasive, in part because Pachakuti and Thupa Inka Yupanki annexed virtually the entire empire, according to the sources used. Moreover, despite the ostensible shortages, even Wayna Qhapaq and Waskhar claimed areas in and near Cuzco for their own palaces and estates. The limitations of Andean transport technology also precluded long-distance shipment of food for daily subsistence. What is described as a concern about a shortage of resources is more plausibly explained as jealousy over royal estates (chapter 6). The situation may well have been cause for political infighting, but it does not work well in explaining imperial origins.

chapter five

The Politics of Blood in Cuzco

Since the days of the Spanish conquest, the Inca government has often been pictured as a finely tuned machine. Whether they admired or deplored Inca rule, authors usually agreed that Cuzco's crowning success was its orderly administration (Moore 1958). In the popular view, an omnipotent emperor presided over a vast bureaucracy that was mostly composed of local elites who had been recruited into state service. By applying the same policies everywhere, the Incas soon molded a cultural patchwork into a homogeneous society. Virtually everything the peasants did from birth to death was supervised by state officials, who called on taxpayer labor to meet state economic and military needs. The officials spoke Cuzco Quechua in public affairs and the people adopted some Inca customs into their daily lives. As for religion, the people's beliefs were eclipsed by a state ideology that elevated the ruler to the status of a god on earth. Since the Incas' society had been simply organized before the great expansion, they had invented a state to rule an empire.

This homogeneous portrait of the realm is still common (e.g., Davies 1995), but an image of uniform and ubiquitous control is an illusion based largely on Cuzco's view of the world. We should not be surprised at that, since both the Incas and their conquerors were preoccupied with the life and times of royalty. While the Spaniards did ask hundreds of petty lords about life before and under the Incas, they gave far more weight to the views expressed by Inca aristocrats, which included a fair measure of propaganda. From the early seventeenth to the mid-twentieth century, Garcilaso's (1966) idealized treatise on the uniform and benevolent society of his ancestors was especially influential. His credibility was based largely on his lineage, however, and not on the accuracy of his account.

Research over the last few decades has shown that some societies were transformed by Inca rule while others continued much as before. Their duties to the state notwithstanding, most subjects spent their lives in everyday activities focused around family and community, and many of them seldom saw a real Inca. And while the Incas did apply standard policies, the land outside Cuzco was actually a mosaic of societies to which they had to adjust their methods (chapters 2, 10). Cuzco's political history also affected the nature of Inca rule. The oral traditions that were dominant in Cuzco from about 1550 onward said that the government was largely the product of Pachakuti's divine genius. In accounts that unabashedly burnished his image, Pachakuti's descendants described a visionary who personally invented the social, political, and ceremonial order of the Inca world. While elements of this vision were surely hyperbole, it is true that the Incas did rule their empire for only a few generations. It is reasonable to believe that a few individuals were instrumental in the design, although the details of Pachakuti's inspired role are still open to question. One reason to raise an eyebrow is that the Incas periodically modified both the ruling hierarchy and the history that accounted for its legitimacy. They were, in fact, just at the point of changing things again when the Spaniards arrived. Because the Incas lacked a writing system and used their past as a political tool, it is hard to disentangle myth from reality – especially for times more than a generation or so removed from the Spanish invasion. The narratives also warn us that Inca rule cannot be explained simply by describing the system that existed in 1532. Tawantinsuyu was in a dynamic phase at the time of its collapse, but it was not the first time that a political cataclysm had occurred.

Tawantinsuyu: The Four Parts Together

Like many Andean peoples, the Incas envisioned their society, history, and land as a unified whole. They divided the world and its people into four parts (*suyu*) whose political and cosmic center lay at Cuzco (figure 5.1). In fact, the name of the realm – *Tawantinsuyu* – means "The Four Parts Together." Each of the parts was headed by a great lord (*apu*) who advised the emperor in Cuzco and directed affairs for his division (Cobo 1979:199). The most populous of the four parts, called *Chinchaysuyu*, took its name from the respected Chincha *etnía* of Peru's south-central coast; it encompassed the lands and peoples of the Peruvian coast, the adjacent highlands, and the north Andes. *Antisuyu* lay to the north and northeast of Cuzco; it was named after the warm forests of the montaña, known in Hispanic form as the *Andes*. *Kollasuyu* formed the largest part of the empire; it ran from Peru's southern highlands through the altiplano all the way to central Chile and adjacent Argentina. This division

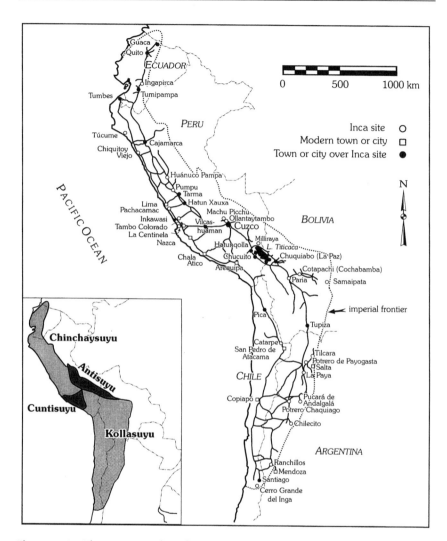

Figure 5.1 The Inca road and provincial installation (*tampu*) system, after Hyslop (1984): frontispiece; the four parts of the Inca realm are shown in the inset map

took its name from the Qolla (Kolla, Colla) peoples who lived on the north side of Lake Titicaca. *Cuntisuyu*, the smallest part, took in the stretch of land that ran southwest from Cuzco to the Pacific; its name corresponded to a province in the same region. Following the arrangement that divided the whole empire into four parts, Upper (*Hanan*) and

Lower (*Hurin*) Cuzco also contained ranked parts. The Upper part included Chinchaysuyu and Antisuyu, while the Lower included Kollasuyu and Cuntisuyu.

Until recently, we did not know where the borders among the four divisions lay around Cuzco. Then, in 1977, Waldemar Espinoza published a document prepared for Viceroy Toledo exactly 400 years earlier, which listed the affiliations of many villages near the capital. A plot of their locations and the positions of known shrines shows that the four parts were laid out neither symmetrically nor along the cardinal directions, even though the Incas had the knowledge to do so. Observers have known since the sixteenth century that the *suyu* took in markedly different fractions of the empire as a whole and this evidence shows that the *suyu* probably differed in size even near the capital (Espinoza 1977; Zuidema and Poole 1982).

Cuzco's Political Organization

Stripped to the bones, the Inca government was a monarchy in which rule passed from father to son. A layer beyond the skeleton, however, takes us into an elaborate hierarchy that fused Inca kinship and ancestor worship with ethnicity and a rigid class structure. In the Inca regime, the mummies of long-dead kings and queens, as well as oracular idols, participated in affairs of state through cults staffed by their descendants. To many Spaniards, this was proof positive of the devil's handiwork, but to the Andeans, their roles were natural, since the world was shared by the living, the dead, the gods, and the spirits.

The emperor and his family stood at the apex of power, below whom were two classes of aristocratic Inca kin and one class of honorary Inca nobility. In 1532, the most exalted aristocrats were ten royal kin groups called *panaqa*. In theory, a new *panaqa* was created with each royal succession as part of a convention called split inheritance. In this custom, the "most able" son of the deceased ruler became the new sovereign, while his other descendants became the custodians of his properties, usually under the leadership of one of his brothers. A *panaqa*'s duties included perpetual veneration of its ancestor and care for his assets through a cult founded around his mummy (see below). Below the *panaqa* were ten noble Inca kin groups who were considered to be distant relatives of the royalty. Cuzco's final elite class were called the Incas by Privilege. They were made up of ethnic groups who had lived in the region when the founding Inca ancestors arrived, according to mythohistory (see Bauer 1992c). Figure 5.2 illustrates the relationships among these social levels.

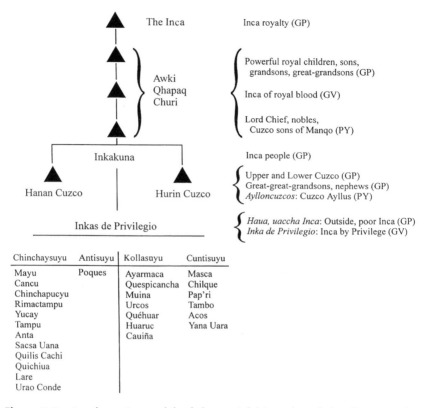

Figure 5.2 A schematic model of the social hierarchy of the Cuzco region in 1532, redrawn from illustration by Bauer 1992c:32. GP: Guaman Poma; GV: Garcilaso de la Vega; PY: Pachacuti Yamqui

The elite kin formed matching halves that were called Upper and Lower Cuzco. When the Spaniards arrived, each of the halves included five royal and five non-royal kin groups. This design probably resulted from one of the periodic reformations that occurred as Cuzco's society grew and changed over time, but it is difficult from our present vantage point to be sure when specific changes occurred. In late prehistory, the *panaqa* of Upper Cuzco were the more powerful and enjoyed the greater fruits of the imperial expansion. Their members lived in the higher part of town and took precedence in politics and ceremony. They dominated the civil, military, and religious hierarchies and their estates were far grander than those of Lower Cuzco. Pachakuti's descendants (*Hatun ayllu*) and Thupa Inka Yupanki's scion (*Qhapaq ayllu*) were especially powerful in the last prehispanic years. The narratives told of an intense rivalry that carried on for decades, which culminated in *Qhapaq ayllu*'s virtual eradication just as the Spaniards arrived (Ziółkowski 1996; see below).

The Ruler: Sapa Inca *("Unique Inca")*

In the final version of Inca government, the king was an absolute ruler – a divine being with a celestial mandate to rule the world. In practice, however, the very human monarch had to work closely with Cuzco's contentious aristocracy to take the throne and rule afterward. The royal epics recounted time and again how rulers had been elevated, counseled, assisted, deposed, and even assassinated by their relatives. The two faces of monarchy – the omnipotent ideal and the negotiated practice – were found throughout the oral histories. Because the Incas drew no neat distinctions among different aspects of power, the emperor melded political, social, military, and sacred leadership in a single person. Ideally, his existence passed through three stages (Gose 1996b). Early in life, he had to show himself to be a warrior worthy of his lineage and the support of Cuzco's noble kin. Once anointed by the Sun to rule the land, he was revered as a deity whose powers and perquisites were unique among the beings who walked the earth. In death, however, his descendants accentuated his perpetual vitality, as he feasted and conversed with the quick and the dead in public during the day and retired to his quarters for repose at night.

When a ruler took office, he assumed a new personal title that replaced his given name. Betanzos (1996:72) wrote that the sovereign was to marry his principal wife at that same time, so that the coronation actually installed a new royal couple. According to narrative tradition, the custom began with Thupa Inka Yupanki, who also instituted the practice of marrying his full sister. The ruler's many titles were intended to advertise his lineage, power, and generosity. The most prominent epithets were *Sapa Inca*, which means Unique Inca, *Intip Churin* or Son of the Sun, *Qhapaq Apu* or Powerful Lord, and *Huaccha Khoyaq*, or Lover and Benefactor of the Poor (Garcilaso 1966:59–60, 62–4; Rowe 1946:258). In the Andean view of things, the king's generosity was just as important as his sanctity and valor, for he embodied the state as a magnanimous patron. All of royal Cuzco lived from his largess both symbolically and literally, since they regularly received provisions from the central storehouses that he controlled. The ruler's relations with provincial lords and subjects also drew on his image as a gift-giver on a grand scale. His principal wife held parallel titles, including *Qoya* or Queen, and *Mamancik*, meaning Our Mother (figure 5.3). Garcilaso explained

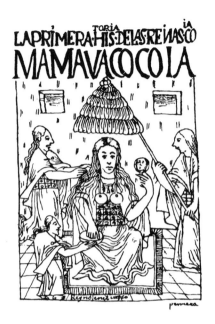

Figure 5.3 Guaman Poma's (1936) stylized illustrations of four Inca queens

that *Sapa Inca* and *Qoya* were matching honorifics, as were *Huaccha Khoyaq* and *Mamancik*. Secondary consorts and other royal women were called *palla*, while princesses or other daughters of royal blood were called *ñusta*.

As befit his station, the emperor's activities were filled with ritual, pomp, and feasting. Among his most important duties of protocol were presiding over the regular feasts in the main plaza in Cuzco, where he hosted the assembled guests from the Upper and Lower parts. According to Inca law, anyone approaching the emperor had to remove his footwear and carry a burden. He often sat behind a screen and spoke through an intermediary when receiving visitors or conducting affairs of state.[1] His attending court was meticulously organized. When the Spaniards had their first audience with Atawallpa at the baths near Cajamarca, he received them while seated on a low wooden throne (*duho*), surrounded by wives and lords who were all positioned according to their rank. The invaders reported that no one dared raise his eyes in the sovereign's presence (H. Pizarro 1959:85).

The conquistadores' observations while Atawallpa was imprisoned help us to understand the emperor's deportment. The Spaniards saw him in daily life and personal political relations, although for obvious reasons they never saw him conduct grand assemblies as head of state. They were duly impressed with his aura of gravity and august manner. Even while captive, Atawallpa received lords who came to pay obeisance and to receive instructions on managing the empire's affairs. Miguel de Estete wrote, "When they arrived before him, they did him great reverence, kissing his feet and hands. He received them without looking at them. It is remarkable to record the dignity of Atawallpa and the great obedience they all accorded him" (translation from Hemming 1970:51).

The King's Appearance

We do not know what the individual rulers looked like – even in a stylized format – except for Atawallpa and Waskhar, who were described by the conquistadores. The Incas did have a tradition of illustrating their history and kings on wooden panels, and Viceroy Toledo sent a number of portraits or tapestries to Spain, but they have since been lost (Molina de Cuzco 1988:7–8; Acosta 1986:323). Chroniclers also recorded oral descriptions of other rulers, but what remains today in graphical form are the illustrations by Guaman Poma and Murúa, who were clearly influenced by European cultural traditions. Guaman Poma's drawings retain many indigenous

continued

Andean elements, for he often took considerable care to represent the clothing and adornments of the individuals. His work is consequently an irreplaceable visual source regardless of the mixture of Andean and Spanish elements and the generalized visages of the persons illustrated.

An emperor had an array of insignia and personal adornments, along with elaborate customs, that marked his office (see Rowe 1946:258). His most important personal effect was a headband of braided cloth (*llauto*), which was sometimes adorned with feathers. It was positioned so that a thick tassel (*mazcaypaycha*) covered his forehead. He wore uniquely large earspools, a symbol of prestige that also marked Cuzco's aristocrats, who were called *orejones* or "big-ears" in the Colonial era. Another important royal symbol was a staff (*sunturpaucar*) that was completely covered with tiny feathers and adorned with three larger feathers that projected from the tip; it was sometimes used at the head of ritual processions to represent the ruler's power. The king had military insignia as well, most importantly a golden mace (*champi*) and a royal standard made of cloth that was painted until it stood stiff (Cobo 1979:244–7). When Atawallpa arrived at Cajamarca's square just before his capture, a soldier placed the standard in front of one of its buildings to declare the royal entry, unaware that the tense Spanish troops were inside, awaiting the order to attack.

When the emperor traveled, he was carried on an elegant litter borne by the Rucanas, who were selected for this prestigious duty because they were thought to have an especially even pace. His fine clothing was often woven for him by the *mamakuna*, members of the land's highest women's institution. Pedro Pizarro (1986:67–8) recalled how carefully Atawallpa was attended while he ate:

(H)e was seated on a wooden duho [stool] little more than a span [nine inches] high. This duho was of very lovely reddish wood and was always kept covered with a delicate rug, even when he was seated on it. The ladies brought his meal and placed it before him on tender thin green rushes . . . They placed all the vessels of gold, silver and pottery on these rushes. He pointed to whatever he fancied and it was brought . . . He was eating in this manner one day when I was present. A slice of food was being lifted to his mouth when a drop fell on the clothing that he was wearing. Giving his hand to the Indian lady, he rose and went into his chamber to change his dress and returned wearing a dark brown tunic and cloak. I approached him and felt the cloak, which was softer than silk . . . He explained that it was made from the skins of bats that fly by night in Puerto Viejo and Tumbes and that bite the natives. (Translation after Hemming 1970:50)

Atawallpa added a regal coda: "Those dogs from Puerto Viejo and Tumbes, what else did they have to do except catch the bats and make clothes for my father?" (ibid.). Pizarro explained that all the clothing that Atawallpa had worn, the bones of the animals and the ears of corn he had eaten, in short all things that he had touched, were gathered and stored in chests. They were to be burned later in an annual ceremony intended to thwart witchcraft against his royal person. The issue came to Pizarro's attention, predictably enough, when the ruler complained that a Spanish soldier had been rifling through the chests.

The installation of a new emperor was attended by all the pageantry that might be expected for the deified ruler of the world. Cobo (1990:154–7) wrote that all the eminent lords of the land who could make the trip attended the ceremonies, which were held once the lamentations for the deceased ruler had been properly observed. As a cleric, the chronicler focused his description on the ritual rather than political dimensions of the ceremonies. He wrote that the participants gathered in the central plaza called Awkaypata, along with the statues of the Sun and other major gods and representatives of all of the important *wak'a*. The sacrifices took the lives of two hundred children aged four to ten and great numbers of camelids, along with elegant clothing, seashells, and many golden and silver serving vessels and statues. The priests made sacrifices to each of the shrines in the city and designated materials for sacrifice in each shrine in the four quarters of the land. Their most important offerings were dedicated to the Creator God Wiraqocha, whose aid was solicited in granting the emperor health and a long life, victory over his enemies, many children to succeed him, and peace in his time. Once they had completed those prayers, the priests of Wiraqocha strangled the children, and then buried them with the gold and silver objects on a hill called Chuquicancha, above San Sebastián. The camelids, cloth, and other materials were burned.

The death of a ruler was supposed to be celebrated in an equally majestic manner. Following the format of Inca epic history, Betanzos (1996:134) explained that Pachakuti put a great deal of thought into planning his funerary rites and the disposition of his remains after death. He first ordered that all of Cuzco should spend a year dressed in mourning once he had expired. At the end of that time, royal Cuzco was to perform a month-long sequence of ceremonies that ensured his passage into the everlasting with the celestial gods. They began by visiting all the lands where the Inca had planted or harvested crops, carrying his clothing, weapons, and adornments. At each place, they were to cry out to him, "Look here at the garment that you used to wear" or " 'See here your weapon with which you won and subjected such a province and so many caciques who were lords there' . . . The most important lord of those who were going there would answer, saying he is in heaven with his father, the Sun." A great ceremony was then held in the main plaza of Cuzco, toward the end of which squadrons of warriors from Upper and Lower Cuzco staged a mock battle in the main compound. The side from Upper Cuzco won the battle, symbolically recapitulating the ruler's actions in life.

The penultimate act to the ceremonies was to be a grand series of sacrifices (Betanzos 1996:138–9). All the clothing that had been used in the mourning rituals was to be consumed in a bonfire in the main plaza, along with a thousand camelids decked out in fine clothes, and a thousand newborn camelids. The throats of two thousand other llamas were to be slit and their meat fed to his supporters, while another thousand were sacrificed and burned in all the places where he had gone in his lifetime. Pachakuti further instructed that ". . . a thousand boys and girls will be brought and will be buried for me in the places where I slept and where I usually enjoyed myself." Finally, all of his table service of gold and silver was to be buried with him and his livestock and stores burned. The goal of the sacrifices, repeated in reduced form until Polo discovered his mummy in 1559,[2] was to ensure that the ruler had food, drink, and servants aplenty in the afterlife. Once all of the funerary rituals had been completed, Pachakuti's survivors dressed his mummified remains in finery and kept it in state at Patallacta, probably the site now known as Q'enqo. Betanzos wrote that his personal golden idol, known as his brother (*wawqi*), was placed upon his tomb, so that people could worship it. His fingernails and hair had been carefully saved during his lifetime and were now formed into a statue, called a *bulto* by the Spaniards. This statue was held in as much reverence as his mummy (*mallki*) itself and could serve as a surrogate for the deceased lord in public affairs.

From his newly sanctified plane, a dead Inca emperor continued to participate actively in Cuzco's ceremonial and political life. The mummies of past rulers were customarily kept in houses in town or in sanctuaries on royal estates. Cobo (1990:39–43) wrote that the mummies and other images of the early rulers had once been kept in dedicated chapels within the main temple. Over time, however, their descendants decided that it would be more proper for each deceased ruler to reside in his own house where he could be better served. When the main Spanish force first entered Cuzco, the scribe Pedro Sancho de la Hoz saw Wayna Qhapaq's mummy comfortably seated in his palace, fronting the main plaza. The dead kings and queens were regularly feted and consulted on matters of importance. Pedro Pizarro (1986:89–90) recalled:

> (m)ost of the people [of Cuzco] served the dead, I have heard it said, who they daily brought out to the main square, setting them down in a ring, each one according to his age, and there the male and female attendants ate and drank. The attendants made fires for each of the dead in front of them with firewood that was worked and cut until it was quite even, very dry, and lighting [them], burned everything they had put before them, so that the dead should eat of everything that the living ate, which is what was burned in these fires. The attendants also placed before these dead certain large pitchers . . . of gold or silver or clay, each as he wished, and here they poured out the chicha that they gave to the mummies to drink, showing it to him, [and] the mummies toasted each other and the living, and the living toasted the dead. When the vessels were full, they emptied them over a circular stone they had for an idol in the middle of the plaza, around which there was a small channel, and the beer drained off through underground pipes.

The mummies or their surrogates were accompanied by a variety of other idols and armaments. And, so that they might communicate their wisdom or make their wishes known, each ruler or *qoya* was served by a male and female medium. The mummies attended only the most solemn festivals, sending their brother images out for less important occasions. As Pizarro explained, the mummies or images were arranged according to their rank in a row in the main plaza, where they were offered sacrifices and chicha. When the urge took them, the mummies and their retinues also visited one another or their living relatives for festivities – a hospitable gesture that was, of course, later returned.

The Spaniards marveled at their preservation when they found several in 1559 (table 5.1). The young Garcilaso apparently saw the mummies when he went to say goodbye to Polo in 1560 before leaving for Spain (Hemming 1970:298). Almost fifty years later, he (Garcilaso de la Vega 1966: pt. 1, bk. 5, ch. 29; pt. 1, bk. 3, ch. 20; from Hemming 1970:298) recalled that:

> (T)heir bodies were so perfect that they lacked neither hair, eyebrows nor eyelashes. They were in clothes such as they had worn when alive, with *llautas* on their heads but no other sign of royalty. They were seated in the way Indian men and women usually sit, with their arms crossed over their chests, the right over the left, and their eyes cast down . . . I remember touching a finger of the hand of Huayna-Capac. It was hard and rigid, like that of a wooden statue. The bodies weighed so little that any Indian could carry them from house to house in his arms or on his shoulders. They carried them wrapped in white sheets through the streets and squares, the

Table 5.1 Inca emperors: their mummies and statues, according to Sarmiento (1960), Cobo (1990), and Betanzos (1996)

Ruler	Name of brother statue	Image	Place where mummy or image maintained or found	Mummies' and idols' fate
Manqo Qhapaq	Indi	falcon	Indicancha or Wimpillay (image)	—
Zinchi Roq'a[a]	Guanachiri Amaro	fish	Wimpillay; house named Acoyguaci	found by Polo in 1559
Lloq'e Yupanki	Apo Mayta	—	Wimpillay	—
Mayta Qhapaq	—	—	Wimpillay	found by Polo in 1559
Qhapaq Yupanki	Apu amayta[a]	—	Wimpillay	found by Polo in 1559
Inka Roq'a	Vicaquirao[a]	—	Larapa (mummy)	found by Polo in 1559
Yawar Waqaq	—	—	—	not found
Wiraqocha Inka	Inga Amaro	serpent	Caquia Xaquixaguana (i.e., Juchuy Cuzco; mummy and image)	mummy burned by Gonzalo Pizarro; ashes collected in jar, captured by Polo along with idol in 1559
Pachakuti Inka Yupanki	Chuqui illa, Indi illapa	lightning, viper	Patallacta (Totocache; mummy)	mummy found and sent to Lima by Polo in 1559; idol broken apart and sent to Cajamarca as part of Atawallpa's ransom
Thupa Inka Yupanki	Cuxi churi	happy son	Calispuquio (idol)	mummy burned in dynastic war in 1532; ashes collected in jar, captured by Polo along with idol in 1559
Wayna Qhapaq	Guaraqui Inga	—	house near Saqsawaman (mummy)	mummy found and sent to Lima by Polo in 1559
Waskhar	—	—	—	none created
Atawallpa	—	—	—	none created

[a] Spelling of brother statue according to Cobo; all others according to Sarmiento.

Indians falling to their knees and making reverences with groans and tears, and many Spaniards taking off their cap.

The High Priest (Willaq Umu)

In 1532, the High Priest of the Sun (*willaq umu*; "priest who recounts") was probably the second most powerful individual in the empire. According to several chroniclers, the office was created or elevated during Pachakuti's reign. Part of his power stemmed from his role in confirming the selection of the new emperor in office. His pious duties hardly restricted him to ceremony, however, for both Atawallpa's and Manqo Inka's chief priests were also their field marshals in the last dynastic war and the neo-Inca era, respectively. At one point, the emperor Wayna Qhapaq deposed the priest and took the office for himself, perhaps to ensure that he could appoint his own successor (see Gose 1996b; Ziółkowski 1996:154, 158–62). The leader of an early resistance movement, Titu Cusi Yupanki, also assumed both mantles in the jungles of Vilcabamba in the 1560s.

The Royal and Aristocratic Kindred

The emperor was theoretically an absolute monarch, but Cuzco's royal kin groups (*panaqa*) were still a political force to be reckoned with. They formed an advisory court and provided many of the officials who devised and applied state policy. Because the *panaqa* could influence the selection of royal successors, candidates and kin groups likely negotiated with one another constantly in the quest for power. The murderous intrigues that punctuated royal successions gave the kin a great deal of leverage in deciding the future direction of the empire (see *Succession Crises*, below). The highest ranking *panaqa* were the kin closest to the current emperor, not to the most ancient.

Earlier, we noted that ten royal *panaqa* and ten non-royal *ayllu* formed Cuzco's elite when the Spaniards arrived. The most widely accepted view today is that a new *panaqa* was added to Cuzqueñan society every royal generation as a result of split inheritance. This custom should have modified the political arrangement, but we cannot be sure how things worked in practice, since one tradition suggested that all ten groups had actually been present from the pre-imperial era (e.g., Betanzos 1996:69–73). In an alternative vision, the royal kin of Lower Cuzco were descended from the first five Inca rulers, while the kin of the later kings formed Upper Cuzco. If that was true, then history was written continuously into the

Table 5.2a The ten royal kin groups (*panaqa*) of Cuzco at the time of the Spanish conquest (modified from Rowe 1985a:64); note that Qhapaq Yupanki's *panaqa* has been shifted from Upper (*Hanan*) Cuzco to Lower (*Hurin*) Cuzco with the addition of the 9th and 10th *panaqa*

Hanan Cuzco		Hurin Cuzco	
Ruler	Descendant kin group	Ruler	Descendant kin group
10 Thupa Inka Yupanki	*Qhapaq ayllu*	5 Qhapaq Yupanki	*Apu Mayta panaqa ayllu*
9 Pachakuti Inka Yupanki	*Hatun ayllu (Iñaqa panaqa)*	4 Mayta Yupanki	*Uska Mayta panaqa ayllu*
8 Wiraqocha Inka	*Zukzu panaqa ayllu*	3 Lloq'e Yupanki	*Awayni panaqa ayllu*
7 Yawar Waqaq	*Awqaylli panaqa ayllu*	2 Zinchi Roq'a	*Rawra panaqa ayllu*
6 Inka Roq'a	*Wika K'iraw panaqa ayllu*	1 Manqo Qhapaq	*Chima panaqa ayllu*

Table 5.2b A hypothetical structure of the eight royal kin groups (*panaqa*) of Cuzco in the epoch of Pachakuti (modified from Rowe 1985a:71)

Hanan Cuzco		Hurin Cuzco	
Ruler	Descendant kin group	Ruler	Descendant kin group
8 Wiraqocha Inka	*Zukzu panaqa ayllu*	4 Mayta Yupanki	*Uska Mayta panaqa ayllu*
7 Yawar Waqaq	*Awqaylli panaqa ayllu*	3 Lloq'e Yupanki	*Awayni panaqa ayllu*
6 Inka Roq'a	*Wika K'iraw panaqa ayllu*	2 Zinchi Roq'a	*Rawra panaqa ayllu*
5 Qhapaq Yupanki	*Apu Mayta panaqa ayllu*	1 Manqo Qhapaq	*Chima panaqa ayllu*

social structure and political hierarchy (Sarmiento 1960).[3] In yet a third version of Inca history, Pachakuti organized Cuzco's existing kin groups into a new dual design when he invented the imperial order. Following this view, Rowe (1985a) suggests that one of Upper Cuzco's royal kin groups may have been shifted to Lower Cuzco every two generations, to preserve the balance between the moieties (table 5.2a, b).

As with so much Inca history, however, any view is beset by all sorts of niggling problems (see below, *Two Inca Kings?*). For example, Rost-worowski (1983:141–5) points out that some royal kin groups may have fallen by the wayside over time. In addition to the core set of ten royal kin groups, the chronicles named several other kin groups that were either called *panaqa* or claimed status as a royal kindred. She suggests that political maneuvering may have removed some *panaqa*, or that some that had existed before the formation of the empire were not included in its original political design. Each option suggests a different way that structure and history could have interacted to produce the system that existed in 1532. Although the data are conflictive, I am most comfortable with the idea that kin groups were added or dislodged over the generations, and that stories of the Inca past were revised to rationalize the organization as it existed at any point. Whichever view best explains the situation, the political arrangement described to the Spaniards was a snapshot – the design as it was frozen in time by the European invasion.

Two Inca Kings?

A number of scholars support Zuidema's proposition that Inca government may have been a diarchy (Zuidema 1964:127; Duviols 1979b; Rostworowski 1983:130–79, 1999:177–81). That is, there were always two Inca kings, one from Upper Cuzco and one from Lower Cuzco. His proposal starts from the observation that Andean social organization, including Cuzco's, featured opposing halves, each of which had its own leader. In addition, the generally reliable chronicler Cieza (1967:111) said that Inca aristocrats claimed that there had always been two kings of Cuzco. Several chroniclers also wrote that Manqo Qhapaq was considered to be the founder of both social divisions. Without taking the latter premise at face value, Zuidema infers that the names of *panaqa* may have been titles for groups holding a particular status, not the names of kindreds in a historical genealogy. From his viewpoint, the narratives described relations of power, not linear accounts of history. His model of Inca government more closely approximates the diarchy illustrated in

continued

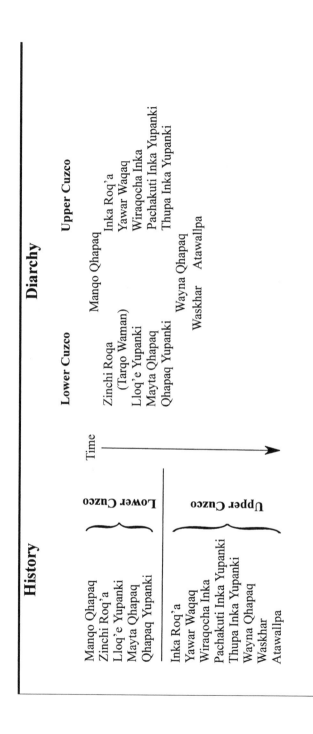

Figure 5.4 Three alternative models of Inca government, redrawn from Gose 1996b, incorporating Zuidema's (1983) diarchy

figure 5.4, than the standard design. If Zuidema is correct, then we cannot assume that each *panaqa* corresponded neatly to a generation (Zuidema 1983; Rowe 1985a; Rostworowski 1983:141–5). Gose's illustration of three perspectives shows how the same basic information can be used to support different views of the central Inca political design (figure 5.4). Although the structural and diarchy models are influential, they remain a minority viewpoint because they require elevating individuals to the Inca king lists who are virtually, if not altogether, absent from most lists of Inca royalty cited in the chronicles. In addition, Lower Cuzco almost certainly had a paramount figure, but studies of kin-based political systems throughout the Andes show that the leader of one social division invariably stood higher in rank than the other and spoke for the group as a whole in external relations and global decision-making.

Royal Alliances: Political Marriages and the Power of the Queen

Women, especially the sovereign's principal wife (*qoya*), were powerful figures in royal life (see esp. Rostworowski 1983, 1999; and Ziółkowski 1996:177–214). According to Betanzos, the *qoya* had to be of pure Inca blood. She had to be "one of his sisters or first cousins" (Betanzos 1996:72). The *qoya* brought a great deal into the marriage, including counsel, status, legitimacy for offspring, and wealth. Once in the alliance, she wielded some independent power and was also a persuasive political adviser for her husband and son who succeeded him. Even though she may well have been voicing the interests of her kin group, a *qoya* mother could also impede the marriage of her daughter to the king. Similarly, a prospective *qoya* could reject the proposal. Both Wayna Qhapaq and Waskhar suffered from this rebuff, at least temporarily. The outstanding feature of Inca royal marriages before the imperial era was probably the bond that they formed with other ethnic groups. In the imperial era, the ruler continued to take many women of other ethnic groups as wives, often with political intent, but only in a secondary status. The later emperors were credited with having hundreds or even thousands of wives or concubines of various statuses. When Wayna Qhapaq traveled north for his Ecuadorian campaigns, for example, he was said to have taken along a mere 2,000 consorts, leaving the other 4,000 behind.

In the political arena, women were instrumental in promoting the case of a selected son as royal successor. The lineage of the candidates' mother was crucial, because sitting rulers did not belong to their father's kin group. Instead, they founded their own *panaqa* and identified closely with their mother's.[4] Those affiliations had enormous significance for alliance formation and for the actions of Atawallpa's generals at the end of the war, described below. The rulers' wives seem to have been the main liaisons between their husbands and their own kin, and the king's mother was also influential, alive or dead. During an Ecuadorian campaign, for example, Wayna Qhapaq berated the military nobility for having let him fall in harm's way and refused them the gifts to which they felt entitled. When they packed up in a huff to go home, the king recruited his mother's image to entreat them to stay; a Kañar woman spoke as the image's medium (Ziółkowski 1996:177–207).

Two changes in marriage practices illustrate how the Inca rulers worked to concentrate power in the face of Cuzco's growing aristocracy (Rostworowski 1960a). One was to designate a principal wife whose male offspring would constitute a small pool of legitimate heirs. While it is hard to know exactly when that shift became formalized, it was sometimes described as one of Pachakuti's reforms. A second innovation was marriage between the ruler and his full sister – a practice that drew mythic legitimacy from the coupling of founding sibling ancestors. Thupa Inka Yupanki may have been the first emperor to wed his full sister (see figure 5.5).

Waskhar's ascent to the throne leads into a report of one of the most peculiarly Andean of weddings. According to the native chronicler Pachacuti Yamqui, Waskhar had his mother officially marry his father's mummy, to provide the young ruler with full genealogical legitimacy. Since Wayna Qhapaq's mummy was regarded as animate and could voice his thoughts through his living mediums, the wedding would have been seen as an expression of his wishes. Whether this story was faithful to the facts is beside the point. What is important is that, in the Inca view of power, the act was plausible and maybe even necessary. The story also highlights the role assumed by the deceased kings and queens in choosing spouses for members of their kin groups. The ancestors and living *panaqa* could advance their mutual interests by forging marriages between the current ruler and the *panaqa*'s women (Rostworowski 1999:106–7; Gose 1996a:4). The ancestral lord and his principal wife, through their mediums, regulated the choice of marriage partners among the *panaqa*'s members and, if fortunate, created marital bonds with the king.

The stature of women in royal politics may also be appreciated by considering the unhappy fates of female relatives of royal combatants. When Wayna Qhapaq's kin elevated him to power in a coup, the displaced heir may have been only banished, while both his mother and

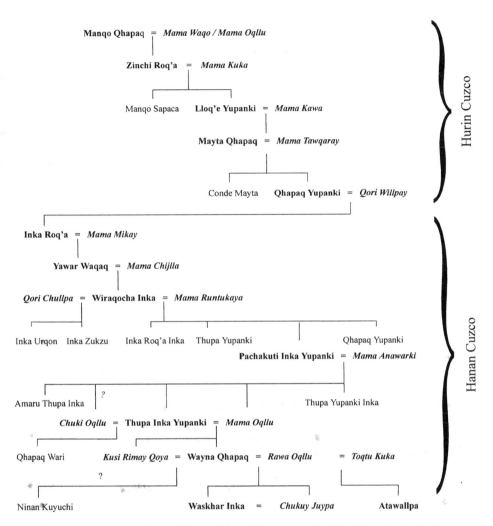

Figure 5.5   A genealogy of the traditional Inca rulers (bold), their principal wives (italics), and principal offspring

another female relative who had forwarded his case were executed (Murúa 1986:107; Ziółkowski 1996:189, 351). In the next generation, Waskhar's power was threatened by a coup, which was to be touched off by his mother's assassination. According to some chroniclers, once Waskhar was finally defeated in the dynastic war with Atawallpa, the only three individuals taken into custody were the ruler, his mother, and his wife. A general pardon was issued to everyone else on Waskhar's side and only later were the bloody mass reprisals carried out. These stories emphasize that adversarial parties viewed women as crucial figures and took steps to remove them at an early opportunity.

The roles of royal women thus suggest that the ruler's principal marriage was not a simple joining of a couple to produce legitimate offspring or the forging of a political alliance. The royal couple formed a ruling pair with complementary roles. Within the marriage, the *qoya* enjoyed wide latitude of choice in some matters and owned significant personal resources, which she could bequeath as she wished (chapter 6). And once the monarch had passed on and his son was installed, the stature and influence of a surviving wife – and later her mummy – may have actually increased.

Succession Crises and the Shaping of Political History

The Incas' political system undoubtedly evolved over time, but their history's flexibility makes it hard to pin down the timing and nature of the changes. Still, the chronicles are our best source for insight into how the practices of power helped to shape the government's structure. They suggest that the royal successions and marriages were the pivotal moments for conflict and maneuver, although certain rulers also tried ideological reformations that would have enhanced their positions (see chapter 7). Some years ago, Rostworowski (1960a) drew attention to the bloody infighting inherent in royal successions, and observed that the situation arose because Andean rules of succession typically favored vigorous actors. Often, a lord passed his station to the son who showed himself most able regardless of birth position, but it was not uncommon for a number of able brothers in a generation to hold office successively. Among the Incas, factional competition meant that successful aspirants won the throne through political intrigue, coup, murder, and even war.

Spanish writers often had trouble grasping the idea that there was no rightful candidate genealogically, because they saw primogeniture as the only legitimate path of succession. Native lords quickly learned to exploit their confusion by claiming rights based on Andean and European customs as the situation warranted. Members of the royal kin groups, for example, soon began referring to eldest-born sons as "legitimate" heirs and discrediting others as "bastards" when the circumstances favored that position. At other times, they asserted that a younger son had been tapped by the sitting ruler and installed as co-regent during the elder's lifetime. Their disputes contributed to the varied Inca histories that are preserved today. Rostworowski (1983, 1999) and Ziółkowski (1996), among others, have paid careful attention to sorting out the political struggles, which are too detailed to cover in more than a sketch here.

If we look at the outline of the imperial successions (see figure 5.5), we can gain a sense of the infighting that characterized royal politics. All the sources concur that the transition from Wiraqocha to Pachakuti was contested, but we do not know if Wiraqocha's displaced son Inka Urqon was simply designated as heir (Sarmiento 1960:230; Cabello Valboa 1951:298–9), treated as if he were all but emperor (Betanzos 1996:27–9), or actually enthroned (Cieza 1967). In any event, Inka Urqon did not figure in the standard king list in the Colonial era nor did he leave a panaqa that was incorporated into Upper Cuzco.

Thupa Inka Yupanki's ascension was also convoluted, beginning with his replacement of an elder brother named Amaru Thupa Inka who had fallen short of expectations (Sarmiento 1960:247–56; Pachacuti Yamqui 1993:228; Cabello Valboa 1951:334–5; Rowe 1985b:221–3; Murúa 1986:224, 317–26). Even though the younger prince had served a military apprenticeship on the northern campaigns, his ascendancy may not have been fully endorsed by Cuzco's families. In Sarmiento's account, Thupa Inka Yupanki required all of Cuzco to pay homage to him upon pain of death. Despite his precautions, the ruler was challenged (unsuccessfully) by another brother and he may eventually have been murdered.

According to some accounts, Thupa Inka Yupanki may have designated his son Qhapaq Wari for the throne, but the heir was thrust aside in a bloody palace coup staged by Wayna Qhapaq's kin (Cieza 1967:206; Sarmiento 1960:259; Murúa 1986:101–3). Since Wayna Qhapaq was still thought to be too callow to govern, his early political career was managed by two paternal uncles. The first of them tried to usurp power for his own son, but he was foiled by the other uncle, who then co-ruled with Wayna Qhapaq until the youth was mature enough to assume the throne alone. Guaman Poma (1980:93) added that this ruler also followed the time-honored expedient of murdering a couple of his brothers to consolidate his position.

The final prehispanic succession was the passage of power to Wayna Qhapaq's sons, which culminated in the great dynastic war between Waskhar and Atawallpa. This conflict brought to a head a long-simmering rivalry between Pachakuti's panaqa, named *Hatun ayllu*, and that of Thupa Inka Yupanki, named *Qhapaq ayllu*. Through their mothers, Atawallpa was closely identified with *Hatun ayllu* and Waskhar with *Qhapaq ayllu* (Rostworowski 1999:106–7). By all accounts, Waskhar's behavior as ruler was deplorable. In addition to repeatedly breaching royal courtesies and abusing the aristocracy (sometimes fatally), Waskhar jeopardized the entire system of privileged wealth when he threatened to bury the mummies of the past kings and alienate all the royal and religious properties (chapter 7). The most politically shocking of Waskhar's moves may have occurred when he divorced himself from Upper Cuzco (including his own kin) and declared his reaffiliation with Lower Cuzco. Using personnel from Lower Cuzco, Waskhar then set about building a new town at Calca, where he planned to live (Betanzos 1996:195).

When Atawallpa's men took Cuzco, his field commander Cusi Yupanki personally supervised the massacre of Waskhar's kin and carried out reprisals against Lower Cuzco. He also directed a house-by-house search in which *Qhapaq ayllu* and many of its priestesses and service personnel were killed. The most telling act occurred when *Hatun ayllu*'s forces dragged Thupa Inka Yupanki's mummy out of its house and reduced it to ashes (e.g., Cabello Valboa 1951:464).[5] Nothing could have been more potent, for Atawallpa's agents had effaced both the living icon of his grandfather's reign and the people who maintained his legacy. The survivors' attempt to maintain some semblance of power and dignity by scraping the mummy's ashes into a jar seems a forlorn gesture indeed.

The different ways that the succession crises were memorialized illuminate Inca politics. Whatever the accuracy of any account, successions involved plotting, successful and failed coups, murder, and a host of other political delicacies. That situation is typical of imperial history everywhere, but the competition that was woven into the fabric of Inca politics virtually guaranteed periodic upheavals in Cuzco. In a polity intent on expansion, selection for leaders in this way may have yielded effective rulers, but in an established empire the practice could be ruinous, as it was in the final dynastic war. Over time, the Incas tried to limit the damage by consolidating power in a small circle of family members. Seen in this light, the marriage of the ruler to his full sister makes perfect sense, since royal incest reduced the pool of claimants in the next generation. Moreover, who but the daughter of a god was best suited to marry the son of the Sun? The devastation visited by the last dynastic war suggests that these designs had only a modest effect. It is hard to say with present information if the scope of the final blood-bath was unique in Inca history. Even so, the narratives suggest that the descendant kin of three (or four, if we count Inka Urqon) enthroned rulers were either wiped out (Thupa Inka Yupanki, Waskhar) or were delayed in their entry into Cuzco's formal hierarchy (Wayna Qhapaq) by successional conflicts. When we consider that those rulers were said to have reigned for as much as two-thirds of the imperial era, that is quite an impact.

chapter six
The Heartland of the Empire

Cuzco, the sacred center of the Inca empire, was a small city of thatched-roof palaces nestled in a high mountain valley (plate 6.1). The city was a planned town designed to awe visitors with its majesty and sanctity. Both the empire's seat of authority and its architectural jewel, Cuzco consisted mostly of temples, plazas, and housing for the empire's royalty, nobility, and their retainers. Ethnic lords and colonists were settled nearby in a dozen neighborhoods that echoed their position in the empire. Tawantinsuyu's most hallowed shrines lay in and about the city on a landscape whose every feature recalled the legendary past (figure 6.1). In a more extended region that took in the lands within the next 60 km lay country homes for living and dead emperors, their kin, other Inca nobility, and privileged ethnic groups. The heartland also housed all the service personnel that the elites needed to keep their lives running smoothly – domestic staff, temple attendants, accountants, and farmers, along with the weavers, metal smiths, potters, and other artisans who crafted objects in a distinctive style that symbolized imperial power.

Cuzco was Tawantinsuyu's center of power when the Spaniards arrived, even though a strong late rival to its pre-eminence was rising at Tumipampa (Ecuador), where Wayna Qhapaq erected a second planned capital. Today, the local tourism industry, with only a bit of hyperbole, proclaims the city the "archaeological capital of the Americas." The urban core was a planned settlement, covering about 40 hectares (figure 6.2). Pachakuti is often credited with devising the plan after turning over command of the armies to his brothers and son Thupa Inka Yupanki (chapter 4). As his descendants explained it to Betanzos, Pachakuti ordered the entire basin vacated and then had much of the existing architecture razed. The ruler then modeled his concept of the central city in clay and assigned architects to execute it. Whether we accept all the details of this vision or not, the city's core was certainly rebuilt during

Plate 6.1 View overlooking Cuzco and the valley to the east in 1931; Neg. No. 334756, photo Shippee-Johnson collection, courtesy Dept. of Library Services, American Museum of Natural History

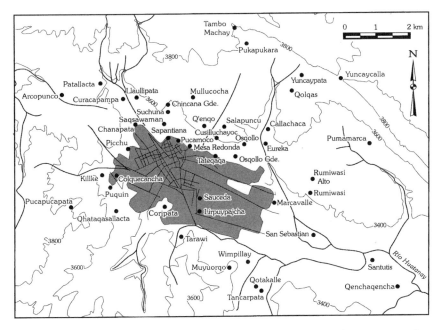

Figure 6.1   Distribution of important Inca sites near Cuzco, after Agurto Calvo 1987

the imperial era following a carefully considered design. The town and its suburbs still incorporate many structures, terraced fields, and intricate networks of canals and baths. Hundreds of cultural and natural landmarks – including hilltops, carved rock formations, temples, and fountains raised over springs – formed elements of a sacred geography that radiated outward from Cuzco's center. Small wonder that Garcilaso said that the Incas called their capital the "navel of the universe."

It may be surprising that our knowledge of Cuzco is still patchy. We understand the basic plan because it was described in the chronicles and was preserved during the Colonial era with some modifications, but many important elements have been lost. The Spaniards began to alter the face of the city soon after taking control in 1533, when they assigned palaces to the officers, granted house lots to the soldiers, and designated other spaces for public use. A conflagration that was deliberately touched off in 1536 during Manqo Inka's effort to evict the invaders and an earthquake in 1650 also ravaged the capital. Some architectural features stand as discordant reminders of the cultural clashes that occurred over the years. The main temple, for example, was converted to the monastery of

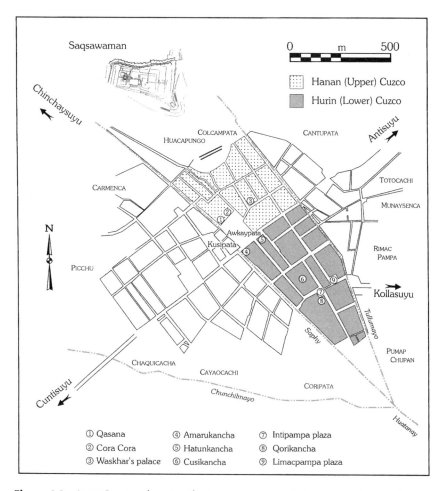

Figure 6.2   Inca Cuzco, showing the two core areas of Upper and Lower Cuzco, the 12 surrounding residential districts, and the roads leading toward the four parts of the empire

Santo Domingo and a remnant wall of Wayna Qhapaq's palace now holds planters in a tourist restaurant. In view of the hundreds of years of modifications, it is difficult – from standing archaeological remains alone – to gain a sense of what the city looked like during the height of Inca power. Historians and archaeologists have been working at the problem for decades, but have yet to produce a comprehensive architectural or settlement analysis or a fine-grained chronology for the valley's imperial occupation.

The Setting and Urban Plan

Within the constraints imposed by a rugged natural setting, the rulers shaped Cuzco and its surrounding landscape to symbolize the cosmos and their elevated place within it. The city lies at an elevation of 3,450 m (about 11,300′). The surrounding valley lands are well suited to growing a standard array of highland crops, while pastures can be found nearby in both rolling uplands and the steeply dissected terrain bordering the valley. The valley's streams are fed by numerous springs whose waters flow through the city in channelized courses and then merge in the eastward-flowing Huatanay River. About 20 km east of the capital, the Huatanay discharges into the Vilcanota's narrow gorge; in its lower course, the river is known as the Urubamba. To the west of Cuzco lies the marshy Pampa de Anta, while the Apurimac river gorge provides a formidable barrier on the south. During the imperial era, the Incas modified the region's topography through landscape engineering, especially for the rural manors along the constricted valley lands and hillslopes of the middle Urubamba. They memorialized pivotal events of myth and history by erecting estates and building shrines that honored a landscape thought to be populated by animistic spirits. Much of the surrounding land was cultivated and storage facilities were built to hold raw materials, produce, and crafts.

Cuzco was unquestionably the grandest center of its time in South America. While the capital formed a spatial metaphor for Inca society and their world, it was also the hub of imperial political, social, and ritual activity. To its visitors, the city's elaborate ceremonial life must have provided stunning witness to the power of the Incas and their gods. Its architectural elegance deeply impressed the Spaniards who saw the capital before events changed its face permanently. Pedro Sancho de la Hoz, Pizarro's secretary, compared it favorably with cities of his homeland in Spain. His companion, Juan Ruiz de Arce (1933:368; translation from Hyslop 1990:34), wrote that "(t)he city . . . would have four thousand residential houses between the two rivers surrounding it and they are on a slope of a mountain, and at the head of the city in the same mountain there is a fort [Saqsawaman] with many rooms." Cuzco is better thought of as extending well into the valley, however, rather than consisting just of the dense core. Sancho de la Hoz (1917:194; translation by Hyslop 1990:35), who appreciated the layout better than his fellow, explained that "(f)rom the fortress one sees around the city many houses out to a fourth of a league, half a league, and a league, and in the valley in the middle surrounded by mountains there are more than one hundred thousand homes." Sancho's estimate should be taken as an impressionistic figure, since the conquistadores often used that number to describe a multitude of people or things.

In 1970, UNESCO carried out field studies that identified many buildings but also confirmed that destruction and erosion have been too severe to permit more precise demographic estimates than the eyewitness accounts (see Hyslop 1990:29–68). As Ruiz de Arce's description suggests, the city core covered a small area, about 1 by 0.6 km between the Ríos Huatanay and Tullumayo (ibid.:36). It was divided into two sectors. *Hanan Cuzco*, or Upper Cuzco, referred to both the last five royal *panaqa* and the sector of Cuzco northwest of the main plazas, where they lived. It was socially and topographically elevated above *Hurin Cuzco* (Lower Cuzco), which lay to the southeast (figure 6.2). Twelve districts surrounded the central sectors, three for each of the four *suyu*, or divisions of the empire (Agurto Calvo 1980:122–8; Hyslop 1990:64–5). The UNESCO report's author, Santiago Agurto Calvo, surmised that the population of the central sector was about 15,000–20,000 people, with an additional 50,000 in a ring of immediately surrounding districts. He estimated, very roughly, that 50,000–110,000 more people may have occupied the suburban area that extended about 5 km beyond the urban neighborhoods. While the evidence to support any population estimate is thin at best, we may judge that greater Cuzco housed somewhere between 100,000 and 150,000 people. The city was thus smallish by the standard of ancient imperial capitals.

The Incas said that their city had been built in the form of a puma, but even sixteenth-century writers were uncertain if that was meant literally or metaphorically. In his official history written for the Viceroy Toledo, Sarmiento (1960:258) accepted a literal view. According to his informants, Pachakuti designed the city so that the puma's body took in the area between the Huatanay and Tullumayo rivers. The confluence of the two rivers is still called *pumap chupan* or the "puma's tail," after the Inca toponym. Pachakuti, in this account, did not construct the animal's head himself, but left the task to his son Thupa Inka Yupanki. The young man took up the challenge with a vengeance, transforming a rocky prominence above the city into the feline's head. On it he built Saqsawaman, the most elaborate single architectural complex in the entire empire (see below). The metaphorical conception is supported by other passages in the chronicles that suggest that the image applied to the people of the greater Cuzco region, not to the layout of the city core. Betanzos's (1996:74) account is probably the closest to a royal vision of any we have. He wrote: ". . . to the whole city together [Pachakuti] gave the name 'the lion's body,' saying that those neighbors and inhabitants of it were the members of said lion, and that his person was the head of it." Some scholars take such comments to mean that the puma was intended as an allegory that has been misunderstood by most chroniclers and modern authors alike (see Hyslop 1990:50–1).

The street plan consisted of straight roads that were irregularly arranged to fit the topography of the sloping land and perhaps the puma figure. The central district contained two main avenues that ran the length of the city and were crosscut by six other streets. None of the central blocks formed by their intersection was square and they varied greatly in size, with a general range of about 30–40 m wide by 45–70 m long (Agurto Calvo 1987; Hyslop 1990:37–42). The streets themselves were narrow, as befit a city in which wheeled or mounted traffic were not concerns. Many were paved with stones and contained stone-lined water channels running down the middle. A persistent Spanish complaint about the city was that there was space for only a single mounted horseman on either side of the canals.

The Central Plazas

Two adjoining plazas, separated by the Huatanay River, lay at the center of ancient Cuzco. *Awkaypata* ("Terrace of repose")[1] was a main locale for open-air ceremonies. *Kusipata* ("Fortunate terrace") lay just to the west across a watercourse; less well known because it was largely built over during the Colonial era, it included the space now covered by the Plaza de Regocijo. Measuring about 190 by 165 m (~3 ha), Awkaypata occupied the space that is today covered by the Plaza de Armas; it is fronted by two cathedrals that have replaced important Inca buildings. In a gesture that brought the mother sea to their capital, the Incas covered the space with a layer of Pacific coast sand at least two and a half palms thick, into which they interred gold and silver figurines and vessels (Polo 1916:109–10). A gilded stone was also situated in the plaza next to which the Incas excavated a hole in the ground. Chicha and other liquids poured into the aperture during rituals drained out through an underground canal system. Awkaypata often hosted the mummies of the dead emperors for ceremonies of state. There, they were seated according to their rank and feted as though they were in living attendance.

Until recently, it was thought that the Spanish efforts had eradicated any traces of Inca constructions within the great plazas. However, excavations in Awkaypata in 1995, associated with the municipal refurbishment of the Colonial fountain, uncovered wall footings as well as a quantity of Inca ceramics and four camelid figurines – one made of gold, two of silver, and one of Spondylus shell. Underground canals were also found in the plaza and in nearby locations, including the terraces

Plate 6.2 Central Cuzco in 1931, with the colonial Plaza de Armas overlying the Inca Awkaypata ("Terrace of Repose") in right-center of photo. Neg. No. 334796, photo Shippee-Johnson collection, courtesy Dept of Library Services, American Museum of Natural History

between the Sun Temple and the Saphy River (Farrington and Raffino 1996:73). Collectively, these finds suggest that there is still much to be learned about Inca Cuzco beneath the modern city.

The Major Architecture

Royal palaces and religious compounds dominated the central architecture. Most were surrounded by a wall that limited access and vision into the interior. The Awkaypata plaza in particular was bordered by impressive compounds or buildings on three sides, but there is no comparable evidence for monumental Inca constructions adjoining Kusipata (plate 6.2; Rowe 1991:84). The two compounds on the southeast of Awkaypata were probably the most impressive. *Hatunkancha* ("Great enclosure") was a magnificent construction with a single entrance that gave onto the plaza. Among its many interior buildings was the house of the *mamakuna* or *aqllakuna*, the most privileged women's orders. One of the structure's walls along modern Loreto Street, known as the Street of the Sun, still contains beautifully cut stonework (plate 6.3). The other grand compound on the southeast, called *Amarukancha* ("Serpent enclosure"), was attributed to a number of rulers by the early sources. Sarmiento (1960:265) assigned it to Waskhar, along with another city palace at Colcampata. Amarukancha apparently contained a great hall that gave onto the plaza. Wayna Qhapaq's palace (*Qasana*) lay on the plaza's northwest side; this complex housed the ruler's mummy when the Spaniards first entered the city. Garcilaso (1966:261) claimed that a courtyard within the complex was large enough to accommodate exercises for 60 mounted Spanish horsemen. In front of the palace were two round structures, with tall thatched roofs, that extended in the plaza. It was bordered on the north by another royal palace, perhaps called the *Cora Cora* (Rowe 1991:87–8).

An elevated terrace lay at the northern corner of Awkaypata, behind and above which lay Waskhar's spacious palace; this compound has been largely destroyed (Farrington 1983). The nature of the architecture on the northeastern side of the plaza is uncertain. The Triunfo Church was built on the site of a large Inca hall, which was converted into the city's first Spanish church. The Inca building has often been associated with the name Wiraqocha, either as the king's palace or as the Creator God's temple (*Kiswarkancha*), but modern scholars generally do not accept either proposition (see Hyslop 1990:40–1; Rowe 1991:86–7). Two other palaces of note, whose location is uncertain, were Pachakuti's residence called Kunturkancha and Thupa Inka Yupanki's urban

Plate 6.3 Finely cut regular ashlar masonry on the exterior of the Hatunkancha compound (left), facing the more uneven masonry of the Amarukancha compound (right)

palace, which may have been found at Pukamarka (Rowe 1967:61; Cobo 1990:55).

There were also residences for the royal kin groups. The ten *panaqa* maintained residences in Cuzco, while the non-royal *ayllu* lived in settlements beyond the center. Within the suburban neighborhoods lived members of a variety of ethnic groups, arranged according to their position in the empire, creating an ethnic microcosm of the realm. For example, the non-royal *ayllu* who had (legendarily) migrated northward with the Incas from Pacariqtambo lived in Cayoache, a neighborhood on the south side of the city. The Chachapoyas and Kañaris, whose homelands lay in the empire's northwest part, were settled in an analogous position in the city. (Conversely, some groups such as the Chilque and Qolla had limited or no access to the city, apparently because of their historical resistance to Inca rule.) Each great lord of the empire was supposed to keep up a house in Cuzco, where he was expected to spend four months a year. One of his sons was also required to live in the capital continuously, so that he could learn Quechua and become enculturated in the ways of the Incas. While in the city, the provincial nobles were expected to maintain themselves with their own servants, who lived nearby (see Rowe 1967).

Temples

Allusion to religious architecture or space in Cuzco is almost a redundancy, for so much of the city was intrinsically sacred or the place of important rituals. Even so, a few buildings occupied a special position in the performance of the official religion. The most important complex by far was the Qorikancha, or Golden Enclosure, more commonly known today as the Temple of the Sun. The last term is a partial misnomer, since all of the major celestial beings were worshiped there and important royal mummies were also venerated in the inner sanctums (Rowe 1967:62, 70; Hyslop 1990:44–7). Located a couple of blocks to the southeast of Awkaypata, the temple was the focal point in the Incas' vision of sacred geography. At the same time that the temple was the empire's most important shrine, the compound enclosed several other sacred objects and locations that were venerated individually in the ceremonial cycle (chapter 7).

The western exterior of the compound was graced with the most famous wall in the realm – an elegant curve of ashlar masonry (plate 6.4). The interior of the complex contained four to eight rectangular rooms of similarly cut stone. Some of the walls were adorned with gold plate, which the first three Spaniards to enter the precinct prised off the

Plate 6.4 The curved wall on the northwest exterior of the Qorikancha ("Golden Enclosure"), known popularly as the Temple of the Sun, over which the Spaniards erected the monastery of Santo Domingo; courtesy Brian Bauer

walls to take back to Cajamarca. There were probably also several other buildings within the compound, since priestesses and other temple personnel lived there. The Temple's rooms housed a variety of effigies, most importantly Punchao or the image of the Sun itself. This statue was brought out into a patio during the day and then returned to its quarters at night. Nearby lay a maize garden with birds interspersed among the plants; the garden was accompanied by a herd of camelids attended by their keepers. All were executed in precious metals (chapter 12).

Despite considerable architectural study and several excavations, we still do not have a secure understanding of the chronology of the Qorikancha. In legend, the original Temple of the Sun was built when the founding ancestor Manqo Qhapaq settled in Cuzco. The epics also recounted that Pachakuti rebuilt the Temple when he undertook his ambitious remodeling of the capital and its environs. The excavations that have been conducted do indicate that there was a pre-imperial Killke component in the location, but have not found clear evidence of a Sun Temple before the imperial era (Rowe 1944; Hyslop 1990:32). The problem has been compounded by the early transformation of the Inca sanctuary into the monastery of Santo Domingo and its subsequent remodeling.

Two other important temples within the city were Kiswarkancha ("Enclosure of the kishwar tree") and Pukamarka ("Red Town"). The first, as noted above, was a temple dedicated to Wiraqocha the Creator God. Some early writers said that it was situated on the northeast side of Awkaypata, but Molina's more trustworthy account suggests that it was a little bit removed from that core area. The second temple contained shrines to the Creator and to the weather/thunder deity, Illapa.

Saqsawaman

On a rocky promontory above Cuzco lay Saqsawaman, the grandest architectural complex in the empire (plate 6.5). Depending on the oral tradition, either Pachakuti or Thupa Inka Yupanki was responsible for inaugurating its construction as the head of Cuzco's puma design. L. Valcárcel's (1934–5) work in the 1930s recovered a great deal of pre-imperial Killke pottery, indicating that the site was occupied by the Incas even before the imperial era. According to Cieza (1967:169–71), Pachakuti began the work and it was carried on by all his successors. He wrote that the ruler ordered 20,000 workers sent in from the provinces on a rotating basis. Four thousand of them quarried stones and another six thousand hauled them into place, while other workers dug trenches or laid the foundations.

Plate 6.5 The Saqsawaman complex, on a rocky promontory above Cuzco (slide by author)

Cieza wrote that Saqsawaman was originally founded as a Sun temple, but the facility was actually a combination of religious architecture, fortress, magazine, and ceremonial complex. Unfortunately, much of the architecture was dismantled for use in the Spanish remodeling of Cuzco even before Cieza saw it, but some early witnesses provided vivid descriptions. Pedro Sancho wrote, in part:

> (T)here is a very beautiful fortress of earth and stone with big windows that look over the city and make it appear more beautiful. In it are many chambers and a main round tower in the center made with four or five stories one on the other . . . There are so many habitations, and the tower, that one person cannot see it all in one day. And many Spaniards who have seen it who have been in Lombardy and other foreign kingdoms say that they have not seen another construction like this fortress, nor a more powerful castle. Five thousand Spaniards might be able to fit inside. On the side facing the city there is only one wall on a rugged mountain slope. On the other side, which is less steep, there are three, one higher than the other. These walls are the most beautiful thing that can be seen of all the constructions in that land. This is because they are of such big stones that no one who sees them would say that they have been placed there by the hand of man. They are as big as pieces of mountains or crags . . . These stones are not flat, but very well worked and fit together . . . These walls have curves so that if one attacks them one cannot go frontally but rather obliquely with the exterior. (Translation from Hyslop 1990:53–4)

Sancho went on to describe the remarkable array of materials that were stored in the complex, including arms, quilted armor, clothing, pigments, cloth, tin, lead, silver, and gold. Recent excavations at Saqsawaman confirm this description, as archaeologists have unearthed a variety of sumptuary craft goods, including tupu pins, knives, other metal objects, and polychrome pottery (Valcárcel 1934–5; Rowe 1944; Van de Guchte 1990:127–9).

The zig-zag walls of Saqsawaman are still one of the archaeological wonders of the Americas (figure 6.3; plate 6.5). The terraces between the walls were wide enough for three carts to pass side by side and today provide a vantage point for re-enactments of Inca sun ceremonies (chapter 13). As grand as they were, the walls formed only part of the facility. Across a grand plaza to the north lay another complex on a rocky hilltop, called Suchuna ("slide"), which contained aqueducts, cisterns, terraces, patios, stairs, and other buildings. One of the most elegantly carved stones in the empire is found on this hill. Popularly called the "Throne of the Inca," it consists of a series of step-planes cut into the bedrock. Just beyond lay the "Tired Stone," another of the most important carved shrines of the empire (chapter 7).

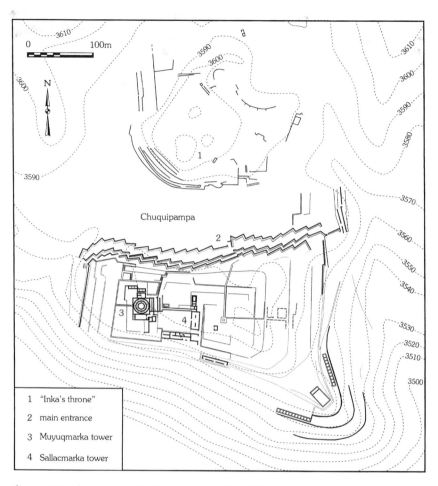

Figure 6.3   The ceremonial-fortress complex of Saqsawaman, above Cuzco; after Gasparini and Margolies (1980)

Other Features

Cuzco was not limited to residential and religious compounds, as a series of sacred agricultural fields also lay scattered throughout the city (Bauer 1996). One field was dedicated to the ritual planting of the first maize, while the harvest of other plots was reserved for various shrines of the city. Cuzco's outskirts also boasted a great quantity of storehouses (*qollqa*). The goods kept there were used to provision the city's residents, ostensibly every four days, and to supply the incessant ceremonial feasts. The *qollqa* also kept supplies for the capital's artisans as well as their finished products (chapters 11, 12). Unfortunately, little evidence of the storehouses remains today.

Greater Cuzco

The imperial capital is best understood as an area extending outward from the urban core for a distance of several kilometers. Within this zone were aristocratic and service residences, hundreds of shrines, agricultural fields, and canal systems. A few estates lay in the Cuzco basin, although the *panaqa* of emperors after Thupa Inka Yupanki held no lands there. Sancho's estimate that more than 100,000 buildings were found in the entire valley is surely an exaggeration, but much of the valley was part of the grand imperial plan. Unfortunately, this surrounding area has not yet been well studied and we do not yet even have a full inventory of the sites. Susan Niles' study of Callachaca, one of several estates owned by Amaru Thupa Inka (brother of emperor Thupa Inka Yupanki), provides an exception to the general lack of detailed information about estates near Cuzco. The manor, which stretched along about 1.5 km of hillslope north of the city center, contained about fifty buildings loosely grouped in four clusters on terraces (Rostworowski 1962; Niles 1987).

Cuzco's organization was also closely tied to both the landscape and the cosmos through an array of at least 332, and probably more than 400 shrines (*wak'a*). Many of the shrines were springs, stones, and mountain peaks, each with its own name and link to Inca history. Jeanette Sherbondy (1994:73–5) has identified over a third of the *wak'a* as water sources or other features associated with hydraulic works. During a year-long ritual cycle, the *panaqa* and affiliated *ayllu* took their appointed turns venerating the powers of the shrines with which they were associated. Hanan Cuzco controlled the water sources and canal systems of the upper half of the valley and Hurin Cuzco the lower. Each water source for the major irrigation canals was a shrine on a line assigned to the *panaqa*, whereas the less important networks received their water at shrines assigned to the lesser kin groups. Particular canal segments were cared for by specific kin groups. For the most part, the waters that ran through each canal system were used to irrigate the lands belonging to the associated group. The landscape, its production, and the social order of the valley's inhabitants were thus integrated through a ritual and agricultural cycle.

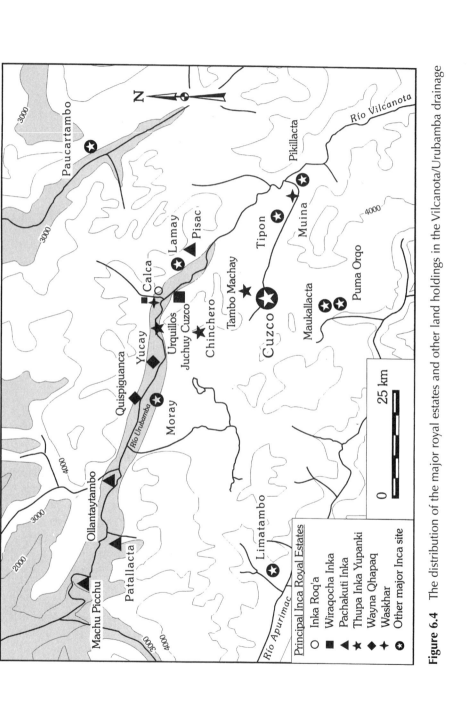

Figure 6.4   The distribution of the major royal estates and other land holdings in the Vilcanota/Urubamba drainage

Royal and Aristocratic Estates

The imperial expansion put vast resources in the hands of the Inca elites, some of which were converted into private reserves for living and dead emperors and other aristocrats (table 6.1). Every province set aside lands for each ruler, but the most elegant estates lay in a 100-kilometer stretch of the Vilcanota/Urubamba drainage between Pisac and Machu Picchu (figure 6.4). This picturesque valley, which lies beneath snowcapped peaks, is often called the Sacred Valley of the Incas. It contains many of the most spectacular archaeological sites ever erected in the Americas – not just Machu Picchu and Pisac, but Ollantaytambo, Wiñay Wayna, Patallacta, and others. The royal estates were used to support the monarchs in a manner suited to their deified stature. Not incidentally, they also provided sustenance and wealth for their descendants and underwrote their political and ceremonial activities. Those needs were weighty, since living and dead rulers and their kin spent a great deal of time visiting each other and performing rituals. Cobo (1990:40–3) commented at length how those visits were needed to rationalize the *panaqa*'s ownership of such expansive resources and their fondness for lazy debauchery.

Every ruler from Wiraqocha Inka onward owned countryside properties, and even earlier monarchs may have also had private manors. Inca Roq'a and Yawar Waqaq's descendants, for example, lived in villas near Cuzco where they venerated the mummies of their royal ancestors (Sarmiento 1960:224; Cobo 1979:125, 129; Rowe 1967: n. 21, p. 68). Rulers claimed their properties in many ways, including carving out new estates and commandeering expanses that had already been developed. Rowe (1990b:143) suggests that Pachakuti founded estates at locations such as Pisac and Ollantaytambo to commemorate his military victories. According to the Inca narratives, this ruler even spruced up an estate at Juchuy Cuzco for his father Wiraqocha Inka, where the deposed monarch could live out his years in relative comfort (Kendall et al. 1992). Thupa Inka Yupanki followed his father's example by claiming five strongholds that he had captured in the altiplano as personal estates.

Rulers could expand their personal holdings at the expense of state institutions and royal competitors. Waskhar, for example, converted state lands and personnel into his own estate, when he claimed a region east of Huánuco in the last few imperial years (C. Julien 1993:209–11). In an especially interesting twist, Thupa Inka Yupanki won some estates through a game of chance played with the Sun himself (Albornoz 1989:175, 182; Cobo 1979:149). He deliberately lost some lands to a son in a later game to give the youth a head start on building his own wealth. Monarchs and aristocrats could also augment their holdings by

Table 6.1 Principal royal holdings near Cuzco, all in the Vilcanota-Urubamba drainage, excepting Chinchero and those of Inka Roq'a (expanded and modified from Niles 1987:14–15)

Ruler	Estate	Location	Comments	Sources
Inka Roq'a	Larapa	near San Jerónimo	mummy found there, estate not confirmed	Sarmiento 1960 [1572]: ch. 19, p. 224; Cobo 1979 [1653]: bk. 2, ch. 9, p. 125
Yawar Waqaq	Paullu	near Calca	mummy found there, estate not confirmed	Cobo 1979 [1653]: bk. 2, ch. 10, p. 129
Wiraqocha Inka	Paucartica Caquia Xaquixaguana Pumamarca	near Calca site of Juchuy Cuzco eastern Cuzco Valley	mummy found there	Rostworowski 1970a:253 Cobo 1979 [1653]: bk. 2, ch. 11, p. 132; Rostworowski 1970a:253 J. Rowe 1997:279–80
Pachakuti Inka	Pisac Guamán Marca, Chuñobamba, Pisiguay	Pisac Amaybamba		Rostworowski 1966:32, 1970a:253 Rowe 1997:280
	Ollantaytambo (Tambo)	Ollantaytambo		Sarmiento 1960 [1572]: ch. 32, p. 237; Rostworowski 1966:32, 1970a:253
	Patallacta	Cusichaca	mummy kept there for a time	Betanzos 1996:138–9; Sarmiento 1960 [1572]: ch. 41, p. 246; Cobo 1979 [1653]: bk. 2, ch. 13, p. 141
	Huamanmarka Wiñay Wayna <26 named parcels	valley below Machu Picchu		Rostworowski 1963; Kendall 1988:458 Protzen 1993:53 Glave and Remy 1983 [1568]; see Rowe 1990b
	Machu Picchu	lower Urubamba	inferred, not specifically named	Glave and Remy 1983 [1568]; see Rowe 1990b

| | | Urubamba Valley | | Rowe 1997:278 |
		from Torontoy (km 91.5) to Cochabamba (km 149)	includes some parcels named above	
Thupa Inka Yupanki	Chinchero	Chinchero		Sarmiento 1960 [1572]: ch. 54, p. 258; Rostworowski 1970a:253, 258
	Huayllabamba	Urquillos canyon		Villanueva 1971:38–9; Rostworowski 1970a:253
	Urcos	Urquillos canyon		Villanueva 1971:38–9; Rostworowski 1970a:253
	Calispuquio		ashes of mummy hidden there	Sarmiento 1960 [1572]: ch. 54, p. 258; Rostworowski 1966:32
	Cozca	Yucay Valley	arbor	Rowe 1997:282
	Tiobamba	near Maras		Rowe 1997:282
	Condebamba	near Amantuy		Rowe 1997:282
	Quebrada of Sorama		held with wife Mama Oqllu	Rowe 1997:282
	Piscobamba	Urubamba Valley	held with wife Mama Oqllu	Rowe 1997:282
Wayna Qhapaq	Quispiguanca	Yucay Valley	mummy kept there for a time	Villanueva 1971:38–9; Rostworowski 1970a:253
	Urubamba			Villanueva 1971:38–9; Rostworowski 1970a:253
	Zurite, Jaquijaguana	Limatambo area		Rostworowski 1983:141
Waskhar	Calca	Calca		Murúa 1986 [ca. 1605]: ch. 46, p. 163; Rostworowski 1970a:253
	Muina Pomabamba	site of Kañaraqay		Rostworowski 1970a:253; Rostworowski 1962 [1555]:134

accepting gifts from subjects, although we may reserve judgment about
the optional nature of the donations (Rostworowski 1962:134, 136;
Conrad and Demarest 1984:139). In addition, Inca kings seized some
estates once the dust had settled from successional infighting. Cabello
Valboa (1951:360), for example, wrote that Wayna Qhapaq's kin appropriated the properties of his uncle Wallpaya and his associates – and put
their families to death – after they staged an abortive coup against the
youthful sovereign. An especially important transfer may have been envisioned at the close of the dynastic war between Atawallpa and Waskhar
(chapter 5). The conflict ended with the virtual eradication of Thupa
Inka Yupanki's *panaqa* (*Qhapaq Ayllu*) and Waskhar's *panaqa* (*Waskhar
Ayllu*) and the survivors' loss of their families' holdings (Rowe 1985b).

Our picture of the prehispanic system of land ownership has been
clouded by native claimants' ready use of European legal precepts to
gain control over lands (Rostworowski 1962, 1963, 1966). Even without
those complications, however, control of resources was an entangled
affair. Inca rulers, kin groups, institutions, and other elite men and
women held estates and there may have been some discretion involved
in passing them on. Most importantly, a deceased ruler's estates were
normally left to his *panaqa*. Following the custom of split inheritance
(chapter 5), the throne passed on to a successor who had to develop his
own kin group's resources. The lands of the queen (*qoya*) were held separately; when she died, they were left to her own relatives. The natural
complexity of the ecology and the slow development of the estates meant
that parcels belonging to rulers, aristocrats, and local communities
were intermingled among one another (Rostworowski 1962, 1963,
1966; Rowe 1990b, 1997). Since the Inca elite were linked through blood
and marriage in many ways, ownership of some lands was especially
complicated. Personal choice may have also played a role in inheritance,
as claimants in early Colonial litigation testified that some bequests
skipped generations at the wish of the benefactor. Over the generations,
the number and types of claims that could be placed on particular plots
must have created fertile ground for intrigue.

From a physical viewpoint, some estates were created through formidable engineering works. Wayna Qhapaq's holdings in Yucay were
largely reclaimed from swamp and Waskhar's estate at Pomabamba
was developed by diverting a river to create new land (Rostworowski
1962:134–5; Villanueva 1971; Niles 1987:13). Even though parts of the
estates attributed to early monarchs boasted major land improvements,
the riverine reclamation projects may have become increasingly important because the best field lands had already been spoken for. At one
point, Waskhar groused that land tenure customs meant that the dead
"had all that was the best of his kingdom" and that no decent expanses

were left for him to claim (P. Pizarro 1986:54). His gripe may have arisen from political rancor linked to his conflict with Atawallpa, but he may have also had legitimate grounds for complaint about limited access to prime lands for rural manors. His proposed solution was to abolish or confiscate both familial and institutional (Sun) estates, with an eye to appropriating them himself. As can be imagined, his threat to destroy all the mummies and seize their lands was not well received by Cuzco's powerful interests.

The archaeological remains along the Urubamba Valley provide magnificent witness to the resources and artisanry devoted to royal estates. The Incas' penchant for melding land forms and structures is one of the most distinctive features of their approach to designing the manors. All exhibit elegant terracing, waterworks, and masonry that is seldom approached in the rest of the empire. The estates were designed to provide access to a wide range of resources. Wayna Qhapaq's holdings in Yucay, described below, contained crop lands, pastures, settlements, forests, parks, a pond and marsh, a hunting range, and salt fields (Villanueva 1971; Farrington 1995). The number of workers committed to the manors was remarkable. At Yucay, 2,400 men and their families were dedicated to Wayna Qhapaq's holdings (Villanueva 1971:94, 98, 136, 139; Rowe 1982:100; Niles 1987:13–15). Even more impressively, Thupa Inka Yupanki had 4,000–4,500 workers at each of three locations in the empire (Rostworowski 1966:32). The assets found on individual estates may be best exemplified by the case of two of Wayna Qhapaq's secondary wives. According to one story, the ruler was unable to pacify the restive populace of the Huayllas region of highland Peru. Finally, he obtained peace by marrying daughters of each of the two regional lords. As part of the pre-nuptial agreement, each wife – upon giving birth to a son – was reportedly granted an estate with 6,000 tributaries free of state obligations (Ziółkowski 1996:206).

A description of some of the estates attributed to the last four emperors before Waskhar will provide a more concrete sense of their nature. One of Wiraqocha Inka's estates was developed at Caquia Xaquixaguana, which archaeologists today identify as the site called Juchuy Cuzco ("Little Cuzco"). This site is spectacularly positioned at 3,650 m on a rock prominence some 600 m above the Urubamba River, with a grand view northward to the white-capped *cordillera oriental* and eastward toward Pisac. As at many estates, an enclosing wall restricted access to the site's core, which lies amidst elaborate sandstone terracing extending to sets of storehouses and smaller sites. The main architecture contains three groups of buildings that include elite dwellings and probable retainer housing. The site plan was modified at least once during the imperial era, when a standardized monumental style was imposed and

Plate 6.6 Terraces at Pachakuti's royal estate called Pisac, about 30 km east of Cuzco (slide by author)

sandstone walls were replaced by finely worked dacite incorporated into adobe walls. Ann Kendall and her colleagues suggest that the changes generally fit the historical account describing a major renovation during the imperial era (Kendall et al. 1992:231). Soon after the Spanish invasion, Gonzalo Pizarro found Wiraqocha Inka's mummified remains and a golden treasure there. He looted the tomb and burned the mummy, but Wiraqocha Inka's caretakers gathered the ashes into an urn. They guarded them along with his personal idol until 1559, when Polo seized them in his campaign to root out vestiges of idolatry and to destroy enduring symbols of imperial power (Sarmiento 1960:230; Kendall et al. 1992:191).

Several of the most spectacular Inca sites have been identified as royal estates of Pachakuti. Most prominent among them are Pisac, Ollantaytambo, and Machu Picchu. Pisac lies about 30 km north of Cuzco, on a rocky promontory extending into the Urubamba Valley (Angles Vargas 1970). The site's principal architecture consists of a set of residential structures and a temple complex built around a large carved rock. The slopes below the settlement are graced with splendid terraces that cascade hundreds of meters downslope (plate 6.6). Across a ravine to the west, the face of an escarpment is pocked with scores of looted tombs, mute witness to the pillaging of the empire. Ollantaytambo, 40 km downriver, exhibits a striking combination of regular layout and architecture tailored to rugged land forms (Gasparini and Margolies 1980:68–75; Gibaja 1984; Hollowell 1987; Protzen 1993). The site was a planned residential settlement with palaces, religious and defensive structures, storehouses, roads and bridges, terraces, and waterworks (Protzen 1993:14). Much of the site lies on an alluvial fan straddling the Río Patakancha just above its confluence with the Río Urubamba. The settlement was protected by forts and high terraces, while entry was channeled across bridges and through narrow gates. Its center is dominated by a trapezoidal street grid on the alluvial fan, which still forms the plan for the modern town (plate 6.7). The town blocks are formed by enclosed *kancha* compounds, consisting of up to six one-room buildings facing onto an open patio. Canals running through the streets provided fresh water and may have carried away effluent.

To the west, a grand set of terraces cascades down a steep hill, where the complexes now called the Fortaleza and its Temple of the Sun were erected. The architecture on this spur is the subject of controversy among Inca scholars. The six exquisitely worked vertical ashlars of pink rhyolite that form the centerpiece of the Temple are unique in Inca construction (plate 6.8). They contain design details that recall masonry at Tiwanaku, the great city on Lake Titicaca's southern margin. Some archaeologists contend that the reported use of Qolla masons, from the

Plate 6.7 The royal estate of Ollantaytambo, where the Inca-era houses and compounds are still inhabited; the temple complex lies at the far end of the terraces toward the top of the image (slide by author)

Plate 6.8 Pink rhyolite monoliths in the unfinished temple complex at Ollantaytambo (slide by author)

Plate 6.9 Machu Picchu, probable royal estate of the emperor Pachakuti, in the lower Urubamba river drainage (slide by author)

Titicaca basin, to build the site (Sarmiento 1960:245) and the similarities in construction and design details (e.g., the step-fret; T-shaped sockets for binding stones together) show that the Inca cut-stone style was a direct outgrowth of Tiwanaku's architecture (Gasparini and Margolies 1980; Hollowell 1987). Others doubt that the link was so clear, citing stylistic differences and a break of several centuries between the demise of Tiwanaku and the rise of Cuzco (Protzen 1993). Whatever the cultural derivation, the finest stereotomy at the site is found at the Temple and in nearby walls.

The treatment of the nearby landscape epitomizes the Incas' bent for modifying the terrain and adapting their designs to existing land forms. Taking advantage of a meander in the Urubamba, engineers diverted the water flow from the left bank to the right and back again and also channelized the Río Patakancha where it flowed through the site (Protzen 1993:22). The eleven expansive terraces that face the settlement gracefully blended in with the natural slope of the piedmont. In 1536, their steep stone walls helped to repel the Spanish expedition sent against Manqo Inka. The Incas even used the waterworks in their defense, as they flooded the valley where the Spaniards were attacking, handing them their only real defeat of the campaign (P. Pizarro 1986:146–8).

Ollantaytambo's architecture also exemplifies the paradoxes of archaeology in the heartland. Although *panaqa* ostensibly had an inviolate right to control their estates, both Pachakuti and Thupa Inka Yupanki were said to have ordered the construction of important buildings. Hollowell's and Protzen's work indicates that the settlement's design was changed over time. There were at least three major construction phases in the imperial era, and structures were still being erected when the Spanish conquest put an abrupt cessation to the labors. The architecture contains at least seven kinds of stone, each seemingly worked in a distinct style with differing degrees of craftsmanship; rarely was more than one kind of stone used in a single cut-stone building. Over time, early structures were dismantled, and many stones were reworked, repositioned, or both (Hollowell 1987). The implications of the evidence are the subject of lively debate, but it is clear that the design of an estate was not inviolate, even when the property pertained to the founding emperor and his *panaqa*.

The magnificent site of Machu Picchu is celebrated as one of the archaeological splendors of the world (Bingham 1930; MacLean 1986). Although much of its stonework was beautifully crafted, it is the spectacular setting high on cliffs in the jungle and the graceful melding of land forms and architecture that impart such grandeur to the complex (plate 6.9). The site came to the world's attention when Hiram Bingham was guided there by local farmers in 1911 and it has undergone intermittent fieldwork and reconstructions ever since.[2] The site contains two architectural complexes on a projecting ridge line: a main, lower site called Machu Picchu ("old hill") and an upper site on a sugarloaf peak called Huayna Picchu ("young hill"). Machu Picchu itself contains two principal sectors: a western set of terraces, and a central complex of dense, elegant architecture laid out around a main plaza.

Machu Picchu illustrates the range of activities pursued at royal retreats. Both the dense architectural sector on the east side of the site and the sector bordering the plaza on the south were likely residential. These compounds contain sets of one-room buildings facing onto enclosed patios; the enclosures were fitted to the rugged topography, so that their shapes and orientations tend to be more irregular than those of Inca sites built on flat terrain. Among the site's most striking features are the fourteen fountains and many carved granite outcrops that were often incorporated into the architecture. Bingham (1913:471) imputed a religious significance to the treatment of stones, a judgment that is shared by some modern scholars. MacLean (1986:72) suggests that the importance of stones in the animistic Inca religion led the architects to situate numerous structures expressly to incorporate the outcrops. The two most prominent rocks are the *intiwatana* – thought by some to be a sun gnomon – at the peak of the temple complex on the west side of the site, and the carved bedrock within and underneath the so-called *torreón* (see chapter 7). The majority of buried individuals recovered during Bingham's expeditions were young women, which has led to a general view that there was a house of the chosen women present, but it is not certain that the young women represent a cross-section of the settlement's residents.

Thupa Inka Yupanki's best-known estate was a rural villa at Chinchero about 30 km northwest of Cuzco, studied by a Spanish team in the 1960s and 1970s (Alcina Franch et al. 1976). The relatively high elevation of the settlement, about 3,400 m, afforded a less hospitable climate than the estates in the Urubamba Valley. Like other sites described as manors, Chinchero was a planned settlement, containing a large central plaza and a platform mound and enhanced with both agricultural and residential terraces. Besides the royal residence, the estate included compounds that Betanzos said were built to house Cuzco's nobility when they came to visit (Betanzos 1996:159). Chinchero was apparently entirely remodeled in the imperial era, as the fill deposits from landscape architecture contain quantities of Inca polychrome ceramics (Rivera 1976:28). In 1540, the site was burned by Manqo II, but was later reoccupied and rebuilt during the Colonial era.

Wayna Qhapaq's main estate in Yucay was centered at the residence called Quispiguanca. The valley enjoys a reputation as a pleasant location, as its floor lies at 2,850–2,910 m, some 500–600 m below Cuzco. The estate is celebrated for its arrays of terraces, but most of the hillsides were actually farmed as sloping fields and lynchets (Donkin 1979:111–14; Farrington 1995:57). Chosen by Francisco Pizarro as one of his *encomiendas*, the estate became the subject of contentious land claims in the early Colonial era, records of which provide many details about its nature (Villanueva 1971:37–9, 51–3; Rowe 1990b:144). The manor was a place of recreation that existed only because of major feats of Inca ecological engineering. Much of the estate consisted of tracts claimed from swamp through channelization of the main river and several tributaries (Farrington 1983). The holdings included 40 named parcels where maize, sweet potatoes, and the warm-weather crops of coca, chili pepper, cotton, and peanuts were cultivated. It included woods that were home to deer, while fish and reeds were grown in an artificial pond. Several of those plants are from environments that are lower, warmer, and more humid than those naturally found in Yucay. Their presence suggests that the Incas were aware of how to manipulate terracing systems to create micro-environments, and used their heat- and moisture-retaining capacities to devise a mini-montaña near Cuzco for the emperor's pleasure.

The architecture of Quispiguanca is modest in comparison to the estates of other emperors, perhaps because Wayna Qhapaq's most elaborate lodgings were in Tumipampa, Ecuador, far removed from Cuzco. The manor (10.4 ha) contains three sectors on a series of terraces and an alluvial fan: an agricultural area, a structural or residential zone, and a lakeside house complex (Farrington 1995). Like other rural retreats, the settlement was obviously executed according to a plan. It exhibits a large central plaza, a platform mound, and residential structures, with a large enclosing wall, along with several sets of nearby storehouses (Niles 1999). One building contains fine polygonal, fitted stonework, as do some of the terrace and enclosing walls. Although it was not nearly so ornate as some of the sites described earlier, Quispiguanca displays some distinctive architectural details of the kind typically reserved for royal constructions, such as human-sized wall niches and elegant staircases in the terraces.

Overall, the royal estates exemplify elite life in the heartland during the imperial era. Their designs, which modified and adapted to natural features, symbolize an intensive interaction between humanity and the powers of the cosmos. They epitomize how prime resources were converted into private domains held first by the ruler and, after his death, nominally held in a trust for his reverence. On an empire-wide scale, the resources committed to the estates were not especially great, but the manors exemplify how an endogamous and exclusionary upper class concentrated power and wealth at the empire's heart.

chapter seven

Inca Ideology: Powers of the Sky and Earth, Past and Present

The Incas, like the rulers of many ancient societies, promoted an official ideology that inspired their actions and gave meaning to their lives. Although the tenets of the state religion were intended to justify their supremacy, the beliefs that the Incas professed were filled with the paradoxes that so often arise when dogma and politics collide. For example, while they fervently worshiped the sun, a line of divine kings, and sacred landmarks from their past, they also consciously manipulated the history that legitimized their rule. Royal families re-imagined the past for political gain and, at least to the Spaniards, ridiculed claims of sanctity by kings belonging to other kin groups. At the end of the last dynastic war, they even destroyed the mummy of Thupa Inka Yupanki as part of an effort to eradicate history. In ancient societies, deceased rulers who mediated with the supernatural were a common phenomenon, but the Inca royalty enjoyed unusually energetic careers after death. With the help of a coterie of assistants, kings and queens carried on as though their spirits had never left them. Royal mummies ate, drank, urinated, visited one another, sat at councils, and judged weighty questions. In the official religion, the Sun cult was the dominant institution, but many other deities were also worshiped and there was even competition among the different deities and their adherents. At times, the Incas sacrificed humans to their gods and ancestors, but the scale of offering never approached the tens of thousands who met a similar end in Aztec Mesoamerica. More commonly, Inca practices demanded immense quantities of goods and llamas for sacrifice.

These practices illustrate that, in order to explain Inca ideology, we have to think about how tradition, history, and politics were interwoven with belief. As with so many elements of their culture, Inca religion drew extensively from local and great traditions. Many Andean peoples believed that they shared the cosmos with the animate dead, the gods, and the spirits of the landscape. They paid careful heed to those powers through sacrifice and prayer – and that was wise, because they saw countless signs that human well-being depended on the deities' good will. The skies were filled with gods, animals, and omens that controlled the weather and augured the future. People created mythic cycles, measured time, planned their crops, and celebrated festivals based on their knowledge and beliefs about the heavens. On the earth, stones could come alive and people could be petrified, so that a mountain peak, a rocky outcrop, or a spring could be an ancestor or a guardian spirit. In Andean eyes, the different beings co-existed as kin or rivals in a world where history was imprinted on the countryside. The relationships between different beings were negotiable, for humans could worship, consult, supplicate, battle, abduct, or even incapacitate gods, oracles, and shrines. The Incas captured all of these things within a single concept – *wak'a* – that is, any thing or place that had transcendent power.

Despite Cuzco's might, religious practice among the general populace still revolved around local deities, shrines, and myths in the sixteenth century. Most people believed that their founding ancestor had emerged from the landscape at a particular spot, called a *paqarisqa* (hispanicized as *pacarina*; see Bauer 1991). They worshiped their progenitors through sacrifices and periodic commemoration of funeral rites when they re-opened graves to make new offerings. Some graves were even built with conduits so that libations could be offered to the dead. The original ancestor for a local society was often embodied in an idol whose capture or destruction could spell disaster. The Incas took this belief quite literally, for they held ancestral idols hostage in Cuzco so that subjects had to travel there to worship their founders and renew their people's vitality. When challenged, the Incas would publicly whip the idols of rebellious provinces until they bowed to Cuzco's will. Local oracles also abounded. Some, such as Chavín and Pachacamac, may have been consulted by pilgrims for one or two thousand years before the Incas incorporated them into their domain.

The Spanish conquistadores soon recognized that the Incas worshiped the sun and that the rulers were thought divine. They also saw people revere idols and converse with oracles – all of this clear evidence to the Christians that the devil had been at work. But the invaders were slower to absorb the complexities of indigenous beliefs. The rifts between imperial and local religion were lost on most Spaniards, as were the intricate relations among ritual, an animate nature, and social power. In their efforts to come to grips with Andean beliefs, the early Spaniards relied on the cultural referents they had at hand. They referred to Inca temples as mosques and drew on Christian and Classical analogs to explain what they saw. Clerics tried gamely to reconcile Andean creation myths with Christian theology, or assigned Andean deities individualized natures like those of the Greek gods, when the native gods were actually multi-faceted and overlapping (see MacCormack 1991).

It took about fifteen years for the Spaniards to begin inquiring closely about Inca religion, but that was unfortunately more than a decade after Cuzco's last major Sun ceremony. Among the first to make the effort were the soldier Cieza and the interpreter Betanzos, but they were soon followed by the lawyer Polo, Viceroy Toledo and his assistant Sarmiento, and the priests Molina, Albornoz, Arriaga, and Acosta, among others. Some Spaniards made earnest efforts to record myths, describe religious practices, and explain Andean views of life, death, and the supernatural. They also worked hard to discover the locations of shrines and mummies so that they could stamp out idolatry. Sadly, they rarely saw an important ceremony – such Manqo Inka's investiture in 1534 or Cuzco's June solstice festival (*Inti Raymi*) in 1535 – and so they relied on the memories of informed survivors. By the time the Spaniards sought detailed information, however, the Incas had realized the perils of public celebrations and practiced much of their religion in secrecy. It was not until the beginning of the seventeenth century that the native authors Garcilaso de la Vega, Guaman Poma, and Santa Cruz Pachacuti Yamqui wrote about indigenous beliefs, and they all wrote as Christians trying to explain a coherent, though theologically flawed, system to a Spanish audience. The existing descriptions are thus heavily filtered, but they still manage to convey images of an elaborate ceremonial life. As with so much of Inca lore, we again need to remember that our information most often comes from Cuzco's fallen aristocrats. When the Spaniards wrote down the knowledge that they had gained, they often conveyed the idea that Inca imperial religion was Andean religion, which was far from the case.

Origins of the Cosmos

Myths of the origins of the world and humanity were as abundant as the Andean peoples themselves. In the mid-seventeenth century, an exasperated Cobo (1990:11) said that he had come across a "thousand absurd stories" that people told about their origins; "each nation," he wrote, "claims for itself the honor of having been the first people and says that everyone else came from them." Today, some forty cycles of Andean origin myths are found in the early sources (Urton 1990:18). The Incas themselves told a variety of stories about the creation of the cosmos, whose contradictory elements even well-informed authors like Betanzos could not sort out.

Most Inca creation myths begin at Lake Titicaca, and run something like this (mostly following Sarmiento 1960:206–8; see also Betanzos 1996:7–11; Molina 1988; Cobo 1990:11–18; Urton 1999:34–7). In ancient times before there was light, the Creator *Wiraqocha Pachayachachic* ("Creator of all things") fashioned a race of giants to see if it would be good to make humans at that scale. He saw that they were too large, however, and so he made humans in his own size. But they were filled with hubris and greed, so the Creator turned some to stone, and others to diverse forms, and some were swallowed up by the earth or sea. And he caused a great flood to cover the land, destroying all that was upon it, save for three men, whom he saved to help him create humans anew. Later, on an island in Lake Titicaca he caused the sun, moon, and stars to come forth. The sun was jealous that the Creator had made the moon brighter than he, so he cast ashes in her face and thus she remains with her brilliance dimmed.

The Creator then crossed over to dry land at Tiwanaku, where he carved and drew images of all the nations that he thought to create on some large stones. He ordered his two servants to memorize the names of the people and the places where they were to appear on the earth. Then he sent one to the coast and the other to the eastern slopes. Wiraqocha himself took the central path, calling out the people from the lakes, springs, valleys, caves, trees, caverns, rocky outcrops, and mountains. He appeared to be a man of normal size, dressed in a white robe, carrying a staff and a book in his hands. At Cuzco, he called forth the Alcabizas and Inca nobles, gave Cuzco its name and continued north. Finally, he reached the Ecuadorian coast, where he told his servants that his messengers would return one day. Together they walked out over the water until they disappeared in the west.

The variations on this myth suggest that the Incas found it necessary to change their theology to bring it into agreement with their expanding world. Rowe (1960) points out that different versions placed the Creator's point of departure on the south coast, at Pachacamac on the central coast, and in Ecuador. He suggests that the different locations probably reflect the retooling of the myth as the empire grew and the Incas had to account for more peoples and places. In a way, the situation paralleled the Spanish experience in the New World, when they suddenly discovered that their theological map covered only a fraction of the world. However we interpret the myths, there is little doubt that the Incas were content to tell conflicting versions of their origins without suffering the angst felt by some chroniclers.

The Inca Pantheon

Wiraqocha, *the Creator*

The loftiest Inca god was the Creator god just mentioned, who had no formal name, but a series of titles. One was *Ilya-Tiqsi Wiraqocha Pacayaciq*, which means "Ancient Foundation, Lord, Instructor of the World" (Rowe 1946:293). The Spanish chronicles usually referred to him as *Viracocha* (table 7.1). Although Wiraqocha was generally removed from daily affairs, he appeared to Inca rulers on a few auspicious occasions. He revealed himself, for example, to the Inca prince Hatun Thupa Inka, who subsequently took the god's name in his imperial title Wiraqocha Inka (Sarmiento 1960:228). Later in that king's life, the Creator (or Sun) appeared to prince Inka Yupanki (i.e., Pachakuti) who used the revelation to legitimize his claim to the throne. The god appeared in human form, with rays about his head, snakes twined about his arms, and puma heads projecting from his body. The image cited most often for this vision is the central figure on the Gate of the Sun at Tiwanaku, whose attributes are much like those of Pachakuti's apparition (Demarest 1981).

The chroniclers often portrayed the Creator Wiraqocha as one of a triad of Inca gods, along with the Sun (*Inti*) and Thunder (*Inti-Illapa*; see Duviols 1977; Demarest 1981; MacCormack 1991). The idea that the three formed a trinity was a Christian imposition on Andean religion, but the gods were clearly intertwined. All three were worshiped in Cuzco's main temple (*Qorikancha*) and were multi-faceted celestial beings with overlapping powers. In Molina's account, some prayers began with the joint invocation, "O Creator and Sun and Thunder." Despite Wiraqocha's importance, the Incas devoted relatively little energy or resources to his worship. No major ceremony seems to have been devoted to him, he had no endowment or elaborate priesthood, and only a few of the shrines in and around Cuzco were dedicated to his sacrifices (Demarest 1981). His most important temple lay between Cuzco and Lake Titicaca.

Table 7.1 Major Inca deities and regional oracles (sources: Rowe 1946:293–6; Demarest 1981; Bauer and Dearborn 1995; Bauer 1998)

Deity	Meaning	Image or associated icons	Themes and roles	Region or culture
Major Inca deities				
Ilya-Tiqsi Wiraqocha Pacayaciq; Wiraqocha	ancient foundation, lord, instructor of the world	male and female aspects; golden statue, puma	creator of heavens, earth, living beings	Inca
Inti	sun	male; *Punchao*: golden statue of young boy; golden disk (questionable)	father of royal Inca lineage; patron of empire	Inca
Inti-Illapa	thunder	male wielding a sling; cat, puma	meteorological phenomena: lightning, thunder, rainbow	Inca
Mama-Kilya	mother moon	female	wife of sun; calendrics	Inca
Qollqa	storehouse (Pleiades)		preserve seed	Inca
Urcuchillay		parti-colored male llama	watch over flocks	Inca
Chaska Cuyllor	shaggy star (Venus)			Inca
Pachamama	earth mother	female	protect and make fields fertile	Inca
Mamacocha	mother sea	female	supports earth, source of water	Inca
Important regional deities or oracles				
Apurimac	Lord Oracle		oracle	Inca: southwest of Cuzco
Vilcanota			place where the sun is born	Inca: 40 km east of Cuzco
Thunupa	thunder	male	creator; meteorological phenomena, puma	Titicaca region
Pachacamac	maker of the earth	statue	creation, oracle	Lurin Valley, central coast of Peru
Catequilla		stone statue	regional patron, oracle	Huamachuco (north Peru)
Wariwillka	sacred ancestor [??]	stone statue	regional oracle	Upper Mantaro (central Peru)

Inti, *the Sun*

Worship of the Sun was a centerpiece of official Inca religion. By 1532, Inti outshone all other Inca deities combined in worship, institutional scale, and properties. Although solar deities had long existed in Andean religions, the Incas' innovative emphasis on solar observations tied in neatly with their claims to cosmological supremacy. It placed crucial sacred knowledge in their hands and backed up their pretensions to be vital to the world's well-being (Pease 1973; Duviols 1977; Ziółkowski 1996). The Inca ruler could claim a direct genealogical link to the Creator through the Sun, since the Creator fathered Inti, who in turn sired the king. In Betanzos's account, Pachakuti was touted as the main force behind the Sun cult, but Sarmiento's sources named Wiraqocha Inka as the ruler who set the Sun's elaborate worship in motion. Pachakuti's contributions, according to most sources, included rebuilding the main temple and fabricating the principal solar idol (Demarest 1981:49).

Inti was a male being reportedly represented as a golden statue or disk. The statue was a seated figure of a small boy, called *Punchao* ("Day"). Solar rays projected from his head or shoulders; he was adorned with earspools, a pectoral (chest ornament), and a royal headband; serpents and lions projected from the body, much like Pachakuti's vision. Punchao tangibly bridged the gulf between humanity and the Sun since the vital organs of deceased rulers were incinerated and cached in his hollow stomach. The figure was housed in the main temple where it was brought out to a patio during the day and returned indoors at night. Molina wrote that it was kept together with the golden images of his wives Inca Ocllo and Palpa Ocllo. The Spaniards never saw Punchao during the conquest, though they searched for it vigorously, because its custodians had spirited it away. In 1536, Manqo Inka took the idol to Vilcabamba to help stage his resistance to Spanish rule. When Viceroy Toledo captured Thupa Amaru, the last ruler of the neo-Inca state, in 1572, the Spaniard boasted that he had finally seized the idol as well. He initially suggested sending it to the Pope, but then reconsidered; unfortunately, we do not know what ultimately happened to Punchao (Duviols 1976b:167). The solar disk, often cited as an authentic Inca creation, was illustrated by the two indigenous authors Guaman Poma and Santa Cruz Pachacuti Yamqui. A Spanish soldier named Mancio Serra even claimed that he carried it off from the temple and later lost it at gambling. Even so, Duviols (1976b) makes a strong case that the disk was actually a Colonial-era image adopted by native Andeans and that an elaborate mythology was built up around spurious claims and misapprehensions.

Inti was the patron of the empire and of conquest. It was the Sun to whom the Incas dedicated innumerable ceremonies intended to ensure the ruler's welfare and to foster bountiful harvests. The foremost priest in the land was the High Priest of the Sun, who was usually one of the ruler's close relatives. The Incas set aside vast human and natural resources for Inti throughout the empire. The temple in Cuzco highlighted Sun worship, although numerous other images were also revered there (chapter 6). Every major installation in the provinces had a Sun Temple served by its coterie of male and female priests. One house of the *mamakuna* (or perhaps the *aqllakuna*, i.e., "chosen women") stands at coastal Pachacamac, where the building has been reconstructed rather more enthusiastically than accurately (Hyslop 1990:255–61). Every province was supposed to dedicate lands and herds to the Sun, and the church had its own set of storehouses that were used to keep supplies for its personnel and sacrifices. The most expansive set of resources dedicated to the church's holdings may have been found on the north side of Lake Titicaca, where an entire province may have been given over to the institution (C. Julien 1993; chapter 10 below).

Mama-Quilla, "Mother Moon"

The second great deity of the heavens was the Moon, the wife of the Sun. Just as gold was the sweat of the Sun, so was silver the tears of the Moon. In some coastal societies, such as the Chimu, the moon was more important than the sun (Rowe 1948). Mama-Quilla was important in calculating time and in regulating the ceremonial calendar (Cobo 1990:29–30), since many rituals were based on lunar cycles adjusted to the solar year. The moon had its own temple in Cuzco and was served by its own dedicated priestesses. The Incas envisioned the moon in female human form and created an image of her that was tended by priestesses dedicated to her worship (Cobo 1990:29). One myth accounted for the dark spots on her surface by explaining that a fox fell in love with the moon because of her beauty. When he rose up to the sky to steal her, she squeezed him against her and produced the patches that we see today (Garcilaso 1966:118–19).

Inti-Illapa, the Thunder God

Another important deity in the Inca pantheon was the god of thunder, lightning, the rainbow, and virtually all other meteorological phenomena. He was visualized as a man in the sky who wielded a war club in one hand and a sling in the other. The thunder was the crack of his sling and the lightning flash the glitter of his shining garments as he moved. Lightning bolts were the sling stones that he cast and the Milky Way the heavenly river from which he drew the rainfall (Cobo 1990:32). His image, Chucuylla, was kept in a temple called Pukamarka, in the Chinchaysuyu quarter of Cuzco, which also held an image of the Creator God (Bauer 1998:58, 63). Inti-Illapa was the deity to whom prayers for rain were addressed (Rowe 1946:294–5).

Other Important Deities

The Incas revered many other deities, including *Pachamama*, the "Earth Mother," a goddess to whom the Incas sacrificed for successful crops. Cobo wrote that farmers commonly worshiped her at a stone altar that they placed in the middle of a field. *Mamacocha*, or "Mother of the Lakes (and Sea)," was also revered by the Incas, although she was less important than for coastal peoples, for whom she ranked as high as any deity (Cobo 1990:32–4). An especially important regional god recognized by the Incas was *Pachacamac*, or "Maker of the Earth," a coastal oracle with two millennia of history before the Incas appeared.

The Incas also built up an elaborate mythology around stars, constellations, and planets (Bauer and Dearborn 1995:101–40; see also Ziółkowski and Sadowski 1989). They visualized figures in both stars and black spaces in and about the Milky Way, which passes high in the sky in the central Andes. The Incas' reverence for the stars and planets was nothing unusual in the Andes, for they were tracked and worshiped before, during, and after Inca rule. The Pleiades and the stars known as Orion's Belt or the Three Marys in western lore were especially important on Peru's north coast (Bauer and Dearborn 1995; Rowe 1948; Salomon and Urioste 1991: sections 372–8). About 1559, Polo composed an extended treatise on native beliefs of which only the abstract remains. He wrote that, "in general they believed that for each [kind of] animal and bird on earth there was a similar one in the sky who was in charge of its procreation and increase" (Polo 1965a:2–5). Herders worshiped a star that they recognized as a multi-colored llama (*Urcuchillay*) that watched over the animals, along with two others they saw as a ewe and a lamb. Forest peoples venerated particular stars for protection against jaguars, bears, pumas, and snakes. Cobo, who used Polo's full treatise, wrote that all peoples sacrificed to *Collca* [*qollqa*, granary], or the Pleiades. The constellation was honored because it gave rise to all other stellar patrons of earthly things, and thus they called it "mother." He continued that "all the power that conserved the animals and birds flowed from this group of stars" (Cobo 1990:30). They also revered a cross, although we cannot be sure that it was the four stars now known as the Southern Cross, since several constellations of that form are known in Quechua star-gazing (Bauer and Dearborn 1995:107–10; Urton 1981:129–50). The Incas also recognized the visible planets. They grouped them in with the brighter stars (*chaska*, shaggy hair) and distinguished all of those from lesser stars (*cuyllor*, star). They took special note of Venus (*chaska cuyllor*) and the Pleiades, whose passage was related to the agricultural/calendrical cycle.

Calendrics and Astronomical Observations

Solar and Lunar Calendrics

The Incas knew a great deal about celestial cycles.[1] They had a good fix on the solar equinoxes and solstices, for example, and seem to have kept track of zenith passages of the sun (i.e., the point where the sun is directly overhead). They also knew that the midsummer sun casts no shadow from a vertically aligned pole on the equator. As for the moon, they understood the lunar cycles and timed many of their celebrations according to the appearance of the new moon. Moreover, they had solved the cycles of Venus and some star groups.

The Incas' annual calendar was based on solar cycles, while festivals were largely built around twelve lunar cycles (table 7.2). The two do not mesh well, since there is an 11-day disparity between 12 lunar months (29.5 days each) and a 365-day solar year. According to several chroniclers, the Incas knew that 12 lunar months fell short of a solar year and made a correction every winter solstice month. Ziółkowski and Sadowski (1989:167–96) have designed a plausible Inca-era calendar in which each lunar month began on a new moon and a short intercalation month was used to bring the solar and lunar years into agreement. Bauer and Dearborn (1995:61–2) express doubts about such a scenario, because it would have put one of the solstices and its associated ceremonies out of synchrony every year. Instead, they infer that the Incas likely used 30-day months (as Betanzos said) and made adjustments on a month-by-month basis, to ensure that the ceremonial and celestial cycles stayed in agreement.[2]

The Incas measured the solstices by making observations from points in or near Cuzco to stone pillars erected on the horizon. Several chroniclers described the four pillars on the hill called Picchu, which forms the northwest horizon from central Cuzco. Unfortunately, their reports of the columns' dimensions and purposes do not coincide, but Bauer and Dearborn judge that two accounts make good sense (1995:69–76). The pillars could have been used to define either (1) the June solstice sunset or (2) a specific sunset in August, as viewed from the Awkaypata plaza, for the inception of the planting season. A few other stone structures in the empire were also likely used for astronomical observations or calendrical purposes (Hyslop 1990:226–9). The most famous is the Torreón at Machu Picchu. This D-shaped building contains a window that is oriented toward the Pleiades rise azimuth (65°) of the fifteenth century. Intriguingly, the edge of a cut stone in the floor may have been used as a solar device. The edge would have lined up nicely with the shadow cast by a plumb line dropped from the window, as the sun rose over a low point in the horizon on the June solstice (Dearborn and White 1983; Dearborn, Schreiber, and White 1987).

Eclipses and Comets

Unlike some Mesoamerican societies, Andean peoples had not worked out the cycles of earth, sun, and moon that would allow them to predict eclipses, so these were frightening events that called for a vigorous response.[3] Cobo (1990:27, 29; see also Garcilaso 1966:118–19) wrote that when a solar eclipse occurred, the Incas would consult their diviners, who usually determined that a great prince was about to die and the Sun had thus gone into mourning. He continued that the Inca reaction was to sacrifice boys, girls, and livestock; the priestesses dedicated to the Sun went into mourning themselves, fasted, and made frequent sacrifices. Lunar eclipses were thought to occur because a puma or a snake was eating the moon. The corrective was to frighten the beast away by shouting, blowing trumpets, beating drums, hurling spears and other weapons toward the heavens, and whipping dogs until they howled.

The Incas also thought that comets were augurs of momentous events. One was seen in Cajamarca during Atawallpa's imprisonment there by the Spaniards. Francisco de Xérez (1985:156), Pizarro's secretary, wrote that Atawallpa foretold the passing of a great lord of the land – and was dead himself within two weeks. About fifteen years later, Cieza de León (1984:201) confirmed the report through interviews with men who had been at Cajamarca. He commented that Atawallpa had also said that a comet portended Wayna Qhapaq's demise. Dearborn and Ziółkowski

Table 7.2 The twelve lunar months of the Inca calendar, according to the chroniclers Betanzos, Polo, and Guaman Poma, modified from Bauer and Dearborn 1995: table 2; and according to Rowe's (1946) synthetic rendition

Month (approx. beginning date)	Betanzos [1557]	Polo de Ondegardo [1585]	Guaman Poma [1615]	Rowe (1946)	Comments[a]
January (23 December)	Hatumpo Coiquis	Camay	Capac Raymi, Camay Quilla	Qhapaq Raymi	"magnificent festival"; summer solstice
February (22 January)	Allapo Coiquis	Hatun Pucyu	Paucar Uaray Hatun Pocoy Quilla	Kamay	disposal of year's sacrificial remains
March (21 February)	Pacha Pocoiquis	Pacha Pucuy	Pacha Pocuy Quilla	Hatoñ Poqoy	"great ripening"
April (23 March)	Ayriguaquis	Antihuaquiz	Ynca Raymi Mamay Quilla	Pawqar Waray	"earth ripening"
May (22 April)	Haucai Quos Quiquilla	Hatun Cuzqu Raymoray	Atun Cusqui Aymoray Quilla	Ayriwa	harvest of sacred maize field
June (23 May)	Hatun Quosquiquilla	Aucay Cuzqui	Haucay Cusqui Quilla	Aymoray	"great cultivation"

July (23 June)	Caguaquis	Chahua Huarquis	Chacra Conacuy Quilla	Inti Raymi; also Awqay-Koski	"Sun festival"; "warrior's cultivation"; winter solstice
August (23 July)	Carpaiquis	Yapaquis	Chacra Yapuy Quilla Quilla	Cawawarkis	sacrifices to water sources
September (23 August)	Satuaiquis	Coya Raymi	Coya Raymi Quilla	Yapakis	sowing of sacred maize field at Sausero
October (22 September)	Omarime Quis	Homa Raimi Puchayquis	Uma Raymi Quilla	Sitowa	Qoya Raymi: "Queen's festival"; Citua: "purification festival"
November (22 October)	Cantaraiquis	Ayamarca	Aya Marcay Quilla	K'antaray	rain ceremonies
December (22 November)	Pucoy Quillaraimequis	Capacraymi	Capac Ynti Raymi	Ayamarka	preparations for Qhapaq Raymi

[a] There are apparent discrepancies in the sequences of months here because the chroniclers were not always precise or disagreed about the correspondence between Inca and Christian calendars. For example, Polo said that Qhapaq Raymi was the first month and corresponded to December, whereas he may have meant that it began in that Christian month. The comments here generally follow Cobo and Rowe.

have independently concluded that a comet probably passed overhead in January of 1528. This timing corresponds well with the report that Pizarro had landed on the South American coast before Wayna Qhapaq died, during an exploratory trip that lasted from 1527 to early 1528 (Ziółkowski and Sadowski 1989; Dearborn and Schreiber 1986; Bauer and Dearborn 1995:147–51).

The Ceremonial Cycle

The Incas celebrated ceremonies tied to both the solar and lunar cycles, as well as irregularly scheduled rituals that were associated with particular events.[4] The lunar months were given a variety of names by the early chroniclers, examples of which are listed in table 7.2. The most important ceremony of the regular cycle fell in the first month of the year, which included the December solstice. The *Qhapaq Raymi*, or "Magnificent Festival," was both the year's first festival and its greatest. During this celebration, the noble Inca boys went through the puberty rites that marked the passage from child to adult (chapter 8). A number of public ceremonies included dancing, drinking, and eating cakes of maize and llama blood said to symbolize the food of the Sun. As this was the year's most solemn event, provincial subjects were required to leave the city for the duration of the rites.

Inti Raymi, or "Warriors' Cultivation," took place in the month that coincided with the June solstice. Like the *Qhapaq Raymi*, this celebration was intended primarily to honor the Sun. In recent years, this festival has been revived as a grand show in Cuzco that merges re-kindled tradition with events staged for tourists. In 1535, a few months after Manqo Inka's coronation, the Spanish cleric Bartolomé de Segovia was among those who witnessed the last great Inca festival to the Sun, which lasted eight or nine days (Segovia 1968:82). His account conjures a vivid image of a grand state ceremony in which all the major figures were involved – the Sun, the Inca, the effigies of past rulers, the nobility, priestesses, and people of Cuzco. Segovia wrote: "they brought out all of the effigies from Cuzco's temples onto a plain at the edge of Cuzco, toward the area where the Sun dawned. The effigies with the greatest prestige were placed beneath rich, finely-worked feather canopies, which had an elegant appearance . . . The space [between the canopies] formed an avenue over thirty paces wide, and all the lords and other principal figures of Cuzco stood in it." The lords, dressed in all their finery, were arrayed in two rows of about 300 each. As the Sun rose, the Inca ruler led off a chant that ascended in volume till noon, and then slowly diminished as the Sun descended. Throughout the day, offerings of meat were consumed in a great fire and great amounts of chicha, coca, and other materials brought out by maidens were given in sacrifice. At one point, a number of llamas were set loose and the common Indians leaped to catch them in a scramble that everyone enjoyed as great sport. As the Sun completed its descent, the Incas expressed great sadness and humility. After sundown, the effigies were returned to their quarters and the canopies that had sheltered the nobility were packed up for the night. At the end of eight or nine days of similar celebrations, the Incas brought out foot plows and Manqo Inka took the lead in breaking the earth. Through this act, wrote Segovia, the Incas inaugurated the plowing season (chapter 11).

According to several chroniclers, during the month known as the *Qoya Raymi* ("Queen's Festival") or *Citua*, the Incas performed a rite of purification. Cobo explained that the ceremony was performed in the rainy season, because that was when people were prone to fall ill. Cuzco's residents began the rituals by striking each other with torches and shaking clothing outside their doorways, as if to rid themselves of malignity. Molina's account explains how social hierarchy and ceremony were played out over space. At one point, four groups of one hundred people ran out of the city carrying sacrificial ashes in the four directions. The procession began with priests in the Temple of the Sun and fanned outward. Members of three royal *panaqa* and three non-royal *ayllu* carried their burdens out on the Kollasuyu and Chinchaysuyu roads, while two of each kindred did the same in the other two parts, Antisuyu and Cuntisuyu (Molina 1988:73–5). When they reached a certain spot, they passed their burdens to people of lower status and so on outward from the city. The last carriers bathed in four major rivers many kilometers away to divest the city and its people of disease and other impurities.

Cuzco's Network of Shrines: the Zeq'e System

Few aspects of the Inca empire have excited as much interest or mystification as Cuzco's network of shrines. Andean people often envisioned geography and features of the landscape in terms of sacred space. Among the Incas, this idea took form initially as a world composed of four parts that converged at Cuzco. The land around them teemed with spirits, while their history was inscribed on the terrain in mountains, springs, caves, stones, and buildings. Hundreds of holy places (*wak'a*) were joined together to form the most elaborate ritual complex in the native Americas – the *zeq'e* (line) system of Cuzco.

The Spanish authorities had known about some major shrines for decades, but their scope and significance really began to dawn on them about 1558–60, when Polo began inquiries into Inca religion. As magistrate of Cuzco, Polo found that the Incas worshiped at more than 400 shrines in and around the city (see Bauer 1998:16–19). As they delved into Andean religion, the Spaniards found that Cuzco's network was only one of untold numbers that native people used to structure their interaction with a sanctified terrain. Polo ventured at one point that every town in the Andes had one. Other Spaniards were also alerted to the complexity of native shrine systems. During an inspection of Chinchaysuyu, the crusading cleric Cristóbal de Albornoz found more than two thousand *wak'a* in the lands of the Chanka and Aymara and recorded them in local ecclesiastical records. The most complete account of Cuzco's shrines is in Cobo's (1990:51–84) magnum opus, into which he copied a list of 332 *wak'a*, probably from Polo's lost manuscript.[5] The catalog includes descriptions of the position and social affiliations of the shrines, their mythical history, and the sacrifices practiced at them (table 7.3).

In outline, the design was straightforward.[6] Shrines distributed across the landscape were linked by *zeq'e* lines radiating out from central Cuzco; most lines originated in or near the Sun Temple. Each line was assigned to a particular social group in Cuzco, which conducted rituals at the appropriate shrines following a ceremonial calendar. Bauer's field research shows that most ran for about 5–11 km and contained between 3 and 15 shrines. Some lines were essentially straight, while others jogged to adjust to the positions of the *wak'a*. That sounds simple enough, but the system's complexity quickly becomes so baffling that many otherwise diligent scholars have been reduced to scratching their heads and trusting someone else's judgment (see below). In fact, Cobo wrote that over one thousand record-keeping specialists were needed in Cuzco to memorize the lore of the holy places, their prayers, rituals, and sacrifices (Cobo 1990:9; see MacCormack 1991:190). To help readers visualize the system, figure 7.1 provides a map of the system's geography, figure 7.2 represents its organization schematically, and table 7.3 lists some of the most important shrines and their roles.

Table 7.3 A selection of important shrines in and around Cuzco, in Cobo's (1990:51–84) list; spellings of shrines according to original, information following Cobo (1990) and Bauer (1998)

Name of shrine	Designation	Gloss	Modern identification	Social affiliation (royal founder)	Form	Ceremonies or significance
Chinchaysuyu						
Patallacta	Ch. 1:2[a]	Terrace Town[b]	Q'enqo site	Goacaytaqui	carved stone and building complex	death house of Pachakuti
Inti Illapa	Ch. 2:3	Sun – Lightning	Toto Cachi district: exact location unknown	Vicaquirao	golden idol	idol of sun taken as brother idol by Pachakuti
Nina	Ch. 3:1	Flame	near Qorikancha	*mamakuna:* priestesses	stone brazier	sacrifices to Sun every morning
Collaconcho	Ch. 4:6	Large Cut-Stone Work	Tired Stone		carved stone	got tired on trip to Saqsawaman
Cusicancha	Ch. 5:1	Happy Enclosure	opposite Qorikancha on Maruri Street, Cuzco	*Iñaqa panaqa*	house?	where Pachakuti was born
Pukamarka	Ch. 5:2	Red Town		*Iñaqa panaqa*	temple	idol of Thunder worshiped there
Haucaypata	Ch. 5:4	Terrace of Tranquility	Cuzco's Plaza de Armas	*Iñaqa panaqa*	plaza	main plaza of Inca Cuzco
Sabacurinca	Ch. 5:6	Unique Golden Inca	"Throne of the Inca" above Saqsawaman	*Iñaqa panaqa*	carved stone	gives view of six sacred mountains of Cuzco
Pukamarka (probably Kiswarcancha)	Ch. 6:2	Red Town (Kishwar Tree Enclosure)	Red Town on Maruri Street, Cuzco	Arayraca	temple complex	sacrifices to Pachayachachi (Creator)
Cajana	Ch. 6:5	Place of Ice	northwest corner of Plaza de Armas	Arayraca	palace	palace of Wayna Qhapaq; sacrifices to wind made in doorway *Guayra* ("wind", Ch. 6:4)
Quiangalla	Ch. 6:9	Near the Rust-Colored (Sunset)	near Cinca, on western horizon of Cuzco Valley	Arayraca	stone pillars	marked sunset at beginning of summer

continued

Table 7.3 *continued*

Name of shrine	Designation	Gloss	Modern identification	Social affiliation (royal founder)	Form	Ceremonies or significance
Antisuyu						
Turuca	An. 1:2	Deer (Stone)	in Qorikancha	*Zukzu panaqa* (Wiraqocha)	round stone	idol of Ticci Viracocha (Creator God)
Amaromarcaguaci	An. 1:7	Serpent Town House	Amaro	*Zukzu panaqa* (Wiraqocha)	house, carved rock outcrop?	house of Amaru Thupa Inka, eldest son of Pachakuti
Tambo Machay	An. 1:9	Lodge Cave	Puca Pucará site	*Zukzu panaqa* (Wiraqocha)	house and enclosures	hunting lodge of Pachakuti
Quinoapuquio	An. 1:10	Quinoa Spring	Tambomachay site	*Zukzu panaqa* (Wiraqocha)	two springs and architecture	universal sacrifice, save children
Chuquimarca	An. 3:4	Gold Town	Salonpunca or Cusilluchayo site	—	carved stone	various sacrifices to Sun
Mantocallas	An. 3:6	Near Red Paint (Tree)	Salonpuncu site	—	carved stone	important rituals for Sun, esp. for Inti Raymi ceremonies
Susumarca	An. 5:8	Reed Town	above Callachaca	Sanoc?	spring	may be Susurpuquio, where Pachakuti had vision of Creator or Sun
Chuquicancha	An. 6:3	Gold Enclosure	Rumi Huasi Alto	—	stone outcrop with buildings	sacrifices to the Sun for Inti Raymi and *qhapaq ucha* ceremonies
Pilcourco	An. 8:11	Many-Colored Hill	near Larapa	Ayarmaca	stone	girls sacrificed for enthronement of new Inca
Kollasuyu						
Limapampa	Co. 2:1	Plain – Speaker	plaza east of Qorikancha	Aguini	open area	maize sowing and harvest festivals
Sausero	Co. 2:3	?	terrace in Cuzco	Hahuanina	maize field	primordial field in Cuzco; initiation of agricultural season

Taucaray	Co. 4:2	(Funerary Bundle) Continually Piling Up	Taucaray hill	Apu Mayta (Qhapaq Yupanki)	tomb	place where dead assembled periodically
Huanacauri	Co. 6:7	Royal Scepter of Expiation	Huanacauri hill	—	stone on hill	petrified brother of Manqo Qhapaq; various pilgrimages, esp. for boys' initiation rites
Matoro	Co. 7:5	?		*Uska Mayta panaqa* (Mayta Qhapaq)	mountain slope	birthplace of Zinchi Roq'a; boys' initiation rites
Cuntisuyu						
Sabaraura	Cu. 1:1	Unique Flame	in Qorikancha	Anaguarque	stone	*pururauca* (petrified stone warrior)
Anaguarque	Cu. 1:7	Exquisite Wavy (Feathered Hawk)	Anaguarque hill	Anaguarque	large hill	boys' initiation rites
Tanancuricota	Cu. 8:1	Valiant, Gold Coca (Warrior Woman)		*qollana*	stone	petrified female warrior: Chañan Cori Coca
Chinchincalla	Cu. 13:3	Near – ?	Chinchincalla hill	—	hill with some Inca remains	stone pillars marked solstice sunset
Other						
Coricancha	—	Gold Enclosure	Santo Domingo/ Qorikancha	—	temple	main shrine to the Sun and other important deities
Tocoripuquiu	—	Provincial-Governor Spring	near headwaters of Saphy River	—	spring	source of Cuzco's water, found underground by Roq'a Inca

[a] The designations refer to the *zeq'e* line of shrines and the numbering of shrines along each line. For example, the designation Ch. 1:2 refers to the second shrine on the first *zeq'e* line of shrines listed by Cobo in the Chinchaysuyu (northwest) part of the empire. The numbering follows Rowe's (1979a) system, also followed by Bauer (1998).
[b] Glosses are by Margot Beyersdorff, in Bauer (1998:179–96).

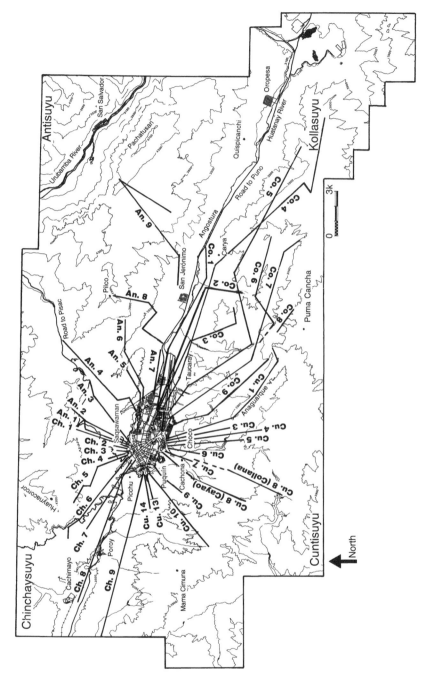

Figure 7.1 The layout of the Cuzco *zeq'e* system of lines radiating outward from the city's center (courtesy Brian Bauer)

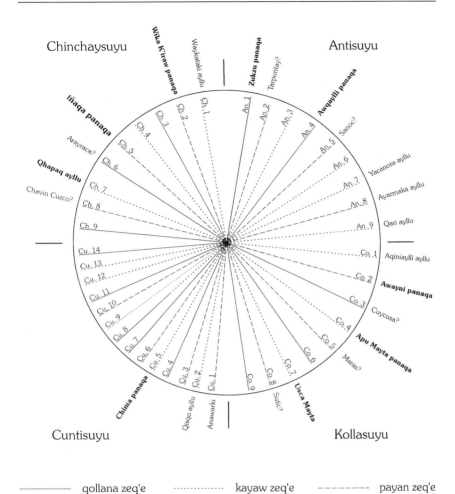

Chinchaysuyu

Antisuyu

Cuntisuyu

Kollasuyu

——————— qollana zeq'e   ············· kayaw zeq'e   — — — — — payan zeq'e

Figure 7.2   The schematic organization of the Cuzco *zeq'e* system

Deciphering the *Zeq'e* System of Cuzco

Modern study of Cuzco's shrines began with Paul Kirchoff's (1949) work in the 1940s, followed up by Manuel Chavez Ballón's mostly unpublished work. Beginning in the 1960s, Tom Zuidema (1964, 1983) proposed that the system simultaneously reflected Cuzco's kinship and marital customs, cosmic space, and ceremonial calendrics. He saw a year-long clockwork in the layout that included

continued

sighting lines for the solar calendar and other astronomical phenomena. Zuidema has worked with the astronomer Anthony Aveni
to test certain of his ideas; some have met acceptance, while others
remain controversial. His student, Jeanette Sherbondy (1992, 1994),
has shown how kin groups high in Cuzco's social hierarchy claimed
rights to water and land through the spring-shrines and canals under
their authority. Another student, Maarten Van de Guchte (1990),
subsequently explored how the Incas carved stone shrines to mediate
their relationship with the animate landscape. Rowe (1979a, 1985a),
conversely, has tried to trace out the system's historical development
in accordance with royal genealogies. His view challenges Zuidema's
approach, which treats the system as if it were largely static. In the
1990s, Brian Bauer (1998) conducted the first comprehensive study
of the system that integrated history and archaeological fieldwork.
He identified many shrines in the field, correlated them with historical discussions of Inca religion, and tested proposals about how
the system worked.

To illustrate the complexities, let me expand a little on the main
text here, condensing from Bauer's (1998) work. Chinchaysuyu,
Antisuyu, and Kollasuyu contained nine lines of shrines each. The
fourth part, Cuntisuyu, contained either 14 or 15 lines. In total, then,
there were 41 or 42 lines. Cobo's enumeration of lines runs clockwise for three of the four parts and counterclockwise for Chinchaysuyu. Within each part, the *zeq'e* lines were grouped into sets of three
lines. Each triad was assigned a status according to a rank order
(*qollana-payan-kayaw*, in descending order) based on the Inca
kinship system. Individual lines in each triad were also assigned one
of the three ranks. In Cobo's list, 23 lines were assigned to social
groups in or around Cuzco, but we do not know if the assignments
were extended to every line. Each social group carried out the sacrifices and other ceremonies associated with the shrines along its *zeq'e*.
In many cases, one line within a triad was assigned to a royal kin
group (*panaqa*) and another to a non-royal *ayllu*.

As entire books have been written on the subject, it should be
clear that these features only skim the surface of the system. Scholars are still uncertain if the asymmetries in the layout arose from historical changes, oddities of the Inca social structure, or recording
error. Another issue concerns whether the *zeq'e* were straight lines
or moved erratically across the landscape. Many of the calendrical
and astronomical proposals that have been put forward assume that
a significant number of lines were straight. Some sight lines almost
certainly were, but Bauer's work indicates that others took crooked

paths. Since only a fraction of the shrines have been located, not all proposals can be tested conclusively. Some shrines, like the main Sun Temple, are unmistakable, but the identity and position of others are open to debate. Another question concerns how flexible the structure was. We can appreciate the adaptability that may have been required if we consider that the whole system of social ranking reported to the Spaniards may have worked only when Wayna Qhapaq was emperor. The unfulfilled addition of his *panaqa* to Cuzco's social system would probably have shifted all of the ranking categories, added new shrines, and maybe displaced or promoted one of the existing kin groups.

The shrines included natural and modified features of the landscape as well as buildings. Not all can be clearly typed, but Bauer groups many on Cobo's list as follows: 96 springs or sources of water, 95 stones, 32 hills and mountain passes, 28 royal palaces and temples, 28 fields and flat places, 10 tombs, 7 ravines, 3 caves, 3 quarries, 3 stone seats, 3 sunset markers, 2 trees, and 2 roads. The two most important shrines were the Qorikancha and Huanacauri. As the Qorikancha has already been described (chapter 6), the discussion here will look briefly at Huanacauri and other shrines.

Huanacauri, an uncarved stone, was one of the most potent symbols of Inca mytho-history. The Incas thought that it was the petrified remains of one of the four original Inca brothers ("Ancestor Chili Pepper") who emerged from the primordial cave at Pacariqtambo; it was thus the second oldest *wak'a* in Inca mytho-history, after the origin cave. Cobo (1990:74) described the stone as being "of moderate size, without representational shape, and somewhat tapering." For solstitial festivals, it was adorned with fine clothes and taken to the hill southeast of Cuzco that was its namesake. Intriguingly, there was little architecture on the hill to indicate its status within the Inca pantheon. The peak is still an important terminus for local ritual pilgrimages (Sallnow 1987). The stone was also often taken to war as the patron of the noble warriors (chapter 9). It accompanied the Incas to Ecuador, but was returned to Cuzco with Wayna Qhapaq's mummified body. The Spaniards later placed it in the custody of their royal ally, Paullu Inca, who built a special house for it in Cuzco, until the Spaniards confiscated the stone. The name Huanacauri was applied repeatedly to locations around Cuzco and to important peaks in the empire, as the Incas imprinted their mythical past on an expanded domain (Van de Guchte 1990:53–4).

Plate 7.1 The site of Q'enqo, above Cuzco, which may have been the death house of Pachakuti called Patallacta

Many other stones were also important in the array of shrines. At least 15 of them were the *pururaucas*, the stones venerated as the warriors who helped the Incas repel the Chankas (chapter 4). Among the carved stones are the beautiful planes of the "Throne of the Inca" above Saqsawaman and the Moonstone (*Quilla Rumi*) of the plain of Anta, west of Cuzco. The designs on some carved outcrops are astonishingly intricate. The site of Qenq'o, which was probably the death house of Pachakuti called Patallacta, contains a large boulder whose surface has been carved in steps, zig-zag channels, and gnomons (plate 7.1). On the interior is a superbly cut passageway with a stone altar, which may have been a tomb. The main sector contains a small amphitheater of finely cut stonework and an enclosed monolith. Another carved stone of note is the "Tired Stone" (*Collaconcho*) above Saqsawaman; according to myth, the stone became fatigued on its way to be incorporated into the Inca fortress, shed bloody tears, and stopped in its tracks.[7] The Stone of Sayhuite, found just to the west of Cuzco's network, is a single boulder that exhibits an elaborate symbolic scene of humanity and the natural and built landscape (plate 7.2). It contains pumas, serpents, lizards, birds, monkeys, maybe lobsters, humans holding beakers, maize stalks, a miniature building illustrating traditional canons of Inca architecture such as trapezoidal niches or doorways and a stone staircase, and canals, among other things. Van de Guchte suggests that its nine-part figurative landscape may have been a graphical metaphor for the Inca world.

Several carved outcrops elsewhere may have been markers that divided the Incas' civilized world from the barbarity beyond. Samaipata, which lies along the eastern Bolivian frontier, contains a remarkable worked rock, carved in planes, steps, niches, channels, and other figures. Coyuctor, in southern Ecuador, is like a small-scale Samaipata; it reportedly contained a stone carved in the form of a park of animals that has been destroyed (Figuencia Pinos 1995; Hyslop 1990:102–28; Van de Guchte 1990:220). Ingapirca, a nearby Inca center, contains both finely carved Inca architecture and sculpted figures and designs in nearby rock outcrops.

Many of Cuzco's shrines were enclosed or canalized springs (Bauer 1998:86–7). Among the most important was Tocoripuquiu, which was the source of the stream that flowed through Cuzco. Another was Susurpuquio, where it was said that Pachakuti had experienced his vision of the Creator God or the Sun on the eve of the battle with the Chankas. A third, now a popular tourist attraction known as Tambo Machay ("Lodge Cave"), was probably called Quinoapuquio ("Quinoa Spring") by the Incas. This lovely little spot contains a spring that has been adorned with dual channels, niches, and terraces of fine stonework. Among the other landscape features in the *zeq'e* system were caves, fields,

Plate 7.2 The Stone of Sayhuite, whose figurative landscape may represent a map of the Inca cosmos (courtesy Brian Bauer)

open places, hills, and viewpoints where Cuzco disappeared from sight as the traveler left the valley.

The built environment had its fair share of shrines as well, within and beyond the main temple of the Qorikancha. One important location was a brazier called Nina, just outside the Qorikancha, where female attendants of the Sun made burnt offerings each morning. Another was Cusicancha, an enclosure that Pachakuti's descendant kin worshiped as his birthplace. A number of the shrines were portable. Next to Huanacauri, the most important was probably a golden idol named Inti Illapa, which was set on a gold litter in a house or temple in the Toto Cachi district (Bauer 1998:54). Pachakuti reportedly took the idol to be his *wawqi*, or symbolic brother (see Ziółkowski 1996). It traveled with him when he went to war and in death accompanied his mummy in the house of eternal repose at Patallacta.

On Cobo's list, the common offering made to the *wak'a* was the sea shell called *mullu*, which was especially important in ceremonies designed to induce rain (Bauer 1998:27). Other sacrificed materials included llamas, guinea pigs, precious metals, textiles, and coca. The most celebrated of Inca offerings – human children – were apparently rarely consecrated and were mostly associated with Sun worship and important events in the life of the Inca (see *Qhapaq Ucha*, below).

Overall, the system of lines and shrines provided a conceptual map for Cuzco's society, the empire, and the cosmos, while the worship of shrines and ancestors grounded Inca history in the landscape. The system organized the annual round of ceremonies that the Incas thought vital to their well-being, and gave the social groups in the capital a place in maintaining relations between humanity, the ancestors, and other sacred powers. Rowe and Bauer point out that as concrete as the system sounds, however, it was actually dynamic. Since it encapsulated history and power, both of which were forever changing, the system had to adapt. The Incas themselves historically associated at least nineteen shrines with Pachakuti; various others were associated with his wife Anawarki and later figures such as his eldest son Amaru Thupa Inka and younger son Thupa Inka Yupanki. Even Wayna Qhapaq's and Waskhar's palaces were *wak'a* on *zeq'e* lines, illustrating that shrines were added even in the empire's last years. In fact, we would be hard put to find a better Andean example of a continuously invented ritual order (Rowe 1979a; Bauer 1998:155–61).

Other Important Shrines

Cuzco's *zeq'e* system formed only a tiny portion of the shrines and ritual pathways found in Tawantinsuyu. For instance, a case has been made

Figure 7.3 The distribution of high elevation shrines in the southern Andes (modified from Reinhard 1985)

that many of the radial patterns among the famous Nasca lines, which antedated the Incas by about a millennium, were ritual pathways organized like those around Cuzco. All told, thousands upon thousands of water sources, peaks, or unusual land forms that had some ritual significance for local peoples were linked together in spatial arrays throughout the Andes. There were also several especially renowned non-Inca oracles or shrines. One lay at coastal Pachacamac, which had been an urban center since the early first millennium AD. According to most accounts, the Incas took control of the area under Thupa Inka Yupanki. While they respected the oracle's power, they also built a Sun Temple, a house of the holy women, the so-called pilgrim's plaza, the "Painted Building," and the Tauri Chumbi sector at the site (Hyslop 1990: 255–61). Intriguingly, coastal myths recorded that the presence of the Inca Sun god had been accepted by Pachacamac himself in deference to his inevitable supremacy and the two gods co-existed in an uneasy relationship. Even so, he demanded human sacrifice in return for the intrusive presence. Atawallpa apparently consented to the idol's destruction by Hernando Pizarro with satisfaction, since Pachacamac had mistakenly predicted Waskhar's victory in the dynastic war (MacCormack 1991:55–61).

Mountaintop Shrines

The attention that the Incas devoted to the sacred landscape is visible in a number of small ceremonial sites at unusually high elevations (figure 7.3). Among them is Llullaillaco (Salta Province, Argentina), which at 6,739 m is the world's highest archaeological site. Work there in 1998 recovered one extraordinarily well-preserved child mummy and two lightning-damaged child mummies, along with gold, silver, and Spondylus shell figurines (Reinhard 1999). Both archaeologists and alpinists have investigated the mountaintop shrines, many of which have been damaged by looters and natural processes (Beorchia 1985; Schobinger 1966, 1995; Reinhard 1985, 1993; Ceruti 1997). The existing remains consist of small platforms, fieldstone structures, and enclosures. Their deposits contain human hair, camelid bones and dung, pottery, wood, grass, coca leaf, rope, carbon, and feathers. The most elaborate artifacts are usually paired human statuettes and llama figurines, modeled in gold, silver, and Spondylus shell (plate 7.3). Johan Reinhard, the leading investigator of the shrines, infers that there was a consistent rationale behind the creation of the deposits, because no other kind of figurine is found at the high sites. It seems most likely that the combination of the two sexes and precious metals was intended to pay homage to the

Plate 7.3 Silver figurine from a mountaintop shrine in Chile; Neg. No. 329852, photo by Boltin, courtesy Dept. of Library Services, American Museum of Natural History

male Sun and female Moon, while the Spondylus invoked Mother Sea. A similar cache of richly dressed figurines has also been found in a structure atop a pyramid at Túcume, on Peru's north coast (Heyerdahl et al. 1995).

Strikingly, but rarely, the sites contain frozen bodies of children, adolescents, and adults of both sexes, who were probably sacrificed in the *qhapaq ucha* ceremony described below. They are known from Cerro el Plomo and Copiapó (Chile), Cerro del Toro, Aconcagua, and Llullaillaco (Argentina), and Nevado Ampato and Mt. Ausangate (Peru). A similar cache with a human sacrifice has been found on Isla la Plata, off the Ecuadorian coast (McEwan and Van de Guchte 1992). One of the best-described sites is Nevado Ampato, Peru, excavated and reported by Reinhard and his colleagues, at an elevation of 6,300 m (Reinhard 1998). Nicknamed Juanita, the teenage girl was adorned with rich textiles, including a dress tied up by a belt and a bright red and white shawl that was fastened with silver pins. Her pigtail had been tied to her waistband by thread of black alpaca, from which carved wooden miniatures of a box, two drinking vessels, and a dog or a fox dangled from threads. Among the other offerings that accompanied her into death were female statuettes adorned with textiles much like those that the girl herself wore, coca leaves in a feather-covered bag, and maize. The girl most likely walked voluntarily to her next life, which came to pass when she was struck on the head while she was in a drunken stupor. The bodies of two other children – probably a boy and a girl – were found a bit below at a staging point along the path to the top. Four statues were found with the burials, each of which was clothed in Inca-style textiles, along with a Spondylus necklace and silver llama figurine. Many of the artifacts in the two burials appeared in pairs. The excavators suggest that the two may have been buried as a symbolically married couple, just as the chroniclers described for the *qhapaq ucha* ceremony.

Reinhard notes that all 50+ sites that have been recorded over 5,200 m lie south of 15° S latitude. This distribution has led some scholars to consider the truly high sites a south Andean phenomenon that the Incas borrowed from local peoples. Reinhard (1985) points out, however, that all of the culturally identifiable remains found above that elevation so far are Inca. Heffernan (1996) also notes that there are some mountain peak sites in Peru, but the highest peaks in the north are permanent snowcaps or glaciers, while many high summits in the south are exposed seasonally. Erecting the sanctuaries was nevertheless a daunting task that challenged even the Andean physiology. The Incas lessened the difficulties by building staging stations a few hundred meters below the peaks on the sheltered sides of the mountains, and made paths to the summits (Reinhard 1985). Thus the final pilgrimage and sacrifice could be accomplished expeditiously, once the propitious moment had arrived.

As Reinhard observes, the high elevation sites provided a wonderful means of meshing religious and political goals. A primary reason for building them, of course, was to pay homage to the mountain deities. From an Andean perspective, however, the peaks were also the perfect context to stake an imperial claim. By building the shrines, the Incas interposed themselves as the mediators between human society and the supernatural world. Since certain peaks were origin places and home to powerful beings and since humanity's well-being depended on their relations with the spirits, the shrines let the Incas lay claim to the cultural foundations of the area's residents. The sanctuaries in this way formed a deft analog to the abduction of ancestor statues.

Human Sacrifice: The *Qhapaq Ucha* and *Itu* Rituals

The Incas offered human sacrifices for ceremonies of great solemnity dedicated to the Sun, to the ascendancy, well-being, and death of an emperor, and to military victory. Specific *wak'a* around Cuzco, such as the petrified ancestor Huanacauri, Pachakuti's birthplace, and shrines dedicated to his wife, could also receive human sacrifices. In all, Cobo reported that 31 of the 332 shrines he described in and around the capital were owed human sacrifice (Dearborn and Schreiber 1989:51). Calamitous events such as earthquakes, eclipses, and epidemics called for the ultimate offering as well, as did critical divinations. The victims were usually boys and girls chosen for their beauty and recruited from the entire land. Prisoners taken in war were also sometimes executed in a gesture that paid homage to the Sun and symbolized Inca power. On infrequent but dramatic occasions – such as the death or investiture of a ruler – the victims could number in the thousands. Even so, the scale of sacrifice never approached that of their imperial contemporaries – the Aztecs of Mesoamerica, among whom a single unusual event may have consigned as many as 80,000 victims to their deaths. The Andean chroniclers referred to maximal sacrifices of 1,000–4,000, and even those figures may have been more symbol than reality.

The rationale underlying human sacrifice in Inca ideology has not been as clearly laid out for us as it was in Aztec religion. Myths from Mesoamerica recount that humans owed a debt of creation to the gods that could only be paid with frequent offerings of human blood. There are no comparable myths in Inca lore, but the chroniclers did explain that the intent was to ensure that humanity's best was sent to join the Creator, the Sun, and other deities, as well as to accompany rulers into death. Cobo (1990:8) reasoned that they could not have sacrificed their own children without expecting some reward, which is a different logic from one in which humanity was repaying an endless debt.

Two Inca rituals stand out in particular for their gravity and attendant human sacrifice – the *qhapaq ucha* and the *itu* (chapter 9). According to Polo and Cobo, the *itu* was conducted in times of great need, against such natural disasters as drought, epidemic, and earthquake. It could also be a positive celebration. For example, a provincial lord whose daughter was being received as wife by the ruler could be granted the right to celebrate the festival. The *qhapaq ucha* epitomized imperial ideology. Nominally, it paid homage to the Creator and Sun, but it also reinforced the legitimacy of the Inca lineage, Cuzco's social structure, and pan-Andean shrine networks. *Qhapaq ucha* ceremonies could be focused in and around Cuzco, but the grandest events encompassed the entire realm (Cieza 1984:100–1; Betanzos 1996:42, 132; Sarmiento 1960:217, 237, 245, 247; Cobo 1979:235–7, 1990:54, 58–60, 67, 70–3, 78, 80–2, 154–7, 170).

The best description of a *qhapaq ucha* comes from Molina (1988:120–8), who placed it in the context of a monarch's ascension. He wrote that all of the towns of the empire were called upon to send one or two boys and girls about ten years old to the capital, along with fine cloth, camelids, and figurines of gold, silver, and shell. The boys and girls dressed in finery and matched up as if they were married couples. The ceremony began with sacrifices in the main temple and an assembly in the main plaza, where the victims paraded solemnly around Cuzco's notables – living, dead, and graven. Molina wrote that the ceremonies in Cuzco included sacrifices to the Creator God Wiraqocha, asking for health, long life, peace, and perennial victory for the new ruler. Some children were strangled while others had their hearts torn out and their blood painted across the faces of the images. Similar sacrifices were made to the Thunder, Mother Earth, Mother Cloud, and the petrified ancestor Huanacauri. Sacrifices of other kinds were then made to all of the other *wak'a* of Cuzco.

Priests were then dispatched to the four quarters with sacrificial items and orders to make offerings to all *wak'a* according to their rank. The parties left the city in straight-line paths, deviating for neither mountain nor ravine. At some point, the burdens were transferred to other porters, who continued along the route. The children who could walk would do so, while those who could not were carried by their mothers. The Inca himself traveled the royal road, as did the flocks. At each shrine in the provinces, the devotees interred gold, silver, and shell objects, while children were sacrificed only at the most exalted locations. And thus the parties continued with their travels and sacrifices, until they reached the markers that defined the edge of the civilized world, at a distance of 500 leagues (~2,000 km) or a little less. To keep account of everything, wrote Molina, the Incas maintained mnemonic specialists (*khipukamayuq*) and keepers of sacred things (*villcakamayuq*). They also required knowledgeable provincials to be present in Cuzco or in the provincial centers so that the ceremonies could be conducted appropriately, since they were changed from time to time.

Archaeologically, the evidence to support sacrifices at this scale is still lacking. In his fieldwork among the *wak'a* of Cuzco, Bauer (1998:31) found surface evidence of human burial at three shrines, but nothing approaching the thousands of victims described in the chronicles has yet been reported. Since systematic excavations at the shrines around Cuzco have yet to be undertaken, he notes that the issue is still open. Even so, Molina's comment that the rituals paid special attention to high peaks has been supported by the archaeological finds just described. The principal offerings recovered from those sites – gold, silver, Spondylus shell, and children – also nicely match the priest's account.

A View from the Provinces

Only one known document, from the sierra east of Lima, describes indigenous religious traditions in a native Andean language. Written in Quechua, *The Huarochirí Manuscript* was prepared for the cleric Francisco de Ávila, who used it to help in his campaigns against the very traditions it described. As Frank Salomon (1991:1) explains in an introduction to the English version, the manuscript tells of the ancient times of the mountain deity Paria Caca and his sister Chaupi Ñamca, when humans were immortal and when cannibal gods preyed upon them. It describes a landscape alive with spirits, recalls the Inca conquest, and tells of the coming of the Spaniards with their gods who displaced the children of the ancient deities. Although the manuscript is very much a Colonial-era document, it is also a lively testament to the memories of ancient traditions. The author begins his account of human origins in this way:

> In very ancient times, there were *huacas* named Yana Ñamca and Tuta Ñamca.
> Later on another *huaca* named Huallallo Caruincho defeated them.
> After he defeated them, he ordered the people to bear two children and no more.
> He would eat one of them himself.
> The parents would raise the other, whichever one was loved best.
> Although people did die in those times, they came back to life on the fifth day exactly.
> And as for their foodstuffs, they ripened exactly five days after being planted.
> These villages and all the others like them were full of Yunca [i.e., warm valley lands, their biota, and their people].
> When a great number of people had filled the land, they lived really miserably, scratching and digging the rock faces and ledges to make terraced fields.
> These fields, some small, others large, are still visible today on all the rocky heights.
> And all the birds of that age were perfectly beautiful, parrots and toucans all yellow and red.
> Later at the time when another *huaca* named Paria Caca appeared, these beings and all their works were cast out to the hot Anti lands by Paria Caca's actions . . .

Also, as we know, there was another *huaca* named Cuni Raya.

Regarding him, we're not sure whether he existed before Paria Caca or maybe after him.

However, Cuni Raya's essential nature almost matches Vira Cocha's. For when people worshiped this *huaca*, they would invoke him, saying,

> *"Cuni Raya Vira Cocha,*
> *You who animate mankind,*
> *Who charge the world with being,*
> *All things are yours!*
> *Yours the fields and yours the people."*

And so, long ago, when beginning anything difficult, the ancients, even though they couldn't see Vira Cocha, used to throw coca leaves to the ground, talk to him, and worship him before all others, saying,

> *"Help me remember how,*
> *Help me work it out,*
> *Cuni Raya Vira Cocha!"*

And the master weaver would worship and call on him whenever it was hard for him to weave . . . (Salomon and Urioste 1991:43-45)

The manuscript continued, in Chapter 4:

In ancient times, the sun died.
    Because of his death it was night for five days.
    Rocks banged against each other.
    Mortars and grinding stones began to eat people.
    Buck llamas started to drive men.
    Here's what we Christians think about it: We think these stories tell of the darkness following the death of our Lord Jesus Christ.
    Maybe that's what it was. (Salomon and Urioste 1991:53)

Concluding Comments

Some years ago, Roy Rappaport (1971) suggested that belief systems are compelling because they draw meaning and legitimacy from untestable premises that are accepted as truth. As they created their official ideology, the Incas put this idea into action. Within the context of Andean beliefs, state dogma plausibly accounted for both cosmic and human history. The Incas embellished traditional ideas of ancestor worship and veneration of the powers of the earth and sky by elevating an existing deity – the Sun – to a position of pre-eminence and by making worship of their ancestors reverence for humanity's past. This does not imply that Inca state ideology was the religion of the people, however. In many regions, it was an alien and unwelcome presence. As soon as the empire disintegrated, Sun worship and use of the solar calendar quickly abated outside Cuzco. The Sun temples and the religious orders fell apart, and the lands tended for the Inca gods were abandoned. Only among the Incas proper did the royal mummies and idols retain the potency that the polity had lost – and they were defended with a desperate vengeance for decades. During the tumultuous early Colonial years, Inca and local beliefs were reformulated as part of resistance movements, but the Sun cult and worship of Manqo Qhapaq's descendants were exposed as a recent veneer laid over hundreds of more resilient local religions. This fact, more than anything else, underscores that the official Inca ideology was as much a political instrument as it was a belief system.

chapter eight
Family, Community, and Class

By 1532, Inca dominion had imposed a host of new noble statuses and a stratified social order on thousands of local societies that were still heavily based on traditional family and gender relations in their home communities (see table 8.1). New overlays of class and ethnic ranking organized life on the grand scale and many societies that had been without an aristocratic class now enjoyed all the new-found blessings of their presence. Even so, for the vast majority of people, daily life revolved around the kin with whom they shared social ties and economic risks and obligations. Most of the highland societies were headed by hereditary local lords, called *kuraka*, who were part of the region's social fabric. Only along parts of the Peruvian coast, especially in Chimor, had pre-imperial peoples lived in a class-based society where aristocrat and commoner stood on opposite sides of an unbridgeable gulf.

For centuries, Garcilaso's and Cobo's chronicles provided most of the information that was used to describe Inca social relations. Since they knew the heartland best, much of what they had to say was most relevant to the Incas proper. Things changed in the late twentieth century, as historians delving into the archives found evidence for many different kinds of social relationships across the Andes. Among the most valuable texts are Spanish inspections and court cases about rights to office, resources, or inheritance, which often show how family and kin relations worked in one region or another. Archaeology has also broadened our understanding of social relations, for example through the study of architecture and settlement planning, which provide avenues for analyzing social interaction. Similarly, mortuary analysis lends insight into how people envisioned social status, gender roles, identity, and relations with the afterlife. Recently, household archaeology, which studies the residues of daily life, has also begun to shed more light on the domestic life of the general populace and relations between local nobility and their peoples.

Table 8.1 Quechua and Aymara terms referring to the nobility (after Rostworowski 1999:140–3)

Quechua: Santo Tomás' and González Holguín's dictionaries			Aymara: Bertonio's dictionary	
Capac or *Capac Capa*	ST	king or emperor	*Hakhsarañani Apu*	lord of great majesty
Capac Apo	ST	sovereign ruler	*Ccapaca Suti*	royal name or great ruler
Çapay Apu	GH	supreme lord	*Ccapaca Cancaña*	king or lord, an ancient term no longer used with this meaning
Çapay Auqui	GH	the principal of or noble gentleman	*Ccapaca*	wealthy
Hatun Kuraka	GH	the highest-ranking lord, best known, oldest, richest man	*Apu*	lord, *corregidor*, prince
Hatun or *Akapac Kuraka*	GH	great lord	*Apu Cancaña*	*señorío*, domain
Appo	ST	great lord	*Auqui*	father or lord
Appocac	ST	great lord	*Taani*	fieldmaster, provider of something, such as a banquet
Yayanc	ST	lord, generic	*Pachpa Marcani Mayco*	rightful and natural lord of the people
Kuraka	ST	lord, principal of subjects	*Cchamani, Sinti, Ataaani*	captain
Atipac	ST	powerful	*Hilacata*	the principal or head of the *ayllu*
Appocta, Sayani, Gui	ST	to be standing before a great lord	*Hisquiquiri*	rich or noble gentleman

Term	Code	Description	Equivalent	Gloss
Auquicuna	GH	the lower nobles, lords	*Huallpani*	captain, or the one in charge of banquet preparations and other aforementioned
Rinriyoc Auqui	GH	*orejón* nobles	*Laa Mayco*	intrusive chief, or one without the right to the position
Kuraka	GH	the lord of the people	*Mallco vel. Mayco*	*cacique*, lord of subjects
Kuraka Cuna	GH	the principals or those who execute what he orders	*Maycoña vel. Mayco*	domain, royal authority
Llactayoc Apu	GH	the lord of the people	*Tataña*	one who plays the role of lord
Llactacamayoc	GH	deputy *kuraka* or one who executes his orders		
Appo Ayllon	ST	lineage of lower nobility		
Llactayok	GH	lords of owner of camelid herds		
Michini Runacta	GH	govern or rule men or be of higher rank		
Ccoripaco Ccorinrincri	GH	the *orejón* captains		
Appoycachani, Gui	ST	to outrank		
Mussoc Capac or Mosso Cappo	ST	newly crowned emperor (young)		
Pacuyok	GH	commoners who were made *orejones* in war		

The different kinds of evidence underscore that an ideal of mutuality and balance permeated social life, whether between males and females, among extended kin, or between people of different social rank. A fundamental symmetry between male and female roles lay at the heart of Andean society. Attuned as they were to Spanish mores, the chroniclers tended to focus on men and their activities, but indigenous cultures generally saw the two genders as complementary parts of a whole, not as a hierarchy. A household was not only conceptually incomplete without a married couple at its center, but the division of labor put any unmarried adult at a great disadvantage in performing the tasks of daily life. At a broader level, kin owed each other assistance, while the nobility owed leadership and generosity to their people, who in turn owed labor and allegiance to their lords. The degrees of ranking varied from one society to the next, but the traditional links between people of different statuses were stronger than the divisions that separated them. As the Incas imposed a class-based structure, the obligations remained, but the social gulf often widened.

The Elites

The most elevated classes in the realm consisted of the Incas themselves and their closest subjects. As described in chapter 6, the topmost ranks included the royal family, the descendant kin (*panaqa*) of past rulers, the non-royal ethnic Incas, and the Incas by Privilege. Both Quechua and Aymara have rich vocabularies for other elites, as did the Muchik language of the Chimu (Rostworowski 1999:138–44).[1] In addition to the decimal officials, the diverse nobility included those whose statuses were distinguished by their lineage, military stature, civic role, or source of wealth (table 8.1). All of these terms were distinguished from the occupational specialists found among the commoners, called *kamayuq* ("master," chapter 12). The terms for the nobility suggest how some social transformations may have occurred, but we need to remember that the lists were compiled decades after Spanish rule began and that there is some borrowing across languages. Rostworowski points out that some terms incorporate the word for "father" (*yaya*), and suggests that traditional kin terms were modified as society became stratified; the terms may have also carried the implication of lord as father/patron. Terms also existed for commoners elevated to noble status for their performance in war, and for individuals who usurped power or who simply played the role.

Peasant Communities

Despite the elites' prominence, peasant families living in towns and villages – farmers, herders, fishers, and artisans – made up about 95–98 percent of Tawantinsuyu's population. There were several layers of ranking or social divisions within peasant communities, but by and large, sharing and mutual responsibility typified their social relations. A highland community (*llaqta*) in the central Andes usually contained one or more *ayllu*, the most important kin grouping in traditional society. The sizes of *ayllu* varied from one to the next, but the largest could contain several lineages and hundreds of households. The *ayllu* were often divided into two parts and their lineages could also hold statuses of different social ranks. The households themselves typically included a male head of the family, his wife, children, and unmarried or widowed adult kin. As described in chapter 2, the *ayllu* and its member households often distributed their members across the landscape to take advantage of several ecozones so that they could be self-reliant for their daily needs (see below, *Making a Living*). The guiding ethic for these communities thus combined self-reliance, kinship, gender balance, social hierarchy, and mutual obligations.

The remains of these settlements are scattered throughout the Andes, but have become subjects of archaeological research only since the 1980s. In the Upper Mantaro Valley, my colleagues and I have recorded more than 125 Inca-era settlements within about a day's walk of the provincial center of Hatun Xauxa. The largest of these towns, Marca and Hatunmarca, each contained about 4,500 residential structures. We estimate that their populations were probably in the order of 4,000–5,000, a reduction of maybe 60 percent from the largest communities in the pre-Inca era. Both study of the settlement patterns and household archaeology illustrate the impact of the Inca occupation on village society (Earle et al. 1987; D'Altroy 1992; Hastorf 1992). One major change was a shift of the villages from defensible, high elevation peaks, to more dispersed communities near the valley bottoms. This shift was reflected in the diet that people consumed, which favored more maize under Inca rule (chapter 11). High-status families adopted some of the canons of Inca status into both the architecture and insignia of prestige. The elites also had access to hundreds of thousands of Inca ceramic vessels, with which they probably sponsored ceremonial feasts partly as representatives of the state and partly as traditional ethnic lords among their own people (chapter 12).

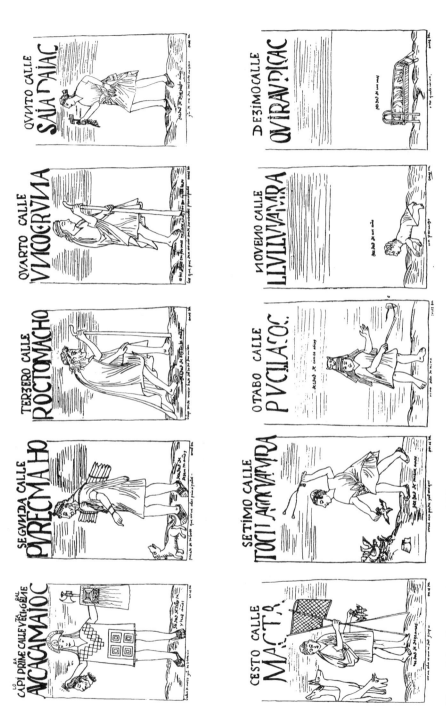

Figure 8.1 Guaman Poma's stages of life ("roads") for males in the Inca realm

The Stages of Life

The Incas kept track of people's ages by following them through stages of life, not by counting their years, which they did not pay much attention to. They were most concerned with a person's ability to work and marital status. Of all the chroniclers, Guaman Poma probably portrayed the customary age-grades the best. Although he was actually trying to describe the Inca census categories for each sex (table 8.2), some of the age-grades he listed were likely based on pre-Inca customs. Rowe (1958:516–17) suggests that he may have split the youngest categories to round the number up to ten, which was the base for Inca accounting. Guaman Poma's first three age-grades included the warriors and their wives, followed by old men and women who were still productive, and then the deaf and drowsy ancients. The chronicler drew the first man as a valiant warrior clutching an enemy's decapitated head (figure 8.1), while the woman is industriously weaving (figure 8.2). Later in life, men could still carry burdens and the women could still weave, but the community's eldest members just whiled away their time. The fourth category, or "road" of life, took in all of the people who were unproductive because they were ill or disabled. The last six roads ran from adolescents to infants, in descending order of their ability to contribute. Guaman Poma showed the marriageable girl in the fifth road spinning, while her male counterpart is drawn as a messenger. Then come female herders, flower gatherers, and girls who could carry burdens, paralleled by male herders and hunters. As he illustrated, even children younger than five were expected to contribute something to the family.

Guaman Poma's list suggests that life's progress was based on the tasks thought appropriate for particular ages and sexes, but the arrangement also ties into the ways that Quechua speakers do their arithmetic. In a study of modern Quechua mathematics, Gary Urton (1997:85–9) has found that the Incas' modern heirs think about ordinal numbers in terms of kinship and descent. When they are putting things into a sequence, the eldest or highest in rank comes first, followed in descending order by the remaining elements. Typically, a set of ranked numbers will be envisioned as a mother and her (four) offspring; two sets of five then make ten, which matches the Inca decimal base. In this way of thinking, adults logically come before children and infants, not the other way around. To put the situation another way, instead of thinking of life stages in terms of the order that we pass through them (i.e., the European way), the Incas thought about age-grades in terms of a hierarchy of importance (i.e., a line of descent).

Table 8.2 The "roads," or life stages, of males and females, according to the native chronicler Guaman Poma, as summarized by Rowe (1958:514–16)

"Road" (life stage)	Male			Female		
	Term	English gloss	Approximate age	Term	English gloss	Approximate age
1	awqa-kamayoq	warrior	25 (or 33) to 50	awqa-kamayoqpa warmin · 'auqayoq warmi	warrior's woman · woman who has a warrior	33 years
2	pureq-machu	old man who can walk	60 or 70	payakuna	old women	50 years
3	roqt'u-machu	deaf old man	80, 100, or 150	puñoq-paya	old woman who sleeps	80 years
4	'onqoq-runa · 'upa · ñawza · makim p'akisqa · hank'a · t'inri wayaqa · k'umu · ch'eqta zenqa	sick person · dumb man · blind man · person with a broken arm · lame person · dwarf sack · hunchback · split nose	people with various infirmities	ñawzakuna · hank'a · 'upa · wiñay 'onqoq · t'inri wayaqa · k'umu · ch'eqta zenqa · q'aqya	blind people · lame · dumb · always sick · dwarf sack · hunchback · split nose · tuberculosis	people with various infirmities

5	*sayapayaq*	helper, companion	18, 20	*'allin zumaq sipaskuna purum thazki*	very beautiful girls of marriageable age / virgin girl	13 years
6	*maqt'akuna*	adolescent youths	12, 18	*qhoru thazkikuna / rutusqa thazki*	girls with their hair cut short / girl with her hair cut	12, 18 years
7	*toqllakoq warmakuna*	children who set net snares	9, 12	*pauau pallac*	[unknown] gatherer	9, 12 years
8	*pukllakoq warmakuna*	children who play	5, 9	*pukllakoq warmi wamra*	female child who plays	5, 9 years
9	*llullu lloqhaq warmakuna*	tender children who go about on all fours	1, 2, 3 to 5 years	*lloqhaq warmi wawa*	female infant who goes on all fours	1, 2 years
10	*wawa k'irawpi-kaq*	infant / one who is in a cradle	1 month, new born	*llullu wawa warmi k'irkaupi-kaq wawakuna*	tender infant girl who is in a cradle / infants	1–5 months

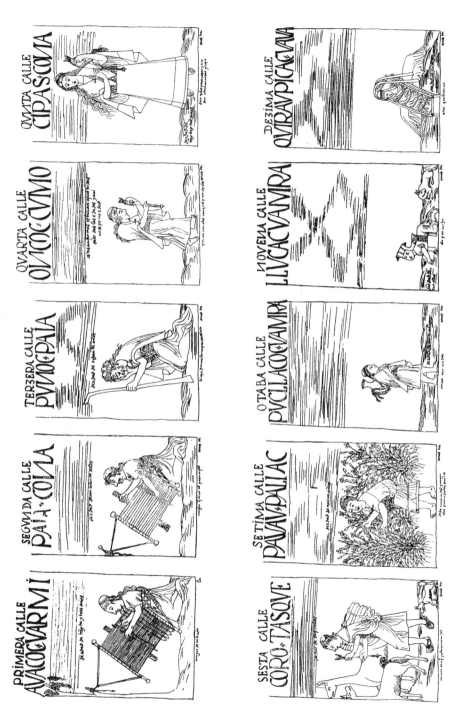

Figure 8.2 Guaman Poma's stages of life ("roads") for females in the Inca realm

Birth and Childhood

Large families were welcome in Inca society both for the emotional attachments that children bring and because of their productivity. Even so, pregnancy and childbirth themselves did not draw much public attention. Women worked right up to the time of childbirth, although it was thought to be bad luck for a pregnant or menstruating woman to walk through a sown field (Cobo 1990:176). As the mother went into labor, she would confess and pray to the *wak'a* for an easy birth. The husband and sometimes the woman would fast until the child was born. Women usually gave birth without the help of a midwife. Immediately after the baby arrived, the mother would wash both the infant and herself in the nearest stream, providing a chilly welcome into their mountainous world (Garcilaso 1966:212). Cobo (1990:200), who was greatly dismayed at the injury done to God's creations, wrote that many people bound their infants' heads to shape them into forms that they found attractive. The Qolla of the altiplano, for instance, wrapped strips of cloth around the head for four to five years to mold them into a cone shape – the better to fit their brimless hats, he commented. Archaeologists sometimes find evidence of such head deformation practices, which can provide a way to help track the movements of ethnic groups under Inca rule.

Cobo wrote that the babies were wrapped in swaddling clothes four days after birth and placed in a cradle. Relatives were then called in to visit and have a drink, but no more elaborate ceremonies were celebrated at that point. The tiny bed was made of a board with four feet; a folded blanket padded the surface and the child was lightly bound to the cradle. It was used to rock the baby to sleep and was also strapped onto the mother's back for travel. Garcilaso (1966:212) recalled that children were treated sternly during their earliest years to make sure that they were up to the rigors of Andean life.

> Every morning when [the baby] was wrapped up it was washed in cold water, and often exposed to the night air and dew . . . The mothers never took the babies into their arms or on their laps either when giving suck or at any other time. They said that it made them crybabies, and encouraged them to want to be nursed and not to stay in the cradle . . . The mother reared the child herself, and never gave it out to nurse, even if she were a great lady, unless she were ill. During this time they abstained from sexual intercourse, considering that it spoiled the milk and caused the baby to pine and grow weak.

When a child was about two years old, it was weaned and given a name in an elaborate hair-cutting ceremony called the *rutuchicoy*. Since

Figure 8.3 The *aqllakuna*, or "Chosen Women," by Guaman Poma (1980); these were young girls taken from their families and trained as weavers and chicha makers in provincial centers

many infants died of respiratory and intestinal diseases and half the children would probably not reach adulthood, we can understand why people might postpone a naming ceremony for a couple of years. Friends and relatives gathered for drinking and dancing, after which the relatives, starting with the eldest and most respected uncle, took turns in cutting off locks of hair and fingernails with a flint knife. The cuttings were gathered and safeguarded, for they were thought to carry the person's essence and a sorcerer could seriously injure or even kill someone by performing witchcraft on the materials (Cobo 1990:201). Most children learned their parents' skills, but did not receive any other special education. Boys were typically taught to hunt and to make the craft objects that their fathers were adept at manufacturing. Girls learned to make thread, to weave, and to perform all the duties of a wife, such as cooking and maintaining the household. Farming and herding, and some crafts such as potting or weaving, were sometimes performed by both sexes, often as complementary tasks.

Children of Inca and provincial nobility enjoyed a more elaborate education. The sons of high provincial lords were sent to Cuzco as hostages, where they were trained as future officials of the realm and were inculcated with Inca values and culture. Along with the sons of Inca aristocracy, they were taught the use of arms, Quechua, Inca religion and history, and *khipu* accounting. Garcilaso says that they were taught by wise men called *amautas*, who passed along their knowledge of the sciences, poetry, music, philosophy, and astrology. Following Blas Valera and Murúa, he described the training as a formal school with a four-year curriculum (Garcilaso 1966:226–7; Rowe 1946:282–3; Rowe 1982).

The only girls to receive formal instruction were the *aqllakuna* (Chosen Women), who were trained throughout the realm (figure 8.3). They were attractive girls taken from their families at about age ten and placed in Inca settlements under the supervision of the provincial governor. In the sequestered House of the Chosen Women (*aqllawasi*), they were taught religion, weaving, cooking, and chicha-making by life-long virgins dedicated to the religious institutions. Cobo said that as many as 200 women of various ages could be found in the largest *aqllawasi*. Although they were well protected, the girls and women were not entirely confined, since they participated in many ceremonies at locations outside their quarters. After about four years, the girls were ready to serve as *mamakuna* (priestesses) or to marry men who merited the honor for their service to the Inca (Cobo 1990:172–4; Rowe 1946:283). The cloth they wove and the chicha they brewed were consumed in great amounts in festivities and sacrifices to the Sun. They began the chicha-making process by chewing maize or other plants; the mash was then spat into a jar where it fermented for a few days. Once decanted, the heady, sweetish brew was ready to be quaffed.

Growing Up

Both boys and girls went through rites of passage in their early teens that marked their transition from childhood to adolescence. A girl celebrated individually at her first menstruation, which occurred at the age of about thirteen or fourteen. Although a girl's ceremonies (*quicuchicuy*) were less elaborate than the boys' collective affairs, they were equally valued. She was required to fast in seclusion for three days, on the last of which she received just a little raw maize. On the fourth day, her mother washed and dressed her in fine clothes made for the occasion. The relatives then came to visit for a couple of days during which the girl served them food and drink. Her most notable uncle gave her an adult name and counseled her to live right and serve her parents well. Favored names for girls emphasized beauty and purity, for example, Star (*Cuyllor*), Egg (*Rontu*), Pure (*Ocllo*), Mark (*Cimpo*), Gold (*Qori*), and Coca (*Koka*; Rowe 1946:284). The ceremonies concluded as he and the other relatives gave her gifts according to their means (Cobo 1990:202–3).

Boys' maturation ceremonies were probably simple for common folk, but were very elaborate for the scion of Inca aristocrats (see Rowe 1946:283–4; Cobo 1990:202). The rite of adolescent passage (*waracikoy*) was celebrated once a year for a community; in Cuzco it coincided with the December solstice festival, called the *Qhapaq Raymi* (chapter 7). Boys who had reached the age of about fourteen were given their breechclout at this time, woven by their mothers. They also received their adult names during these rites. Among the preferred names for Inca boys were Condor (*Kuntur*), Snake (*Amaru*), and Hawk (*Waman*). The royalty were given names that included Happy (*Kusi*), Powerful or Wealthy (*Qhapaq*), Honored (*Yupanki*), and Jaguar (*Uturunku*), among many others.

The ceremonies for the sons of Inca nobility and royalty featured pilgrimages, sacrifices, and physical feats of daring and prowess. A month before the main ceremonies, the boys made a pilgrimage to the sacred mountain named Huanacauri to seek approval to go forward with the rites. During the preparations, the boys made slings and helped to chew maize for the chicha that would be consumed during the festivities. A second pilgrimage to Huanacauri marked the beginning of the month-long ceremonies; the journey was highlighted by sacrifices of camelids and was followed up by a dance in Cuzco's central plaza. Additional pilgrimages to other nearby mountains continued throughout the month, where the boys made sacrifices of llamas, their wool, and other materials. Periodically, their adult sponsors would whip them on the legs, admonishing them to be brave and to serve the Inca and the Sun with honor. One of the high points of the month was an hour-long race down a mountain face that often resulted in injury. The boys were spurred on by young maidens, who waited at the bottom with chicha. As the rituals came to a close, the boys received gifts from their adult male relatives – each one accompanied by a single whip stroke – and had their ears pierced for the large earspools that marked them as nobility. Thus they were known in adult life as *orejones*, or big-ears.

Marriage and Adult Life

Marriage marked the passage to full adulthood. In pre-Inca times, most young people probably chose their mates with the consent of both sets of parents. It was important to find someone from the other side of the (flexibly defined) *ayllu*, so that resources could be kept within the large kin group. In traditional society, marriage bonded both the individuals and their extended kin groups; the relations between in-laws were important links that could be activated when assistance was needed. Men typically married at some point between their late teens and mid-twenties, while the girls married somewhat younger. After the Incas asserted their rule, marriages were supposed to be approved by the provincial governor. In some regions, he reportedly lined up the eligible young men and women in separate rows and let the boys choose mates one by one. If two boys wanted to marry the same girl, the official would investigate who had the superior claim and settle the matter. Elsewhere, the boys made arrangements with the parents of their prospective wives, but the governor's sanction was reportedly still required. In practice, official supervision may have been applied unevenly (Cobo 1990:204–10; Rowe 1946:285–6). The marriage ceremonies were typically simple and varied from one society to the next. In the altiplano, wrote Cobo (1990:206), the groom presented a bag of coca leaves to his future mother-in-law. When she accepted it, the marital bond had been secured. The new couple took up residence in their own household and were counted among the taxpaying populace. Although trial marriages were common in many places, full marital status could only be achieved with the formal sanction of the Inca or his delegate.

Love Poetry and Other Oral Literature

Andean peoples enjoyed composing and reciting oral literature that included love poetry, ballads, narrative history, myth, and religion. The Incas held accomplished orators and storytellers in great esteem. There was a special group of orators in Cuzco called *amautas*, who wove together the deeds of past kings and queens into captivating sagas recited at the court's request. The Incas also seem to have performed dramas in their public ceremonies and dances, but no securely prehispanic piece is known (Rowe 1946:321). In his letter to King Carlos V, Guaman Poma recorded some verses that were preserved from Inca times or composed in the prehispanic style early in the Colonial era. The following love poem is an example of Quechua verse from the Colonial period (Guaman Poma 1936:317; translation by Rowe 1946:322–3).

> *What evil fortune separates us, queen?*
> *What barriers separate us, princess?*
> *My beautiful one, for you are a chinchiroma flower,*
> *In my head and in my heart I would carry you.*
> *You are like the sparkling water,*
> *You are like a mirror of water.*
> *Why don't I meet my loved one?*
> *Your hypocrite mother causes our unbearable separation;*
> *Your contrary father causes our neglected state.*
> *Perhaps, queen, if the great lord God desires,*
> *We will meet again and God will bring us together.*
> *The memory of your laughing eyes makes me sicken.*
> *A little, noble lord, just a little!*
> *If you condemn me to weeping, have you no compassion?*
> *Weeping rivers, over the cantut lily, in every valley,*
> *I am waiting for you my little beauty.*

Among the ethnic Incas, the marriage ceremony took place after the harvest was in. Cobo wrote that the groom and his relatives visited the bride's home, where all of her relatives had assembled. He placed a sandal on her foot, of wool if she were a virgin or of ichu grass if she were not, and then he took her by the hand. The whole group then made their way to the groom's house, where the bride presented him with a fine wool tunic, a headband, and a metal ornament, which she had secreted under her sash. After the groom had donned his new apparel, the elders counseled each of them on the responsibilities of marriage. The pact was sealed with gifts from both sides of the family and celebrated with feasting and drinking.

Among Inca and provincial nobility, the men could have several wives, but only one could serve as his principal wife. The rest had the status of secondary wife, even if the principal wife had died. The most prestigious way a man could receive a secondary wife was through the order of the emperor. A man who had several wives was considered wealthy, because of the household labor that he could command. A commoner whose wife died was in serious trouble. Not only had he lost his life partner, but there was no one present to maintain the household. Even worse, a wife's death was often treated as suspicious and he was blamed. Not until he remarried was he back on his feet socially and economically. Divorce of the principal wife was not possible if it had been sanctioned by the Inca, at least in theory, but secondary wives could be divorced easily (Rowe 1946:285). Not surprisingly, the sources that provide detailed information on the married rights of men are essentially silent on the lives of women who were divorced or widowed.

Death and the Afterlife

In the high Andes, a common person's status changed when he died, but he did not ascend into an incorporeal heaven or sink into eternal torment. Instead, the thirsty spirit of an ancestor still inhabited the land, requiring libations of chicha and other attentions (Gose 1993). Despite the spirit's continuing presence, relatives dressed in black mourning clothes and grieved at the death of a family member; the nobility wore black for a full year. Cobo (1990:250–2) wrote that the lamentations for the dead could last for a considerable number of days, depending on the status of the deceased. Accompanied by flutes and drums, mourners would sing laments, fortified by drink and foodstuffs provided by the surviving family members. Women would cut off their tresses or tear out their eyelashes in a gesture of grief. The funeral party would visit the places that the deceased had enjoyed the most or where he had achieved his greatest successes; there, they recounted the key events of his life for everyone to hear. Cobo said that lords were dressed in their finery for burial and were accompanied into death by their wealth and occasionally by wives and servants. A commoner's burial furniture was considerably less extravagant, and some of his belongings may have been burned at the time of his interment.

Archaeologists have long recognized that the mortuary context provides the perfect opportunity for making social statements about the living and the dead. Rather than being a mirror of one's position in life, a burial is an idealized synthesis of the images that the survivors wish to convey. The Incas' mountaintop shrines are an exaggerated version of this practice, but their combination of chicha jars, cups, and individualized serving plates, gender-appropriate clothing, and offerings to the sun, moon, and sea, epitomized what was considered valuable in Inca culture. Many other graves in Inca times also contained artifacts that were associated with one gender or the other, for example, weaving kits and fastening pins for women. Similarly, the continuity between the ancestors and their surviving descendants was emphasized time and again by the preservation of mummies in caves and the periodic reopening of tombs for offerings.

The variety of burial customs recorded archaeologically throughout the Andes is so complex as to defy description. Regrettably, however, the conquistadores and their successors were so effective at sacking Inca tombs that we have almost no mortuary evidence from the Inca elite classes themselves. An entire cliff face at the royal estate at Pisac, for example, is pockmarked with looted tombs. The relatively few burials recovered intact from imperial sites in the heartland, such as those excavated by Eaton (1916) at Machu Picchu, tend to contain the remains of service or institutional personnel, not the aristocracy. The evidence from those burials and the few cemeteries at provincial sites that have yielded much material indicate that individuals were buried with goods appropriate to their ethnic group and duties to the state.

Morris (1972) has observed that one of the outstanding features of Inca provincial centers is their apparent lack of a cemetery. He attributed that situation (reasonably in my view) to the fact that even the ethnic Incas considered their presence there to be temporary. Andean peoples considered their proper burial place to be their ancestral kin's homeland, so that many individuals may have been transported home for proper treatment after death. As a result, many of the burials with Inca material culture that have been recovered intact in the provinces come from ceremonial contexts, such as the high elevation shrines described in chapter 7. At the oracular coastal site of Pachacamac, the Incas sacrificed and buried about a score of young women at the entrance to the Sun temple and in the temple itself; some of their burial goods suggest that they may have been from coastal societies (Cornejo 2000). Similarly, about a century ago, Juan de Ambrosetti excavated 202 burials at the site of Puerta de La Paya, Argentina, where he recovered the most spectacular array of Inca grave lots yet found in northwestern Argentina. The goods that were recovered include hundreds of Inca-style ceramics, bead strings, and 35 metal objects. Most of the metal was tin bronze in such forms as axes, awls, tweezers, and *tumis* (crescent knives); only one silver and two gold objects were included in the inventory. More interesting were the thousand-plus spindle whorls and other tools for carding wool, spinning, and weaving, found in the tombs of young women. These burials almost certainly contained the remains of *aqllakuna* set to work by the Inca (Ambrosetti 1902, 1907–8; Calderari 1991; González 1979; González and Díaz 1992).

In the provinces, Inca-era mortuary practices varied widely in the degree to which they modified traditional practices to incorporate Inca elements. Among the Lupaqa of Lake Titicaca, the lords adopted rectangular floor plans and the cut-stone ashlar masonry characteristic of the finest Inca architecture into their above-ground crypts. The goods interred with these favored lords included a significant proportion of fine Inca polychrome vessels (Hyslop 1990:247–9). In Peru's Upper Mantaro Valley, where the local lords were also highly esteemed, tombs of the elite included cooking, serving, and storage vessels in the Inca style, as well as a variety of metal goods, such as tumi knives, also in the imperial style (Owen and Norconk 1987). Nonetheless, the majority of the tombs contained objects primarily in the local style.

Gender and Kin Relations

Male and female roles were inseparable complements in Inca life (see Silverblatt 1987 for an extensive discussion). We saw earlier that age-grades paralleled one another and that rites were celebrated for each sex at various stages in the life cycle. In some Andean kinship systems, descent was reckoned through both male and female lines (ambilineality), so that men were thought to be descended from their fathers and women from their mothers. Among the Inca royalty, the female line was especially important, because sitting emperors were most closely identified with their mother's kin group and drew their wives from the same kindred. In contrast, the non-royal *ayllu* of the Incas proper seem to have been patrilineal rather than ambilineal, and most other highland peoples also reckoned descent through the male line (Rowe 1946:253–6; cf. Zuidema 1964, 1977b; Rostworowski 1999:19).

Various kinds of labor were envisioned as efforts shared mutually by men and women. In agriculture, men broke the soil and women planted the seeds, while mining teams recorded in Colonial documents sometimes contained equal numbers of men and women (chapter 11). Certain other tasks were apportioned to each sex. In the mountains, women made beer, collected firewood, and did most of the spinning and weaving, while men hunted and were responsible for military duty, often accompanied by their wives. In some tasks, such as pottery manufacture and metallurgy, both sexes seem to have been involved. Control over the products of labor was not necessarily equally divided, however. For example, women controlled the household larder, while the men controlled the distribution of most status and politically related goods.

The balance between male and female was enshrined symbolically in many ways. As we saw in chapter 3, the origin myths told of four pairs of ancestral sisters and brothers who emerged from the origin place at Pacariqtambo. The Creator God Wiraqocha was conceived as having both male and female aspects, while the two most powerful celestial beings, the Sun and the Moon, were married. Two of the most powerful terrestrial deities were females: *Pachamama* ("Earth Mother") and *Mamacocha*, or "Mother of the Lakes (and Sea)," while the earthquake deity (*Pachacamac*) and weather deity (*Inti Illapa*) were male. The various deities' human servants included both male and female orders. Silverblatt (1987) suggests that females were generally associated with symbols of fertility, although the male spirits of the mountains (*apu* or *wamani*) were also intimately associated with fertility as the owners of the flocks and the source of the rain.

Despite the many parallels between men and women, their relations were not entirely equal. Public roles, such as access to political office and power and the disbursement of natural resources that arose from those positions, were generally reserved for men. Among the Incas proper, there is no evidence for a queen as ruler and the presence of a woman as the paramount leader in other societies was rare enough to warrant special mention (Rostworowski 1999:73–6). Even so, the Queen Mother and the Queen were enormously powerful figures, immediately below the sitting ruler in authority (chapters 5, 6).

The terms that individuals used to refer to one another depended on the sex of the speaker and that of the person to whom he or she was referring, as well as on their generational relationship. Broadly speaking, Inca kin terminology was ego-centered, meaning that kin terms depended on the speaker. In some contexts, however, the terms were defined in relationship to an important personage. For example, the status of royal Inca kin groups was defined by their kin relationship to the sitting ruler. Within families, a father used different terms for children of different sexes (son: *churi*; daughter: *ususi*), but the mother used only one term (*wawa*) for all children. Both sexes called their father *yaya* and their mother *mama*. Brothers called each other by a reciprocal term (*wawqi*) and their sisters by another word (*pana*), just as sisters called each other by a reciprocal term (*ñaña*) and their brothers by another (*tura*). Those and other terms were extended out to other relatives in different ways. First cousins, for example, were called "brother" and "sister," while father's brother was called "brother" and father's sister was called "aunt." By the time that a young man and woman had reached three or four generations of separation (i.e., they shared a great- or great-great-grandfather), they were thought to be distantly enough related that they could marry (Rowe 1946:249–51; Zuidema 1964, 1977b; Lounsbury 1986).

For the Incas, their kin terms were not simply a way of describing social bonds, but provided a conceptual vocabulary for all kinds of relations. As we have seen in other contexts, for example, Inca rulers kept statues as their alter egos. Called *wawqi* ("brother"), the statues could stand in for the ruler in ceremonies and accompanied them into death. Similarly, celestial beings and features of the landscape were envisioned as ancestors, while the deities themselves were kin to one another. Today, Quechua speakers carry out their arithmetic and weaving designs in kin-based terminology, which is probably a legacy of prehispanic times (Urton 1997). Kinship, gender balance, and hierarchy thus permeated Inca relations with all of humanity and nature.

Making a Living

In the Highlands

FARMING

In Inca times, highland peoples followed land use practices much like those used by today's Andean peasants (chapter 2). A family had the right to farmlands and pastures because one of its adults was an *ayllu* member by birth. The amount and kinds of land they had depended on the family's status and size and on how productive the lands were. Garcilaso (1966:245) wrote that each newly married couple received a *tupu* of maize land, which was the area they needed to feed themselves for a year. He equated that to 1.5 times the Spanish *fanega*, which was a little more than half a hectare (1.59 acre/ha).[2] As convenient as that conversion sounds, it was probably too simple, since the size of a *tupu* varied according to local ecology, especially the length of a fallowing cycle. Andean farmers often resisted describing their holdings in European measures, because the Spaniards tried to fix areas that should have remained flexible in the native view of things. According to one Cuzqueñan farmer, for example, warm potato lands could be sown only one year in five and the coldest only one in ten. As a result, a farmer needed twice the area in a cold-lands *tupu* than in the warm lands, to allow him to rotate among fallow and cultivated plots without degrading the soil (Murra 1980a:280–1).

Garcilaso (1966:245–6) went on to say that a married couple received another *tupu* when a son was born, but only half a *tupu* came with a new daughter. When the children married and formed new households, their natal family's allotment would be reduced and the land reverted to the *ayllu*'s communal holdings. When the last member of a family generation died, the rights to the resources also went back to the *ayllu*, so that the lord could distribute them as needed. Although the Incas themselves apparently passed most rights from father to son, inheritance varied widely among Andean peoples. Among some societies, for example, a husband brought use rights from his father's *ayllu* into the marriage, and the wife brought rights from her mother's kin group (bilateral inheritance; see Murra 1980a).

Early colonial inspections suggest that higher-status households held more lands in a wider range of zones than did most common folk (Tomka 1987). The elites' right to more than one wife also meant that lords could have more children, which in turn reinforced their prestige, and household labor force. Before the time of the Inca, the highland lords were entitled to pastoral, agricultural, and household service. In return, they were supposed to provide authority in war and peace, ceremonial leadership, and wise judgment in settling community disputes. The lords confirmed or modified land use rights for each household annually and assigned rights to newly formed families. When we take the variations described for different regions into account, Garcilaso's formula is too neat, but he was still on the mark about the core principles of peasant life – use rights were based on kinship, status, and family size.

Farmers' tools were simple – principally a foot plow, a hoe, and a clod breaker. Men wielded the plow, called a *chakitaqlla*. It was made of a pole about 2 m long with a pointed end of wood or bronze, a handle or curvature at the top, and a foot rest lashed near the bottom (Rowe 1946:211). The farmer drove the point into the ground using both arms and a foot, and then levered up to break the soil. Both the hoes and clod breakers were typically made of river cobbles. The hoes were hafted like adzes while the clod breakers were attached to the end of long poles. When a hoe became blunted, it could be resharpened simply by knocking off a few flakes with a hammerstone after which it could be reused until it was exhausted. In Peru's central highlands, some farmlands are still littered with thousands of fragments of the hoes and clod breakers (Russell 1988).

Farming was a social activity that was celebrated with rituals, sacrifices, and songs (Garcilaso 1966:244; Cobo 1979:213–14). Typically, a team of seven or eight men from a family or neighborhood group would work in a line to prepare the fields. Each man used a plow to break the soil and the women followed in another row, breaking the clods and planting the seeds. By teaming up, the work group could share the labor and lighten their burdens. While they worked, they sang and chanted, striking the earth in unison. Cobo recalled being able to hear their singing from a distance off, and Garcilaso professed that the Spanish priests found the songs so pleasant that they were incorporated into church services. During the growing season, the hoes were used to weed the plants as needed. Harvesting inspired the same kinds of labor-sharing as planting did. Once the harvest was in, it was a time of public celebration, called the *Aymoray* (Rowe 1946:213–16). Such gender-based teamwork remains a common sight in the highlands where traditional farming implements are used. Among modern farmers, it is not unusual for them to go for days with little sleep when it is time to get the harvest in ahead of the frosts.

HERDING

Many chroniclers accepted the Incas' broad claim that they owned all of the flocks in the empire, but there is little doubt that the empire's subjects had herds of their own (Murra 1975:117–44). The chroniclers refer to herds owned by both individuals and the community, and there were probably several kinds of ownership practices among Andean peoples. It seems especially likely that the lords retained their rights to personal herds under the Incas. Most clothing came from the herds' wool, but camelid meat was not part of the normal daily fare, despite the abundance of the animals. It was reserved instead for local elites and for special occasions (Garcilaso 1966:202). Tending the herds was primarily the task of the adolescents and children of the community. Guaman Poma wrote that boys up to about 20 years of age and girls up to about 18 saw to their care, a view affirmed by other chroniclers (Guaman Poma 1980:180–1, 200–1; Cobo 1979:246). Adults were certainly involved in their husbandry, especially during birthing and shearing, but the day-to-day rounds were in the hands of the young.

EXCHANGE OF LABOR AND GOODS

Local autonomy was the ideal, but Andean households depended on each other for a host of activities. And, since not all communities could produce everything they needed, exchange networks linked people living in complementary ecozones. Native witnesses in the Huánuco region, for example, said that people who had lands in only a few zones would produce extra coca, *ch'arki* (jerked, or freeze-dried meat: chapter 2), or other local specialties, which could be exchanged with trade partners elsewhere (Ortiz de Zúñiga 1967:31, 63, 73, 179, 219, 329).

Altiplano peoples traded llamas, *ch'arki*, and wool for lowland products, including cotton, pepper, and coca (Burchard 1974). In one of the more intriguing practices, some special resources such as salt and coca were obtained from colonies who lived several days' walk from their home communities, in what is called an archipelago settlement pattern. In some cases, the colonies housed members of several ethnic groups, who kept up their affiliation with their homelands (Murra 1972; Masuda et al. 1985). Families also arranged labor exchanges with real or fictive kin or through links to people of different social statuses. Close relatives often pooled their labor efforts for farming, herding, rituals, or house construction, working on each household's tasks as needed. This kind of balanced exchange, known as *ayni*, is still a common practice. In the asymmetric relationship called *minka*, a family head would work for his in-laws or a low-status household would work for a higher-status family; their labors were repaid with a share of the produce (Alberti and Mayer 1974).

A particularly important kind of mutual reliance came into play when workers were away, for instance when they were called up for military duty for the Inca. At those times, their fields were tended by their neighbors and the products were stored, so that when the soldiers came home, they found their produce nicely stored away and awaiting them. Similar extensions of neighborly support were extended to community members who could not fend for themselves, such as the aged and infirm without family. A household that could call on the labor of a full nuclear or extended family could work a wider range of lands than one formed of old, single, or orphaned individuals. The smaller households had to rely on social relations to get what they needed, or they would have to do without. Cobo commented approvingly that the Lake Titicaca villages that kept up the mutual support practices a century after the Inca collapse were especially well-off and organized.

Relations between local lords and their subjects also provided ways for households to get goods that would otherwise be hard to obtain. Beyond his political, military, and ritual leadership, a good lord was supposed to be a generous host. To the degree that he could, he would dispense cloth, chicha, or other valued materials through ritualized generosity. He might also distribute products such as coca and peppers which could be procured only from great distances, sometimes from the colonies mentioned above. Some of the most noteworthy colonies of the sixteenth century exploited the guano islands off the south coast of Peru. The products were usually gathered or produced by people who worked directly for the lords, who then distributed them along social or political lines. It needs to be stressed that this largess did not substitute for subsistence production or a market system. Instead, it bonded groups, reinforced unequal statuses, and provided commoners with special products.

DOMESTIC ACTIVITIES

Household life revolved around family care, cooking, and weaving. Within the household, the woman was the dominant figure. Each household produced most of its own food and daily goods, although more extended kin often worked together and shared in the products. A typical complete household included a male head of family (*hatun runa*), his wife, children, and unmarried or widowed adult kin. It was normally part of the larger kin group called the *ayllu*, which held its farmlands, pastures, and other resources in common. Like their modern descendants, prehistoric *ayllu*s sought access to several ecozones, for example, maize, potato, and herding zones in the highlands, and coca lands lower down. This allowed most families to be self-reliant for their daily needs.

Women and girls spent a great deal of time collecting firewood or llama dung to be used for cooking. The foods that they made were predominantly vegetarian. Cobo wrote that maize was toasted or cooked in small cakes; popcorn was thought to be a delicacy. Potato dishes were reconstituted from freeze-dried *chuño* or were made with fresh dried potatoes (Cobo 1979:27–8, 1990:198–9; see Rowe 1946:220–1). Grains such as quinoa and cañihua were also staples of the highland diet, along with other tubers, such as oca, mashua, and maca. Many of the dishes were flavored with herbs and chili peppers obtained from distant plots or through exchange. Stews made with fish were popular, but meat was reserved for special occasions and for the elites, although *ch'arki* (freeze-dried meat) was a staple on the road. The maize and other foods were ground with rocker mortars or mortar and pestles. Fermented beverages, broadly called chicha, were so much part of the cuisine that Cobo said that being forced to drink water was a form of punishment. Families typically ate twice a day, once at about 8 or 9 in the morning and again an hour or two before sunset (ibid.). When a commoner family ate, the dishes were placed on the floor, but a lord would eat off a cloth spread on the ground. The husband and wife sat back to back and she served the food and drink as he requested.

Archaeological evidence from 29 late prehistoric households in the Upper Mantaro Valley, Peru, paints a similar picture (D'Altroy et al. 2001; see below). All households, whether elite or commoner, shared a basic set of tools: cooking, storage, and serving pottery, grinding stones, weaving tools, and casual flaked stone tools for cutting and scraping. Just before the Inca conquest, most of the Xauxa populace lived in high-elevation settlements that were protected by defensive walls. Christine Hastorf (1990) has been able to show that plant remains recovered from their residences closely matched a set of crops that could be grown nearby, mostly tubers and quinoa. Where maize was found, it was concentrated in the elite houses. Similarly, Elsie Sandefur (1988) has shown that the people who ate in elite households – whether the residents or their guests – got finer cuts of camelid meat. Under Inca rule, many people moved downslope into areas better suited to maize farming, which was reflected in household botanical remains. Not everybody gained equally, however. Analysis of human bone collagen shows that adult males benefited more than anyone else because, Hastorf suggests, the Incas gave them maize beer as part of their institutionalized generosity (Hastorf and DeNiro 1985). The status differences in meat consumption disappeared under the Incas, but we do not know if the diets were really equalized or if the elites were eating meat elsewhere, such as at the nearby provincial center. In any event, the elites still managed to display their rank through food, for they roasted much of their meat, while the commoners ate theirs in less prestigious stews.

HOUSEHOLD CRAFTS

Despite the scale of state production (chapter 12), most goods and tools produced under Inca rule were made, used, and discarded in village economies in which the Inca had no interest. The written record took little notice of those activities, because they were marginal to Inca or Spanish concerns. With respect to the bigger picture of Andean life, however, household remains are a reflection of most people's daily affairs. The discrepancy between a vision of the Inca state involved in all aspects of domestic life and household residues could hardly be more conspicuous. The typical Andean household had no access to the cultural equivalent of Fabergé eggs, Wedgwood china, Chinese silks, or sterling silver. Instead, householders made their own homespun clothes and made or traded for the whole range of tools and utilitarian goods that they needed for daily life. Cobo said that a person owned just one set of clothes, which he or she never changed or washed; the peasants' state of constant filth offended his sensibilities. Even where we know that the local population was organized to perform state duties, goods of state manufacture are rare. The difficulties of identifying Inca-era occupations at local settlements is a key reason that we still do not have as fine an understanding of subject life under the empire as we would like.

This situation does not mean that daily life among Andean peasants did not change under Inca rule, but that the shifts were more subtle and less pervasive than imperial propaganda might lead us to expect. For a case study, we return to the Upper Mantaro. To get most of their craft goods, peasants in the Mantaro relied on a mix of their own manufactures and regional exchange. In the classic vision of an Andean woman, whether sitting at home, nursing a baby, or walking, she was invariably spinning wool to make cloth. Archaeologically, the ubiquity of spinning and weaving is confirmed by the ceramic spindle whorls found in all households and by other bone tools and bronze needles (Costin 1993).

It is less widely appreciated that families relied on chipped stone tools right through the Inca era, for cutting, chopping, drilling, and scraping. Bronze tools complemented lithics, but did not replace them entirely. All households seem to have made casual stone tools for cutting and scraping, and some villages also made certain tools for exchange with neighboring settlements. Glenn Russell (1988) has shown, for example, that both before and during Inca rule, the Mantaro town nearest the main chert quarry made special blade tools that were probably used for the grain harvest. The scale of production was prodigious, as more than a million tool blanks were roughed out before being taken home for finishing work during the centuries that the quarry was mined. However, almost none of those tools found their way to Hatun Xauxa, the Inca center. In fact, stone cutting and scraping tools are uncommon at Inca installations throughout the empire. The reasons for this are unclear, but it may be that the crafts pursued at state centers did not require them or that lithics were considered low status and were replaced by objects made of bronze. Many Mantaro households also contain vitrified sherds (wasters), which are evidence of the manufacture of pottery. As with the chert blades, large-scale potting was focused in single towns before and under the Incas. In contrast, the valley's finest pottery style was a special product made to the south that was replaced by Inca polychromes under Cuzco's dominion (Costin 1986, 2001).

The Mantaro evidence shows that craft production before Inca rule, where specialized, was organized along community lines. With Inca rule, the state intervened only in crafts that were part of the political economy, that is, in metals, prestige ceramics, and textiles. They seem to have utterly ignored the production of stone tools, which were essential to agriculture. None of the lists of labor assignments includes lithic tool production, and the farm workers seem to have carried their own tools to state fields. Overall, the pattern suggests that some village specialization was treated as part of local self-sufficiency, which the Incas were more than content to leave alone.

On the Coast

The social and economic relations of coastal communities were intimately linked, just as they were in the highlands. The decapitation of the Chimu empire along the north coast did not completely dismantle the strict social hierarchy, however. Some coastal lords owned entire valleys and their subjects had access to lands only through their relationship with the lord, not through the communal land holdings that prevailed in the mountains (Rostworowski 1999:152). There were differences in other rights, too. For example, coastal farmers measured both field size and standing crops by the number of feeder canals that watered them and not by the flexible highland measure called *tupu*. People of higher social status had preferred access to the finer lands, especially those toward the canal intakes, which could yield more than one crop per year (Netherly 1978:288, 1984:239).

In sharp contrast to the mountains, entire communities could specialize as potters, weavers, farmers, fishers, traders, and sandal-makers. Rather than being self-sufficient, they would exchange their products for those gathered, grown, or made by other communities. One of the other interesting distinctions lay in the production of maize beer. On the coast, men made chicha for trade or to present to their lords, while women made the beer in the highlands for communal or institutional uses. Rostworowski shows that kin groups often gained access to diverse resources by organizing their holdings lengthwise within valleys. Access to more distant resources could also be enhanced as lords up and down river exchanged the rights to cultivate maize and coca fields in one another's territories (Rostworowski 1977:240–1, 1990).

Another important difference lay in the long-time presence of special-purpose money and more sophisticated weights and measures than those found in the central Andean highlands. It is not clear how widely the currencies were used in prehistory. There is no evidence, for example, that land or labor could be purchased until the Colonial era (Hosler et al. 1990; Salomon 1986, 1987; Netherly 1978). The Incas themselves did not adopt the currencies for the state economy, although they used large amounts of the shell and gold for political and ceremonial ends. Instead, they either left things alone or manipulated the situation politically to give favored groups an advantage. Coastal life thus differed in important ways from that of the adjacent highlands. Overall, however, the ideas of community focus and collective resource management, along with mutual commitments between lords and subjects, typified the coast as much as they did the highlands.

chapter nine

Militarism

Diplomacy, reward, and enculturation were essential ingredients in the Incas' formula for creating Tawantinsuyu, but warfare still lay at the heart of the process both symbolically and practically. Triumphant campaigns put untold resources at Cuzco's disposal, showered glory on the elites, and gave common folk a rare chance to better their station in life. Although the Incas negotiated dominion over many societies while shedding little blood, their armies met considerable opposition and a few especially redoubtable societies fiercely resisted Inca rule for many years. Effective Inca military strategy thus required mobilizing thousands of military and auxiliary personnel for campaigns that could last months or even decades. To meet their military goals, the Incas created a network of internal garrisons, frontier forts, and a remarkable logistical system of roads, support facilities, and depots. Those military activities collectively placed enormous, though sporadic, demands on the human and natural resources of the Andes throughout Inca rule.

The earliest chroniclers wrote extensively on military affairs largely because they were fortune-seeking soldiers themselves. Despite the Spaniards' initial successes, the course of events rapidly compelled their respect for the Incas' military prowess. In 1536, besieged Spanish forces in Cuzco and Ciudad de Los Reyes (Lima) narrowly escaped annihilation and several expeditions were wiped out in the mountainous terrain. Under the circumstances, it is small wonder that Inca militarism gained a conspicuous place in early accounts. Some modern authors nevertheless suggest that the conquistadores' martial bent and the Incas' efforts to glorify their history have biased our views toward militarism as the power that forged Tawantinsuyu. They point out that the Incas formed many ties through ceremonial exchanges and that the same stories of conquest and rebellion tended to be repeated from one chronicle to the next (e.g., Pease 1982; Rowe 1982; Morris 1982, 1998; Rostworowski 1999:65–86). Their persuasive skills notwithstanding, the Incas' power and their own self-image hinged on their military capacities. The recitals of accomplishments by past sovereigns highlighted their conquests, and the names of forts captured in military campaigns were memorialized in *khipu* accounts. After his death, an emperor's funerary rites celebrated his life through pilgrimages to the sites of his great victories, while rulers without military conquests to boast of were not honored as were the more vital leaders. Gose's (1996a:4) characterization of Inca rulers is apt: "(A)n Andean king began his career as a living warrior and matured into a dead deity."

In this chapter, we will explore how Inca militarism worked. At the outset, it should be pointed out that the Incas owed much of their success to strategy and logistics, not to tactics, training, or technology. It was in their preparatory organization that the Inca military excelled, for their battlefield command and conduct drew from traditional methods applied on a grander scale. Even in 1532, the army consisted mostly of modular units of conscripts, using their own weapons and led by their own lords, waging war as labor duty to the state. That method of recruitment, along with linguistic barriers and the challenges of transportation, limited the Incas' tactical options, which they partially addressed by creating a support system and professionalizing the army over time. Even so, the dynastic war between Waskhar and Atawallpa was fought largely by farmers and herders pressed into duty.

Military Strategy

We are on firmer ground in discussing the Inca military strategy of the early sixteenth century than for earlier eras, but clues about pre-imperial warfare can be found in the royal sagas and archaeology. As described earlier (chapters 2, 3), the settlements of the Late Intermediate Period (LIP) were situated on high peaks throughout much of the Andean highlands, suggesting that localized conflict was endemic. To judge from the narratives, early Inca war was indistinguishable from that of other highland contemporaries. The tales portray the local leaders as warlords, called *zinch'i*, who mobilized their kinsmen and communities for booty and glory. Pillaging the neighbors' crops, wealth, and women was said to have been the main goal of war, along with the social stature that martial glory brought. The offensive and defensive elements of early Inca militarism were mutually reinforcing, because successful raids could provoke retaliation or dissuade attacks.

When the Incas expanded out of the Cuzco region, they faced great obstacles, for they were neither the most populous, the most powerful, nor the richest people of the central Andes. The Qolla and Lupaqa of the Lake Titicaca basin probably surpassed them in most ways and the coastal Chimu polity was vastly larger, wealthier, and more complex. The military situation dictated that the Incas economize in their use of force, because they lacked the resources to enforce hands-on control over all the societies that they dominated. The early imperial-era successes probably owed much to alliances, conscription of defeated foes, and confrontation of target societies with overwhelming force (e.g., Bram 1941; Rawls 1979; Espinoza Soriano 1980; Rostworowski 1999). The shift from looting to annexation was probably a decisive change in policy. Most chroniclers ascribed the policy to Wiraqocha Inka and Pachakuti, although some said that Inca lords had begun to attach lands three or four generations earlier (see chapter 4). The practical methods of annexing new subjects coupled diplomacy and coercion. Customarily, an army that was mobilized in the agricultural off-season approached a targeted *señorío* with overwhelming force. Messengers sent by the Inca commander would offer favorable terms of surrender: compliant subject elites received gifts and could expect to retain or enhance their status, while communities were allowed to keep many of their resources (e.g., Cieza 1967:163–4; Toledo 1940a:19–20). Polo (1917:118) astutely observed that a key to early success lay in the inability of Andean *señoríos* to coordinate resistance to Inca advances. In most confrontations, the Incas could marshal armies capable of overpowering whatever force the opponents could muster. The newly subject populace would have to pledge loyalty to the *Sapa Inca*, agree to supply labor service, and pay homage to the Sun.

Tawantinsuyu's rapid expansion may have thus owed as much to perceptions of Inca power as it did to the reality. The general principle was to be generous with those who capitulated, and to punish those who resisted harshly. Many stories describe ethnic groups succumbing in the face of Cuzco's forces, if not meekly, at least without pitched battle (Rostworowski 1999:69–72). For example, several valleys along Peru's southern coast from Chincha to Moquegua were also said to have been absorbed through diplomatic ventures, although the sources disagreed over the particulars. Similarly, an army of 30,000 soldiers reportedly took much of the agriculturally rich Upper Mantaro Valley of central Peru and its 200,000 residents without opposition. Only at the Xauxa stronghold of Siquillapucara – probably the archaeological site called Tunanmarca – did the residents resist fiercely. There the Incas were said to have won a desperate battle, after which they deported their adversaries en masse (Cieza 1967:163–4; Toledo 1940a:19–20; Espinoza Soriano 1972:38; Rowe 1985b:224). The archaeological data fit the notion of a forced abandonment of the area, as Inca remains are lacking in Tunanmarca and several nearby LIP towns, even though well over a hundred other sites with Inca ceramics lie within half a day's walk (Earle et al. 1987; D'Altroy 1992:186–95). The success of the Incas' diplomacy elsewhere similarly hinged on their ability and willingness to crush resistance. In part to deter rebellions and perhaps to make examples, they massacred some especially obdurate foes, such as the Guarco of coastal Cañete and the Cayambe of Ecuador (chapter 4).

As the empire matured, the Incas moved from expansion to more stable dominion. Governance shifted from a low intensity, low control approach in most areas toward a high intensity, high control strategy, especially in the central and northern highlands (Rawls 1979; D'Altroy 1992:71–83). Broadly speaking, the goals of military policy shifted from acquisition toward pacification and securing frontier areas. These goals were met in part through founding garrisons, resettling restive societies, and fortifying frontier hot spots. The need to sustain large forces at great distances from home for extended campaigns also favored development of a network of storage depots along the roads (see *Logistics*, below). Even so, incidents of resistance, alliance, submission, and rebellion combined with the nature of existing societies and geography to make distinct policies appropriate in different times and places. Shifts in Inca military policy are thus better understood as changes of emphasis in regional theaters than as a sequence whose phases occurred concurrently throughout the empire (Dillehay and Netherly 1988).

The overall system toward the edges of imperial control can best be characterized as a strategy of defense-in-depth (Rawls 1979:146). This approach relies on self-contained strongholds and mobile forces deployed between or behind them. Forts formed hard points in a defensive perimeter that was intended to impede passage into the territory, if not stop it altogether. Defense-in-depth offers more security for the provinces than a strategy that relies on threat and retribution, but it reduces flexibility in the disposition of resources and requires an investment in fortifications and supply facilities (Luttwak 1976). If we can accept the narratives, elements of this strategy may have been introduced fairly early in the imperial era. Even though frontier problems were a concern, the principal threats to the stability of the state after the major conquests were insurrections and dynastic wars of succession (Murra 1986). The Lake Titicaca ethnic groups and the Chachapoyas were reportedly prone to reasserting their independence at every opportunity. The persistence of such rebellions led the Incas to install loyal colonists, who provided control over refractory subjects. The move toward a more professional force of militarily specialized ethnic groups also helped meet the need for a dependable army (see *Military Specialists*, below).

The provincial centers between Cuzco and Quito aided military activity by facilitating movement of goods, people, and messages between regions. The centers often lay at the intersection of natural conduits of travel, adjacent to open valleys or plains where armies could be conveniently bivouacked. Because many provinces were never truly secure, Hyslop (pers. comm. 1990) has suggested that major centers were situated partially as a tactic to reduce the threat of uprisings and to support reprisals when they did occur. As the support system was developed, the state's ability to mobilize large armies was markedly improved. Even so, armies could not be moved simply at the will of the commanders, and the resources of the immediate vicinity of the conflicts were occasionally exhausted even in well-planned campaigns. The development of roads, storehouses, and waystations was therefore fundamental to Inca military strategy.

Fortifications and Garrisons

Fortified strongholds are not abundant in most of Tawantinsuyu. Forts were built near hostile frontiers, but the Inca realm did not have a fixed border in the sense that modern nation-states do. Instead, the Incas maintained flexible relationships with societies beyond their control, leaving the frontiers permeable or hardening them as the situation warranted. The limits of effective Inca rule often lay at retrenched positions, to which the troops had withdrawn after exploratory ventures. In fact, Morris (1988) has pointed out that most areas lay at or near a frontier at some point and that incorporation was an irregular process, so that some front-line forts eventually lay 1,000 km or more behind the empire's limits. The restricted use of forts makes sense in terms of the largely offensive character of Inca warfare. The Incas did not have to defend a home territory against invasions by major powers, as did many Old World empires. Instead, they usually carried the battle to the enemy, so that military construction was often attuned to logistics. Forts were used as forward bases of operations for campaigns, field camps in hostile territory, front-line redoubts used to support frontier advances, hard-point defenses, perimeter guard posts, and occasional internal garrisons. That is a varied list, to be sure, but strongholds were more important in the military arsenal of the Incas' targets than for Cuzco's strategy.

Few truly fortified Inca sites are known for the heartland, though many sites north and east of Cuzco lie in strategically and topographically defensible positions. Two important sites that played military roles in the early colonial wars – Saqsawaman and Ollantaytambo – may have been only partly designed as fortified redoubts, if at all, but they served that purpose well enough when the need arose. Scholarly opinion is split about the military functions of the estates and other settlements lining the Urubamba Valley for 200 km below Cuzco. Some writers note that they could have served to limit traffic into the heartland, even if they were not specifically designed as fortifications (Rawls 1979). It has sometimes been proposed that the walls that enclosed the spectacularly situated Machu Picchu were intended for defense, but MacLean (1986:34–40, 82–6) argues that they are better understood as barriers protecting sacred or private spaces or as terrace support walls needed because of the precipitous terrain. Even without any explicitly military architecture, however, the Urubamba sites would have placed the stamp of Inca dominion on the eastern slopes.

Despite the rarity of strongholds away from the frontier in highland Peru, garrisons at major centers were important even near the heartland. Their lack of defensive architecture suggests more that the Incas did not expect the centers to come under military threat than that they had no military functions. The structures most appropriate to military uses are *kallanka*, large rectangular buildings that sometimes served as barracks. Vilcaswaman was said to house 30,000 soldiers, but archaeological studies have found no fortifications there (González Carré et al. 1981). No Inca fort is known in the Upper Mantaro Valley either, even though a large army was stationed at Hatun Xauxa in 1532–3 (see below). Similarly, there are no fortifications at Huánuco Pampa or Pumpu, while the Spaniards found Atawallpa's army in Cajamarca quartered in an orderly array of tents, but mentioned no fortifications.

In their earliest campaigns, the Incas may have made use of existing facilities, such as Cuismancu's fort at Cajamarca, Peru, or the series of redoubts built by the altiplano societies alongside Lake Titicaca. Nonetheless, documents and archaeology both suggest that the permanent forts were mostly a late phenomenon. The perceptive Polo (1916:98–9) provided a brief list of the regions where the Incas conducted warfare that corresponds neatly to both the locations of known forts and Wayna Qhapaq's campaigns. Excepting a few prominent sites in Peru, such as Saqsawaman above Cuzco and Inkawasi in the coastal Cañete Valley, the forts cluster mostly in northern Ecuador and along the perimeter of Kollasuyu, in Bolivia, Argentina, and Chile (Hyslop 1990:146–90) (figure 9.1).

An especially high concentration of Inca forts lay near Quito. In total, 37 forts identified archaeologically have been attributed to the Incas' Ecuadorian occupation. Plaza Schuller (1976, 1980) suggests that many were originally built by the indigenous societies, but were then taken over by the Incas to sustain their advances farther north. The complex of 14 fortified hilltops at Pambamarca, 32 km northeast of Quito, was by far the most extensive array of strongholds concentrated in one region (plate 9.1; Hyslop 1990:165–73). The site was probably the historical

Figure 9.1   The distribution of known Inca fortified settlements

settlement of El Quinche, where the Incas installed colonists from half a dozen Peruvian and Ecuadorian societies (Salomon 1986:163; see Espinoza Soriano 1975).

The concentration of fortified sites in the southern Andes, in contrast, reflects an intense Inca concern for military security. Among the most important fortified sites east of the altiplano were Incallacta, Pocona, Batanes, and Incahuasi. Incallacta was unusual in that it seems to have

Plate 9.1 View of Unit 12 at Pambamarca, showing four concentric walls and a central platform; photo by John Hyslop, courtesy Division of Anthropology, American Museum of Natural History

been both a regional administrative center and a fortified stronghold. In northwest Argentina, the easternmost array of forts also lies along or just below the crest of the mountains, beyond which roads, waystations, and farms extended for well over 100 km (Raffino 1993:213–34). Several major sites in Kollasuyu's intermontane valleys were also fortified, among them the stronghold at Cortaderas, which was transformed into an administrative complex as their hold on the valley became more secure (Hyslop 1984:175–7; D'Altroy et al. 2000; Acuto 1994). Pucará de Andalgalá and Pucará de las Pavas are impressive Inca citadels in the Bolsón de Andalgalá, and numerous other forts were also built or coopted. The Chilean forts at Cerro del Inga, Chena, and Angostura stand out as local sites at the southern margins of the empire that were taken over by the state (Stehberg 1976; Planella et al. 1991). Many of the strongholds formed a line of defense well inside the eastern margin of the empire; beyond them the Incas maintained economic or cultural relations for distances of several hundred kilometers. Until we have fine-tuned the chronology better, it will be hard to assess if the positioning of those sites represented an early stage of the Inca occupation, beyond which economic activities were extended, or if the intent was to provide a cordon of hard points behind the active frontier.

Most frontier fortresses were neither large enough nor manned with personnel adequate to preclude all potential incursions by outside forces. Instead, they seem to have been designed to deter raids or cut them off from behind. Forts were typically positioned to control traffic through key natural points of transit, especially mountain passes. Pambamarca (Ecuador), Incallacta (Bolivia), Cortaderas and Pucará de Andalgalá (Argentina), and Cerro del Inga (Chile) were all situated in such locations. In some cases, the forts may have been no more than temporary facilities, such as the encampments that Wayna Qhapaq's armies built in their descent into the woodlands of northern Peru and Ecuador (Cieza 1967:187). The site of Inkawasi, in the coastal Cañete Valley, was the most elaborate temporary facility erected expressly for military purposes (Hyslop 1985). According to Cieza, it was built when entreaties and assaults failed to take the local stronghold at Ungará. A planned settlement containing about 800 structures, Inkawasi was one of several installations christened a "New Cuzco." The site housed a small garrison during the summer, when the highland armies suffered from the heat and withdrew to the mountains. When campaigns were conducted in the cooler months of several successive winters, the site was the regional base of operations. Inkawasi was abandoned when the campaign drew to a successful close, suggesting that forts were not a central part of the Inca strategy for ruling within their relatively secure lands.

Permanent Inca forts were usually not elaborate affairs, though they were well tailored to the kinds of threats that Andean armies could mount. The Incas could expect attacks with projectiles of limited range and power, such as arrows, spears, and sling stones, but did not have to cope with explosives, mounted attacks, or siege machinery, such as battering rams or catapults. Frontal attack by shock troops was the preferred method of taking a stronghold in Andean war, so forts were designed to repel waves of soldiers in close combat. They usually consisted of walled enclosures with broad open areas and spare architecture, set on hilltops or at the crest of steep slopes. Many had several concentric walls, moats, and revetments. The encircling walls were often built with bends and salients to gain multiple shooting angles on assaulting troops (Hyslop 1990:163–90). Behind the walls, the Incas typically erected elongated platforms and cached piles of sling stones. Entry was channeled through doorways that were sometimes offset or laid out in zigzag patterns to foil massed attacks. The largest forts each encompassed no more than about 10 ha, which limited the number of people who could seek refuge, but kept the perimeters relatively short. They were not designed to bivouac large numbers of soldiers for any length of time, and armies on the move typically slept in tents.

Military Organization

Even in 1532, the Inca command structure was not complex by the standards of ancient empires. Much of the command's simplicity arose from the lack of a standing army for most of Tawantinsuyu's history, the drafting of peasants as soldiers, and the difficulties of communication in the polyglot empire. The emperor was the commander in chief and occasional field general. Below him was a hierarchy of officers ranging down to ethnic leaders of the fighting units. The highest officers were usually royal kin, although non-Inca ethnic elites sometimes held high ranks. Choosing relatives may theoretically have ensured common interests between the ruler and his officers, but delegating command of a large army to competent soldiers with a potential royal claim was a chancy business. The more effective a commander was, the more potent a threat he posed, since the military often held the key to settling claims to the throne.

In light of this situation, it is intriguing that the military commanders executed by sitting rulers were those whose power or glory potentially threatened the throne, not those who had failed in their duties. The most celebrated case occurred when Qhapaq Yupanki, Pachakuti's brother, returned to Cuzco after vainly pursuing the deserted Chankas through the central highlands of Peru (chapter 4). Sarmiento suggests that Qhapaq Yupanki was killed nominally because he had failed to keep the Chankas in line and because he exceeded the territorial limit that Pachakuti had set for the expedition. Rowe (1946:206) points out, however, that Pachakuti may have seen his brother's victories as a threat and decided to take preventive action. According to Sarmiento, Pachakuti also ordered the execution of one or two of the soldiers who accompanied his son Thupa Inka Yupanki, at the close of the great northern campaigns. The rationale was that they had kept the young man away from Cuzco for so long, but Sarmiento (1960:252) offered the opinion that the ruler was jealous of their glory and riches. In contrast, failed generals seem to have been relieved of command in disgrace, but not executed. Wanka Awki's string of resounding defeats from Tumipampa to Xauxa, for example, resulted only in his humiliating dismissal.

The king's military role changed in emphasis from battlefield command to strategic planning as Inca warfare shifted from chiefly predation to imperial expansion. Many chroniclers wrote that Pachakuti increasingly delegated military command to his brothers and finally ceded it entirely to Thupa Inka Yupanki, his son. Thupa Inka Yupanki in turn was acclaimed for leading the armies, but the northern campaigns typically ascribed to his leadership occurred before he assumed effective military command and his uncles seem to have kept the heir a safe distance from the battlefield. Such protective action is not to say that heirs apparent were always removed from peril, however. Candidates for the throne accompanied military actions to represent the crown and to learn the dangerous practice of war. Atawallpa's disastrous sortie into the Ecuadorian forests provides a case in point (see chapter 4).

The rulers did go on campaign selectively throughout Tawantinsuyu's reign and even put themselves in the midst of conflict on a number of storied occasions, such as Wayna Qhapaq's miscarried assault on the Caranqui, when he was unseated. Atawallpa's first battle at Tumipampa, when he was captured and his ear damaged, and Waskhar's final defense on the banks of the Apurimac also saw the principals on the battlefield. In those situations, the paramount's role as charismatic leader and perhaps tactician may have been crucial to the success of the ventures. Despite his frequent absence from the battlefield, the king's presence on campaign was important, as leaders accompanied their men into some of the most difficult lands that the Andes have to offer. Even so, Inca monarchs only intermittently got close enough to the action to be in much personal danger. They usually directed operations from a headquarters some distance removed from the battlefield. Campaigns in northern Peru under Thupa Inka Yupanki's titular leadership and in highland Ecuador under Wayna Qhapaq were directed from Cajamarca and Tumipampa, respectively. Expeditions sent into unfamiliar lands were often headed by subordinate officers, for example into Pasto territory in the north, the temperate forests of the Araucanians in the far south, and the eastern lowlands of Bolivia and Argentina. Similarly, except for the first few and the last engagements of the dynastic war, neither Waskhar nor Atawallpa was present at the battleground.

In keeping with the dual organization that pervaded Inca rule, two or four commanders were often appointed to lead a campaign or army. How authority was divided among the commanders is uncertain. If military practice followed social convention, one individual was dominant. The chroniclers used distinctly European terms to describe such individuals, but their expressions may conceivably reflect the broad scope of duties assigned each position. Cabello Valboa (1951:430, 442), for example, described Atawallpa's two commanders in the war against Waskhar as Field General or Field Marshal (Challcochima) and Master of the Camp or General Administrator of the Army (Quizquiz). At least in late campaigns, military units were organized in a decimal structure, which also had civil applications. The units were usually made up of soldiers from particular ethnic groups led by their own lords. The smallest unit contained 10 heads of household (*hatun runa*), under the command of a *chunka kamayuq*. The next order up was 100 soldiers, under a *pachaka kuraka*. One thousand men were commanded by a *waranqa kuraka*, and 10,000 by a *hunu kuraka*, but it is not clear how often that many men were ever fielded at one time from any ethnic group. Each division contained two halves, each with its own leader.

For practical reasons, ethnic elites led their own men on the battle-field. There were scores of distinct languages in the domain and even the main dialects of Quechua were not mutually intelligible. Using Cuzco Quechua as a *lingua franca* among the elites helped matters, but most of the common troops could not be expected to speak it. Linguistic and personal familiarity between commanders and their troops was therefore necessary for effective battlefield conduct. Moreover, group cohesion and competition with other fighting units fostered an *esprit de corps*. The downside of using compartmentalized fighting units and scores of eth-nically distinct low-level officers was a limited flexibility in battlefield command. Almost certainly, there were severe limits on the kinds of tactical control over the troops that come with standardized, profes-sional, training exercises, such as those practiced by the Roman legions. Although maneuvers were planned and the troops were arrayed accord-ing to their weapons, once a battle was engaged, only the simplest changes in plan were possible based on up-to-the-minute information.

Scale of the Armies

Both Inca oral histories and Spanish accounts state that the Incas could field armies in excess of 100,000 at a time, although we should view the high-end estimates skeptically. Regrettably, only a couple of the figures seem to have been taken directly from *khipu* tabulations. In one case, Atawallpa's force at the battle of the Yanamarca Valley was tabulated as 140,000 men, plus servants and porters, whereas the opposing army was estimated to include 130,000 soldiers (Cieza 1987). The other tally involved Challcochima's contingent, which was bivouacked at Hatun Xauxa following Atawallpa's final victory. When the first Spaniards on the road to Cuzco paused there, the army's *khipu kamayuq* counted off 35,000 soldiers for the visitors' benefit (H. Pizarro 1959:89). At the same time, Quizquiz headed a force of 10,000 at Cuzco, having dismissed the other 30,000 under his command (Xérez 1985:121).

For armies seen first-hand by the Spaniards, estimates of many scores of thousands are common, although we need to be cautious about the accuracy of any figure, since the participants on both sides were prone to exaggerate for effect. Cristóbal de Mena (1937:84) reported that there were more than 80,000 effectives at Cajamarca when the Spaniards arrived, while others put the figure at about half that or a little more (see Xérez 1985:92, 108; P. Pizarro 1986:32; Trujillo 1967:202; see Hemming 1970:36). Drawing from interviews fifteen years later, Cieza (1987:128) wrote that Atawallpa's army had totalled 87,000 men: 12,000 in a vanguard, then 5,000 to capture the Spaniards' horses, and 70,000 in the main body. He added that 30,000 servants, plus women, were also present. Such a profusion of porters and camp followers, common in Inca warfare, added to the size and unwieldiness of the imperial forces (see below). Some of the largest Inca armies may have been those under Manqo Inka that set siege to Cuzco in 1536. De Mena gauged that 100,000 soldiers and 80,000 auxiliaries were present. Pedro Pizarro put the figure at 200,000, which is the same figure that Molina cited for the army that Manqo Inka was preparing to mobilize for a renewed summer siege.[1] At the same time, an immense force assembled on the outskirts of Ciudad de los Reyes (Lima). Even after the siege of Cuzco collapsed, remnant armies in the eastern Andes reportedly contained upwards of 20,000 soldiers.

Estimates for earlier eras should be taken even more guardedly. The figures for armies of conquest range from the 10,000 Thupa Inka Yupanki was said to have used to take the Mantaro Valley (Toledo 1940a:19) to the less credible 250,000 reported for Thupa Inka Yupanki's first campaigns against the Kañari and Quitos (Sarmiento 1960:250). Even if we take these grandiose estimates with a large dose of salt, the two *khipu* accounts and the scale of forces besieging Cuzco and Lima give us ample reason to believe that scores of thousands of soldiers could be mobilized for individual campaigns and that more than 100,000 effectives may have been engaged in single battles.

Recruitment of Personnel

General Mobilization

Military service under the Incas was a broad, but not universal, labor duty of adult males (Polo 1916:98–9). In principle, all sound married males whose age-grade fell in the range of 25–30 to 50 years were subject to call-up on a rotating basis. Those men, called *awka kamayuq* ("warriors"), formed the bulwark of the army as foot soldiers. They were often accompanied on campaigns by their wives or other close kin, who cared for their personal needs. On long campaigns, it was not unusual for children to be born and travel with the soldiers. Unmarried men whose age-grade fell in the range of about 18–25 (*sayapayaq*) bore messages and cargo (Guaman Poma 1980:171, 179; RGI 1965:1:346; Murúa 1986:362–5; Rowe 1958; Murra 1980b:89; Spurling 1982:3).

Some chroniclers explained that boys were trained in the martial arts in their home communities so that they would be capable warriors when called upon. Bartolomé de Las Casas (trans. from Bram 1941:46), probably with some exaggeration, wrote that "(i)n every settlement there were instructors in the art of fighting and manipulating weapons. They had charge of all the boys from ten to eighteen, who at certain hours of the day, were ordered to fight among themselves in serious or sham-battles . . ." Cobo (1990:215) reported a more likely scenario, that many captains and officers were found in the provinces to train the youths. Ritual battles in Cuzco were part of the young men's initiation ceremony (Guaman Poma 1980:231; see Rowe 1946:308–9). The battles helped distinguish the best warriors, who would later be tapped for duty. Such staged conflicts were widespread in the Andes well into the Colonial era and have even been recorded in the ethnographic present; the blood that was spilled and occasional fatal outcomes were thought to add potency to the rituals (Gorbak et al. 1962; Sallnow 1987:136–9).

Typically, when a campaign was being planned, the military leaders sent out word to the lords of selected ethnic groups to mobilize the personnel required. Because some Inca campaigns were raised against rebellions, the call to duty could come at disconcertingly short notice. The disruption caused by rapid mobilization was likely greatest for campaigns whose timing was unpredictable, but any military service was surely a burden for a farming populace, especially if one or both parents were taken away from children who could not travel with them. The lands of those on duty were supposed to be farmed by the remaining members of the community. Fractions of ethnic groups were called to service by the state, not individual heads of household. The actual proportion called up at any point undoubtedly varied, but some idea may be gained from information gathered for Spanish inspections. In 1549, the Chupachu and Yacha of Huánuco, Peru, reported that about one eighth to one quarter of the heads of household were committed to military duty. Out of their 4,108 households, they provided 200 guards against the Chachapoyas, 200 more for Quito, and 68 for Huánuco Pampa. Five hundred also reportedly went with the king to Quito and elsewhere, but it is not clear if the last figure was a summary or a separate tabulation (Ortiz de Zúñiga 1967:306–7). Similarly, the Lupaqa of the altiplano stated that they had sent 6,000 soldiers out of their population of 20,000 households to the northern campaigns. Of those, only 1,000 returned home, for a net loss of a quarter of the adult male populace (Diez de San Miguel 1964:106). As Murra (1982:53) observes, such burdens were truly onerous.

Warriors recruited from the Upper Mantaro Valley for Spanish military operations in the early Colonial decades were taken in proportion to the population of the province's three political divisions (Murra 1975:246). The working figure (266) is very close to one percent of the tabulated taxpaying populace, estimated in 1586 to have been 27,000, suggesting that it was a standard proportion for calling men to war. Gifts and supplies presented to the Spaniards were also tendered in proportion to the population of the three *saya*, but porters were not. Remarkably, the baseline for mobilizations remained intact during the demographic catastrophes of the first 25 years of Spanish rule. The resiliency of the system after the Inca collapse is testimony to its utility, and it is a fine irony that it was used so effectively against Cuzco's dominion.

The Inca's Personal Guard

Drawn from Cuzco's aristocracy, a few thousand *orejones* ("big-ears"), trained from youth as warriors, formed the army's elite corps and emperor's guard until late prehistory. Perhaps mindful of the not-so-latent threat posed by their close kin, later rulers also supplemented their guard with warriors from other *etnías*. Thupa Inka Yupanki reportedly enlisted Charkas, Karakaras, Chuis, and Chichas from the southern altiplano, while Wayna Qhapaq used Kañaris and Cayambes from Ecuador along with Chachapoyas from northern Peru, and Waskhar employed Kañaris, Chachapoyas, and the central Peruvian Wankas (Espinoza Soriano 1980:175; Spurling 1982:9–11). In the neo-Inca era, Manqo Inka used the cannibalistic Quillacingas from Ecuador in that capacity (Hemming 1970). The Quillacingas had earlier proved their terrifying worth when they ate the bodies of three Kañari lords at Atawallpa's request before their defeated troops (Betanzos 1996:201). The use of non-Inca subjects to protect the emperor may be a telling comment on the trustworthiness of Cuzco's nobility. When Wayna Qhapaq reviled the *orejones* for letting him fall into danger against the Caranqui, he may have inflamed tensions that had been building as Cuzco's military elites found themselves increasingly removed from unimpeded access to the ruler.

On campaign, the guard was a well-ordered force in the low thousands.[2] Cristóbal de Mena (1937:83) recalled that Atawallpa's lodgings near Cajamarca in 1532 were "surrounded by squadrons of pikemen and halberdiers and archers; and another squadron had Indians with throwers and slings; and others with clubs and maces." The honor guard preceding Atawallpa for his entry into the center consisted of 1,000 soldiers in a dazzling livery of red and white tunics that vividly reminded the Spaniards of a massive, mobile chess set. Atawallpa himself said that

7,000 of his guard were killed in the square when he was captured (Ruiz de Arce 1933:261).

Military Specialists

Inca armies included few military specialists other than officers and the *orejones*. The notion of a voluntary career soldier or mercenary in the rank and file was outside the scope of Andean military practice, but the Incas instituted two policies that moved them toward a more professional military. They created islands of loyal *mitmaqkuna* in areas otherwise hostile to the Inca; these were especially important in Ecuador and along the frontiers. Late in their rule, they dedicated especially redoubtable ethnic groups to soldiery (Espinoza Soriano 1975, 1980). Murra (1986:53) has suggested that general conscription lost its attractiveness over time as a recruiting principle, perhaps because of the increased distances that the armies had to travel to campaign or because recruitment was hard to enforce. Moreover, the great conquests had been completed, so that the common soldier's economic and prestige incentives for military service had become curtailed. Standing out in military roles were the Chachapoyas and Kañari, long-time Inca foes in the northern Andes who were subdued over the few last decades of the empire. Ultimately, up to half of the two ethnic groups was dispersed as permanent military personnel. Some were installed in the Yucay Valley (Cieza 1967:189; Murra 1986:55–6), just north of Cuzco, while others formed garrisons elsewhere, such as in the Upper Mantaro Valley (Toledo 1940a:22). A particularly privileged duty lay in acting as personal bodyguards to Wayna Qhapaq (Murra 1980b:159). In the civil war, both ethnic groups sided with Cuzco, for which Atawallpa exacted horrific revenge on the Kañari. When the Spaniards met Atawallpa in Cajamarca, he had 15,000 Chachapoyas in his camp, apparently destined for resettlement.

Exemptions from Service

As useful as they are, individual cases cannot be extrapolated directly to determine how armies were mobilized throughout Tawantinsuyu. The notion of equally apportioned, universal service masks the actual recruiting practices. As we have just seen, some ethnic groups suffered oppressive levies while others were dedicated wholesale to military duty. In contrast, many adult males were exempted from service, because they were privileged, were assigned other duties, or their people were thought unreliable. Even among the groups that contributed many troops, the Incas separated out the better warriors and dedicated others to auxiliary duties such as portage. The most sweeping exclusion included most of Peru's coastal societies, which removed a third or more of the empire's populace from the rolls. When the Spaniards arrived, the peoples of the north coast were forbidden to carry arms, ostensibly because the Chimu lords had rebelled (Zárate 1862:472). This law was apparently part of a policy, intended to reduce the Chimu threat, that included the dismantling of the coastal empire into its constituent valleys. Coastal troops are almost never listed among those who contributed to Inca conquests or the civil war, and they were conspicuously absent from the army that set siege to Lima in 1536.[3] Apart from being untrustworthy, or holding favored statuses as did the Chincha, the lowland peoples may have fared poorly at high elevations. The converse is certainly true – the highland soldiers suffered from heat and disease in campaigns on the coast (Marcus and Silva 1988:27). Several highland ethnic groups were also partly excused from military duty. Speaking generally, Cobo (1979:234) wrote that groups rich in particular resources or skills could work off their entire obligation to the state through intensive exploitation and thus presumably were not obligated for military duty. Polo (1916:98–9) mentioned that the Rucanas were exempted because they had a good pace for litter-bearing and the Chumbivilcas were exempt because of their dancing skills. The much-despised Urus of Lake Titicaca were little used because they were thought inept.

Ritual and Ideology

Ritual and ideology pervaded Inca militarism from strategy to tactics. The Incas themselves proclaimed that they were driven by a divine mandate to spread the religion of the Creator God Wiraqocha, the Sun god Inti, and the other deities, to the rest of humanity. Rowe (1946:280) notes that such a directive sounds suspiciously like crusading Christianity, but that there is little doubt of its aboriginal character by the early sixteenth century (Polo 1940:132). What we cannot resolve from our present vantage point is how much such a charge truly galvanized the expansion or formed an expedient rationale.

The preparation for campaigns incorporated divination, fasts, feasts, and sacrifices. In an effort to see the future, the Incas sacrificed black llamas that had been starved for some days. According to Polo (1916:38), the weakening of the llamas' hearts was thought to correspond to the loss of the enemy's courage. If certain flesh near the heart did not diminish from the fasting, it was an ill omen for the coming campaign, and a number of dogs were then sacrificed to overcome the bad fortune. An especially solemn ceremony called the *itu* was performed when the emperor went to war. For two days, everyone in Cuzco fasted and refrained from sex. After all the provincials and women who had dogs and other animals were sent out of the city, the images of the gods were brought into the Awkaypata plaza. Two llamas and sometimes children were sacrificed, followed by processions by boys under twenty, resplendently garbed in red tunics of *qompi* cloth, feather crowns, and shell ornaments. During the processions, coca was scattered on the ground and, once the ceremonies were complete, there was an enormous feast with copious drinking (Cobo 1990:151–3; Acosta 1986:377–8; Rowe 1946:311–12). On occasion, children were also sacrificed in the *qhapaq ucha* ceremony as a precursor to war (see chapter 7). Other divinations were also undertaken to ascertain the result of military ventures. According to Montesinos, "(i)f the King desired to learn of the outcome of some war, or battle or some other event, they [the priests] placed the [maize] grains as usual [in a large flat ceramic vessel called a *kallana*], naming the captains and saying certain words. The grains themselves then had a great fight, some against others, until the conquered were driven out of the vessel, and then the wizard told the outcome as if he had seen it . . ." (Montesinos 1920:88–9, bracketed expressions added by this author).

Priests played key military roles, in keeping with Inca practice that did not neatly divide responsibilities into civil and military or religious and secular categories. Atawallpa's chief priest, Cusi Yupanki, for example, led an expedition against the province of Rata, Ecuador, and directed the execution of Waskhar's kin at the end of the dynastic war (Betanzos 1996:200, 242–6). Later, Manqo Inka's chief priest of the Sun (Villac Umu), likened by many chroniclers to the Pope, accompanied Almagro and Paullu Inka to Chile but then organized the siege of Cuzco in 1536 (Anónimo, Sitio del Cuzco 1934:6, 15; Hemming 1970:177, 187).

Religious belief and ritual practice also had an effect on battle tactics. For example, the Incas reserved the night of the new moon for ceremonies, even during campaigns. The Spaniards were quick to recognize the practice and used it to their advantage in the siege of Cuzco, capturing Saqsawaman on the night of the new moon on May 18 or 19, 1536. Whenever the Incas marched into battle, they carried an array of idols, or *wak'a*, with them. The most important were the images of the Sun itself, of Thunder, and of the mythical Manqo Qhapaq and Huanacauri. Each emperor also had his own named battle idol (Ziółkowski 1996:136–40). The *wak'a* were items of great potency, as they were not simply symbols of a society, but embodied spirits. Seizing the enemy's idols signified capture of his power. The Incas kept the captured icons in Cuzco so that their subjects would recognize their domination and have to travel to the imperial capital to worship their own gods. A sense of the reverence the people held for the idols may be seen in the phrasing both Sarmiento and Murúa used to describe General Yasca's mobilization of an army to retake the troublesome Guaraní frontier about 1520. As the chroniclers put it, Yasca took the *wak'a* from various regions with him and the people came along with the images (Sarmiento 1960:263–4). Similarly, when Atoq left Cuzco to engage Atawallpa in Ecuador, he took the statue of the Sun with him and made the Kañari swear allegiance to Waskhar before it (Cabello 1951:427).

The Army on Campaign

On the Road

When the Incas set off on campaigns, they dispatched multiple contingents, stretching out their departures. The staggered approach to the march moderated the impact on the supplies and support personnel along the way, as well as limiting the turmoil inevitably entailed in moving large forces. Wayna Qhapaq's major campaigns in Ecuador began with an inquiry into the state of affairs in the provinces, followed by notice to all the societies along the planned route to prepare supplies and lodgings (Cieza 1967:213–14). That communiqué prepared the way for a vanguard from Cuzco, after which larger contingents were dispatched over an extended period. The principal forces accompanying the emperor followed in a grand procession. Wayna Qhapaq reportedly took along 2,000 concubines and a vast array of servants, leaving another 4,000 wives in Cuzco. The main force was said to contain 200,000 men, plus servants and camp followers. Even allowing for some literary license in the estimates, the scale and character of such an army on the move had little to do with a lean fighting force (see below, *Logistics*).

Porters, wives, servants, and other personnel formed a substantial entourage that may have approached the number of combatants.[4] Such large auxiliary groups relieved the soldiers' burdens by cooking and carrying loads, but they placed additional demands on the logistical system. It is little wonder that the Inca armies sometimes left their supply train and camp followers behind, when pressed for rapid movement. That occurred at least once in the final battles of the civil war, when Atawallpa's army left its train at Vilcas in a rapid flanking move to the battlefield at Chaquixampa. The army paid dearly for the decision, because a contingent of Waskhar's soldiers found and sacked the camp (Betanzos 1996:217–18).

Zárate's (1862:483) description of the disposition of Quizquiz's forces across the mountainous terrain east of Hatun Xauxa in the 1530s provides a concrete example of how an Inca army on the move was organized. A Kañari *kuraka* warned the Spaniards that Quizquiz's army exceeded 12,000 members, a figure that Almagro dismissed at the time; it is not clear if he was referring to soldiers or total personnel. Zárate wrote that a vanguard contained 2,000 with 3,000 on the left flank and 3,000–4,000 more in a rearguard. He did not estimate the size of the main body of the army, which included many women and service personnel. The lead force preceded the main body by about two or three days' march, while the rearguard followed it by two days. During the march, the flanking contingent foraged among the towns in the region. In all, the troops were said to be spread over 15 or more leagues (60 km), which suggests that they were covering about 12–15 km per day. In a running conflict with Almagro, Quizquiz abandoned more than 15,000 animals along with more than 4,000 male and female prisoners, and burned all the textiles his forces could not carry into their hastily built high forts.[5]

The road and *tampu* system was designed largely to assist military operations, but even the provincial centers were not equipped to shelter thousands of soldiers. Settlements such as Huánuco Pampa and Pumpu did have barracks-like structures, called *kallanka*, but they could have lodged only a fraction of the assembled forces. The large armies apparently camped in tents, such as those the Spaniards observed at Cajamarca. The soldier Ruiz de Arce (1933:359; translation by Hemming 1970:32) wrote of his impression of a first view of the encampment: "the royal center of the Indians appeared on one side of the river, a very beautiful city, for they all had their tents . . ." Atawallpa's lodgings themselves were surrounded by white tents for half a league around (Mena 1937:83).

Discipline among the troops was a mixed thing. While on the road, the soldiers were said to be forbidden to stray from the road or to take any goods from the countryside, on pain of death (Rowe 1946:279). The Spaniards at Cajamarca were witness to capital punishment for disciplinary infractions, as 30–40 of Atawallpa's guard were executed when they broke ranks in the face of a display of horse-charging bravado by Hernando de Soto (Ruiz de Arce 1933:361). Atawallpa himself remained regally impassive when de Soto approached so close that his horse's breath fluttered the emperor's fringe (Mena 1937:83). Regardless of the order exhibited on the march and in the camp, discipline broke quickly on the battlefield and looting was the order of the day following victory.

Logistics

Few aspects of the Inca empire impressed the conquistadores more than its supply and transport system. Besides the road network, the most renowned aspect of the Inca supply system was the array of storehouses, which stockpiled an enormous variety of food, arms, clothing, and other items throughout the empire (Morris 1967; LeVine 1992). Each soldier was supposed to receive a set of clothing and sandals annually, and some weapons were also provided. They were also issued blankets, maize, peppers, and coca leaf (Murra 1980b:76, 102). The difficulties of transport in the rugged Andean terrain required that the storage facilities be replicated regionally. The massive scale of the system is best exemplified by the hundreds or even thousands of storehouses at each major center from Cuzco to Tumipampa, and adjacent to state farms in Cochabamba, Bolivia, and the Lerma Valley, Argentina (chapter 11). Each small waystation located every 20 km or so along the roads also stored goods for state travelers.

The Incas relied on llama caravans and human porters for transport. The state owned hundreds of thousands of llamas and on occasion individual pack trains could include thousands of animals (Zárate 1862:483; Murra 1980b:46). Although the camelids are supremely well adapted to the rigors of the mountains, there are limitations to their uses. For example, llama caravans cover only about 20 km per day, that is, the average distance between *tampu*. Typically, two loads of 30 kg each will be rotated among three adult males, but they still break down with disconcerting frequency and will refuse to budge when tired. As a consequence, humans may have actually carried the majority of portage on their backs. They were more reliable and could carry heavier loads (Murra 1980b:48), but had to be fed from local supplies or carry their own. Both colonial and modern figures suggest that porters could carry upwards of 30 kg for 20–25 km per day (see Hyslop 1984:294–8; D'Altroy 1992:85–6). Both male and female porters accompanied the army on long-distance treks, the women usually as soldiers' wives. In 1575, Atienza (1931:49–50) reported acerbically that Ecuadorian women customarily carried enormous loads alongside their unburdened husbands. In another routine, porters carried supplies from one end of their territory to the next, where their neighbors assumed the burdens. The second form of transport did not wear down the porters, but both forms required drawing on food along the road to transport the loads.

The slow transport, together with the bulkiness of foodstuffs, meant that porters would have had to be replenished every few days with food from the countryside. Under those circumstances, the best solution to the logistical challenge was to develop a regionally based supply system and to mix pack trains and human porters. Armies and other state personnel could then travel in the expectation that their supply needs would be met without having to forage or make resented demands from the countryside.

Battle Tactics and Weaponry

Our information on Inca battle tactics comes mostly from the late prehispanic Ecuadorian campaigns, the dynastic war, and early encounters with the Spaniards, where the Incas followed a number of sound principles. In order to inform themselves as best as possible of what lay ahead, they attempted to spy out the land and made clay models of the terrain. The armies then presented an overwhelming force at the point of attack. When Manqo Inka's forces invested Cuzco in 1536, for example, he waited several weeks for his full army of 100,000–200,000 to arrive, even though they were attacking only 190 Spaniards and a few thousand native allies (Hemming 1970:190–2). Most battles for which we have accounts were described as either great melees on open terrain or assaults on fortified strongholds. Two favorite tactics were feigned withdrawals coupled with pincers counterattacks, and flanking maneuvers. Both approaches indicate that the Incas used surprise to their advantage and concentrated force on the vulnerable flanks and rear of forces.

The battles were noisy, colorful affairs. The soldiers from each *etnía* were clothed in their distinctive martial vestments. Cobo (1990:216) wrote that the warriors adorned themselves with finery: "Over this defensive gear, they would usually wear their most attractive and rich adornments and jewels; this included wearing fine plumes of many colors on their heads and large gold and silver plates on their chests and backs; however, the plates worn by poorer soldiers were copper." Before the actual fighting, both sides typically postured belligerently, trading insults and martial songs, sometimes for days. Passages in the narratives also record impassioned, if apocryphal, oratory by emperors or generals before their men, firing their ardor for the fighting to come. Various instruments fashioned from bodies of defeated opponents were used to terrorize the enemy. Guaman Poma (1980:287) wrote that the soldiers celebrated their valor in song: "We will drink from the skull of the traitor, we will adorn ourselves with a necklace of his teeth, we will play the melody of the pinkullu with flutes made from his bones, we will beat the drum made from his skin, and thus we will dance."

The Inca battle formation was organized by ethnic group, each one of which specialized in its own arms (Mena 1937:83; Cabello Valboa 1951:308; Cobo 1990:218; Rowe 1946:276–7). Flurries of arrows, sling stones, and javelins preceded hand-to-hand combat by troops who wielded maces, clubs, and spears. Some stones were large enough to fell a horse or break a sword in half at a distance of 30 m (Hemming 1970:192–3). The emperors were carried into combat on litters, wielding slings or spears (figure 9.2). The Incas' preferred weapon was a stone or bronze star mace mounted on a wooden handle about 1 m long. Another favorite was a hard, double-edged, palmwood club shaped like a sword. The bow and arrow were a late addition to the Inca army's repertoire as warriors from the jungle were drafted into service. Troops defending fortified locations responded with a similar array of weaponry, to which they added large boulders rolled down onto advancing forces. Piles of hundreds of sling stones lining the interior of defensive walls can still be found at various Inca forts, such as Cerro del Inga, Chile (Planella et al. 1991:407). Soldiers often wore quilted cloth armor that was so effective against Andean weapons that many Spaniards discarded their own metal plate in favor of the lighter protection. Warriors also frequently carried shields and protected their chests and backs with plates of metal and their heads with cane helmets.

A sketch of one engagement will illustrate the kinds of tactics employed on fortified strongholds. In an effort to take a Caranqui fort north of Quito, the Incas prepared the field by taking control of the surrounding country and then launched a frontal assault (see chapter 4). The first strike was repelled and an unexpected counterattack unseated Wayna Qhapaq from his litter, who was saved only by the heroic action of a number of *orejones*. After another unsuccessful assault, the Incas withdrew to Tumipampa, desolating the area around the stronghold (Sarmiento 1960:262). According to Cabello, Awki Toma's forces then set siege, but a prolonged, bloody assault failed when he fell mortally wounded. When some of the besieging forces withdrew for lack of food, the defenders broke out to resupply themselves and reinforce the fort (Cabello Valboa 1951:377–8; Murúa 1986:122–5). Wayna Qhapaq led the next force himself, finally gaining victory by drawing the enemy out of their fort with a feigned withdrawal and pincers counterattack by hidden forces. The difficult terrain and the distances involved meant that the forces had to take circuitous routes and appear on the morning of the fifth day. At the appointed time, the Incas under Wayna Qhapaq attacked the fort frontally and then withdrew as if they had been routed. When the Caranqui pursued the fleeing enemy, they were set upon from

Figure 9.2 Guaman Poma's illustration of the emperor Wayna Qhapaq wielding a sling as he is carried into battle against the *etnías* of highland Ecuador

the flank and rear by the two other forces. The defenders were then slaughtered in a nearby lake (called *Yaguarcocha*, or Lake of Blood), in which they had sought refuge. Similar surprise attacks and flanking maneuvers characterized a number of the battles, most notably the final battle on the Apurimac when Waskhar was captured by Atawallpa's men.

The attack on Lima in 1536 provides an example of late Inca tactics in open terrain. The general Quizo Yupanki had amassed an immense army on the surrounding hills in an effort to overwhelm the Spaniards by force of numbers. Accompanied by a brilliant array of banners, the army advanced from the north, east, and south. The general himself rode a litter and wielded a lance at the head of his hand-picked troops in the eastern force. The Spaniards waited until the army had begun to enter the streets of the town and then attacked with two contingents of cavalry. They chose the Inca command as their target, which marched at the army's head. In short order, Quizo Yupanki and 40 officers were killed and the attack was broken. With their leaders gone, the native army melted into the hills that night and the siege was lifted. In addition to the Spaniards' superiority in such terrain, several features typical of Inca warfare stand out from this battle: the concentration of massed force, the physical leadership of the army by its officers, the three-pronged attack, and the collapse of the army's discipline with the loss of its command (Hemming 1970:212–13, 575; Murúa 1986:206).

Triumphs and Rewards

Victories in war were celebrated in grand fashion, most prominently by triumphs in Cuzco led by the generals or the emperor himself. To show off the defeat of a foe, the Inca trod upon his head in the Golden Enclosure or in the main plaza in front of the massed throngs of Cuzco's residents. Particularly dangerous enemies were killed, some by imprisonment in a dungeon of snakes, while others were sacrificed to give thanks for the victory (Rowe 1946:279–80). In a highly personalized expression of victory, Inca rulers had the heads of obdurate foes fashioned into drinking cups. Cristóbal de Mena saw Atawallpa drink chicha from the skull of Atoq, the commander sent to confront him at the inception of the dynastic war. A golden bowl had been set in the general's skull and a silver spout emerged from his mouth. Defeated lords were also flayed and the skins of their bellies made into drums that were taken into battle or played at ceremonial events in Cuzco. Individual valor was elaborately rewarded, though clear distinctions were made between the awards granted to nobility and to commoners, reinforcing the class structure of Inca society. Clothing, gold and silver breast- or backplates, and captured women, weapons, and flocks were rewards for commoners; marriage to an *aqlla* was a sign of special favor. Nobles, on the other hand, could be awarded administrative sinecures, lands, multiple wives, and privileges such as riding in a litter or sitting on a stool (Guaman Poma 1980:164; RGI 1965:1:177; Diez de San Miguel 1964:106; see Rowe 1946:279–80).

Summary

As the Inca polity developed, the leaders faced a shifting array of challenges that were addressed through military action. Up to the proto-imperial era, warfare was focused on localized raiding. Once the Incas shifted their goals to annexing lands, warfare – combined with alliances, diplomacy, ceremony, and gift exchange – became the linchpin of Tawantinsuyu's expansion. The emperor himself drew much of his personal prestige from his perceived success as a military leader, while valor in battle was the principal means by which commoners could move up the social ladder. In the latter decades of the empire, after the main conquests had been completed, threats to Cuzco's power came largely from insurrections, not from external attack. The commitment of relatively small forces to the perimeter and large contingents to internal garrisons and armies of pacification suggests that the Incas saw the greatest threat in rebellion, not invasion. Thus, the logistical infrastructure took center stage in most of the empire. Fortified military architecture was useful, but only for limited circumstances, primarily along the frontiers.

chapter ten
Provincial Rule

The Administrative System

As their domain expanded, the Incas were faced with the challenge of governing societies that ranged from villages to states and a population that ultimately outnumbered them by about a hundred to one. In chapter 1, we outlined a range of policies that imperial rulers have chosen to address similar problems, ranging from the extractive, hegemonic approach of the Aztecs to a full-fledged civil bureaucracy, such as that developed in Han China. The Incas opted for a mixed strategy, ruling the central part of the empire directly, but applying less intensive rule along the populous north coast and in much of the far north and south Andes. At the heart of the provincial system was an administration that is often – misleadingly – called a bureaucracy. In actuality, the government consisted of an umbrella of Inca officials who supervised a hierarchy of hereditary ethnic lords drafted into state service. Most taxpayers were assigned to units of 10 to 10,000 households in an organizational pyramid used for labor taxation and military recruitment. By 1532, millions of people had also been resettled for political and economic ends and to defuse threats to Inca dominance. To keep track of the population, the Incas took censuses, kept detailed accounts, and imposed an official language. And to provide a physical framework for their rule, they built a network of roads, provincial centers, and waystations.

As novel and rigorous as some of those policies may seem, Morris (1982) points out that the approach really consisted more of shuffling about existing ethnic groups than inventing a new government. Political relations between the Inca and the provincial lords relied heavily on personal bonds, while supervision of the general populace depended as much on ritualized exchange, pageantry, and state-sponsored revelry as it did on law or compulsion. Moreover, because social and political conditions differed from one place to the next, so did Inca policies. A single model of Inca rule thus fails to capture the nature of the empire, and some cases will be sketched out in this chapter to illustrate the variety of provincial relations.

The Provinces

There were at least eighty provinces in the Inca realm, distributed unevenly among the four parts.[1] Chinchaysuyu was the most populous and contained the most provinces, while Cuntisuyu was the smallest. The Incas thought of a province as an enumerated population which was typically based on the societies that were native to a region. As an extension of this logic, the colonists who moved to distant territories were still counted on the census rolls of their homelands. Each province was divided into two or three ranked parts called *saya*. The partitions also corresponded in some way to ethnic divisions, although they could include more than one group or parts of several. The goal was to create units whose composition came as close as was convenient to multiples of decimal figures (Murra 1958; Julien 1982, 1988). Ideally, each *saya* consisted of 10,000 heads of households, so that a province nominally contained 20,000 or 30,000 households.

After claiming a new region, the Incas defined the limits of the province and groups within it; two kin groups from Cuzco seem to have had a special responsibility for surveying and setting out markers (Van de Guchte 1990:323). Provincial subdivisions also had bounded territories, but officials sometimes had to intervene in land disputes that were frozen when Inca rule was applied (Cieza 1967:215). Betanzos (1996:110) wrote that when a local population needed more resources than were available to them, Inca officials were supposed to send a painting of the lay of the land to Cuzco, accompanied by the local lords, so that an equitable adjustment could be made and the markers reset. Those who lost land would be compensated as the Inca saw fit.

A governor (*tokrikoq*) conducted the affairs of each province with help enlisted from local elites and functionaries, such as the record-keepers called *khipu kamayuq*. The governor was usually an ethnic Inca, although the rare non-Inca could find a place near the top; ability was a prime consideration in making his appointment (Rowe 1946:262; Wachtel 1977:75–9; Schaedel 1978:300–6). He had broad responsibilities and authority, most importantly supervising the census and mobilizing labor for whatever tasks his superiors required. He was supposed to administer the colonists, along with the lands of the state and maybe the Sun, but probably not the private estates of the *Sapa Inca*, the *panaqas*, or other aristocrats. Additional duties included making sure

Table 10.1   Officials in the Inca decimal hierarchy

Title of official	Scope of jurisdiction (heads of household)
hunu kuraka	10,000
pichkawaranqa kuraka	5,000
waranqa kuraka	1,000
pichkapachaka kuraka	500
pachaka kuraka	100
pichkachunka kamayuq	50
chunka kamayuq	10

that the roads, bridges, and support facilities were in good order, so that people who passed through on state business would find their needs anticipated. He also judged all the cases that were related to state interests and had the authority to pass sentences up to and including the death penalty (Cobo 1979:194–202; Moore 1958:115).

The Decimal Administration

In much of the realm, the Incas organized able-bodied heads of household men into units of 10, 50, 100, 500, 1,000, 5,000 and 10,000 (table 10.1). Both Cieza and Polo, who inquired closely on such matters, credited Thupa Inka Yupanki with the design (Rowe 1958:500). The Incas used the hierarchy to tabulate labor for both civil and military duties, including farming, herding, and artisanry, as well as portage, guard duty, and war service (Rowe 1946:264; Murra 1958:33–4; Wedin 1965; Julien 1982, 1988; LeVine 1987). The officials were responsible for maintaining state facilities and for leading their men into battle. Each unit was headed by a hereditary local elite called a *kuraka*. According to some chroniclers, no official took his post without the direct approval of the Inca or his governor, but Cobo wrote that those who had charge of 100 or fewer households were appointed by their lords of 1,000 (Cobo 1979:201). In practical terms, individuals in line for positions under local customs generally filled state offices. The guiding rule seems to have been to keep power within elite families by selecting the most appropriate adult male at times of transition. Most commonly, he was the most able son of the prior lord, but brothers of the past lord could hold the position until it passed on to the ablest son of the first. If an official was unwilling or unable to carry out his duties, he was replaced by a more compliant individual who was usually also drawn from the local people. Drafting the *ayllu* leaders into the state hierarchy meant that the Incas could rule without interfering unduly in community life, but it also meant that the government reached deep into existing political structures.

As might be imagined, the decimal structure had to be adjusted to local conditions. It was installed throughout the central empire, but in the far north and south, it may have been regularly applied only among the colonist communities (Salomon 1986; see Lorandi 1991). The program's uneven application probably arose from many factors. For one, as Murra (1958) points out, it was simply not feasible to rearrange the empire's people into a neat structure by administrative fiat. Local intransigence also played a role. The Chachapoyas, for instance, resisted Inca rule for decades but were finally subdued late in the empire's run. Their leaders were made into *yanakuna*, or personnel committed to serve the Inca personally for life, rather than decimal officials (Pease 1982). Elsewhere, toward the margins of Tawantinsuyu, the population or resources may not have warranted the administrative effort. There is no evidence for decimal officials in Chile and Argentina, for example.

Lords of 100 households or more received benefits according to their standing. Although the sources differ somewhat on the details, in general their lands were worked and herds tended, and they were granted household service at a rate of one servant for every 100 households supervised. They could also receive wives and personal estates, whose maize, coca, and peppers fields were essential to the hospitality expected of a lord. Symbolic paraphernalia, such as wooden seats and elegant tunics, also marked the status of lords in the hierarchy. For especially meritorious service, an individual could be named an Inca by Privilege, although that designation was largely reserved for certain ethnic groups from the Cuzco area. The foremost provincial lords were supposed to make an annual journey to the capital, where they lived for four months supported by their own retainers. While there, they exchanged gifts with the Inca himself, especially cloth.

The Census

Because accurate census records were crucial to Inca administration, keeping track of births, deaths, marriages, and other changes of status was among the most important of official duties. People of each sex were assigned to one of ten categories that corresponded to their life stage or ability to do useful work, not to their chronological age (chapter 8). Registering males and females separately was vital because the members of each sex were recruited for different purposes. Some young girls were tapped for the women's orders, for example, while boys were destined for courier or hunting duties. Garcilaso (1966:329–33) recalled that the Incas kept separate *khipu* for each province, on which a pendant string recorded the number of people belonging to each category. He added that the *khipu kamayuq* would sometimes attach subsidiary strings to indicate, for example, how many men or women of a given age-grade had been widowed. The provincial officials were expected to report their tabulations in Cuzco annually at the December solstice festival, and an independent check on the census may have been made every three to five years (Polo 1965b:55). Rowe (1958:501) makes the reasonable assumption that the decimal hierarchy and the census were initiated together, since they were conceptually so closely linked.

Inspectors and Judges

Cuzco also appointed a centrally controlled set of inspectors (*tokoyrikoq*, "he who sees all") who checked on affairs in the provinces. Betanzos (1996:110–11) wrote that the sons of the ruler were charged with the inquiries. The highest-ranking official may have been the "Inspector General" of the conquered territories, a position that was sometimes filled by the emperor's brother. The existence of these independent agents implies that the rulers evidently did not fully trust the provincial officials to conduct all affairs with the best interests of the *Sapa Inca* and the state in mind.

Maintaining Social Order

Although the Incas aspired to regulate many aspects of life, they did not create an elaborate legal code or a separate judiciary. Instead, they applied many of their own customs to society at large and invented new measures to protect the interests of the ruler, aristocracy, state, and religion.[2] It is often pointed out that the chronicles are filled with social dictates and sanctions for unacceptable acts, but the scope of state interest was still limited. Local societies were left to their own affairs to judge many disputes and misdeeds beneath the mantle of state oversight. Official strictures were often designed to guard specific symbols, property, and personnel of the elite: for example, hunting on the Inca's lands, removing gold or silver from Cuzco without permission, or having sexual relations with the women of the Inca or the Sun were proscribed. Some status articles, such as *qompi* cloth, were reserved for the Inca elite or members of the state institutions, unless the right to use them was explicitly granted. The Incas assumed the right to condemn individuals to death, and only the provincial governors and their superiors had that authority. Other rules were intended to keep tabs on the populace. According to Cobo (1979:206), a resettled colonist was tortured if he returned home and a two-time offender was executed. The existence of a second sanction, of course, indicates that the policy was resisted. Additional rules governed conduct that might be thought of as customary, such as the choice of clothing or headgear, especially among colonists. The purpose again was to identify taxpayers and thereby control their movements.

Further aspects of law emphasized the cleavages of status found in Inca society (Moore 1958:74–5). In general, any individual in the state hierarchy could be judged only by someone of higher rank. Moreover, royalty and aristocrats were granted latitude to behave in ways that were sanctioned for commoners. If an act was widely condemned, the nobility were punished less severely. Incest, for which commoners were usually supposed to be executed, resulted only in reprimand for the nobility, and was required of the later rulers who were supposed to marry their sisters. If a commoner male committed adultery with the wife of a commoner, he was beaten, but if his partner was the wife of a noble, he was executed. Various homicides committed by a commoner were punishable by death, but an official who killed someone under his jurisdiction was only disciplined physically for a first offense. Despite his frequent regard for Inca accomplishments, Cobo (1979:207) commented acidly that the unequal penalties were "due to an illusion . . . that a public reprimand was a far greater punishment for an Inca of noble blood than the death penalty for a plebeian."

Men and women were reportedly punished in different ways for the same crimes. For example, incest committed by certain kinds of cousins resulted in both being beaten and shaved, after which the man was sent to the mines and the woman to temple service. Blas Valera's (1945:58–9) vivid description of the consequences of different kinds of rape or sexual relations may be indicative of the Inca views on gender relations, but it is also notable for the Spanish clergy's absorption with scandalous behavior. There were also explicit sanctions concerning property crimes and proscriptions against witchcraft and other misuses of supernatural powers. For example, it was forbidden to move the markers that denoted boundaries, even among local peoples. Cobo (1979:203) wrote that the entire household of a person who murdered through sorcery was executed along with the guilty party, on the assumption that they all knew the craft. The punishment was carried out as a public event to dissuade others from similar acts.

Even in this society of unequal rights, there were supposed to be protections for commoners. For instance, soldiers on the march were prohibited from stealing food upon pain of death for themselves and their captains (Betanzos 1996:108–9). Officials were ostensibly punished for abusing their subordinates, and the official who failed to ensure that the *tampu* under his jurisdiction were well stocked would be punished. He, however, would then discipline those under his sway for their dereliction of duty. Among commoners, a man who killed his wife for adultery could be forgiven and an individual whose goods were stolen was entitled to restitution. Regrettably, it is hard to know if such rules were truly obeyed in the breach.

Moore observes that most penalties involved physical punishment, such as stoning or torture, or public humiliation for nobles. Polo attributed the relative lack of economic sanctions to the rarity of private property, which was reserved only for the most elite. In one of the most fabled punishments, individuals accused of especially heinous acts, such as treason against the *Sapa Inca*, were thrown into a special dungeon stocked with snakes and other wild animals. Although we cannot track Inca law over time, one major change clearly lay in the state's removal of the right to resolve major disputes over property and life from the hands of the native elites. Murra (1958) points out that enacting such policies did not end conflicts, but simply moved their resolution out of the hands of local peoples into those of the state. Blood feuds and local political violence were thus reduced at the cost of sovereignty. We do not know if specific rules were applied evenly throughout the realm, but a few chroniclers described some of the diversity in locally acceptable behavior. The peoples of the altiplano and the Chimu region, for example, reportedly engaged in sexual practices that the Incas found repugnant.[3] Not surprisingly, however, the codes of the pre-Inca Chimu state protected the persons, perquisites, and properties of the ruling class, just as Inca rules did (Rowe 1948).

The Infrastructure: Provincial Installations

The Incas managed provincial affairs of state through a network of regional centers and secondary facilities that were connected by the highway system. Cieza de León (1553/1984:237–8; trans. by Morris 1982:154), who saw much of the north, wrote:

> For it was their custom, when they traveled anywhere in this great realm, to go with great pomp and be served with great luxury, as was their custom. It is said that, except when it was necessary for their service, they

did not travel more than four leagues [~20 km] a day. And so that there would be sufficient provisions for their people, at the end of each four leagues there were lodgings and storehouses with a great abundance of the things that could be had in this land; and even if it was uninhabited there had to be these lodgings and storehouses.

All of the installations are usually called *tampu*, although the term refers most properly to lodgings. Hyslop (1984:277; 1990), who studied the roads and settlements more comprehensively than anyone else, estimates that there may have been 2,000 or more *tampu*. Although no comprehensive list of the sites was recorded in the Colonial era, Vaca de Castro compiled a partial inventory in 1543 and Guaman Poma pictorially divided over 200 *tampu* into five ranks in his 1608 letter to King Carlos V. At the apex of Guaman Poma's list lay cities with royal installations, followed by large towns with royal lodgings, smaller towns with royal lodgings, royal lodgings, and small lodgings. Unfortunately, his list contains enough significant errors that it is risky to trust his hierarchy too closely (Hyslop 1984:278–9).

Morris (1972) has pointed out that the provincial centers formed a kind of artificial urbanism and quickly fell into disuse after the Inca collapse. He notes that they were usually founded in locations without significant local occupation and lacked independent craft, residential, or market activity. Their positioning often reflects more concern for interregional contacts than for local affairs, for they were located at strategic points for long-distance movement, sometimes two or three days' walk from the people they administered. During most of the year no more than about a quarter of the housing may have been used. The architecture often used local techniques and materials, but their layout, masonry, and material culture were largely foreign to the social landscape. The great storage facilities and emphasis on temporary housing underscore that they were designed to support traveling armies and part-time occupants. Finally, Morris observes, none of the centers on the main highway had a significant cemetery, indicating that even the Inca personnel felt that they were present only temporarily.

We do not yet have a reliable grasp of the system's development, but the evidence that is available suggests that upgrading the roads became policy as early as Thupa Inka Yupanki's reign and that many of the *tampu* and road sections were built at the same time. According to Sarmiento (1960:257), Hatun Xauxa and Tiwanaku occupied a symbolic second tier below Cuzco under Thupa Inka, but none of their archaeological remains suggests that they held such an elevated position. It also seems likely that the elaboration of the route between Cuzco and Quito owed much to Wayna Qhapaq's late campaigns in the northern Andes. By the early sixteenth century, both Cuzco and Tumipampa functioned as imperial capitals. Their roles diverged during Wayna Qhapaq's reign, for the political and military power lay in the north, while the royal kin groups and principal religious institutions were still concentrated in Cuzco.

The major provincial settlements were the seat of a provincial governor and administered large regional populations. The grandest centers lay along the main mountain highway. North of Cuzco were Vilcashuaman, Hatun Xauxa, Pumpu, Huánuco Pampa, Cajamarca, Tumipampa, and Quito. South of Cuzco lay Hatunqolla, Chucuito, Chuquiabo (La Paz), Paria, and Charcas. Along Peru's south-central coast, Inkawasi and Tambo Colorado stand out as planned installations. No important *tampu* were built on the populous north coast of Peru and only a couple of military sites south of central Bolivia exceeded about 35 ha. Although archaeologists and architects have studied the network for decades (e.g., Morris 1972; Gasparini and Margolies 1980; González Carré et al. 1981; Raffino 1983; Hyslop 1984, 1985, 1990; Morris and Thompson 1985; LeVine 1985; Raffino 1993; D'Altroy 1992; Matos Mendieta 1994), most of the centers have not been adequately investigated because they have been covered by later settlements. Of all the mountain centers, only Pumpu, Huánuco Pampa, and Paria are exposed and only Huánuco Pampa has been excavated intensively. Below these large sites were smaller provincial centers, such as Tarmatampu and Acostambo, and the main installations at provinces of lesser importance, such as Conchucos and Guaylas. At least a third and fourth level of smaller Inca settlements and waystations also lined the road system.

Hyslop (1990:291–309) suggests that, conceptually, several Inca settlement systems may have lain on top of one another in the provinces. One consisted of the state administrative and ceremonial centers, another of sanctuaries and other religious facilities, a third of production and storage facilities, another of private estates, and a last of military facilities. In some places, several functions coincided, but often they did not. He infers that the Incas drew selectively from an array of principles – not a standard package – in making their decisions about the design of each site. Most important were the site's major activities, its topography, the amount and proximity of the local labor pool, and local cultural circumstances (Hyslop 1990:306). He also suggests that the scale of each center was proportionate to the size of the regional taxpaying populace. LeVine (1985:458) has noted a similar correlation between plaza size and regional population for some sites, but proposes that it arose from the intended scale of ceremonies. They may both be right.

Plate 10.1 The *kallanka* adjoining the central plaza at Huánuco Pampa; courtesy Craig Morris and the American Museum of Natural History

Planning and Architecture

Inca centers were designed around what Gasparini and Margolies (1980:195–305) call the *architecture of power* – buildings and spaces intended to reinforce the image of the empire's might. Unlike some other pre-industrial states, the Incas did not dedicate buildings to purely administrative functions, such as accounting or holding audiences. To the contrary, most centers reflect an intense preoccupation with ceremony and sacred space. At least six sites were called "New Cuzcos," built in the conceptual, if not actual, image of the capital: Huánuco Pampa, Quito, Tumipampa, Hatunqolla, Charcas, and Inkawasi. Models of spaciousness, the centers were laid out around immense rectangular or trapezoidal plazas that hosted civic-ceremonial functions. At Huánuco Pampa the plaza measured 550 m by 350 m, that is, about 19 ha or almost 30 city blocks (Morris and Thompson 1985:58). The pyramidal platform that was invariably erected in the center of the plaza or to one side of it was a stage from which officials could preside over state ceremonies. The imperial highway typically took a southeast-to-northwest passage through the plaza, just as it did in Cuzco.

Residential and work sectors surrounded the open areas, often enclosed by high walls. The most common Inca architectural element, called a *kancha*, is a rectangular compound that contained one or more one-room structures (Hyslop 1985:282–4, 1990:16–18). At residential sites, the *kancha* housed permanent residents, while at *tampu*, it provided housing and craft quarters. Special sectors of some centers were also designed to house the *Sapa Inca* and his retinue when they passed through. A second unit, called the *kallanka*, is an elongated rectangular building with an undivided interior space; one side opens onto a plaza (plate 10.1). Common in the north, the *kallanka* housed mobile groups, such as soldiers on the move, and provided space for feasts. In contrast, Inca sites in the south Andes often had a single *kallanka*. Hyslop has suggested that *kallanka* may have been built mostly along roads with large transient populations, especially the main highway that served Wayna Qhapaq's operations in Ecuador. A third form, most prevalent in the south, is a large structure (over 100 m long) divided into about twenty cells, whose function remains unclear (de Hoyos and Williams 1994). Other important architectural forms were religious structures, such as the temples to the Sun, and sequestered sectors devoted to the *aqllakuna*.

The elegant cut-stone masonry seen in Cuzco is rare in the provinces. In most cases the architecture was built from locally available materials, especially the fieldstone used in *pirka* masonry. At coastal sites, the standard material was adobe. Such a result could be expected because most provincial installations were built and maintained by the labor of local residents. As a consequence, the architecture's materials and masonry could vary a great deal from one installation to the next.

The Road System

The Inca royal highway (*qhapaq ñan*) was a wonder of Bronze Age engineering that unified the empire physically and conceptually. Built using wood, stone, woven, and bronze tools, and without benefit of precise surveying equipment or draft animals, the network linked together about 40,000 km of roadway (Hyslop 1984:224). Hyslop's study, which built on the work of Raymondi (1875), Strube Erdmann (1963), and Regal Matienzo (1936, 1972), showed that the network was based on two north–south highways (see also Kosok 1965). The eastern route took a high path through the puna and mountain valleys from Quito to Mendoza (Argentina). In most of the north, another artery ran along the coastal plain, but deserts made that route impassable in northern Peru and Chile. In those stretches, the road hugged the western foothills where water was more readily available. The major highways were bridged by more than twenty routes that traversed the western mountains, while other roads crossed the eastern cordillera and ran into the montaña and lowlands. Some of the lateral roads ran through passes that approach 5,000 m in altitude. Along the east, a few roads ran well beyond the last significant state sites into the jungles or plains, where they seem to have been used to aid military expeditions or as ties to people beyond Inca control.

To build their highway, the Incas claimed exclusive rights over numerous traditional routes, including some that had been built centuries earlier. Some ran right through Wari centers such as Pikillacta and Azángaro, leaving no doubt as to their original cultural associations (Schreiber 1987, 1992). Even so, the Incas' unrivaled vision is exemplified by the highways built where none had previously existed and there was no local population to serve. A prominent new road ran through Chile's Atacama desert, for example, as well as alongside the Nudo de Azuay in the Ecuadorian páramo, on the Peruvian puna south of Huánuco Pampa, and along the western margin of Lake Titicaca (Hyslop 1984:270–4; plate 10.2). Scholars have often commented that the central Andean roads were far more ostentatious than was needed for the practicalities of travel (e.g., Thompson and Murra 1966; Morris and Thompson 1985). The intent of the elaborate design may have been in part to impress travelers and workers called to the centers for labor service.

Plate 10.2 Inca royal highway near Huánuco Pampa, Peru; photo by John Hyslop, courtesy Division of Anthropology, American Museum of Natural History

The roads provided conduits for rapid communication, personnel movement, and logistical support. Soldiers, porters, and llama caravans were prime users, as were the nobility and other individuals on official duty. Other subjects were allowed to walk along the roads only with permission and tolls were charged at some bridges. Relay messengers, called *chaski*, were stationed at intervals of about 6 to 9 km to carry everything from news from the battlefront to fresh marine fish for the ruler in the sierra (see below, *Measurement*). Rowe (1946:231) estimates that they could cover about 240 km per day. Since a message carried from Quito to Cuzco would have required about 375 transfers (Hyslop 1984:308), some means must have been found to reduce the garbling that would accompany an oral report transmitted by so many locally drafted couriers. Estete and Garcilaso said that the chaski carried *khipu* along with the spoken message, which implies that some knot-records could be read with minimal oral input (chapter 1). Despite the chaskis' renown, we cannot even be sure that the runners were used along all of the major highways, since Hyslop was unable to locate roadside relay stations (*chaskiwasi*) along several important and well-preserved stretches. He concluded that we can only be certain that runners were stationed along

Figure 10.1 Woven suspension bridge spanning the Apurimac River west of Cuzco; engraving from Squier 1877

the main highland route and a couple of routes to the coast (ibid.), although additional surveys may turn up more sites.

Inca roads varied greatly in their scale, construction techniques, and appearance. For the most part, Hyslop found that road widths varied between about one and four meters. Thousands of drains and culverts channeled water alongside or under the roads and, where necessary, the Incas built buttressing walls or causeways over wetlands. The roads were flattened and clearly delineated by walls, stone markers, wooden or cane posts, or piles of rocks. In a number of locations, there were two or even three parallel roads. Although the highway has a reputation for ignoring obstacles in the interest of straightness, Hyslop found that straight stretches rarely ran for more than a few kilometers and that the roads are filled with minor adjustments to the terrain. The grandest highways were neatly paved with cobbles or flagstones, but much of the network employed dirt, sand, grass, and other natural surfaces. The finest paved roads were concentrated between the altiplano and Ecuador and along the routes that linked that stretch of highway and the coast. Early travelers, such as Cieza, marveled over the stone staircases that mounted the steep western passes. The technical skill seen in some roads was so great that they are still used for foot traffic or as the foundation of vehicular routes.

The dissected topography, rivers, and marshy areas of the Andes spurred considerable ingenuity as people sought ways to traverse watercourses. Polo commented that, "(o)f the four roads leaving Cuzco, there is none which is crossed by a river easy to ford unless by a miracle" (Polo 1965b:52). In some important valleys, such as the Mantaro, crossing points over fast-running rivers lay 50 km or more apart. To get over wide, meandering rivers along the coast and in the highlands, people commonly used rafts (Regal Matienzo 1972; Hyslop 1984:317–34). In marshy highland areas, the Incas built bridges of stone or floating reeds. The suspension bridges were built of braided cables that supported floors of wood, fiber, and brush; some had full side walls. The most famous bridge spanned about 45 m across the Apurimac River, west of Cuzco (figure 10.1). Even when they were well kept up, the longer suspension bridges may not have been passable during much of the day, when winds set them to swinging (see Squier 1877:545). And when the breezes were still, the bridges could support only a few people at a time. Those conditions meant that large numbers of soldiers or support personnel could not always travel easily across the landscape. Some chroniclers noted that many suspension bridges, like roads, were built in pairs; they suggested that the separate courses were designated either for the nobility and commoners or for each sex. The most unnerving means of crossing ravines was the hanging basket, or *oroya*. The basket could span greater distances than any bridge (over 50 m), but could move only a few passengers at a time; a single failure of materials spelled disaster (see Hyslop 1984).

Measurement

Inca measurements were attuned to specific applications rather than being standardized in ways that might have facilitated relating length to area or volume, for example. Measurements of relatively short length, for example, were based on parts of the human body, while those pertaining to travel over any significant distance were related as much to time spent on the road as to a linear measure. Similarly, measurements of land area depended on productivity. The shortest measure may have been the finger (*rok'ana*), although that length is mentioned in Bertonio's Aymara dictionary and not in the early Quechua lexicons (Rowe 1946:323–4). The next largest measurement was the distance between the tips of the outstretched index finger and thumb, which amounted to about 12–14 cm. Then followed the *k'apa*, about 20 cm and roughly equivalent to the Spanish *palmo*. The next largest measure was the *khococ*, which was about 45 cm. Finally came the *rikra*, which measured about 1.62 m; it was divided into two units. Rods a *rikra* long were reportedly used as a standard measurement for land and for constructions requiring precise lengths. In a test of this premise, Farrington (1983) found that architecture and terraces in Cuzco and on the Urubamba estates were regularly based on multiples of 1.6 m. Some of the central platform mounds at provincial centers along the main highway between Cuzco and Quito were similarly designed. The platform at Huánuco Pampa, for example, is 32 × 48 m at its base, while the best preserved side of the platform at Hatun Xauxa also measures 32 m.

The shortest unit used to measure travel distance was the pace (*thatki*). Rowe (1946:325) suggests that it was counted as one step with each foot and may have equalled about 1.3 m. Another term, *tupu*, was used both for longer distances and for units of area. The length of a *tupu* is uncertain, since it was often described in the early sources as 1.5 times the Spanish league, which itself was a measure of uncertain distance. The chronicler Murúa wrote that 6,000 *thatki* were equal to a *tupu*, and Hyslop's (1984:296–7) review of the literature suggested that a league usually fell between 4.1 and 6.3 km. If we take those numbers, then a pace would have fallen between about 1.0 and 1.6 m and a *tupu* would correspond to about 6.2–9.4 km. Hyslop (1984:294–303) points out, however, that Andean concepts of travel distance were influenced by the amount of time needed to traverse a stretch. Rough terrain would have shortened the linear distance assigned to a *tupu*, while flat surfaces would have extended it. The Incas may have also used the concept of a day's walk, since that distance was supposed to lie between adjacent *tampu* along the road. Although there was a substantial amount of variation, Hyslop found that the majority of *tampu* lay between 15 and 25 km apart. Since that is less than Andean people can easily traverse in a day, he suggests that the spacing was tightened up to accommodate the distance that a llama caravan would normally cover.

The *tupu* as a measure of area was probably a flexible unit that was adjusted to the agricultural productivity of the lands that it was measuring. Some of the chroniclers used European terms to describe the *tupu*, but they varied in the expanses that they cited. Cobo said that it was 50 fathoms by 25 fathoms, while Garcilaso suggested that it was equivalent to 1.5 Spanish *fanegas*.[4] Garcilaso's estimate (0.94 ha) unfortunately works out to almost three times that of Cobo's (0.33 ha). Although Rowe suggests that Cobo was more likely to be right, Murra points out that Andean farmers often resisted fixing their land area according to European measures. Instead, they considered a *tupu* to be the amount of land a couple needed to support themselves for a year, which Garcilaso also noted. Since the land's agricultural output varied markedly from one ecozone to the next, the area encompassed by a *tupu* would have varied accordingly (Murra 1980a).

Cobo also wrote that the Incas had no unit of liquid measure, but did have one for grain. That measure was usually a large gourd that contained about half a Spanish *hanega*, that is about 28 liters. The Incas also seem to have used the Roman balance, which they may have borrowed from coastal peoples, but do not seem to have developed a set of standard weights (Rowe 1946:325; Rostworowski 1960b). They also seem to have avoided use of commodities that combined the functions of media of exchange and standard of value. Even so, coca was widely used as an exchange good in the Andes and the Incas dispensed it as part of their obligation to the taxpayers who put in their labor duties to the state. Along the coast and in Ecuador, there was also a long pre-Inca tradition of fabricating bronze axe-monies (*hachas*) in units of 2, 5, and 10 (Hosler et al. 1990). It is not certain if the axe-monies were still in use by the Inca era, but shell beads (*chaquira*) used as media of exchange were certainly in circulation in Ecuador and along the north coast. In neither case, however, did the Incas adopt the currencies into their economies.

Resettlement

No state policy affected the Andean social landscape more than resettlement. According to Cobo, Inca officials as a rule selected six or seven thousand families from each new province to be moved elsewhere. That figure is too general to be useful for any particular region, but his estimate that about a quarter to a third of the population was resettled may be about right on average. The most renowned program moved entire communities hundreds or even thousands of kilometers to create enclaves of settlers called *mitmaqkuna*. Occasionally, the Incas moved people to lands that were ecologically similar to their places of origin, presumably to ease the adjustment, or exchanged groups from two locations with one another.

A principal reason for resettlement was to disperse societies that posed threats to Inca security (e.g., the Qolla, Ayaviri, Chachapoya, and Kañari). Many colonists were assigned to internal and frontier garrisons. A second goal was to congregate economic specialists whose products were destined for state use. Among them were artisans, such as weavers, potters, and metal smiths; farmers, especially for maize, coca, and peppers; and herders, masons, and miners. Wayna Qhapaq seems to have markedly expanded this program, since he was named as the founder of the largest farms and artisan communities. Another motive lay in the Incas' interest in claiming a divine mandate over the Andes. That vision found its most conspicuous form in the ethnic microcosm created at Cuzco, but the sanctuary at Copacabana with 42 ethnic groups may have been designed for the same purpose.

The colonists were supported from state resources only until they could sustain themselves on the lands they received – perhaps a year or two. The Incas went to some lengths to make sure that the *mitmaqkuna* owed their allegiance to the state. They were required to wear their traditional clothing and to speak their own languages, and their interaction with the local societies was restricted. The colonists were often bitterly resented, since they received prime lands at local expense. Even so, the *mitmaqkuna* sometimes forged relationships with their neighbors to obtain goods that they might otherwise be unable to get.

Such a program might be expected to produce a patchwork quilt of ceramic types, house forms, and mortuary practices across the Andes as ethnic groups were intermixed. Surprisingly, however, if it were not for the many witnesses who testified to the program, we could easily underestimate the scale of resettlement by a factor of a hundred. *Mitmaqkuna* communities are notoriously hard to find archaeologically and it is often easier to recognize local shifts from hilltops to valley flanks. In recent years, stylistic and chemical sourcing analyses of pottery have helped to identify settlers who made pots in their home styles in new settlements (e.g., Lorandi 1984; D'Altroy and Williams 1998), but the lack of a clear archaeological signature for colonists suggests that perishable textiles most clearly distinguished one group's material culture from another's.

Local resettlement complemented the long-distance program. During the Late Intermediate Period, many densely packed villages had been situated at high elevations, often perched on hilltops. Once the Incas were in control, many a community moved downslope, which had the potential to serve everyone's interests (e.g., D'Altroy 1992; Parsons 1998). The Incas gained by reducing their subjects' capacity to rise up and workers could be moved around more easily. From the local viewpoint, a loss of freedom was mitigated when lands became available that had been off limits earlier. A "neon lights" effect may have also been at play, as the lords and peasantry alike were attracted to the power, ceremony, or opportunities that a closer tie to the state provided.

The Varieties of Provincial Rule

To illustrate how the varieties of Inca rule worked in practice, we will take a capsule look at a cross-section of regions, beginning with the best-known Inca province, Huánuco, Peru.

Huánuco, Peru

Huánuco's rich historical (Helmer 1955–6; Ortíz de Zúñiga 1967, 1972) and archaeological (e.g., Morris and Thompson 1985) records provide an exceptional opportunity to study Inca provincial rule. The elaborately planned regional center, Huánuco Pampa (3,800 m), is the grandest Inca site preserved anywhere outside the heartland. Guaman Poma called it one of the "New Cuzcos" and Cieza (1984:234) wrote that it had charge of several adjoining provinces. Built on virgin terrain, the city covered about 2 sq km, within which more than 4,000 buildings were erected. Pathways radiate out through architectural sectors from an immense rectangular plaza, so that the city can easily be divided into two, four, eight, or even twelve parts (figure 10.2). Morris (1990) suggests that the design may have reflected the relationships among the ethnic groups administered by the settlement, in a scheme analogous to Cuzco's ethnic

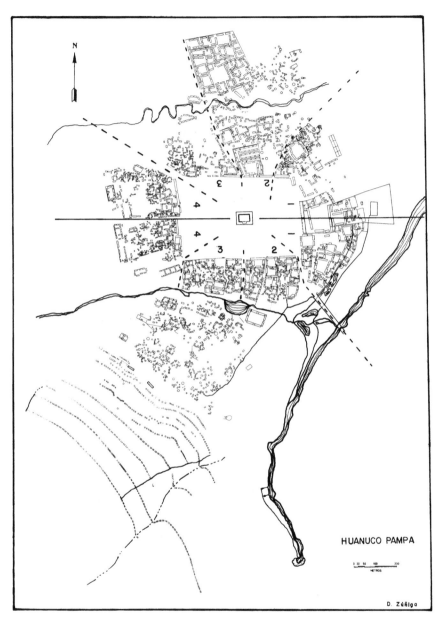

Figure 10.2 Plan of the Inca provincial center of Huánuco Pampa, divided to show potential partitioning of the Inca layout of sacred and social space into two, four, and eight parts; courtesy Craig Morris and the American Museum of Natural History

microcosm. Even though the site could house up to 15,000 people, the permanent population was probably only a fraction of that. Many people came in for a few weeks at a time to fulfill their labor duties or to participate in political and ceremonial functions. Archaeological evidence suggests that one important group of permanent residents were the *aqllakuna*. A well-built compound in the north sector, with a single narrow doorway, contains 50 exceptionally regular buildings. Excavations there recovered weaving and spinning tools, along with large quantities of the kind of jars used to brew and store chicha – just the kind of remains one would expect from the Chosen Women's duties (Morris and Thompson 1985).

The elegant stepped platform (32 × 48 m at its base; plate 10.3) in the plaza's center was built with a facade of dressed stone, but the site's finest ashlar buildings lie in the royal residences of the eastern sector. In one of the more imaginative details, portals through eight unevenly angled walls line up neatly along the site's east–west axis. The alignment runs from a cut-stone bath in the royal sector directly toward the central platform. This sector was probably rarely occupied, which surely reminded the other residents that there was a greater power elsewhere (Morris and Thompson 1985). Despite the site's elegance, the artistry was only skin-deep, since even the finest stereotomy did not extend beyond the visible surfaces. Moreover, many structures toward the perimeter were circular buildings of rough fieldstone built in the local style. On the hill slopes south of the city lie 700 storehouses (30,000 m³) laid out in rows, which housed the supplies used to support state activities.

Huánuco Pampa administered at least five, and perhaps many more, ethnic groups. Inca rule among those societies reflects a full array of standard policies; local lords appear to have held the offices for all units from 1,000 households on down (Julien 1982, 1993; Grosboll 1993). C. Julien (1993:210) describes the effects on one ethnic group: "First of all, 1,110 of the 4,108 Chupachos households were in Cuzco. Another 580 resided out of the province on a full-time basis. Another 918 were out of the province on at least a temporary basis, including the 500 assigned to army service. Those who remained, except perhaps the 500 assigned to do agricultural service, were permanently relocated to specialized communities within Chupachos territory." In the empire's final years, Waskhar claimed the entire populace as a personal estate (Julien 1993:206, 209–11; see Helmer 1955–6: 24, 26–8, 30–1, 35–6, 38). Altogether, Inca policies altered the social landscape in ways that would have been unimaginable to the indigenous peoples beforehand.

The province's roads and waystations were especially elaborate. The roads featured extended paved surfaces, paved staircases, stone drainage channels, retention walls, bridges, and causeways. In some areas, the

Plate 10.3 Pyramid platform in the center of the great plaza at Huánuco Pampa; courtesy Craig Morris and the American Museum of Natural History

paved highway was 15 m wide and one paved staircase was 16 m wide, while two roads ran parallel along some stretches. Hyslop remarked of one 20-km section, that he "has never seen, nor is aware of publications reporting, such a monumental sector of Inca road anywhere else in the Andean highlands" (Hyslop 1984:74, see 68–84; see also Thompson and Murra 1966; Morris and Thompson 1985:109–18). Intriguingly, there is little material evidence for Inca rule away from the grand center and roads. Grosboll (1993:74–5) observes that the Incas invested most effort in the northeast, which was favorable for maize and coca cultivation and for exchange across the frontier. That is where two hundred ethnic Incas from Cuzco were settled and where the most elaborate irrigation and terracing systems are found. The only local village (Ichu) that contains much pottery or architecture in the Inca style was home to the highest-ranking ethnic lord in the early Colonial period (Thompson 1967; Morris and Thompson 1985; Grosboll 1993).

Coastal Peru

Peru's north coast presented a different challenge, for this region had already seen 1,500 years of state society. Chimu resistance to the Inca advances was stout and the Incas distrusted most of the coastal populace. A key Inca goal was therefore to eliminate resistance orchestrated by native elites. To that end, they held the Chimu king hostage in Cuzco, while dividing control among local lords who each headed up a territory roughly corresponding to a valley (Rowe 1948; Netherly 1978; Hyslop 1990:249–51; Ramírez 1990). Irrigation engineers were sent to the south coast to oversee canal systems, while other colonists went to work at *tampu* or to make pots in nearby mountain provinces (Espinoza Soriano 1975; Ramírez 1982, 1990; Rostworowski 1990). Two other policies deliberately weakened the coastal lords. First, coastal peoples were forbidden to carry weapons. Just as important symbolically, some upvalley coca fields were transferred to the jurisdictions of highland peoples, so that the lords lost some of their ability to dispense this vital product (Rostworowski 1983, 1990).

For the most part, the Incas governed the dense coastal populace from installations at least partway into the highlands. In the Chillón valley, the main Inca site lay at Huancayo Alto, about 30 km up the valley. This small settlement lay in lands occupied by the Yauyos, a highland people who kept up good relations with the Incas and were granted the lowlanders' coca fields (Dillehay 1975; Rostworowski 1990). Sites built according to Inca canons are virtually absent near the coast. The Incas built no major centers there and, in fact, their most elaborate construc-

Plate 10.4 Coastal Inca center of Tambo Colorado, in the Pisco Valley, Peru (photo by author)

tion was probably the tapia-walled desert road (Xérez 1985:82–5; Hyslop 1984:37–55). The lacuna is all the more striking when we consider that the coast is incredibly rich in archaeological remains, where the desert climate has preserved even delicate organic remains for millennia. Three important sites in the lower valleys with Inca elements are Túcume, Tambo Real, and Chiquitoy Viejo.[5] Each site had a prior occupation into which the Incas installed a state sector, but local architectural styles and artifacts still dominate (see Conrad 1977; Hyslop 1984:49, 1990:327, n. 6). The cache of brilliantly decorated Inca figurines found at the top of Túcume's main pyramid speaks more of an ideological claim to power in the productive Lambayeque Valley than to direct administration.

The intensive rule on Peru's south coast contrasted starkly with these policies. The Chincha, for example, were so esteemed that their foremost lord fell at Atawallpa's side in Cajamarca's plaza. The Chincha were granted trading privileges along the Ecuadorian coast to obtain Spondylus shell and other goods from extra-territorial peoples. A Spanish expedition ran into one such trading raft a few years before the invasion of Peru was mounted. On the balsa, they found shell, emeralds, and a host of other fine goods (Sámano-Xérez 1937:65–6). The shell, called *mullu*, had many uses – as currency in the north, as decoration on cloth for the Incas, and as raw material for statues and rain ceremonies in the mountains. The Chincha grant was thus a major concession.

Physical evidence of Inca rule in Chincha is concentrated at La Centinela, where a small Inca sector was erected at the heart of the pre-Inca center. Like the compound at Túcume, it seems to have been intended for the ceremonial and political activities that legitimized both Inca rule and the privileges enjoyed by the valley's aristocrats (Morris 1998:296–7). In the adjacent Pisco Valley, the Incas built two new centers, called Lima La Vieja and Tambo Colorado (plate 10.4). The latter is the classic coastal Inca site. Its adobe architecture flanks a large trapezoidal plaza, with the platform situated at the downvalley edge. Traces of brilliant red and yellow clay still adhere to some walls, providing hints of the colorful vision the settlement presented when it was occupied. Two other sites were important in Inca relations with coastal peoples. Inkawasi (Cañete), one of the "New Cuzcos," was built for the express purpose of conquering the resistant Guarco people. Once that goal was achieved, the site was vacated (Hyslop 1985). The other great site was Pachacamac (Lurin Valley), which was an important city and oracle for 1,500 years before the Incas. There, the Incas intruded five architectural sectors, including a temple and enclave of priestesses, but allowed the local society an unusual degree of independence (Cornejo 2000).

The Lake Titicaca Basin

The Lake Titicaca region held abundant attractions for the Incas. While the lake lay at the center of the Incas' vision of their genesis, the altiplano's wealth made it an early target for Cuzco's expansionist aspirations. In 1532, the peoples living around the lake had been formed into about thirteen provinces. As a result of their early alliance with the Incas, the Lupaqa enjoyed a privileged position. The Lupaqa province was composed of two *hunu* of 10,000 households each, but the Incas adjusted to the local demography by organizing the hierarchy around seven population centers. Local Aymara-speaking lords held positions of power in all levels of the hierarchy. Resettlement and militarism devastated some of the other peoples of the basin. Since the Ayaviri had vigorously resisted Inca domination, they were savaged and the province was nearly vacated (Julien 1983:88). Cieza wrote that the survivors "went through the sown fields calling upon their dead ancestors for a long time, and lamented their ruin with groans of profound emotion . . ." (Diez de San Miguel 1964:64–6, 106, 170; see Julien 1983:89–93). The rebellious Qolla were employed as masons and soldiers from Cuzco to Ecuador, while Thupa Inka Yupanki claimed five of their towns as personal estates. The most variegated pocket of colonists lay at Copacabana, where members of 42 ethnic groups were resettled from all over the empire (Ramos Gavilán 1976:43). In addition, seven altiplano groups south of the lake provided 14,000 workers for Wayna Qhapaq's farms at Cochabamba, Bolivia (Wachtel 1982).

The archaeological record also reflects the Inca impact on the basin. Cieza's report that the Incas forced the local societies to quit their fortified hilltops is supported by field studies that show that the populace on both the western and southern sides of the lake moved closer to the water's edge. Surveys along the western lakeshore found that most of the Inca-era populace lived there. Nevertheless, the uplands were still essential for the basin's economy, as vast herds were put to pasture there (Cieza 1967:83; Hyslop 1984:119; Albarracín-Jordan and Mathews 1992:215–42; Stanish 1997:210–11). The most prominent center in the northwest basin was Hatunqolla. This settlement, now buried by a modern town, covered about 50 ha, that is, about one-eighth of Huánuco Pampa's area (Julien 1983). Chucuito was even more spacious, covering about 80 ha. Both of these provincial capitals and likely all the Inca sites along the two roads that ran around the lake were founded in pristine locations. They were provisioned with both high quality Cuzco-style pottery and regional styles (Hyslop 1984:116–25). The basin also contained many religious installations. The settlement at Arapa and maybe even the entire province of Chiquicache were dedicated to the Sun (Polo 1940:182; C. Julien 1993:184). Likewise, the province of Copacabana, located on a promontory extending into the lake, was an Inca sanctuary (Ramos Gavilán 1976:43). The temples on the Islands of the Sun and the Moon provide witness to the importance of the lake in state ideology, and Cobo described Tiwanaku as a universal shrine (Cobo 1990: bk. 1, ch. 19, p. 100). Another kind of state facility consisted of artisan colonies set to work making textiles and ceramics (e.g., Milliraya) and metals (e.g., Pila Patag; see chapter 12; Murra 1978; Espinoza Soriano 1987b; Spurling 1992; Hyslop 1984:130–1). Altogether, the evidence from the basin illustrates that the Incas developed extensive independent facilities that were set apart from the local societies, no matter how privileged they were.

The South Andes

Southern Kollasuyu, the empire's southeastern quarter, is often considered marginal to Inca interests, because of its low population, relative lack of large installations, and distance from Cuzco. That perception is in part well founded, but the region's thin documentary record (Bibar 1966; Valdivia 1960; Matienzo 1967) has led many scholars to overlook the richness of the Inca archaeological remains. Because some peoples resisted Spanish dominion for about 130 years, Inca rule was only a distant memory in oral traditions when the first written accounts were taken down. Even so, we may infer that the Argentine and Chilean lands were divided into only four or five provinces (Lorandi 1988; Lorandi and Boixadós 1987–8). There is no mention of the decimal hierarchy anywhere, but we do not know if that stems from gaps in our knowledge or if, as in Ecuador, the Incas never installed the hierarchy among native peoples. The prominent mention of *mitmaqkuna*, however, indicates that some important positions were filled by colonists.

The infrastructure was not as ambitiously developed as it was in the north, but it still reflects considerable effort carried out within a global conception. Regional surveys have now recorded close to 400 Inca sites or settlements with Inca sectors in south Bolivia, Chile, and Argentina. In recent years, field workers have found many previously unknown Inca sites by surveying high elevations, transverse road networks, and the eastern slopes (Raffino 1983, 1993; C. Vitry pers. comm. 1998). A key Inca tactic was to found settlement clusters at agriculturally productive locations from which travel and communications could be controlled. At some settlements, such as Turi (Chile), Tastil, Quilmes, and Fuerte Quemado (Argentina), the Incas simply installed sectors within existing towns. Chile was mostly administered from sites high in the mountains, paralleling the indirect approach applied to Peru's north coast. In contrast to many important sites in the north, the Incas relied heavily on local material culture at their centers, so that ceramics or other artifacts made in the imperial style are far less common in the south.

The Incas intensified mining, farming, herding, and artisanry in and around the state centers. Raffino estimates that three-quarters of the Inca sites in the mineral-rich south Andes were involved in mining or metallurgy, but some large state farms also lay there. They also improved security by erecting fortresses, such as Pucará de Andalgalá and Pucará de las Pavas, along the upper edge of the eastern slopes. On both the east and west, the line of forts lay well up in the mountains, above other Inca settlements and farms. It is hard to say at present if the lower settlements were founded only after the forts had assured security, or if the forts were a fall-back designed to foil any incursion into the mountains.

Resettlement also reshaped the demography of the south. In the Calchaquí Valley, for example, the Pulares gained status and resources at the expense of the Calchaquíes, who resisted Inca rule. Settlers from Tucumán and Santiago del Estero of the eastern lowlands were moved into the intermontane valleys, while altiplano societies, such as the Churumatas and Chichas, were resettled along the eastern fringes. Canas and Canches *mitmaqkuna* from as far away as Peru (1,200 km) were also settled in Chicoana and Quiri-Quiri (Lorandi 1991). Finally, the Incas claimed the sacred landscape by constructing many shrines on the highest peaks (Schobinger et al. 1966; Beorchia 1985; Reinhard 1985; Ceruti 1997). In addition to their ritual purposes, the shrines served a political end by interjecting the state between the indigenous peoples and their founding ancestors, who were thought to have descended from the peaks.

Highland Ecuador

The Incas fused two extremes of imperial strategy in highland Ecuador: indirect rule through local chiefs, and construction of their second capital at Tumipampa, which took its name from Wayna Qhapaq's kin group (Salomon 1986:172–86, 1987). The chiefdoms were often intransigent foes who occupied difficult terrain and posed administrative dilemmas. They were politically autonomous, but were linked to one another through regional marketing systems; many traded outside imperial territory for Spondylus, gold, feathers, and other materials that the Incas wanted (Idrovo 1984). Salomon judges that, initially, the Incas found it effective to rule each area through a paramount chief who was sometimes elevated to represent a pooled set of smaller chiefdoms. Over time,

Cuzco tried to shift toward a policy of social and political integration. Some local elites resettled in Quito were granted estates and trading privileges, which gave them a vested interest in maintaining the state economy. Small versions of the state tribute and political systems were also set up within the chiefdoms. There is more evidence of those efforts around Tumipampa than in the north, which likely stems from the longer Inca occupation in the south (esp. Salomon 1986:185; Idrovo 1988). Despite the Incas' efforts at civilizing the region, the decimal hierarchy was found largely among the colonists, not the natives (Espinoza Soriano 1975:387; Salomon 1986:172). The resettlement program altered the ethnic composition of the south Ecuadorian highlands as much as any part of the empire, as the entire landscape around Tumipampa was reformed (Truhan 1997).

There are notable Inca sites in Ecuador, but the recorded archaeological remains are inconsistent with the intensity of rule described in the sources. Tumipampa and Quito were the most important centers, but both unfortunately lie under modern cities. Tumipampa was also the locale of heated battles at the inception of the war between Atawallpa and Waskhar, when Inca armies deliberately destroyed much of the city (Hyslop 1990:264–5). Documents indicate that Tumipampa (a "New Cuzco") shared several toponyms with the original imperial capital (Arriaga 1965:24).[6] For instance, the core part of both sites was laid out between two rivers that flowed northwest to southeast, one of which was named Huatanay in each city (Idrovo 1984, cited in Hyslop 1990:140–2). Only modest amounts of ashlar masonry are to be found in standing architecture, but Idrovo's excavations have uncovered deposits that suggest that cut-stone work was prominent. The fact that about 80 percent of the excavated pottery was in the Cuzco polychrome style underscores the state's high status (Idrovo 1984:98). Ingapirca is more spectacular. Situated about 40 km north of Tumipampa, this site consists of an Inca ceremonial and residential complex built over an important Kañari settlement (Hatun Cañar) that had been occupied for several hundred years. Excavations indicate that the Incas demolished the existing surface architecture, perhaps in part as retribution against the recalcitrant Kañari. Fresco and Cobo suggest that the rock prominence upon which the great oval structure was erected was considered to be the origin place of the Kañari. By building on the outcrop, the Incas may have been paying homage to the ancestral power while claiming precedence in mediating between this and other worlds (Alcina Franch 1978; Fresco 1984; see Hyslop 1990:261–4). Other recorded sites are dedicated to military activities, transportation and communication, ceremony, and royal residence, but Inca settlements related to agricultural and craft production, herding, colonies, and residential sites with imperial ceramics are largely missing from Ecuador's archaeological register.

Frontier Relations

The Incas enjoyed a geographic advantage unique among pre-modern empires – at the apex of their power, no foreign competitor could threaten their dominance. There was no analog to the Tarascans for the Aztecs, the steppe nomads for the Chinese, or the Germans, Parthians, and Sassanians for the Romans. Even so, Tawantinsuyu's frontier traversed over 4,000 km of mountains, jungles, and plains, across which the Incas had to deal with scores of societies. The Incas maintained a flexible array of relations with those people and in many areas promoted economic and cultural ties beyond the limits of their military and political control (see papers in Dillehay and Netherly 1988). Regional hostilities called for a hardened border in some places, but for the most part the frontier was a permeable membrane across which the Incas regulated, but did not shut off, traffic.

The northern perimeter of the empire is conventionally set at the Río Angasmayo in Pasto territory, near the Ecuador–Colombia border, across which the Incas seem to have maintained open relations (see Salomon 1986). In the rough terrain of the eastern Ecuadorian slopes, Cuzco's armies ran into fierce resistance, and it appears that the relatively secure edge of the empire lay along an eastern cordon of forts bordering the Quito basin (Salomon 1986:148–51; see Renard-Casevitz et al. 1986). In Chachapoyas territory, local documents state that Thupa Inka Yupanki once visited and claimed lands toward Moyobamba, about 100 km into the jungle (RGI 1:166–75). Recent survey in the region shows that the Incas built several small outposts well into the forest and there is historical mention of small forts along the borderlands in Huánuco (Schjellerup 1997:112–67). Farther south, coca fields claimed by the Mantaro Valley societies lay about 50 km into the jungles, but no forts are known along the eastern slopes there (RGI 1).[7] How far to the north and east of Cuzco the Incas applied their rule is also unclear, because survey of the eastern slopes has been rare. The *tampu* typical of highland provinces are unknown below about 1,800–2,000 m, but a section of Inca road has been found 200 km down the Río Urubamba from Cuzco. Several sources suggest that expeditions ventured well into the tropical lowlands now occupied by the Piro and Machiguenga, and societies within the empire traded there for forest products (Ortiz de Zúñiga 1967, 1972; Rowe 1985b; Renard-Casevitz et al. 1986:68, 71; Camino 1989; Pärssinen 1992:107–18). Overall, it appears that the frontier in lands now part of Peru was not heavily defended and that the Incas tried to extend their relations into the jungles peaceably once conquest had failed.

In Bolivia, there is a great disparity between the locations of state settlements and the farthest Inca advances into a larger territory. Thupa Inka Yupanki reportedly marched 800 km into the lowlands east of Cuzco, along the Madre de Dios river. The most distant named point, Paititi, lies about 400 km beyond the forts that line the eastern cordillera. Inca sites are also strung out along the upper Río Beni, suggesting that Cuzco may have tried to establish control into the *llanos de Mojo* (Saignes 1985:18). Samaipata is the easternmost major Inca site in the region. The Incas said that they had won over some groups even farther out through gifts and alliances, an effort that was stimulated by the discovery of gold. They sent 1,000 miners into the lowlands along with 5,000 *mitmaqkuna* to provide their sustenance, but the settlement was later overrun (see Saignes 1985:20; Pärssinen 1992:130–1). A similar situation existed along the Argentine frontier – a string of forts in the eastern mountains, beyond which expeditions advanced onto the plains without annexing them (see Raffino 1983, 1993 for a review of Inca sites in the south Andes). In both Jujuy and Salta, the Incas gained enough control over the piedmont to establish extensive farms and associated facilities with hundreds of storehouses (Boman 1908; Fock 1961; González 1983; Mulvany de Peñaloza 1986; Mulvany de Peñaloza and Soria 1998). The people living in the Tucumán piedmont allied themselves with the Incas for protection against the plains dwellers, and were dispersed throughout the south Andes as military and economic settlers.

Writers from the sixteenth century to the present have puzzled over the empire's southern limit, placing it anywhere from the Río Maipu, just south of Santiago, to the Río Bío Bío, 300 km beyond. The most southerly major Inca site is the fort called Cerro del Inga, about 80 km south of Santiago in the Cachapoal drainage (Planella et al. 1991; Planella and Stehberg 1994). However, Inca-style copper axes and ceramics have been found as far south as Valdivia, 700 km beyond Santiago. Dillehay and Gordon (1988) point out that the problem of fixing a border in Chile evaporates if we drop the idea that political, military, and economic frontiers coincided neatly. For the far south, they suggest that economic and cultural ties with the Araucanians extended well beyond the military and political limits of the empire.

Frontier relations at the fuzzy limits of dominion were thus complex and varied, because they met imperial needs that changed over time and space. It is especially interesting that the Inca advances to the north and south halted at the edge of rich agricultural expanses. The temperate lands of the Mapuche were richer and more populous than those farther north in Chile, and the societies of Colombia north of the Pasto were wealthy chiefdoms. It seems most likely that logistical obstacles, the great distances from Cuzco, and formidable local resistance combined to halt the progression of Inca rule.

chapter eleven

Farmers, Herders, and Storehouses

> When the Inca settled a town, or reduced one to obedience, he
> set up markers on its boundaries and divided the fields and arable
> land within its territory into three parts, in the following way:
> One part he assigned to Religion and the cult of his false gods,
> another he took for himself, and a third he left for the common
> use of the people. It has not been possible to determine whether
> these parts were equal in any towns and provinces; however, it
> is known that in many places the division was not equal, but
> depended on the availability of land and the density of the popu-
> lation . . . The Inca had the same division made of all the
> domesticated livestock, assigning one part to Religion, another to
> himself, and another to the community; . . . he did the same with
> the grazing lands and pastures in which the livestock was pas-
> tured, so that the herds were in different pastures and could not
> be mixed.
>
> **Cobo 1979:211, 215**

Father Cobo's description of farming and herding, in which all resources
were divided into three parts, is the classic sketch of an orderly Inca
economy. In Garcilaso's more idealized account, no one ever went
hungry, because the community and state provided for everyone's welfare
from resources that were adequate for every need. The priest did not
share Garcilaso's romantic vision, but did comment approvingly that
communities that practiced the ancient ways of mutual assistance were
far better off in the seventeenth century than those that did not. There
was truth in both chroniclers' portrayals, but Cobo simplified things,
while Garcilaso glossed over the effects of labor exploitation, loss of
prime pastures and fields, and the forced removal of millions of people
from their ancestral lands. For a more accurate view, we need to consider both the vast resources commanded by the state, church, and aristocracy, and those held by the common folk in the variegated Andean

environment. Equally important, we need to disentangle utopian myths from the grind of daily life in a demanding land.

In some early empires, the heartland's economy was markedly more complex than that of the provinces and the capital was a vacuum for provincial production. The core cities of the Aztec Triple Alliance, for instance, housed great markets and quarters for artisans and merchants (Smith 1996). Their immediate hinterlands included garden-like farmlands and towns that specialized in particular crafts, such as pottery, textiles, or obsidian tools. Taxes in cacao and cloth from farther afield poured into the center, where elites consumed them or exchanged them for other goods. Similarly, Rome was the hub of a circum-Mediterranean marketing system (Garnsey and Saller 1987). Its populace, subsidized by a public dole, consumed much of the grain and wine output of entire regions, including Egypt, the Crimea, eastern Spain, and southern France. Many of its provinces shifted toward a more fully monetary economy, in part because some taxes were levied in widely used currencies. In these and other cases, the empire's economy was focused on consumption at the core.

Tawantinsuyu was unusual in these respects. The Incas did not have a large urban population to support in Cuzco, nor could they move bulk goods across great distances as part of a regular subsistence system. Even so, the conquests gave them access to the labor of millions of workers, expanses of farmlands and pastures, and the Andes' mineral wealth. How best to take advantage of the human and natural resources was the issue. When the Inca expansion began, economic activities in the highlands were organized community by community or at most by a regional polity. Highland societies did not typically have markets, taxation in goods, a temple economy, or any other institution that would allow the Incas to easily divert their products to Cuzco's ends. People living on the coast, on the other hand, had economies that were more specialized and interdependent, which the Incas were ill-equipped to supervise directly.

Caught between societies with much simpler and more complex economic systems, the Incas chose to intensify the highland economies they knew best and left the more integrated systems largely alone. Beginning with his classic doctoral thesis, John Murra (1980b) has shown how the Incas used the language of kin-based production and exchange to represent their economy as if it were just an extension of familiar obligations. A few observers that he drew from, especially the astute Polo (1940; see also Falcón 1946; Garcilaso 1960; Cobo 1979), took pains to explain to their superiors how things differed from Europe. Some elements of Andean economics struck the Spaniards as novel, bizarre, or idolatrous, for example the ritualized exchange and hospitality that were intertwined with political relations, and the ceremony that accompanied everything from shearing wool to tilling the fields.

Polo and his compatriots described how the Incas claimed farmlands, pastures and flocks, and all the wild and mineral resources of the land for themselves. The peasants paid their taxes in labor on a rotating basis, while the products of their own fields and flocks were untouched. In return, the state owed largess, security, and leadership in all its forms. To make the system work, the Incas periodically counted the empire's heads of household and organized many of them into a pyramid of tax-paying units that encompassed from 10 to 10,000 households (chapter 10). Over time, state officials also resettled entire communities of farmers and artisans who were set to work for particular needs. Although they annexed lands with markets, money, and specialized communities, the Incas did not adopt market features into their state economy. Instead, they created an independent set of state resources and institutions that provided for their needs.

Labor Service

Darrell La Lone (1994) has suggested an apt phrase for the Inca economy – *supply on command* – because it was designed primarily to meet institutional goals, rather than follow the supply and demand motivations of market economics. As they did with so many elements of their rule, the Incas drew from earlier Andean statecraft in designing their economy. The Moche, Wari, and Chimu, for example, had all increased the intensity of farming, herding, and artisanry within their domains (Moseley and Cordy-Collins 1990; Schreiber 1992; Shimada 1994). Even so – and even though they relied on customary principles – Andean economics were radically modified under Cuzco's rule.

By declaring that they owned everything, the Incas devised a rationale that gave people access to their traditional lands only in return for labor duty. The peasants' household output was untouched by Inca demands, but their resources and labor were not. As Murra (1980b) observes, many people did not happily digest the idea that they could use their ancestral lands only by the grace of the Inca. Most of the services and products that the Inca state required were obtained through a corvée system that tapped the heads of households for rotating labor service, called *mit'a* ("to take a turn"). Cobo (1979:234) explained the situation this way:

> One thing that should be pointed out with respect to the amount of tribute that they brought to the king, and it is that there was no other rate or

limit, either of the people that the provinces gave for the *mita* labor service or in the other requirements, except the will of the Inca. The people were never asked to make a fixed contribution of anything, but all of the people needed were called for the aforementioned jobs, sometimes in larger numbers, other times in lesser numbers, according to the Inca's desire, and the result of those labors was the royal tribute and income; and in this way the people extracted all the gold and silver that the Incas and the *guacas* [*wak'as*, sacred objects and places] had.

To make things work, officials required current information about the size of the taxpaying population and the natural resources at their disposal. They also needed to be familiar with subjects' skills and to understand what goals could be met without undermining communities' self-sufficiency. Those needs were met through the census and a flow of information between the higher authorities and their subordinates (chapter 10). Where the data are preserved, the accounting of both labor and goods seems to have been proportionate to the numbers of households within the units (see below).

The labor tax was levied on hale heads of household, called *hatun runa*. These were the married men who belonged to an age category that corresponded to about 25–50 years of age. Since they made up about 15–20 percent of the empire's population, the Incas could call on the labor of about two million workers. A householder's duties typically required two or three months of work each year, but Incas did not require that the *mit'ayuq* (laborer) work for a specified period or even discharge his obligations by himself. As a result, whole families could take on some jobs and the larger the family, the more quickly the task was done (Cobo 1979:235). Thus, a man with a large family was thought to be well-off. That advantage, among others, gave couples a strong incentive to have a lot of children.

Some early sources wrote that there were standard categories of duties, which were reported in an order that generally reflected cultural importance rather than the numbers of personnel involved. Falcón (1946:137–40) itemized 32 duties for coastal societies and 37 for the highlands, not counting general farming and military service, which claimed the greatest energies. Both his and Murúa's (1986:402–4; see also Guaman Poma 1980:183) list regularly distinguished between artisans who produced fine quality objects and more ordinary goods. From our present perspective, it is hard to be sure that the Spanish reports precisely reflected Andean categories of importance, since the lists do not conform exactly to the local labor assessments that are available.

All taxpayers were supposed to render some labor duty, but in practice many were exempt from the standard corvée service. Officials with responsibilities over 100 households or more were excused from labor service entirely and certain ethnic groups were favored for particular duties because they were thought to have special talents (chapter 9). Among the highland peoples, the Rucanas were employed as litter bearers, some of the Lake Titicaca Qolla as stonemasons, the Chumbivilcas as dancers, and the Chachapoyas, Kañari, Chuyes, and Charka as warriors (Rowe 1946:267–9; Espinoza Soriano 1980). Rostworowski (1989:273) suggests that all coastal artisans were exempted from rotating labor service and were put to work on their specific crafts for the state. Other groups were required to render natural products, such as the spears made of *chonta* palm and the gold dust produced by some jungle peoples. Still others were thought to be virtually useless for state purposes, but were put to work anyway. The Urus, who lived on the southern margins of Lake Titicaca and on the north side of Lake Poopó, were renowned for their ineptitude. The word *uru*, in fact, means "worm" in Quechua and was used as a pejorative by the Incas. They were assigned to fish for the state, as well as to gather reeds and help make cloth, but did not participate in public works projects. In one of the more eccentric duties, one society with nothing else to render had to turn in a basket of live lice every four months, ostensibly so that they would learn the imperatives of service (Cieza 1967:56).

Over time, the Incas modified the ways in which they extracted labor service from their subjects. Although the Incas initially depended on the productive capacities of the general populace for their needs, in the latter decades of their rule they increasingly augmented and even replaced rotating corvée workers with permanent specialists (see Murra 1980b:183–6). They also created several specialized labor statuses, the most important of which were the *mitmaqkuna* (colonists), *yanakuna* (lifelong servants), and the *aqllakuna* (chapters 7, 10). There was also some flexibility in the way policies were applied. According to Santillán (1968), local officials assigned duties to the taxpayers under their supervision. Polo (1916:102) added that a new set of miners was called up at every royal succession to work alongside the miners still committed to the estates of the deceased rulers. Rather than select the workers, the new Inca left the choice up to the ethnic lords. Moore (1958) comments that this kind of discretion provided lords a great deal of leverage in local relations, since notions of equal service could be construed in many ways in practice.

Our best evidence on how labor was assigned locally comes from Spanish inspections, called *visitas*, recorded in the first few decades of the Colonial era. The inspections of 1549 and 1562 in the Spanish province of León de Huánuco (Helmer 1955–6; Ortiz de Zúñiga 1967, 1972) and the 1567 inspection in Chucuito (Diez de San Miguel 1964) are especially rich in detail. Julien (1988) has shown that officials in both locales were supposed to apply duties according to the number of tax-payers on the census rolls and that labor duty rotated among households. In Chucuito, witnesses said that the Incas annually specified the area to be farmed, or the amount of seed to be sown, and the amount of wool to be woven by local communities. As was the case with the house-holders' rights within *ayllu*, we may suspect that those amounts were adjusted intermittently, but confirmed annually.

If we explore the numbers a little, we can see how the tax system worked locally. According to the first Huánuco inspection, the Chupachu and 300 Yacha together made up 4,108 households in the last Inca census, which probably dated to the mid-1520s. That figure included four units of 1,000 households (*waranqa*) made up of 40 units of 100 households (*pachaka*). Julien (1988:264–6) suggests that one percent of the taxpayers was the base for assessing levies, since many duties were assigned to 40 households or a multiple. Table 11.1 shows the house-holds dedicated to the wide range of services that were demanded of the Chupachu. Julien points out that we need to keep in mind that some duties, such as farming, lasted only a couple of months a year, while others, such as construction at Cuzco, required continuous duty. LeVine (1987) has also shown that when people made cloth, pots, and other goods, the levies were assessed evenly by units of 100 households. On the other hand, services such as guard duty and portage were assigned evenly among units of 1,000. The difference suggests that tasks that yielded products were tailored to local resources, but service duties did not have to take environmental detail into account.

For archaeologists, the figures are worrisome. Only one of every nine taxpayers performed work that produced architecture and pottery – the two kinds of remains that archaeologists rely on to study the Incas. More than 40 percent performed services that would leave few traces in the archaeological record, such as guard duty and portage. Moreover, every one of the 400 workers assigned to roads and buildings was sent to Cuzco, even though the people came from the province whose center, Huánuco Pampa, was the most elaborate in the empire. The disparities between the tabulated labor duties and archaeology remind us that the most visible remains of Tawantinsuyu are only indirectly related to what people were doing when the Spaniards arrived.

Farms of the State and the Sun

At some point after the Incas took over a territory, state officials set about ensuring a steady supply of food, chicha, textiles, and other supplies.

Table 11.1 Labor service provided to the Incas by the Chupachu of central Peru, as reported in 1549 and 1562

Assignment	Total households	1549					1562
		Extraction	Manufacture	Agriculture	Building/ maintenance	Service	
gold miners: 120 men, 120 women	120	120					+
silver miners: 60 men, 60 women	60	60					+
construction (Cuzco area)	400				400		+
agriculture (Cuzco area)	400			400			
retainers of Wayna Qhapaq (Cuzco)	150					150	+
guards for body of Thupa Inka Yupanki (Cuzco)	150					150	
guards for weapons of Thupa Inka Yupanki (Cuzco)	10					10	
garrison in Chachapoyas	200					200	
garrison in Quito	200					200	
guards for body of the Inca (Cuzco)	20					20	
feather workers	120	120					+
honey gatherers	60	60					+
weavers of tapestry cloth	400		400				+
dye makers	40		40				
herders of Inca's flocks	240					240	+
guards for maize fields	40					40	+
pepper cultivators	40			40			
salt miners (varied: 40, 50, 60)	50	50					+
coca cultivators	60			60			+
hunters for royal deer hunt	40	40					

continued

Table 11.1 *continued*

Assignment	Total households	1549					1562
		Extraction	Manufacture	Agriculture	Building/ maintenance	Service	
sandal makers (Cuzco, Huánuco)	40		40				+
wood workers, products to Cuzco	40		40				+
potters, products to Huánuco	40		40				+
guards for Huánuco Pampa	68					68	
porters carrying loads to Huánuco	80					80	
guards for women of the Inca	40					40	
soldiers and litter bearers	500					500	
cultivators of Inca lands	500			500			
makers of weapons and litters (Cuzco)							
processors of dried, salted fish							+
snare makers for the hunt							+
women in service to the Inca							+
Subtotals	4,108	450	560	1,000	400	1,698	
Percentage		11.0	13.6	24.3	9.7	41.3	
Total	4,108					4,108	

Sources: Helmer 1955–6, Ortiz de Zúñiga 1967; modified from LeVine 1987:23, Julien 1988:265; D'Altroy 1994b:184–5. The figures for miners are ambiguous, since the inspection lists 120 and 60 individuals of each for gold and silver mining, respectively, whereas other figures appear to cite men only. Because this table represents households, I follow Julien in citing 120 and 60 households rather than 240 and 120 individuals.

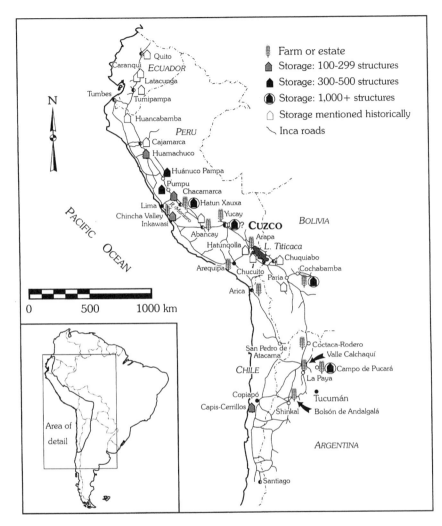

Figure 11.1 Distribution of major state farms and storage facilities in the Inca realm

Many of the state farms were located near provincial centers, but some were also created in especially favorable locales for particular crops (figure 11.1). State and Sun lands often lay next to one another, but the resources and their products were apparently separated both physically and administratively. For the most part, the farms were tended by corvée workers as part of their rotating labor duties, although thousands of colonists were also called upon for this purpose in the empire's later years

Plate 11.1 Vast unfinished terrace system at Coctaca-Rodero, northwest Argentina, possibly an Inca state farm

(Murra 1980b). Both state and Sun lands were distinct from the royal and aristocratic estates created in many parts of the empire, even though they too were maintained by *mitmaqkuna* and *yanakuna* dedicated to lifelong service.

The state farms at Cochabamba, Bolivia, may have been the most extensive in the entire realm (Wachtel 1982; Gyarmati and Varga 1999). In a tour of the south soon after his coronation, Wayna Qhapaq ordered most of the native residents removed from the western part of the valley. Witnesses testified to Polo that 14,000 farm workers were brought in to work fields for the state, mostly from the adjacent altiplano. They said that both permanent colonists and corvée laborers from seven ethnic groups were employed, but did not explain how many people lived there year round or came in only for the peak seasons. The colonists were allocated tracts to support themselves and could also farm along the margins of the state's fields. The farms were divided into 77 narrow strips that ran across the valley and particular groups were assigned to work specific strips. Polo was told that the farms were used to grow maize for the Inca's armies, although we may suspect that "maize" was a shorthand expression for a range of crops. In addition to more than a hundred known Inca-era sites in the valley, the Incas built 2,400 storehouses at Cotapachi, where the produce was stored before being shipped to Paria, Cuzco, and wherever else it was needed (Céspedes Paz 1982; La Lone and La Lone 1987). The permanent colonists had charge of the storehouses in addition to their agricultural labors.

Farms at Arica, Arequipa, and Abancay were also dedicated to military uses (RGI 1965:338; Espinoza Soriano 1973; Spurling 1982:14; La Lone and La Lone 1987). The farms in the warm Abancay Valley were also said to have been founded by Wayna Qhapaq to help sustain his war efforts in the north. Rather than producing maize, the plots were principally dedicated to growing coca, cotton, peppers, and various fruits. The Incas claimed the best bottom lands for themselves and made hill slope fields available to the colonists brought in to work them.

Extensive Inca farms have also been identified archaeologically in the Upper Mantaro Valley, Peru and in Argentina (plate 11.1). In the Upper Mantaro, productive lands within about 5 km of the provincial center (Hatun Xauxa) were virtually empty of subject villages (D'Altroy 1992:154–78). The few that were present contained great numbers of farming tools, such as hoes and clod breakers, but no evidence of other kinds of production typical of villages, such as weaving, metallurgy, or potting. The same area contained thousands of state storehouses, suggesting that the zone surrounding the center was dedicated to Inca farms (plate 11.2). At Coctaca-Rodero, Argentina, a massive terraced field system covers about six square kilometers on the alluvial fans and

Plate 11.2 Storehouses on the hill slopes overlooking the Upper Mantaro Valley, central Peruvian highlands (photo by author)

piedmont (3,700 m) just below the altiplano. Because many terraces were abandoned before completion, it seems likely that the farm was developed late in the empire's run and may never have been put into use (Albeck and Scattolin 1991; Albeck 1992–3; Nielsen 1996). Large tracts may have also been farmed at the Campo de Pucará, in the Lerma Valley of Argentina's eastern piedmont (Boman 1908; Fock 1961; González 1983). Their location suggests that the area was peaceful enough that they could be worked with little danger from the mobile bands who lived on the eastern plains.

Fields were also supposed to be set aside for the religious institutions in every province. Some of those farms were well known and may have been quite large, while hundreds of small plots were also dedicated to the gods. Polo (1916:58–9) mentions a farm for the Sun at Arapa, on the north side of Lake Titicaca, and the entire province of Chiquicache may have also been dedicated to Inti (chapters 7, 10). State and Sun farms were also established south of Cuzco near Raqchi, where a famous temple was built for the Creator God Wiraqocha (La Lone and La Lone 1987). Perhaps more typical were small plots dedicated to nearby temples. In Peru's Chillón valley, residents said that a small coca patch was planted for the Sun and its leaf was offered to the deity while it was still green (Murra 1982:253). We cannot be sure how much land was committed to each kind of farm, but the Sun's resources were probably less than the state's. In one effort to resolve this question, Polo (1916:58–9) compared the storehouses of the state and church in many locales and concluded that the Sun's holdings were much smaller.

Inca farms on the coast were apparently smaller than those in the highlands, and how the Incas got their coastal lands is mostly unclear. In their report on the Chincha valley, Castro and Ortega Morejón (1974) wrote that every 1,000 households ceded 10 *hanegadas* of irrigated lands to the Inca. Roughly speaking, that would have worked out to 190 ha,[1] which is not a small amount, but certainly nothing approaching the farms in the mountains. The Incas nonetheless did intensify some coastal production, as they transferred *mitmaqkuna* with experience in canal engineering from the north coast of Peru to the south (Rostworowski 1990).

If we took the chronicles at face value, we would imagine that maize and coca were essentially the only crops grown on farms of the state and the Sun, with the occasional exception of specialized farms like those at Abancay. The placement of major farms in warm valleys certainly fits that view, and there is little doubt that the maize consumed in chicha and the coca distributed to the armies and state workers were vital to state activities. The Incas even experimented with varieties of maize and appear to have distributed Cuzco flint maize throughout much of the realm. Because the reports to the Spaniards tended to emphasize what was culturally important, however, the emphasis on those two crops is probably misleading. Even on fertile soils, maize must be rotated with other crops to keep the nutrients from being depleted rapidly. Moreover, the botanical evidence from storage facilities suggests that the Incas grew a mix of crops that was locally suitable, even the low-status tubers (see below).

Ceremonial and Agricultural Cycles

The Incas approached farming with weapons in their hands and prayers on their lips. They envisioned agriculture as warfare – a victory claimed by disemboweling the earth (Bauer 1996). At the same time, successful crops could be assured only through supplication to the powers of the earth and the sky. Their agrarian cycle was arranged around a calendar tied to astronomical observations at Cuzco and to the turning of the seasons. It officially began with an August ritual, when the *Sapa Inca* turned over the soil in a sacred field called Sausero within the capital city. This plot, which belonged to the Sun, was revered because the primordial ancestors had first planted maize there. The Incas accompanied the tilling of the land with songs and rituals in which they sacrificed llamas and guinea pigs and poured libations of chicha onto the soil (Cobo 1990:143–4). Garcilaso (1966:151) wrote that the Incas sang verses "which they performed in honor of the sun and their kings; all were composed regarding the meaning of this word 'haylli', which . . . indicates 'triumph', in the sense that they triumphed over the earth breaking it and plowing it, so that it might produce. In those songs, they mixed refrains about discreet lovers and brave soldiers, all with the intent to triumph over the soil."

The emperor or highest Inca noble present took the lead in tilling the soil with a gold-tipped plow, and the Queen and her ladies broke the clods. The king soon retired from his exertions and other lords took up the tasks according to their standing, after which everyone enjoyed a grand banquet. In the provinces, Cuzco's representatives performed similar rituals. The lowest officials and taxpayers worked all day, but farming for the state was festive even for the common folk, as the Incas displayed their generosity by plying them with food and drink at the end of their labors (Cobo 1979:212). The close link among farming, reciprocal obligations, and ritual can be seen in two meanings of the Aymara word *haymatha*. This term is glossed both as "to go and work in the fields which are planted communally, like those of the lord . . . or the poor" and as "to dance in the ancient way particularly when they go to the fields of their leaders" (Bertonio, translation by Murra 1968:134).

To ensure that the life-giving waters continued to flow, the Incas prayed and made sacrifices to the springs and rivers. Cobo (1990:111) recorded a typical entreaty: "O source of water who have irrigated my field for so many years, and by means of this benefaction that you confer upon me I obtain my food, do the same this year, and even increase the amount of water so that the harvest will be more abundant." When the crops were ready to be brought in at Sausero, the activities were once again attended by elaborate rites. The harvest was begun by young men who had recently made the ritual passage into manhood and was followed up by all of the city's nobility. Cobo (1990:140) wrote that the field was then plowed and "they returned with great rejoicing to the main square, wearing the tunics that they had won in war." Molina (1988:118) commented that the maize was used to make chicha for the cult of Mama Waku, one of the founding Inca ancestors.

Several chroniclers explained that the Incas specified a strict order in which the lands were to be worked. The sequence usually described for the highlands said that the church's plots were tilled first, followed by the state fields, and then those of the workers. For the coastal Chincha valley, Castro and Ortega Morejón (1974) reported that the lands of the Inca came first, then those of the state religion and the regional lords, and finally the lands of the "poor," or general peasantry. Despite its repetition, there are ecological reasons to doubt that highland farmers could have adhered strictly to the sequence. Mitchell points out that the formulas run afoul of conditions that require that crops be tended in a staggered sequence according to elevation and maturation time (Mitchell 1980; see also Hastorf 1992). Higher fields normally must be planted before lower lands, because of temperature and rainfall patterns. On a practical basis, farmers could not have worked all state fields from the uplands to the valley bottoms before turning to their own crops. It is possible that state lands were often concentrated in a few ecozones near state centers, or that state lands in any given niche were worked first, or even that the convention applied just to maize fields, in which case the sequence could be a fair representation. Nonetheless, as Mitchell observes, it is likely that the reported labor sequences reflected the elite ideologies of hierarchy more than the details of crop scheduling.

Landed Estates and Grants

Rural manors and other elite resources provide an important contrast to the institutionally and communally held resources. The best-known estates were situated near Cuzco, in the Urubamba drainage. Some of the most celebrated Inca sites, such as Machu Picchu, Pisac, and Ollantaytambo, were royal estates (chapter 6). The development of the manors, especially for the royal kindreds, was part of a trend that converted prime resources into aristocratic holdings. The estates' productivity was needed to maintain the deceased emperor and his descendants and to underwrite their political/ceremonial activities.

Grants of land or other resources were not limited just to the Incas proper. The Incas also used them as an instrument of policy to entice subjects to cooperate with Cuzco's rule. For instance, the Incas gave lands to people who had distinguished themselves in war or who had performed some service of special merit to the crown, such as building a bridge, canal, or road, or who had a valued skill. Children of lords could also receive grants. Polo (1916:73–4) commented that such grants were concentrated in the Cuzco region and that they were passed on to the collective heirs, not to an individual (see also Cobo 1979:213). In northern Ecuador, the Incas awarded lands near Quito to a number of local lords, thinking to draw them closer to imperial control. The lords balked at taking up residence, perhaps because the private gain would have exacted too heavy a political concession (Salomon 1986). Elsewhere, local elites did take advantage of the opportunities. The lords of the Upper Mantaro Valley held lands in the montaña where their personal farmers grew coca and peppers (RGI 1965). Similarly, the paramount Lupaqa lords of the west side of Lake Titicaca sent colonists to live in the warm coastal valleys. There, they grew maize, collected guano, and cultivated or gathered other products that could be shipped up to the highlands for distribution at the lords' discretion. Even as late as 1567, colonists were working for them along the coast (Diez de San Miguel 1964; Murra 1968). Lords on the east side of the lake, in contrast, were awarded lands in the warm eastern valleys.

The Flocks of the Inca

In the Andes, camelids were wealth, transport, food, clothing, and prestige on the hoof (plate 2.2). Because the llama and alpaca lay at the heart of the Inca economy – both culturally and practically – it is small wonder that considerable energy was devoted to breeding large herds that could be used for the armies, sacrifices, and other ends. Unlike some of the lands turned into farms, however, the Incas could not cast about for under-used flocks, but had to requisition herds from conquered peoples (Polo 1916:61–2). Murra (1980b:52) suggests that, since the greatest flocks grazed in the altiplano, the Incas turned their eyes to that region in particular to enhance the herds already husbanded near Cuzco. In the early Colonial era, residents of the Charkas area and the Huamanga Valley testily recalled how the Incas had taken herds from their ancestors.

Although the vast state and Sun herds were carefully tabulated, it is hard to come by reliable numbers. Román y Zamora (1897:122) stated that the Sun had more than a million animals, a figure that may not have been meant literally. Nonetheless, a witness in Chucuito commented that even the altiplano's pastures were sometimes inadequate for the great flocks of the Inca era. In 1567, a middling lord there was reputed to have 50,000 animals (Diez de San Miguel 1964:50; Murra 1968:120), so an estimate of hundreds of thousands or even a million might not be out of line for the church's holdings altogether. The Incas certainly knew how many they had, for they did a census of state and temple animals every November that coincided with ceremonies intended to help the herds multiply (Cieza 1967:101). They also made an effort to introduce flocks into areas where they were unknown as part of the indigenous economy, especially in northern Peru and parts of highland Ecuador (Cieza 1967:52–3, 56).

The prime uses of the herds were military. Armies on the move regularly used trains of thousands of llamas to pack supplies and to supply food when they were no longer needed for portage. Earlier (chapter 4), it was noted that Pizarro ordered Cajamarca cleared of camelids after capturing Atawallpa, because the animals were making a mess of the camp. Zárate also reported that Quizquiz abandoned some 15,000 animals in the eastern mountains after a battle in the first years of the Spanish conquest. The llamas and alpacas were also the principal source of wool and leather for state personnel, especially soldiers. Much of the wool sheared annually from the herds was turned over to women in subject households to spin and make into rough cloth that was turned back to state overseers. Many animals also found their end in myriad sacrifices and in feasts at state installations throughout the empire. To judge from the age profiles of camelid bones recovered from the Calchaquí valley, northwestern Argentina, Inca feasts featured cuts of meat from animals in the prime of life, rather than from the aged animals often eaten in local communities, once their working life was over (D'Altroy et al. 2000).

Herding for the state was at least partially a specialized duty conducted by adults. In some pastures near Cuzco, the herders were *yanakuna*, the lifetime servants (Murra 1980b:56). Those situations contrasted with the typical community practice, in which children and adolescents tended the flocks.

State Storage

A vast storage system provided the bridge between state-sponsored production and use throughout the empire. Because the Incas did not have inland boats or wheeled vehicles pulled by powerful draft animals, they could not regularly move bulky commodities over long distances as part of a subsistence economy. Nor did they have the purchasing power or flexibility of money. Having committed themselves to a staple finance system, in which most supplies came directly from state resources, the Incas had to reproduce their supply system from one province to the next. As with farms and herds, the state and church storehouses were separated from one another administratively and probably physically. Most of the storehouses, called *qollqa*, were built in just a few contexts: at Cuzco, at installations along the roads, and next to state farms (plate 11.2). Cieza (1967:143–4) provides us with a sense of the scale involved:

> ... in the more than 1,200 leagues of coast they governed, they had the delegates and governors, and many lodgings and great storehouses full of necessary things, which were for provisioning the soldiers. Because in one of them, there were lances, and in others darts, and in others sandals, and in others the remaining arms they had. Moreover, some storehouses were filled with rich clothing, and others with more goods and others with food and all manner of supplies. In this manner, once the lord was lodged in his housing, and his soldiers nearby, not a thing, from the most trivial to the greatest, was lacking, because it could be provided.

Cieza highlights the main uses of state stores: supply of the military, administrative and religious personnel, specialists working for the state, and corvée laborers. Craig Morris (1982) has suggested that the Incas' approach to ceremonial politics provided another reason for stockpiling certain supplies. The relationships between the Incas and their subjects required hospitality and generosity on a vast scale, all lubricated by state food and drink. Another important, but irregular, use of state storage was as a fallback for the general populace in times of privation (Polo 1916:127).

As ever, the Incas drew on centuries of Andean practice in devising their storage system. Several Wari sites, including Pikillaqta and Azángaro, contain hundreds of cell-like structures, many of which were probably used for storage (*ca.* AD 600). Once the Incas adopted the idea, they elaborated it to an unprecedented scale. According to Betanzos (1996:51), the Inca state storage system was initiated in the mid-fifteenth century, when Pachakuti ordered facilities built to expedite the construction of Cuzco. We may reserve judgment on that point, since the royal tradition that Betanzos relied on tended to attribute the origin of most everything in Tawantinsuyu to Pachakuti's energies and organizational genius.

In the 1960s, Morris initiated the archaeological study of Inca storage, working at facilities at Cuzco and provincial installations along the highway to Quito. The great provincial centers all contained hundreds of *qollqa* arrayed in rows on the hill slopes just above them, but the vast facilities in the Mantaro Valley were unusual even for the Incas. The valley was a breadbasket for the highlands and home to a major provincial center. All told, 2,753 *qollqa* have been recorded in the basin, about half just above the center and the other half in 48 other sites lining the valley. Collectively, the buildings contained about 170,000 m^3 of storage space, making it one of the largest storage complexes recorded archaeologically in the prehispanic Americas (Morris 1967, 1981; Browman 1970; Earle and D'Altroy 1982; D'Altroy 1992).[2] Facilities adjacent to some of the state farms even surpassed those of most centers. Cotapachi, next to the farms of Cochabamba, contained 2,400 buildings in two sets, and the Campo de Pucará (Argentina) contained 1,717 (Snead 1992). Storage facilities of a few buildings up to several hundred have also been recorded at scores of other Inca installations throughout the Andes. In fact, a road station without storage would have been an anomaly. When we consider that there were more than 2,000 such *tampu* throughout the empire, the scale of state storage becomes astonishing.

The Spaniards were certainly impressed. One of our best eyewitness accounts of Cuzco comes from Pedro Sancho de la Hoz (1917:194–5; translation from Morris 1992:ix–x), a secretary who saw the empire while it still functioned. He wrote:

> From the fortress [of Saqsawaman, above Cuzco] one can see many houses ... and many of these are the houses of pleasure and rest of the past rulers and others are of the leaders or chiefs of all the land who now reside in the city: the others are houses or storehouses full of blankets, wool, weapons, metals and clothes – and of everything that is grown and made in this realm ... and there is a house in which are kept more than 100,000 dried birds, for from their feathers articles of clothing are made ... There are shields, beams for supporting tents, knives, and other tools; sandals and armor for the people of war in such quantity that it is not possible to comprehend how they had been able to tribute so many and different things.

The scale of the facilities at Cuzco is hard to estimate, because so many of the region's archaeological sites have been reduced to rubble over the centuries. Pedro Pizarro (1986:99–100) remembered that they were so vast that it seemed impossible that the supplies could have ever been

Figure 11.2 Guaman Poma's illustration of a storehouse accountant reporting to the emperor Thupa Inka Yupanki

exhausted. Even granting some descriptive licence, the storage at the capital must have been enormous, if only because its residents were said to be supplied every four days from the *qollqa* (Polo 1940:147).

Accountants were responsible everywhere for keeping tabs of everything that went into and out of storage. Guaman Poma drew one of his relatives, Apo Poma Chaua, giving an account of the storehouse contents at Huánuco Pampa to Thupa Inka Yupanki (figure 11.2). In his hand, he holds a *khipu* from which he was presumably drawing his detailed information. The chronicler explained that the inspectors did not belong to the Inca nobility, but were among those residents of the Cuzco region elevated to the position he called "Inca by Privilege." The fact that storehouses were also attended by watchmen and surrounded by expanses of exposed ground suggests that theft was a concern.

In many ways, the storehouses epitomize state planning, since the design of the system aided accounting. *Qollqa* basically came in two modular one-room shapes, round and rectangular, which were laid out in discrete series paralleling the land's contours. Even though they varied regionally, *qollqa* tended to be standardized within any region, as though a functionary had a measurement template and instructed local workers to replicate it. In the Mantaro, we have been able to use airphotos to measure the length of rows, divide that value by a standard length and distance between *qollqa*, and calculate exactly the number of structures in complexes containing up to 100 buildings. For structures built of fieldstone alongside maize and potato fields, that degree of replication is remarkable. Morris's (1967, 1992; see also D'Altroy and Hastorf 1984) excavations show that storehouse architecture was designed to preserve perishable contents as long as possible. Their placement on open hill slopes put the goods in cool, well-ventilated locations. Many structures were also built with gravel subfloors and drainage canals that kept the atmosphere dry and cool (Morris 1981). These practices allowed untreated foods to last a year or two without significant degradation, and freeze-dried foods about twice that long. Polo (1916:59) said that some goods were kept in storage for up to ten years and were shuttled about from facility to facility as the need arose.

Exactly how much of which supplies were actually kept in the storehouses remains a bit of a mystery, although food probably headed the list in most places. Maize was the food most frequently mentioned by chroniclers, followed by *ch'arki*.[3] However, Morris's excavations at Huánuco Pampa found mostly potatoes, which were locally grown, and our own limited tests at Hatun Xauxa found quinoa most often. The disparities between documents and archaeology probably again stem from differences between cultural values and practice. Judging from tests in more than one hundred structures at Huánuco Pampa, Morris has suggested that maize was stored in circular structures and potatoes in rectangular buildings, although evidence from half a dozen buildings in the Mantaro did not match that pattern.

Remarkably, the Inca storage system continued to function for decades in some areas after the empire's collapse. When a Spanish force arrived in the Mantaro Valley in late 1533, the Inca general Chall-cochima was bivouacked outside Hatun Xauxa with an army that the record-keepers tabulated at 35,000 soldiers for Hernando Pizarro's benefit. The valley's residents had unhappily been on the losing side of the war between Atawallpa and Waskhar and were ready to see the Spaniards as saviors. In one of the time's most curious acts, Challcochima agreed to accompany the Spaniards to Cajamarca where his sovereign was in bondage, thus consigning himself to his own death. Soon there-after, his army was routed and the valley's lords began to supply the Spanish forces occupying Hatun Xauxa. The lords kept the production and storage system working until 1554, furnishing the Spaniards with food, prestige goods, and utilitarian supplies, even while rogue bands of soldiers periodically ransacked the facilities (Espinoza Soriano 1972). In 1547 – fifteen years after the fall of Inca power – President Gasca stayed in the valley for a hundred days with an entourage of 2,000 men. Col-lectively, they consumed 15,534 *hanegadas* (878 m^3) of supplies and com-mented with amazement that it was hard to tell that they had even made a dent in the stored goods. That is small wonder, however, when we con-sider that the northern valley's *qollqa* alone could have stored enough food to support Challcochima's entire army for many months.

After twenty years, the supplies in the storehouses finally ran out and the lords filed petitions in Lima's Royal Court to gain restitution. In their briefs, they listed all the goods and services that they had provided the Spaniards in specific episodes over the years. Murra (1975:243–54) rec-ognized that the lists, read directly into the record by *khipu kamayuq*, were apparently ordered by the goods' cultural significance. First came gold and silver, then adult and young camelids, fine cloth, blankets, maize, quinoa, potatoes, two kinds of sandals, bags, rope, large and small ceramics, game birds, rough and fine firewood, charcoal, grass, straw, chicha, "all fruit," salt, and fish. As early as 1537, the Mantaro natives had also started to supply goods of European origin, such as chickens. Significantly, the lords turned supplies over to the Spaniards in proportions that directly reflected the size of their taxpaying populations. This suggests that provisioning of goods, as well as labor service, was intended to be consistent with the number of households in each politi-cal unit. The Mantaro lords' ability to operate the supply system for two decades into the Colonial era also shows that they were thoroughly involved in its management during Cuzco's reign. Their status gave them the power and knowledge to make the arrangement work for their own interests long after the Inca state had been obliterated. Such was the Incas' repute, however, that Polo (1916:76) suggested that many lords actually kept the system working because they feared that the Incas might return some day and call them to account.

Trickle-down Effects on Households

In closing this chapter, I would like to consider what happened to the household economy of the millions of people whose resources and labor were appropriated by the Incas. There is no doubt that the loss of lands disrupted many people's lives, especially in areas such as Cochabamba, Vilcashuaman, and Ayaviri, where the residents were moved out en masse. In some areas, however, production for the state may not have strained community resources as heavily as we might expect. The Incas often placed their fields in areas that were probably not used very heavily during the preceding period.[4] In some cases, farms next to the state installations were carved out of virgin terrain and new canals were built to water them. This approach must have moderated the impact on local villages, and the Inca peace even seems to have allowed farming and herding in areas that had been off limits during the bellicose Late Intermediate Period, especially in Peru's mountain valleys.

What about the impact of taxes? In states where peasants had to pay taxes in money or in kind, such as a tithe on grain, their food may have been stretched in lean years. The Incas' subjects did not normally give up their own produce, but they may have faced a different kind of shortage – disposable labor needed at crucial times in the agrarian schedule. The ecology of the mountains causes farmers to cultivate their plots in a sequence set largely by the choice of crop, the agricultural cycle, and location of the fields. Because the windows of opportunity for planting and harvesting can be counted in days, families may well have felt a labor squeeze at those times. Several responses were possible to such scheduling dilemmas, aside from ignoring calls to service. One option would have been to alternate working on state and personal tasks according to the job immediately at hand. Alternatively, subject households may have tried to increase their size to reduce their per capita obligations by having larger families or delaying marriage. Although data on this subject are scant, witnesses from the Mantaro did say that their populace grew under the Incas (Toledo 1940a:14–37).

Recognizing the problems that ensued, the Incas may have seen that it was in their interest to create an independent economy. Nearly 50 years ago, Murra (1980b) drew attention to the Incas' shift away from corvée-based production to state farms staffed by dedicated workers. In this way, the Incas could have reduced travel time between the villages and state lands at the same time that they improved obedience. In the final analysis, however, the Inca economy was still built upon the skills and hard work of their subjects and on resources taken from communities. The Incas tried to mask the exploitation by using the language of traditional obligations, but their subjects had memories long enough to complain to the Spaniards about how their flocks and fields had been taken away, decades after the Inca collapse.

chapter twelve
Artisans and Artistry

In one cave they discovered twelve sentries of gold and silver, of the size and appearance of those of this country, extraordinarily realistic. There were pitchers half of pottery and half gold, with the gold so well set into the pottery that no drop of water escaped when they were filled, and beautifully made. A golden effigy was also discovered. This greatly distressed the Indians for they said that it was a figure of the first lord [Manqo Qhapaq] who conquered this land. They found shoes made of gold, of the type the women wore, like half-boots. They found golden crayfish such as live in the sea, and many vases, on which were sculpted in relief all the birds and snakes that they knew, even down to spiders, caterpillars and other insects. All of this was found in a large cave that was between some outcrops of rock outside Cuzco. They had not been buried because they were such delicate objects.

Pedro Pizarro (translation modified from Hemming 1970:132)

The smiths who crafted those exquisite objects made up just a tiny fraction of the artisans who worked for the Incas. The state retained skilled craftsmen to create works of beauty, as a means of mass production, and as an instrument of policy. There were thousands of metal smiths, weavers, carpenters, sandal makers, lapidary workers, potters, pigment workers, and dyers. Others made weapons, drinking cups, earspools, and hunting nooses, all from raw materials that were reserved for the Incas' use. In addition to their utilitarian value, many of the items expressed messages about social identity. In a land where status was often rigidly enforced, people used craft goods to make statements about their place in the cultural landscape – about their mythic history, ethnicity, class, gender, occupation, ritual, and relations with the supernatural. In Tawantinsuyu, standardizing some kinds of visual information became crucial because the people spoke so many different languages and had no common symbolic system. Textiles were the favored medium for such expression, but items executed in many other media also met the dual ends of practical use and symbol.

The Incas do not seem to have created many works simply for display, but aesthetic expression is obvious in their material culture. With rare exception, items made for the Incas were more elegant than local wares and provided a conspicuous stamp of imperial presence. In contrast to other empires, where mass production often yielded simple and inelegant objects, crafts made for the Incas combined high quality with labor intensity and mass production. Inca artisans created a distinctive style for portable objects that drew initially from the pre-imperial Killke style of the Cuzco area and from the Titicaca basin and then was refined into a new style of its own. The consistency of the products suggests that state supervisors insisted that the artisans pay careful attention to the canons of the imperial style. The simplicity and repetition of the basic elements lent themselves to duplication by artisans throughout the empire. Designs on textiles and ceramics featured geometric forms in symmetric layouts, executed in bold, solid colors (see Morris 1991, 1995). The realistic, personalized portraiture seen in earlier Andean styles, especially the Moche, is not preserved in known Inca art. The successions of kings were recorded on panels and tapestries, but we do not know how representational they were.

The system worked because the Incas put artisans skilled in all the arts to work in varied settings. It helped the Incas that many tributaries were already masters (*kamayuq*) of a particular craft and that weaving was the essence of Andean women's skills. In the *mitmaqkuna* program, communities that could include hundreds of households were moved en masse to new locations. Espinoza's studies of sixteenth-century court cases chronicle how the Incas stationed weavers, potters, smiths, and other craftsmen on lands alienated from the local peoples (chapter 10). Artisans who worked with different materials were sometimes placed nearby, but their workshops were separated physically and administratively. Specialized workshops seem to have been founded early in the imperial era, but many craft enclaves were part of a late change in economic organization orchestrated under Wayna Qhapaq (e.g., Espinoza Soriano 1970, 1973, 1975, 1976, 1983, 1987a, 1987b; Murra 1980b). Among the other specialists who went to work for the state and the Sun were members of the women's institutions. The products were then used to supply state activities or aristocrats or were distributed through ceremonial largess to favored elites or individuals who had distinguished themselves in service to the state.

The ruler and other lords also retained personal artisans who produced goods for household consumption or gifts. Even so, most artisans worked part-time at their crafts, alternating farming and herding with seasonal or intermittent craft work. Full-time artisans working for themselves, the state, or elite patrons were rare, perhaps even in Cuzco or on royal estates. Because the early sources often did not distinguish neatly between the resources held by the *Sapa Inca* as the personification of the state and those he held in private, it is hard to estimate how many artisans were institutional or members of estates. The difference may not have mattered in many cases, since the ruler had rights over the possessions of the state.

This chapter will focus on textiles, metals, ceramics, and stonework. Those represent only a portion of the material arts, but they cross-cut mass produced and individually crafted items, goods that had symbolic and utilitarian value, and portable objects and the built environment. In thinking about Inca artisanry, it helps to keep in mind how intricately technologies were related (Melissa Hagstrum, pers. comm. 1997); just as ceramic innovations improved metallurgy, metal tools aided weaving and textiles were used for stone working. Feathers or beads of metal and shell were woven into some fabrics, while metals were inlaid with stone and shell, painted, adorned with feathers, or covered in cloth. To speak of individual media would often miss both the cultural point and the visual impact of many objects. In addition, we need to be aware that innovation often arose in the service of making ceremonial or status objects, not from efforts to make tools more efficient. In the Andes, even metallurgy was only occasionally driven by improving the efficiency of weapons, farm tools, or transportation (Lechtman 1984). Mass production did not result from efforts to reduce costs in a market economy, although exchange was widespread. Instead, large-scale production combined utilitarian value, social messages, and artistry in a wide variety of packages.

Despite the scale of the imperial economy, we need to remember that peasants still produced and consumed most of the material culture of the Inca era in their own styles. They lost access to some resources, to be sure, but they were expected to be self-sufficient. Artisans sometimes copied elements of the Inca style into their own, emulating the power of the state, but the effects of imperial rule are virtually invisible elsewhere. In coastal Chimor and in many highland villages, artisans often rejected or were forbidden to use Inca stylistic elements in their own products. As a result, distinguishing pre-Inca and Inca occupations can be difficult, especially since real imperial goods moved in limited circles. One thing is sure, however – much of the archaeological record outside Cuzco does not bear the obvious imprint of state involvement, even at the empire's height.

Community Production for the State

The Incas obtained many goods by applying a household labor tax similar to that described for farming and herding (chapter 11). They put tributaries to work at their home communities or at provincial centers, using materials drawn from state and church holdings. Because the workers' skills were varied, officials sought out individuals, communities, and entire ethnic groups who had expertise in one craft or another. Some communities made certain goods because suitable resources were available nearby. In Huánuco, for example, certain villages made sandals, rope, or pottery, because the fibers or clay could be readily procured (see LeVine 1987; C. Julien 1993). Elsewhere, ethnic groups were assigned to gather items such as specially colored woods and bird feathers. Overall, while labor assignments were made on the basis of population, the state adapted its requirements for craft production to environmental variations.

The most common material made for the state in local communities was ordinary cloth. Every year, each family received wool from state stockpiles that the women used to spin yarn and then weave cloth. One shirt per year may have been the normal output. Cathy Costin's (1993) archaeological studies of Xauxa households in central Peru support this picture of a tax on women's labor. Densities of spindle whorls and related tools show that weaving doubled under Inca rule, even though most of the Xauxa had moved several kilometers away from good pastures. Common cloth ranked high among the materials that the valley furnished the Spaniards in the 1530s, but its production is missing from the 40-odd labor duties on specific provincial lists. It is possible that household weaving was so much a part of the cultural landscape that it did not need mentioning, or that some women's work was not thought worthy of tabulation. Other evidence on the status of women's labor is mixed. Some activities viewed as women's work were often less highly valued than those performed by men. For example, there was no term for spinner, which was mostly a female activity, but there were several for weavers, who were drawn from both sexes. Women were listed for other standard duties, such as mining, and some women held high-status positions whose duties included fabricating material goods. The most outstanding of those were the *mamakuna*, who wove the most valued cloth in the realm (see below). Whatever the value of the work itself, as Costin (ibid.) points out, distributing the products seems to have been mostly under men's control.

Specialized Production

Textiles

Weaving was perhaps the most valued art in Tawantinsuyu. Cloth was usually made from cotton on the coast and in the eastern lowlands and from wool in the highlands, but some coarse textiles were also made from rougher materials, such as maguey fibers. Unfortunately, textiles in the Inca style from the heartland are rare because organic materials disintegrate quickly in the highland climate. Most of the preserved Inca textiles come from the coast or from high elevation shrines. The Incas also valued their cloth so highly that they burned it rather than let it fall into Spanish hands. As a result, relatively few Inca textiles are available for study, but Guaman Poma's drawings provide valuable information, because he took meticulous care to depict the tunics that were appropriate to individuals of particular social groups or statuses.

In 1962, John Murra wrote a classic paper that explored the roles of textiles in Inca culture and the imperial economy (see also A. Rowe 1978; J. Rowe 1979c; Morris 1991, 1995). He observed that woven materials had many functions, such as clothing, blankets, footwear, and carrying bags, but cloth took on its greatest significance in the social and ceremonial aspects of life. It was used in all rites of passage, for instance to celebrate the naming of a child or as gifts in puberty rituals. Weddings typically included the presentation of cloth by the groom and his kin to the family of the bride. Many societies buried their dead in specially woven new clothes, along with sandals, bags, headdresses, and, with women, needles, spindles and whorls, skeins of yarn, and the woven baskets that held them.

WEAVING CLOTH

Making textiles in the Andes did not require complex tools. To make thread, the prepared (cleaned, teased, and organized) wool was wrapped around the wrist or placed on a distaff. The spindle was spun free in the air or rested on a pottery plate. For most Andean textiles, the thread was first spun clockwise (z-spun), then doubled, and twisted counterclockwise (s-plied). Special ceremonial cloth was sometimes spun and plied in the reverse directions (Cobo 1990:223; J. Rowe 1946:241). Needles were typically made of sharp cactus spines or bronze. Andean peoples used three different kinds of looms (Cobo 1990:224–5; Rowe 1946:241). The earliest and simplest was a backstrap or body-tension loom (figure 8.2). In this technique, the weaver used two rods to support the longitudinal threads (warp). One was attached to a post or wall and the other was tied to a belt that passed around the weaver's back. A second type, used primarily among Aymara speakers, was a horizontal loom that consisted of two rods attached to posts set into the ground. The cloth was suspended above the ground. In both of these types, heddles were used to separate the warp threads that formed the ground weave structure, so that the weft threads could be passed through easily to form patterns. The third loom was a vertical frame of four poles that was used to weave the finest cloth.

KINDS OF CLOTH

The coarsest of the Inca textiles (*chusi*) was a thick cloth that was used for blankets and other materials that required a durable weave (Cobo 1990:223–6; Rowe 1946:242). A single length of *chusi* served as a bedroll and, when doubled back, as a blanket. Father Cobo was scandalized that the entire family was accustomed to sleeping under a single cloth. The next grade up was common cloth, called *awasqa*, which was simply dyed or decorated, if treated at all. Woven in large quantities by housewives, it was the most commonly made craft item produced for the empire.

A more elegant cloth, called *qompi*, was a tapestry weave made from both cotton and the finer wools. Some of the most luxurious *qompi* incorporated viscacha fur and bat hair. Feathered cloth and other paraphernalia, such as shields and lances, were especially associated with the military (Murúa 1986: 349–50). The most valued textiles were made with beads or bangles of gold, silver, and Spondylus shell woven tightly into the fabric. Half a century after the conquest, Pedro Pizarro (translation modified from Hemming 1970:135) still remembered the storehouses of textiles and raw materials at Cuzco with wonder:

> There were deposits of iridescent feathers, some looking like fine gold and others of a shining golden-green color. These were the feathers of small birds hardly bigger than cicadas, which are called "pájaros comines" [hummingbirds] because they are so tiny. These small birds grow the iridescent feathers only on their breasts, and each feather is little larger than a fingernail. Quantities of them were threaded together on fine thread and were skillfully attached to agave fibers to form pieces over a span in length. These were all stored in leather chests. Clothes were made of the feathers, and contained a staggering quantity of these iridescents. There were many other feathers of various colors intended for making clothing to be worn by the lords and ladies at the festivals ... There were also cloaks completely covered with gold and silver chaquira [beads], with no thread visible, like very dense chain mail, and there were storehouses of shoes with soles made of sisal and uppers of fine wool in many colors.

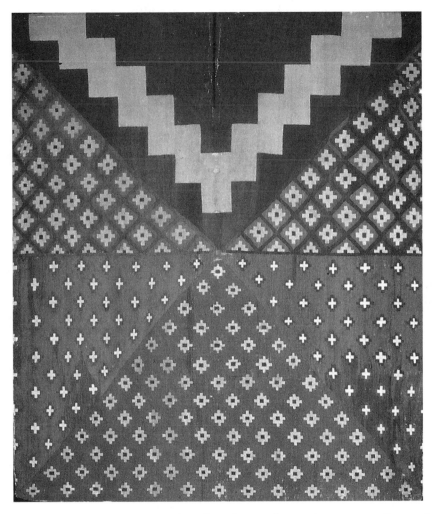

Plate 12.1   Inca men's tunic; photo by John Bigelow Taylor, courtesy Dept. of Anthropology, American Museum of Natural History

Inca tapestry tunics were standardized in decoration and structure (J. Rowe 1979c; A. Rowe 1997). Two common designs were black and white and "Inca key" checkerboards, while more elaborate patterns contained rows of square or rectangular geometric designs with internal repetition (plate 12.1). The designs, or rows of them, were known as *t'oqapu*. They were executed in bold colors of red, black, white, purple, orange, and yellow. Even the tunics' background hues apparently were significant, for Guaman Poma went to some effort to specify whose tunic had been executed in which colors. The designs' regularity has suggested to scholars that the encoded information was closely linked to the Inca social hierarchy. It has even been suggested that the codes approximated a writing system, but that interpretation is not widely accepted.

USES OF CLOTH

The military were probably the major consumer of cloth and other woven goods, such as bags. Soldiers were regularly issued blankets, in addition to one or two annual sets of clothes and sandals. Murúa wrote that the *awasqa* cloth was typically given to soldiers. Warriors who distinguished themselves in battle were also awarded finer textiles, as well as camelids, drinking cups, and jewels (Murra 1962:717). Some fabrics were reserved for the *Sapa Inca* alone, whose most important insignia was a red woolen fringe (*mascaypacha*) that was placed on his head and partially concealed his eyes. According to Murúa (1986:348–9), royal concubines wove the emperor's vestments, which were embroidered with gold, silver, and feathers; one room of the imperial palace was reserved for storage of his most ornate fabrics and jewelry. Each of the deceased lords of the empire was also dressed in the finest clothing, as were the statues of stone or nail clippings that represented them (Murra 1962:719).

Many ceremonies and social interactions among Cuzco's nobility included exchanges or gifts of the finest textiles. When the *Sapa Inca* took a bride, he consecrated a woman's *qompi* garment and fastening pin, golden chains, and other objects in the Golden Enclosure. Accompanied by a musical procession, he made his way to the house of his bride's mother, where he presented the gifts to his betrothed. She reciprocated by giving him a tunic made by her own hand and they both donned the clothing. The rites of passage into manhood celebrated by Cuzco's aristocratic youths were also accompanied by gifts of clothing from relatives, which were changed at each step of the month-long ceremony. The colors, designs, and fabrics all made symbolic reference to royal genealogy and history (Murúa 1986:382–3; Murra 1962:719).

The Incas also consumed untold quantities of textiles in religious activities, especially ritual sacrifices. Santillán (1968:111) wrote that camelids and cloth, both of which were burned, constituted the two principal offerings. Cobo added that fine clothing was part of nearly every major sacrifice and that both men's and women's garments were made expressly to be consumed in specific ceremonies. The maize harvest ceremonies on a hill outside Cuzco (Mantocalla) included the immolation of llamas on fires fed by "many bundles of carved firewood dressed

as men and women and a great quantity of maize ears made of wood"
(Cobo 1990:117; see Murra 1962:714). The children and youths or
paired golden and silver statuettes buried in high elevation offerings were
also dressed in finery (Reinhard and Alvarez 1996).

Textiles were put to more explicitly political ends as well. The only
way that a non-royal individual gained the right to wear *qompi* was
through a gift from the Inca. Upon being incorporated into the empire,
newly subjected lords would be given gifts of cloth, drinking cups, and
jewelry. When provincial lords visited the capital, they were given gifts
of cloth and other fine objects, just as they presented textiles and other
crafts to the ruler. Cieza (1967:74) wrote that transplanted colonists were
awarded gold and silver bracelets, woolen and feathered clothing,
women, and various other privileges, perhaps to help alleviate the pain
of dislocation. As J. Rowe (1979c:240) points out, the Incas typically
made the quality of the gifts appropriate to the rank of the recipient. The
reciprocal exchange of these items bonded the ruler and his subjects,
while reinforcing the status differences that lay between them.

CLOTHING

Clothing signified group identity and social status among Andean
peoples, while nudity was shameful among many coastal and mountain
societies, though not among many peoples of the eastern lowlands. Cobo
wrote that:

> (t)he men and women of each nation and province had their insignias and
> emblems by which they could be identified, and they could not go around
> without this identification or exchange their insignias for those of another
> nation, or they would be severely punished. They had this insignia on their
> clothes with different stripes and colors, and the men wore their most
> distinguishing insignia on their heads; each nation was identified by the
> headdress.[1]

To tolerate the cold and windy conditions in the highlands, both sexes
dressed in layers of simple and untailored wool clothing. In the warmer
lands, both men and women typically wore clothing woven from cotton.
Women's clothing consisted primarily of a long rectangular cloth that
was wrapped around the body and under the arms; its corners were
pinned over the shoulders. A long sash, called a *chumpi*, was wrapped
around the waist several times. Over this wrap, women wore a mantle
which they fastened with thorns or a *tupu* pin made of copper (bronze),
silver, or gold. Besides providing warmth, the mantle was an all-purpose
carrying tool, used to haul everything from infants to potatoes.

The standard men's garment was a rectangular tunic (*unqo*) worn over a loincloth wrapped around the pelvis and groin. The loincloth became part of a male's wardrobe when he passed through a puberty ritual in his early teens. The tunic was a single piece of cloth that was sown on both sides, with room left at the corners for the arms to pass through and a vertical slit left for the wearer's head. To fend off the cold, men would wrap themselves in a heavy cloak. Both men and women sometimes wore leather sandals, which were tied with cords of wool, cotton, or other plant fibers; its cords were often gaily decorated.

WEAVERS

The production of so many textiles required tens of thousands of people working at coordinated tasks. The raw materials came from state or church farms (e.g., cotton) or herds (llama and alpaca wool), or gathered resources (e.g., vicuña wool, hummingbird feathers, dyestuffs). In some instances, such as at Huamachuco and Chinchis, the weavers and herders lived nearby (Spurling 1992:233). Elsewhere, the raw materials were accumulated, stored, and dispensed to the artisans as needed. Many of the tasks involved in making textiles were restricted by gender, but just about everybody in the family could get involved in some way. Young boys, for instance, collected bird feathers and girls the dyestuffs (Guaman Poma 1980:182–3, 202–3).

Different kinds of cloth were woven by women and men (Murra 1962; Spurling 1992:221–2). While male weavers (*qompi kamayuq*) wove many of the finer grades of cloth and the feathered textiles, the *mamakuna* made the finest, most valued *qompi* for sacrifices, idols, and the ruler himself (J. Rowe 1979c:239). Other women holding special rank, especially *aqllakuna*, also made many textiles. At Puerta de La Paya, Argentina, Ambrosetti's (1902, 1907–8; Calderari 1991) excavations a century ago recovered over a thousand spindle whorls and other weaving tools from the tombs of young women. The wives of lords, even those of the Inca, also wove fine cloth. As Polo (1940:146) reported, "(t)here was no one who was an administrative official who did not send the Inca every year a set of garments made for his person by the hands of the official's wives" (translation by J. Rowe 1979c:239).

SPECIALIZED COMMUNITIES

To meet an insatiable demand, the Incas set entire communities – up to a thousand households – to weaving. The best-known facility was Milliraya, situated just northeast of Lake Titicaca, described below. Other enclaves were installed on the altiplano, because of the region's weaving tradition and the proximity of the great herds (Spurling 1992:234–6; Diez de San Miguel 1964:106). Peru's central highlands also contributed many weavers to state institutions or royal estates. One Wanka lord claimed that his ancestor had presided over 500 weavers in the Yucay Valley (Cuzco), where Wayna Qhapaq had an estate (Toledo 1940b:71). Chupachu witnesses from Huánuco also said that 400 of their members, i.e., 10 percent of the enumerated taxpayers, went to work as weavers for the Inca.

The Milliraya enclave lay on the border between two political divisions, but took lands from only one ethnic group (see Murra 1978; Espinoza Soriano 1987b; Spurling 1992). Spurling suggests that the point was to foster local tensions that would help prevent the reformation of an alliance that had put Inca rule in jeopardy a few decades earlier. One thousand tapestry and feathered cloth weavers and 100 (or maybe 300) potters were settled in different parts of Milliraya's lands under Wayna Qhapaq's direction. Rather than being brought in from afar, as often happened with colonists, the *mitmaqkuna* were transplanted from nearby altiplano communities. Each group received irrigated fields, pastures, lakeshore lands, and lowland maize fields, from which they were expected to support themselves (Spurling 1992:182). The artisans worked under an Inca-appointed provincial governor, a Lupaqa lord named Cari. Spurling (ibid.:197–203) points out, however, that none of the artisans was an ethnic Lupaqa – an early Inca ally – illustrating a way that the Incas rewarded cooperative subjects. Below the governor were an overseer (*jilaqata*) and an accountant-manager (*khipu kamayuq*) who kept the land and population records, apportioned clay to the potters, and told them what vessels to make. None of those officials actually lived in the town, but two pottery overseers did, as well as other lower officials who represented the settlers' *ayllu* of origin.

How did the Incas determine how much cloth to weave or how many potters to install? There are hints that some changes arose from the demand for specific projects. The weavers at Milliraya were reportedly installed to help outfit Wayna Qhapaq's campaigns in Ecuador, but the potters said that they distributed their products to other groups living around the north end of the lake. More generally, the Incas appear to have estimated their needs and put artisans to work until the required amounts were produced. If the amount produced did not match the quotas, they could add more workers. The output stockpiled from cadres of artisans such as these was remarkable. Xérez wrote that the storehouses that he saw at Cajamarca were filled with "so much cloth of wool and cotton that it seemed to me that many ships could have been filled with them," and people drew from the Mantaro Valley stores for thirty years after the empire's collapse (translation by Murra 1962:717).

Metallurgy

In Inca cosmology, gold was the sweat of the Sun and silver the tears of the Moon. To the Spaniards, the metals embodied earthly riches. Those differing values meant that a century's creativity in precious metals – modeled figures, idols, serving vessels, personal ornaments, and architectural adornments – disappeared into the Spanish forges in a matter of months. Today we know about Inca metallurgy from the few pieces that survived Spanish diligence, from eyewitness descriptions, and from inferences based on earlier objects, which are preserved in greater numbers.

To make their wares, the Inca smiths drew from millennia of Andean knowledge, which was the most sophisticated in the Americas. The smiths of Peru's north coast were especially proficient. By Moche times (*ca.* AD 100–600), artisans were using sheet metals to create copper-gold and copper-silver alloys and had developed gilding and surface enrichment techniques (Lechtman 1984). The products that they made were primarily symbolic, decorative, and status-related, rather than utilitarian. Both archaeology and the art market show that many items reached a final resting place as grave goods with society's elite or with individuals who symbolized key ritual positions (Alva and Donnan 1994). Copper (actually copper-arsenic bronze) tools, such as needles and tweezers, were common but not very important culturally or economically. Later craftsmen created a remarkable array of pieces decorated with repoussé designs, filigrees, and inlays of shell, turquoise, lapis lazuli, and emeralds. Along the coast and in Ecuador, there was also a long pre-Inca tradition of fabricating bronze axe-monies (*hachas*) in units of 2, 5, and 10 (Hosler et al. 1990).

In Tawantinsuyu, precious metals were wrapped up in an elaborate symbolic system, which the Incas embellished to their own ends (Morris 1995). Because metals were considered to be the gift of the earth, the Incas prayed to the rich mountains as well as to large nuggets or ore-laced rocks, called *mama acha*. In one coastal Andean myth, the Sun came to Earth, where he placed a golden egg that gave birth to noblemen, a silver that bore noblewomen, and a copper that bore commoners (see Rostworowski 1983:147). Inca rulers, who called themselves "the son of the Sun," symbolically inaugurated the agricultural season by rending the soil in the primordial field in Cuzco with a gold-tipped plow. Appropriately, the most sacred temple in the land was "The Golden Enclosure" (*Qorikancha*), which housed a variety of idols made of precious metals. Nearby was the Temple of the Moon, where priestesses held the positions of honor. With such an array of beliefs built around the powers of the two celestial bodies, it is small wonder that the Incas placed great emphasis on mining and metallurgical artistry.

METAL OBJECTS

Many of the treasures that the Spaniards saw before the sack of Cuzco would be the most remarkable products of Inca material culture in existence today, had they survived. The Qorikancha housed the golden sun image, named *Punchao* (Midday Sun), which was brought forth to greet the sun each day and then returned inside at night. This effigy held the ashes of the internal organs of past Inca emperors. The first Spaniards who arrived in Cuzco were astounded and delighted to see that the temple's interior had been covered with golden plates half a meter or more in length:

> These buildings were sheathed with gold, in large plates, on the side where the sun rises, but on the side that was more shaded from the sun the gold in them was more debased. The Christians went to the buildings and with no aid from the Incas – who refused to help, saying that it was a building of the sun and they would die – the Christians decided to remove the ornament . . . with some copper crowbars. (Hemming 1970:133)

The 700 plates that the Spaniards removed weighed about 2 kg each, which would be worth about $11,000,000 today. When the main Spanish army arrived to sack Cuzco on Saturday, November 15, 1533, the temple was still filled with an array of metal statuary and vessels (ibid.). One golden altar that was still in place weighed over 19,000 pesos. The display that excited the greatest wonder was a full garden of maize, with birds flying among the plants, wrought in gold and silver. Nearby stood the flocks of the Inca, along with the herders, all executed to life-scale in precious metals. It is one of the great losses to the modern world that none of those pieces escaped the furnaces to survive to the present day. Even when the conquistadores had the grace to send King Philip 18-carat golden figures of a woman and a llama along with other objects of precious metals (ibid.:131–2), they too met a fate in the royal flames in Spain.

Many metal objects were serving vessels fashioned for the church and the royal families. The royalty were said to drink their chicha from silver and golden tumblers. It was primarily from the *panaqas*' assets that Atawallpa's ransom was gathered, since he specified that his father's assets were not to be touched. The amount of gold and silver that was fed into the forges at Cajamarca ultimately totaled 13,240 lbs of 22.5

Plate 12.2 Silver alpacas; photo by John Bigelow Taylor, courtesy Dept. of Anthropology, American Museum of Natural History

carat gold and 26,000 lbs of good silver (ibid.:73). One elegant golden fountain, dismantled for transport to Cajamarca, weighed over 12,000 pesos by itself. At today's values, the gold would be worth about $60,000,000 and the silver a little more than $2,000,000. The take at Cuzco was even greater.

Because the Spaniards hunted down the Inca treasures so thoroughly, and perhaps because the Incas successfully hid what was left, only a few pieces are found in museum collections. Readers who have seen other publications on Inca artistry may have noticed a suspicious tendency for authors to use pictures of the same items. Scholars' habit of repeating each other aside, those objects appear because they are just about all that remains. Fortunately, recent discoveries of ceremonial offerings at high altitudes have begun to expand our knowledge. When metal objects are included, they usually consist of paired male and female figures made of gold or gold and silver, sometimes accompanied by llamas or alpacas executed in the same materials (plate 12.2). The idols are simply designed, with ovoid heads and stocky, unelaborated bodies. To judge from the well-preserved examples, they were usually clothed in gender-appropriate attire and decked out with feathered headdresses and other adornments (Reinhard 1985; Reinhard and Alvarez 1996).

MINES AND MINING

Chroniclers often reported that the Incas made a blanket claim to all mineral resources, but that was more an assertion of sovereignty than reality. Cobo's (1979:249) comment is more to the point: "Some of these mines were worked at the expense and under the auspices of the Inca himself, and others, constituting the majority, were worked at the expense of the caciques [lords] of the districts in which the mines were located. This was so that they would have things to give as presents to the Inca." Berthelot's (1986) studies suggest that the Incas took the richest, most concentrated sources for themselves, while the community mines were more scattered. The Incas' mines were distributed throughout their domain; copper deposits are distributed in bands along the length of the Andes, but gold and silver occur in more restricted deposits. Tin, which was used widely in the empire to make bronze, was concentrated in southern Bolivia and northern Chile.

Just as they did with food, coca, and cloth, the Incas claimed raw resources for institutions and estates and set men and women tributaries to work on a rotating basis.[2] Santillán (1968: item 42, p. 39, and item 51, p. 42) wrote that the standard practice in provinces where the Incas had mines was for the local lords to call up one percent of their taxpayers, although the numbers of miners actually varied in practice. Apparently distrustful of the lords' interest in rendering accurate accounts, the Incas installed their own supervisors to collect and weigh the ore daily as the miners left for home. One of the most elaborate operations lay about 100 km east of Samaipata, Bolivia, where the Incas reportedly installed 1,000 miners and 5,000 other colonists to support them (Pärssinen 1992:130–1). When the Spaniards arrived in 1533, the gold operation at Chuquiabo (La Paz, Bolivia) totaled more than a hundred people of both sexes from four different tributary groups. The Huánuco inspection reported that the Chupachu committed 120 men and 120 women (3 percent of their tributaries) for the nearby gold mines and 60 more men and their wives for the silver mines in the adjacent Yaros territory (Berthelot 1986:74–6). Betanzos, Sarmiento, and Pedro Pizarro all wrote that the main purpose of the Inca ventures into the south was to procure mineral wealth, although a little hindsight may have slipped into that explanation. Archaeological surveys support the view that the Incas took advantage of mineral wealth in the south. Raffino (1983:243, 259–62) enumerates 68 Inca-era sites in Argentina and 58 in southern Bolivia and Chile that were involved in mining gold, silver, copper, galena, zinc, tin, and other minerals.

Some mines were apparently designated as the *Sapa Inca*'s personal property. Polo (1916:102) implied that an important fraction of all mining operations serviced the emperors, living and dead, along with their retinues. He wrote that when an emperor died, his successor sent out another battery of miners to start producing for his own estate, alongside those of the prior ruler. Thupa Inka Yupanki had one such mine on his estate at Asillo, north of Lake Titicaca. Local lords seem to have set their own tributaries to work their personal mines, as part of the regular labor service to which they were entitled (see Berthelot 1986).

Mining techniques were simple. Where the ore was found in veins, the miners dug galleries that were so constricted that only one person could enter at a time. Fall-ins, poor lighting, and bad ventilation made tunnel mining a risky business, but gold, silver, and copper were all extracted that way. At some open air mines, gold was recovered by sluicing river gravels (see Berthelot 1986:77–80). As always, the Incas were prepared to invest enormous amounts of their tributaries' labor to achieve their goals. Confronted with a perpetual lack of water in ore-rich Tarapacá (northern Chile), they sent engineers to lay out a canal that would carry water from the altiplano to the coastal valley. The intent apparently was to improve the region's ability to support permanent residents, not to assist in mining operations per se. The canal was never finished, as its construction was cut short by the Spanish invasion (Berthelot 1986:80; Núñez 1986:31–2).

For the most part, mining was a seasonal affair, because of the extreme cold found at high elevations and because workers needed to tend their fields back home. Based on his experience in southern Peru and the altiplano, Polo (1940:165) stated that mining was solely a summer occupation. At Chuquiabo, they worked only from December to March and just from noon to sunset. Where the climate permitted, such as at Huánuco, mining could be a year-round enterprise (Berthelot 1986: 74–5).

Much of the ore was sent to Cuzco, where it was worked by the Incas' smiths and jewelers into service vessels, architectural adornments, and other objects. Some important state installations, including Hatun Xauxa (Peru), had resident smiths as well. Waste fragments of gold and bronze have also been recovered archaeologically from Inca centers in the south (D'Altroy et al. 2000).

LOCAL METALLURGY UNDER THE INCAS

Cuzco's rule left a heavy imprint on local metallurgy. Provincial lords lost control over many mines and much of the local product became part of the obligatory gift exchanges between the Inca and his subjects. Just as important was the loss of the artisans to state activities. The heaviest blow may have fallen on Peru's north coast, but the south Andes may have given over much of their artisans' labor as well. A major technological development was a broad shift from copper-arsenic bronzes to tin bronzes, even at local communities. Many copper deposits in the Andes have a high natural arsenic content, but a tin alloy is less toxic and makes the bronze more workable. Since tin was concentrated in a relatively small area in Bolivia and Chile and was under the Incas' control, this technological change was fundamentally a product of state intervention and supply (Lechtman 1984). The bronzes were often used to make tools, among them needles and chisels. Many of the decorative objects made and used by subject peoples were given Inca forms, in particular the *tupu* pins that were used to secure women's clothing (see Howe and Petersen 1994; Owen 2001).

A brief look at the Upper Mantaro Valley will illustrate what happened in one province. Owen, Howe, and Petersen have shown that the Incas altered the local production and use of metals, but did not take over the craft entirely. Excavations in 29 households recovered 267 objects of arsenic bronze, tin bronze, silver, and lead from the late pre-Inca and Inca periods. More than half of the items were used for adornment and display, such as *tupu* pins, pendants, and disks that were probably attached to cloth. Among the utilitarian objects were needles, bola weights used for hunting, chisels, ceremonial *tumi* knives, and a lead fragment that may have been used to repair a vessel. A substantial amount of metal production debris was also recovered, such as ore, sheet scrap, and casting debris. The debris was found in both elite and commoner households in both phases, suggesting that metalworking was a fairly common skill among the valley's inhabitants. Under Inca rule, bronzes shifted from native arsenic to tin alloy (Owen 2001). The amount of copper and lead in circulation increased, while the ratio of finished products to debris doubled, suggesting that some production was moved elsewhere or that the local populace received items made under state auspices.

In sum, metallurgy encapsulates the selective intervention of the Incas in Andean artisanry. While gold and silver provided a crucial symbolic link between the Incas and the cosmos, they were also alloyed with copper and their surfaces were often covered. The Incas claimed all mineral resources, but local societies maintained their own independent mining and metallurgical industries. And while those local industries flourished, the Incas both commanded many of the products and controlled the technology of bronze alloys.

Ceramics

Textiles and metals were more important in Inca culture, but Cuzco-style polychrome pottery is the archaeological hallmark of Inca presence throughout the Andes. Inca polychrome ceramics are abundant in the heartland and in provincial centers from Cuzco to Quito; they are also found in small amounts in thousands of local settlements. At some provincial sites, such as Huánuco Pampa (Morris and Thompson 1985:71–80) and Hatun Xauxa (D'Altroy and Bishop 1990; D'Altroy 1992), provincial variants of Cuzco wares formed over 98 percent of the ceramic assemblage. On the coast and in the southern Andes, they often formed a small component, as the assemblages at state sites consist mostly of local types. Although it might seem odd that the distributions of Inca-style pottery and architecture only partially match, a lack of fit between them should not be that surprising, since they served different purposes (Hyslop 1993:339; Morris 1995).

Inca pottery had a narrow range of uses outside the heartland. The vessels were to brew the beer, prepare the food, and to serve these items in state-sponsored feasts. They were also used for long-term storage, to hold offerings of food, and as grave goods (Morris 1995:523). The pottery's use at provincial centers emphasized the importance of the state as both the symbolic and physical sponsor of political and ceremonial activities. Ceramics were also given to privileged lords, but Inca vessels were not used in the peasants' everyday affairs. The finer Inca ceramics were almost invariably the most elegant vessels in use, no matter the context. Such visual displays, like *qompi* cloth, were ways of expressing the state's presence, especially where many people could not speak the language of their rulers (DeMarrais, Castillo, and Earle 1996).

The most distinctive Inca vessels are flared-rim jars with constricted necks (often called aryballoid jars or *aríbalos*: figure 12.1, plate 12.3 left), open-mouth jars, open and closed bowls, plates with duck head and tail appendages (plate 12.3 center), drinking cups or tumblers (*keros*; plate 12.3 right), bottles, and pedestal-based cooking pots (see Valcárcel 1934–5; Rowe 1944:47–9, figure 18–19; Rowe 1946:243–4; Hyslop 1993:340). The collection from Chinchero, one of Thupa Inka Yupanki's estates near Cuzco, has yielded 28 distinct shapes of pots, illustrated here in figure 12.2 (Rivera 1976:29). The full set of vessel forms found in the Cuzco area does not appear to have been reproduced anywhere else in the empire. That probably occurred, as Hyslop (1993:339) suggests, because state personnel in the heartland were involved in a wider range of activities and held higher statuses than those in the provinces.

Figure 12.1   Illustration of Inca woman carrying an aryballoid jar; from Bingham 1930

Plate 12.3   Left: ceramic flared-rim jar; center: ceramic duck-head plate; right: wooden drinking cup; all from Cuzco; photos # B/8248, # B/8294, # B/9180, courtesy Dept. of Anthropology, American Museum of Natural History

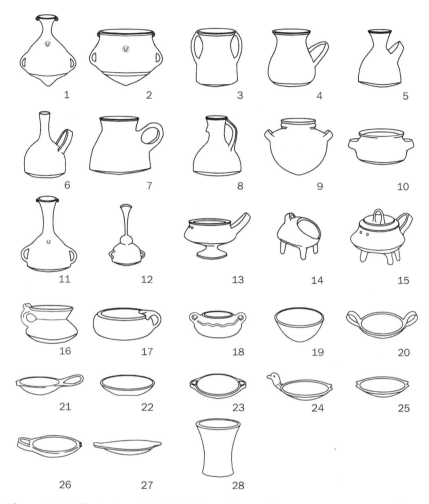

Figure 12.2 Illustration of the 28 different forms of Inca ceramics recovered from Thupa Inka Yupanki's estate at Chinchero; redrawn from Rivera 1976

Inca pottery is usually distinguished by its high technical quality and regularity. It is generally well-fired and burnished, contains low proportions of temper, and is decorated with lustrous, opaque slips. As with the textiles, motifs most commonly consist of geometric forms, such as solid bands, rows of diamonds or pendant triangles, concentric diamonds, large expanses of solid color or highly polished buff areas, the "fern motif" on flared-rim jars, and hatching. The result was a labor-intensive, visually distinctive ware of high quality. Apart from rendering the pottery instantly recognizable, the repetitiveness of form and decoration aided duplication by potters performing their labor duties, although regional variants in style and quality can still be readily distinguished. Potters' tendencies to combine elements of Inca pottery with regional styles led to a welter of Inca-related ceramic types throughout the Andes.

Despite its archaeological importance, polychrome pottery manufacture was a minor component of the Inca economy. Although pot-making figured on standard lists of labor duties, it was ranked lower than all activities associated with weaving, feathers, and metals. In the two cases where we have figures for artisans dedicated to specific tasks – Huánuco and Milliraya (see above) – there were ten times as many weavers as potters. While that difference surely reflects cultural values, it is also true that pots can be cranked out more quickly than tapestry-weave textiles.[3]

Several artisan communities provide evidence for state ceramic production. At Cajamarca (Peru), an important center along the sierra highway, the Incas transplanted 100 potters from the north coast of Peru. The best-documented workshop in the south is Potrero-Chaquiago, Argentina, where pottery, textiles, and metal working were carried out in separate sectors of the site (Lorandi 1984; Williams and Lorandi 1986; Williams 1996). Intriguingly, the settlement had a fair amount of locally made, but non-Inca pottery that resembles styles from other regions in the south Andes, probably made by *mitmaqkuna* in the styles of their homelands (Lorandi 1988, 1991).

The Incas also valued pottery made in the styles of some other ethnic groups. Pacajes ceramics, made on the altiplano south of Lake Titicaca, were apparently especially esteemed. Featuring rows of little camelids, the plates were widely distributed in small amounts at Inca sites throughout the southern half of the empire. Similarly, Chimu blackware has been recovered from Inca sites in a number of locations in the north Andes. This style is found among the burials at Machu Picchu, which included pottery made in the styles of at least four different locales. Lucy Salazar (pers. comm.) suggests that the people buried there may have been interred with objects from their homelands as a mark of the people annexed by the Incas.

There are very few places in the empire where subjects had access to a large number of state vessels. One such location was the Upper Mantaro Valley of Peru, which we know had a privileged status. The region's two largest towns, Hatunmarca and Marca, each housed about 4,500 residents and were probably home to important local lords, whose houses incorporated typical Inca architectural features. Fieldwork at the two towns indicates that their ceramic assemblages each contain one to two million sherds in the polychrome style. Even so, the percentage

Plate 12.4 Cyclopean ashlar masonry in the lowest tier of Saqsawaman; the author provides scale (slide by author)

of Inca pottery never exceeded more than about one-quarter in any residential compound. This pattern suggests that high social status conferred the privilege or, less benignly, the obligation of using state pottery in political and ceremonial activities. High status did not grant elites the right to be sustained at home with goods made entirely in the state style.

Stone Working

Visitors to Cuzco and nearby sites are often astonished at the beauty and ingenuity of Inca stone working. Whether in architecture, worked boulders, or carved bedrock, Inca stereotomy was unsurpassed in the Americas and perhaps in the entire ancient world. The precision cutting and scale of Inca stone working are so confounding that writers have attributed the feats to everything from lasers to space aliens (see Lee 1990). Modern architects, however, have described a range of simple techniques that Inca masons could have used to shape their works (see esp. Gasparini and Margolies 1980; Protzen 1982, 1993; Lee 1990; Agurto Calvo 1987; and Hollowell 1987). Profuse clues to their methods are preserved in the quarries and the rocks themselves. The building blocks were shaped from existing rocks or hewn out of bedrock. The tools were usually simple – hammerstones, ropes, and logs. Distinctive scarring on the blocks' surfaces indicates that shaping was accomplished mostly through pounding, rather than abrasion or cutting. Unfinished rocks in the quarries and along the roads leading to Inca sites indicate that blocks were first shaped in the quarries and then finished on site. Abrasion marks suggest that the rocks were moved by dragging with ropes. That staging of work is illustrated by the constructions at Ollantaytambo, where the cut stones for an entire wall remain laid out on the ground, ready for mounting. Similar techniques of pounding and, occasionally, polishing were used to carve rocks in place.

The work probably moved along more rapidly than one might suspect. Using hammerstones found at the Kachiqata quarry, which provided stone for Ollantaytambo, Protzen (1982:189) dressed five sides of a small block in an hour and a half. Inca masons would likely have been quicker. His experiments have shown that the beveled edges that impart such beauty to Inca ashlar masonry may actually be a consequence of the dressing technique; their angles would have also helped prevent fracture of the edges during transportation and handling. Some questions still remain. How did the masons fit blocks so precisely that a knife blade often cannot be introduced between adjoining, unmortared stones? How were the gargantuan blocks installed (plate 12.4)? We do not have definitive answers yet, but Vincent Lee suggests a credible scenario, based on his study of construction sequences and shape details. Both he and Protzen infer that, in Saqsawaman and other sites, the rocks in an upper course were trimmed first and those in the course below were shaped to receive them. Each upper rock could have been raised with the help of dirt ramps and supported by a log scaffold. A scribe-and-cope (kept true with a plumb) could then be used to follow the contours of the upper rock and mark the fit on the rocks below. Once the bedding and rise joins were matched, the upper rock could have been lowered into place, attaining a neat fit without prolonged trial and error. This is an unromantic vision of Inca cyclopean masonry, to be sure, but it is a more persuasive scenario than shifting 15-ton rocks about in repeated experimental fittings, as is often proposed.

One of the unexpected implications of this approach to stereotomy is that regular courses of masonry – such as those on the famous curved wall of the Qorikancha (chapter 7) – would have posed a greater challenge than the irregular shapes that seem such a marvel. A more beneficial result of the masons' painstaking work is the architecture's resilience to the earthquakes that strike the central Andes with unnerving frequency. Despite many violent temblors, numerous Inca ashlar walls still exhibit no ill effects of the earth's movements, although they are not immune.

Other Crafts

As described in the introduction to this chapter, artisans of many other skills also worked for the Inca in materials ranging from wood, to stone, to organics. An extended description of those crafts is beyond this text, but among the finest objects that they produced were the wooden drinking cups known as *keros*, the large earspools that denoted high status, and musical instruments such as pan pipes and drums. Some of the finest objects were stone vessels and animal figurines. Conscripted artisans were also responsible for making a wide variety of military supplies, including sandals, armor, weapons, and shields.

chapter thirteen
Invasion and Aftermath

The invasion of South America that brought down the Inca empire was not launched in a day or even a decade. Over a period of about fifteen years after Vasco Núñez de Balboa first saw the Pacific in 1513, Spanish adventurers had been pushing the limits of European exploration southward from Panama. A series of expeditions, some led by Francisco Pizarro and his partner Diego de Almagro, had haltingly worked their way into Colombia and down the Ecuadorian coast to little profit. By 1528, however, Bartolomé Ruiz had captured a treasure-laden raft along the Ecuadorian coast that gave promise of a rich land just beyond the Spanish view; his expedition also captured a number of young boys who would later serve as interpreters for the first encounters with the Incas. News of Ruiz's success helped Pizarro to obtain a royal concession as governor of the unknown land and to attract financial support and men back in Spain. Even so, the trying climatic conditions and earlier failures daunted many hardy individuals reared in a society in which the men of recent generations had been tempered in the Reconquista of Spain and the conquest of Mexico. It was no accident that the captains of the expedition typically had ten to twenty years of experience in the New World and that only thirty of the 168 men in the force that Pizarro finally led into the Andes had just come over from Spain. Many had already lived through hazards like those they would face in the invasion and were willing to risk health, money, and life in a quest for wealth. These men were as much entrepreneurs as soldiers or adventurers, especially the horsemen who had spent respectable sums to buy their mounts, an investment that would entitle them to a larger share in any of the booty that they might find.

In 1531, Pizarro's force made its way to Coaque, on the Ecuadorian coast, which they attacked and occupied. They settled down to wait for reinforcements for several months, but many succumbed to local diseases in the interim. By early 1532, several new boatloads of men had joined the vanguard and the expedition had worked its way southward to Tumbes, on Peru's north coast, which had already been scouted four years earlier. Once again, the Spaniards settled down and began to inspect the surrounding territory. It was only at this time that they began to see concrete evidence of a major civilization – roads, storehouses, and state installations. Again, the Spaniards moved forward with a characteristic mix of caution and bravery, founding a new settlement at San Miguel (now Piura), about 100 km farther south, and planning an expedition into the heartland of the empire whose existence became more apparent with every passing day. By November of 1532, Pizarro had finally gathered the resources, men, and boldness to ascend the Andes and meet the Inca prince Atawallpa, who was known to be in Cajamarca along the royal highway in northern Peru. The knowledge was mutual, of course, for the Spanish pillaging and murder along the coast had been angrily noted in the highlands. In fact, gifts with threatening overtones had been sent to the Spaniards and 20,000 men under Atawallpa's general Rumiñawi dispatched to meet the expedition along the road.

The company finally arrived at Cajamarca on November 15 and entered the plaza in the center of town. While most men took shelter from a hailstorm, Pizarro dispatched Hernando de Soto, fifteen horsemen, and the interpreter Martín to greet the Inca lord at the hot springs outside of town. After first passing through the thousands of soldiers lining the way, the Spaniards approached Atawallpa, who was seated on a small wooden throne, surrounded by his court. Captain de Soto made a brief speech that was translated and then offered the prince a ring as a sign of friendship. Atawallpa did not deign to reply to him but did converse with Hernando Pizarro, once he understood that he was the Governor's brother, and invited the Spaniards to dine with him. They declined, but after some hesitation accepted a drink. A fine display of horsemanship by de Soto met with royal approval, but Spanish appeals for Atawallpa to accompany them back to the town fell on deaf ears. Thus ended the first day of contact (Hemming 1970:32–5).

A Deity in Captivity

Even after de Soto and Hernando Pizarro's encounter with Atawallpa, the Spaniards were undecided about their best course of action.[1] They ranged from feigning friendship and postponing military action for a more propitious moment, to demanding that Atawallpa declare obeisance to the king of Spain, to launching a surprise attack. In the end, they agreed to let Francisco Pizarro judge the best course of action once events were underway. Fortunately for the invaders, Inca settlement planning and architecture provided a wonderful opportunity to conceal their intentions. Access to the main plaza at Cajamarca was restricted to a few passages that could be blocked, and elongated halls that opened onto the plaza had numerous doorways that could permit a rapid charge by a wall of horsemen and foot soldiers hidden from view. The Spaniards took advantage of the layout to station men in the entryways to the plaza and to hide artillery, men, and horses inside the buildings. For his part, the Inca was making similar plans to feign friendship and then take the Spaniards prisoner. During his captivity, he explained that he had intended to torture and kill a number of them and castrate the remainder for the service of the women's institutions. A happier fate was planned for the horses, which he planned to breed (Hemming 1970:37–45).

When Atawallpa entered the plaza late in the afternoon of November 16, he was accompanied by some of the highest-ranking lords of the land and several thousand of his personal guard. Garbed in elegant tunics, he was carried on a luxurious litter decorated with parrot feathers and plates of gold and silver. He ordered his bearers to halt in the center of the plaza and waited while much of the remaining open space was filled by his entourage. Surprised to find no Spaniards in sight, Atawallpa thought that they had hidden out of fear. But then the Dominican friar Vicente de Valverde, accompanied by the interpreter Martín, approached Atawallpa and began to explain how he had been sent to reveal the word of God to the people of the land. Valverde handed a closed breviary to the Inca, who succeeded in opening it only after some effort. After conversing briefly with the priest, Atawallpa cast the book to the ground and rose in his litter to ready his men. At that, Valverde rushed back toward the hidden Spaniards and cried out for them to avenge the affront to the holy word.

Pizarro gave the signal for the men to charge – firing small cannon into the midst of the crowded square – and the armed Spaniards stormed out to their battle cry, "Santiago." Riding horses, protected by their armor, and carrying superior arms, the Spaniards were almost invulnerable against the massed Andean soldiers. Atawallpa was personally captured by Pizarro, who took a wound while deflecting a Spanish blow intended to fell the Inca. In the two hours of carnage that followed, as many as 7,000 Andeans may have been killed, at the loss of not a single Spaniard. Atawallpa was immediately protected by his captors, for they judged that their own safety depended on keeping the ruler alive. As night fell, the Spaniards were in such complete control within Cajamarca that Pizarro invited Atawallpa to dine with him (ibid.).

As the Spaniards' passion for gold and silver quickly became obvious, Atawallpa responded by offering an immense ransom in exchange for his freedom. Xérez (1985:122), Pizarro's secretary, wrote that the Inca promised to have his subjects fill a room about 6.2 m × 4.8 m to a white

Plate 13.1 This room in Cajamarca is shown to tourists as the building that Atawallpa promised to fill to half its height with gold and silver to secure his ransom; photo by John Hyslop, courtesy Division of Anthropology, American Museum of Natural History

line set at half its height, or about 2.5 m, with gold objects (plate 13.1). The room's volume was to be filled twice over with silver objects gathered from the entire empire over the next couple of months. Pizarro agreed to the proposal with alacrity and both sides settled down to wait, while planning their moves for the time when the ransom had been paid. The Spaniards were willing to let the process drag out for an extended period, while reinforcements could be mobilized from Panama and they could learn more about the political and military situation in the Andes. Atawallpa, in the meantime, was managing the affairs of state from captivity and planning to avenge himself once free from Spanish hands.

As the ransom trickled in, the two sides got to know one another. The Spaniards watched Atawallpa receive visitors and rule his domain, and conversed with him at length about a wide range of subjects concerning the land. For his part, the Inca expressed a certain degree of interest in things Spanish, even learning to play chess. The information that the conquistadores gleaned during the eight months of Atawallpa's captivity led them to correctly believe that they could exploit the divisions that lay between the two Inca factions. Over time they also came to see how to use the resentments harbored by many Inca subjects, who were eager to see the Spaniards as saviors from imperial rule. During this time, Pizarro sent expeditions to Cuzco and coastal Pachacamac. Along the road, the three soldiers sent to the capital had an interview with the imprisoned Waskhar, but declined to act on his plea for freedom. The other expedition, led by Hernando Pizarro, traveled to coastal Pachacamac, where they destroyed the oracular idol. On the return trip, they persuaded Atawallpa's general Challcochima to accompany them from Hatun Xauxa back to Cajamarca, which essentially consigned the commander to his death. Both expeditions, especially the trio sent to Cuzco, returned to Cajamarca with golden evidence of the empire's wealth.

By late April, 1533, Diego de Almagro, Pizarro's partner, had arrived from Panama with reinforcements and Hernando Pizarro's expedition had reappeared. It seems to have become clear to Atawallpa at that point that the first company of Spaniards was only the vanguard of a much larger invasion and that the prospects of his release were dim. In June and July, the accumulated hoard of gold and silver treasures was melted down and carefully accounted for to ensure that the royal fifth was taken out. Each horseman received about 41 kg of gold – roughly half a million dollars – and each foot man half that. Francisco Pizarro took seven times that of the horsemen, but Almagro's new arrivals received only token awards (Hemming 1970:73).

Finally, by the end of July, the situation in Cajamarca had reached a decision point, since the ransom had been melted down and new action was called for. The Spaniards later testified that they had heard rumors that Atawallpa had ordered Rumiñawi to move on Cajamarca in an effort to free him. Almagro's newcomers took the position that Atawallpa had become a liability whose continued presence exposed the Spaniards to perpetual danger. Conversely, many members of the initial expedition were more loath to kill the Inca. Pizarro himself preferred to keep the Inca as a hostage while the Spaniards made their way to Cuzco to claim the capital and its remaining riches; he even may have considered packing him off to Spain. In the end, Pizarro seems to have panicked and gave in to the demands to execute the Inca. On Saturday, July 26, 1533 Atawallpa was convicted of treason in a hastily convoked trial. He was garroted forthwith, having been spared burning at the stake only after agreeing to be baptized.

On to Cuzco

The Inca's death triggered all manner of response. The Incas in Cajamarca were bereft at the loss of their sovereign and appalled at the small-scale Christian burial that he was accorded – entirely out of keeping with the vast ceremony that he should have enjoyed. On a more personal note, a number of his wives cast about his lodgings, softly calling out for him to reappear until they sadly conceded his death. Crown officials in Panama and King Carlos V himself were outraged that a sovereign should have been so unceremoniously dispatched by social nobodies; Pizarro was later called to account and forced to defend himself. Among the Andean populations, Waskhar's supporters and numerous ethnic groups were overjoyed at the news, while Atawallpa's partisans were devastated and angered. An especially significant consequence was that the major impediment to Inca attacks on the Spaniards had been removed, so that Quizquiz, Rumiñawi, and other military leaders were free to attempt to rid the land of the invaders (see Hemming 1970:86–99).

Atawallpa's death also left the Spaniards without a recognized native leader through whom to rule, and the Incas without a sovereign. Pizarro took steps to remedy the situation immediately, by installing one of Waskhar's younger brothers, named Thupa Wallpa, as a puppet ruler (Sancho de la Hoz 1917). They then set south toward Cuzco, meeting their first significant military resistance near Hatun Xauxa in the Mantaro Valley. The engagement graphically illustrated the divisions that split the Andes. While Atawallpa's army of occupation tried to burn down the town and put up resistance on the far side of the river, the native Xauxa and Wanka populace, who had sided with Waskhar's cause, celebrated in the streets (ibid.). The local people immediately allied themselves with the Spaniards and began to supply them from the royal warehouses, a practice they kept up for two full decades (chapter 11). Pizarro bivouacked at the town for a couple of weeks, which in 1535 became the first Spanish capital of the Andes. During their stay, the invaders suffered a serious setback, as Thupa Wallpa succumbed to an illness. His death plunged the land into another quagmire of intrigue wholly reminiscent of the Incas' own entangled successions.

Despite the young ruler's death, the Spaniards pressed southward. Their speed allowed them to surprise and defeat a retreating Inca army stationed at Vilcaswaman, but an advance Spanish force was surprised as it approached Cuzco and the Spaniards suffered their first real defeat of the invasion. Fortunately the survivors lasted the night and, joined by reinforcements, routed the attacking forces the next day. As the Spaniards approached Cuzco itself, Quizquiz's warriors initially managed to repel them at a pass that controlled access to the city, but the demoralized Incas soon abandoned the city's defense. Unopposed, Pizarro's men marched into the navel of the universe on November 15, 1533, a year to the day after marching into the Inca camp at Cajamarca (Hemming 1970:117).

Cuzco under Co-Rule

In the days just preceding their entry into Cuzco, the solution to one of the Spaniards' most vexing problems presented himself in person. Manqo Inka, yet another of Wayna Qhapaq's sons, had escaped the massacre in Cuzco inflicted by Cusi Yupanki on Atawallpa's behalf (chapter 4). The conquistadores' appearance provided him a chance to lay claim to the throne at the same time that it offered the Spaniards another apparently compliant puppet through whom they could govern. The force marching into Cuzco thus contained both Inca and Spanish representatives of power. Pizarro quickly set about assigning most of Cuzco's palaces and other buildings to members of his party and the Spaniards undertook their search for booty with a vengeance. They looted the Qorikancha over the strident protests of its priests and generally stripped the imperial capital of its wealth. Only a few of the Spaniards were perceptive enough to lament the destruction (Segovia 1968; Hemming 1970: 134–5). That December, Manqo Inka was formally installed as the Inca ruler, with all of the elaborate ceremonies that attended the coronation of a new monarch. Among the most attentive participants were the embalmed mummies of his ancestors, each crowned and dressed in finery and carried on his own litter (Estete 1967). The festivities lasted for a full month, after which the Spaniards and new *Sapa Inca* settled into an uneasy co-rule of the land.

Throughout the next year, the Spaniards met considerable resistance in their efforts to pacify the land. In Ecuador especially, the Inca armies led by Rumiñawi and Quizquiz led a prolonged series of campaigns against the Spaniards. Ultimately, Quizquiz's men rebelled against the continuation of the resistance and killed him, while Rumiñawi was captured and executed by the Spaniards under Benalcázar. At the same time, the Spaniards in Cuzco had renewed their incessant quarrels and Manqo Inka was having difficulty in gaining full support among the remaining Incas. All of these situations had many complications, far too intricate to detail here. The most important outcome of these events, however, was the dispatching of Almagro to complete the conquest of the southern Andes, accompanied by another royal brother, Paullu Inka, and the high priest of the Sun, Villac Umu.

Over time, Manqo Inka came to realize that his role would never achieve equal status with that of the Spaniards. To the contrary, he would remain a puppet at best. He therefore began to plot a way to escape Spanish supervision and take on the role of leader of the resistance. After one abortive attempt, he managed to escape from Cuzco and began to assemble an army intended to expel the Spaniards, not just from the capital but from the entire land. The resistance came to fruition in 1536, as massive armies were assembled to lay siege to Cuzco and attack the newly founded Ciudad de Los Reyes (Lima) on the coast. The siege of Cuzco was a lengthy affair, sustained by somewhere between 200,000 and 400,000 soldiers and other personnel. Within the desperate capital, there were only a few hundred Spaniards supported by barely more than 1,000 native auxiliaries. The Incas employed all manner of tactics, including burning the city and flooding the surrounding lands to counter the Spaniards' advantage on horses. After some time, the Spaniards recognized that they could reduce the direct attacks by capturing the fortified citadel of Saqsawaman above the city. Led by the young Juan Pizarro, who lost his life in the assault, the Spaniards drove the Incas out of the citadel through daring mounted attacks and by scaling the walls with ladders and winning hand-to-hand combat. In the end, however, the Spaniards survived the siege because of the demands of the agricultural cycle. Slowly, but inexorably, the besieging soldier-farmers disbanded to tend their fields at home. The next year, another siege was mounted, but it too failed to take its objective. On the coast, the attack on Ciudad de Los Reyes in 1536 failed when the Inca commanding officers were targeted and wiped out in a direct attack on the city. Leaderless, the army scattered into the hills in a single night.

In retrospect, the early Spanish victories over the Incas can be assigned to a coincidence of historical, technological, and cultural factors. From the point of view of history, the Spaniards could not have arrived at a more opportune moment. The victorious Incas in Cajamarca simply underestimated the threat posed by the small band of invaders. Later, once Atawallpa had been removed from the picture, perhaps half of the people of the Andes were willing to ally themselves with the Spaniards to save themselves from the bloody retribution that Atawallpa's armies had already visited on many of Waskhar's adherents. These new allies provided thousands of seasoned warriors, along with support personnel and supplies (see Espinoza Soriano 1972). The conquistadores also had enormous technological advantages in their weapons and armor, but the horses gave them the greatest initial tactical advantage. Native soldiers and battle tactics were simply no match for mounted Spaniards on open terrain and several early engagements amounted to little more than slaughter. The Incas soon learned to dig pits on open fields and restricted many engagements to the kinds of broken terrain that favored their weapons and negated the horses' utility, but those gains simply prolonged the conflict and did not turn the tide in the natives' favor. The Spaniards had another early tactical advantage – their willingness to take the initiative at every opportunity, which ran contrary to the deliberative Inca approach to warfare. Often, their attacks in the face of overwhelming odds helped to break the morale of the native soldiers. A number of cultural features also contributed to the conquistadores' early successes. One was the personalized and deified nature of Inca leadership. With the sovereign held hostage, his subordinates were handicapped in their ability to undertake military initiatives. Once Atawallpa was gone, no leader existed who would be recognized by all and who could marshal a unified resistance. In the end, the practice of mobilizing soldiers seasonally from farmers and herders meant that it was difficult, if not impossible, to maintain pressure on Spanish enclaves ensconced in Inca installations and the resistance movement stalled.

The Neo-Inca State

The early Inca defeats did not end Andean aspirations for self-rule, but simply sent the resistance into the eastern forests or underground. For 36 years after their unsuccessful efforts to throw the Spaniards out of Cuzco and Lima, the Incas maintained an independent state at Vilcabamba, about 200 km down the Urubamba river from Cuzco (Guillén Guillén 1994; Lee 2000). Founded by Manqo Inka after his escape from Cuzco, Vilcabamba provided a safe haven for the Incas to preserve their liberty and foment plans for regaining their lost lands. For decades under Manqo Inka, Titu Cusi, and Thupa Amaru, they mounted campaigns that harassed the Spaniards from the eastern slopes and punished their Andean collaborators through raids and massacres. Any number of diplomatic and military expeditions were sent into the forests in an effort to bring the holdouts into the Spanish realm peaceably or otherwise, but to no avail. Vilcabamba finally fell in 1572 to an expedition mounted by Viceroy Toledo, for whom the continued existence of a free Inca society had become an insufferable affront to the Crown. The last Inca ruler, Thupa Amaru, was captured and transported to Cuzco, where he was rapidly convicted of treason and sentenced to death. A considerable number of Spaniards interceded on his behalf in an effort to save his life, but Toledo was apparently convinced that the only definitive way to break the spine of Inca rebelliousness was to execute the king. Thus, on September 24, 1572, the last of the Inca kings was marched into the plaza of his ancestors' majesty and beheaded, bringing an end to the lineage that had descended from the Sun to rule the earth.

The Imposition of Spanish Rule

While the Incas maintained their independence on the eastern side of the Andes, the Spaniards set about killing one another in a series of civil wars that were slowly and erratically supplanted by stable Colonial government. The account of that era is a complicated story in and of itself, but a few key developments can be highlighted here. Francisco Pizarro, architect of Tawantinsuyu's overthrow, did not live long to enjoy his hard-won status as governor of the new land. He soon fell out with his partner, Diego de Almagro, the elder, who seized Cuzco from Pizarro in 1537 and installed Paullu Inka as a new puppet ruler. The first chapter of this conflict came to an end the next year, with Almagro's death at the hands of Hernando Pizarro, but Almagro's adherents took their vengeance by murdering Francisco Pizarro himself in 1541. The decade of the 1540s continued to be plagued by a series of other Spanish insurrections that were ultimately dampened by the arrival of new officials from Spain with the mandate of bringing peace to the troubled land. The last major rebellion was staged by Francisco Hernández Girón in 1553–4, whose defeat came about largely because of the military action of the Wankas allied with the Spanish Crown.

As the late 1540s gave way to later decades, the Spaniards undertook a series of inspections of their new holdings that, along with other documents, provide some details of life after the loss of Inca dominion and before the Colonial administration really took hold. For Andean peoples civil wars, forced labor, and pestilence wrought devastation on the populace. Within about 40 years of the invasion, the population had declined by about 50 percent (Cook 1981). In some coastal valleys, the population ultimately fell to as little as 5 percent of its size in 1532. During the earliest years of Colonial rule, the native peoples were granted to individual Spanish soldiers, more than a few of whom treated their vassals as little more than a source of labor to make the new lords rich. The widespread abuse of the native populace, coupled with the theft of their lands, increasingly insupportable tax burdens, death in the mines, and the destruction of the Andean way of life, has understandably given rise to an image of a black time in the former Tawantinsuyu. Even so, there were many instances of alliances between Andean and European, as they adjusted to the changing circumstances. Moreover, the Crown and some of the religious institutions took an interest in protecting the well-being of the native population, who turned to the new political structure to resolve disputes among themselves. Many of those disputes, intriguingly enough, arose from multiple claims to prime resources by the colonists installed by the Incas and the local peoples who were trying to reclaim the lands of their ancestors (see, e.g., D'Altroy 1994a).

Beginning in 1551, the Spanish Crown dispatched a series of Viceroys to bring order to the land, which was still riven by civil wars among the last of the conquistadores. Slowly, civil administration was installed and the Spaniards began to take a closer interest in Andean culture. One of the most perceptive of the administrators was Juan Polo de Ondegardo, the Magistrate of Cuzco who has been mentioned often in this text. It is Polo who has provided us with much of our knowledge on Inca political organization, economics, religion, and social customs, and who made the startling discovery in 1558 that the descendants of the Inca kings were still worshiping their ancestors' mummies. Horrified, he launched a successful campaign to find the mummies and dispatched them to the coast (table 5.1). The most sweeping reforms occurred, however, under the administration of Viceroy Toledo, in 1570–2. Among the many changes that he instituted were the *reducción*, or resettlement, of native peoples out of their traditional communities into new villages near Spanish centers, where they could be supervised more closely for signs of rebellion and lapses from Catholicism. With Toledo's reforms and his destruction of the neo-Inca state of Vilcabamba came the end of any semblance of Inca independence in their once proud land.

The Inca Reborn

Shortly after the discovery and capture of the Inca mummies, a new clandestine movement came to light called the *Taki Onqoy*, or "Dancing Sickness" (Mumford 1998). The Taki Onqoy was a millenarian movement intended to reject all things European and restore the traditional Andean order. In its visible activities, the movement featured ecstatic dancing during which the participants went into trances as if possessed; its leaders also seem to have encouraged the accumulation of weapons as part of an anticipated rebellion. Thus, it was both a response to Catholic efforts to rid the Andes of indigenous religious traditions and an effort to throw off Spanish rule. In an odd twist of confused allegiances, however, the Taki Onqoy was discovered when a participant revealed its existence in the Catholic confessional. The alarmed priest quickly got word to Lima and the Spanish authorities undertook an intensive campaign to find the weapons and call the perceived leaders to account. In the end, the popular uprising never occurred, but its threat fed into careers and conflicts among the Spaniards. The crusading cleric Cristóbal de Albornoz, through whose writings we know the movement, for example, used its suppression as a platform to advance his career. As memory of the Incas as living, oppressive rulers began to fade from the popular consciousness, another image of late prehistory as a glorious epoch began to coalesce among Andean peoples, not just the Incas themselves. Over the centuries of Colonial rule, the myth of *Inkarrí* began to take form. He was a syncretic figure who blended the Inca with the *rey* (Spanish king), a man who would return to the Andes to free the native peoples from the bondage into which the Spanish conquest had cast them. Even in modern times, ethnographers have recorded cycles of myths about *Inkarrí* recalling a glorious past that can still be reborn (Urton 1999:73–5).

The Inca Legacy

Despite the violence, disease, and cultural transformations that Andean peoples experienced during the Colonial era, the legacy of Tawantinsuyu continues to shape the people and cultures of western South America, especially in the Peruvian highlands where many communities still follow traditional ways of life. The most deeply embedded features still lie within the social fabric of local communities and the cultural philosophies that give meaning to relationships among people and between them and the land. Most importantly, life is still defined by links among close kin and an ethic of mutual support. It is not unusual for peasant communities outside the larger towns to be divided into moieties comparable to the upper and lower divisions of ancient times and for young men and women to look for a marriage partner across divisions of local kin groups (e.g., Isbell 1978). Many highland villagers today still rely on cooperative ownership of resources and share the risks and rewards of making an agricultural or pastoral living in the demanding environment (e.g., Flores Ochoa 1978). Similarly, civic tasks, including rebuilding walls, cleaning canals, and maintaining public spaces are still divided up among *ayllu* (G. Urton, pers. comm. 1997).

Plate 13.2 Pilgrims ascending snow fields in the annual ceremonial trek to the high peaks during the festival of Quyllor Rit'i; photo courtesy of Vicente Revilla

The relationship of the people to the land and sky still retains a vibrancy that is expressed in the knowledge, beliefs, and cycles of ceremonies practiced by many communities. Gary Urton (1981), for example, has found that the people of Misminay, not too far from Cuzco, still observe many of the same constellations and celestial passages that formed part of the Inca cosmology in the sixteenth century. Similarly, offerings of coca and chicha are often made to Pachamama, the earth mother, throughout the highlands to give thanks for successful harvests. In Cuzco itself, the celebrations of Quyllor Rit'i and Inti Raymi have regained a vitality that was dampened in centuries past by the Catholic Church. Some of the celebrations can be attributed to events staged for the tourist trade, but the pilgrimages to high elevation shrines are clearly not a reinvention of an ancient tradition, but part of a living belief system (Sallnow 1987). Residents of the towns on the high slopes within a day's walk of Cuzco still follow the well-trodden ritual pathways to the summits of Huanacauri, Nevado Sinakara, and nearby peaks to make offerings to the ancient powers that inhabit the landscape. These are not events to be taken light-heartedly, even though they feature music and dancing, since the climbs to the summits through permanent snow fields occasionally claim the lives of pilgrims who have lived in the high communities since birth (V. Revilla, pers. comm. 2000; plate 13.2). Many of the ritual calendars have been blended with those of the Catholic Church, of course, but the cycles are still attuned to the ebb and flow of the seasons and stars.

The Incas still retain enormous potency in the self-image of the Peruvian nation as well. For a time in the 1980s, the national currency was called the *inti*, named after the Sun God of the Incas, and the currency of recent times is still named the *sol*, i.e., the Spanish word for the sun. There are also many referents to the prehispanic past in popular culture. For example, the national soft drink of Peru is a cream soda called Inca Kola and there are many regional variants that draw on ancient names, such as Chavín Cola and Ccori (golden) Cola. References to Inca glory pervade modern politics as well, as even presidential candidates dance to the ancient pipes and drums. There is no more compelling reminder of the cultural weight of the Incas in modern society, however, than the protests surrounding the presidential election in Peru in 2000. The election pitted the sitting president against a Peruvian-born but Stanford-trained economist whose personal appearance and cultural vision harked back to the times when the Incas ruled themselves. When a massive rally was staged in Lima to protest the political process, it was called "La Marcha de los Cuatro Suyos" or "The March of the Four Parts." The Inca legacy is alive.

Glossary of Foreign Terms

This glossary contains most of the non-English terms used in the text, with the preferred definition for this book listed first. Because translations and meanings of the terms vary, a range of definitions is provided, but this glossary should not be taken as an exhaustive survey. Specific quoted definitions, attributed in brackets, are derived from Cerrón-Palomino 1976a [CP]; González Holguín 1952 [1608] [DGH]; Urioste's glossary-index in Guaman Poma 1980:1075–108 [GP]; Haggard and McLean 1941 [HM]; Hornberger and Hornberger 1983 [HH]; Hyslop 1990:333–4 [JH]; and Murra 1980b [1956]:191–4 [JVM]. Cerrón-Palomino's dictionary refers to the modern Quechua of the Junín region, while the Hornbergers' dictionary is based on the modern Quechua from the Cuzco region. Languages are Arawak (Ar), Aymara (Ay), Quechua (Q), and Spanish (S). Words in square brackets in the text are this author's insertions.

allawqa (Q; also *allauco* [CP: p. 26]): right.

altiplano (S): high elevation plain in Bolivia and far northwestern Argentina.

Ananwanka (Q): upper (moiety) division of *Wanka* ethnic group; southernmost of three political divisions of Inca province of *Wanka Wamaní*, populated principally by *Wanka* and *Xauxa* ethnic groups.

Antisuyu (Q; also *Andesuyo*): northeastern part of Inca empire, generally corresponding to warm lowlands.

apu (Q, also sp. *apo*): "great lord or superior judge" [GP: p. 1076].

aqlla (Q; plural *aqllakuna*): "woman chosen for state and religious service" [JH: p. 333]; "hidden" [GP: p. 1076].

Atawallpa (Q): son of 11th Inca emperor Wayna Qhapaq, won dynastic civil war against half-brother Waskhar, but not formally enthroned as emperor.

awasqa (Q): rough cloth; "common, thick cloth" [GP: p. 1077].

ayllu (Q): localized descent group, varying in inclusiveness, frequently subdivided into moieties, lineages, or both; "division, genealogy, lineage, or kinship" [GP: p. 1078, after DGH: p. 39]; "kinsman, family relation" [CP: p. 33].

Aymara (called *Haquru* by its speakers): one of three principal Andean languages, spoken primarily from far southern Peru through Bolivian altiplano.

cacique (Ar): leader, a term frequently applied by Spaniards to anyone in a position of indigenous authority.

cacique principal (A-S): paramount leader of sociopolitical unit.

ceja de la montaña (S): upper forested area on eastern slopes of Andes.

ceja de selva (S): upper fringe of the jungle.

chala (Q): coastal environmental zone.

ch'arki (Q): freeze-dried (jerked) meat.

chaski (Q): "postal messenger" [GP: p. 1079].

chicha (Ar): "a fermented beverage, generally of maize, originally a Caribbean word" [JH: p. 333]; in Quechua: *aqha, aswa* [GP: p. 1079].

Chinchaysuyu (Q): northwestern part of Inca empire, generally corresponding to the Peruvian and Ecuadorian highlands and coast.

chullpa (Q): above-ground tomb.

chunka kamayuq (Q): official at head of 10-household census unit.

chuño (Q): freeze-dried potatoes.

Cuntisuyu (Q; also sp. *Condesuyo, Kuntisuyu*): southwestern part of Inca empire, generally corresponding to the southernmost Peruvian highlands, and the south Peruvian and northern Chilean coast.

encomienda (S): early Spanish grant of the labor service of native peoples to Spanish recipient.

etnía (S): Spanish term referring to named ethnic group, corresponding unevenly to self-identified prehispanic groups.

hanan (Q): upper half or moiety of dual units characterizing Inca sociopolitical organization.

hanega (S): a dry measure approximating 1.60 bushels [HM: p. 76], 56.6 liters, or 43.6 kg for shelled maize.

hanegada: measure of land corresponding to 0.64 ha or 1.59 acre (HM: p. 77).

hatun (Q): big.

hatun runa (Q): "adult, married male" [GP: p. 1081]; "'Male peasant' [DGH: p. 154]. An adult male, married and enumerated in the Inca census. Literally 'big man'" [JVM: p. 192].

hunu (Q): unit of 10,000; often used to refer to census or sociopolitical unit ostensibly consisting of 10,000 households.

hunu kuraka (Q): official at head of 10,000-household census unit.

hurin (Q): lower half or moiety of dual units characterizing Inca socio-political organization.

ichuq (Q; also sp. *ichoca* [CP: p. 56], *lloq'e* [HH: p. 386]): left.

indios (S): generally, the indigenous commoner population.

janca (Q): the highest elevation environmental zone, without permanent human occupation, characterized by glaciers and sparse biota.

kallanka (Q): "a long hall, often with a gabled roof" [JH: p. 333].

kancha (Q): "an enclosure; several rooms placed around a patio, generally within a rectangular perimeter wall" [JH: p. 333].

khipu (Q; also sp. *quipu*): "cords with knots used [as a mnemonic device] in Inka accounting" [GP: p. 1086]; "knot, ancient Andean recording system" [HH: p. 89]; from "*Qquipuni*. To count by [use of] knots" [DGH: p. 309].

khipu kamayuq (Q): official responsible for keeping records on knotted strings.

Kollasuyu (Q; [HH: p. 188], also sp. *Collasuyo, Qollasuyu*): southeastern part of Inca empire.

kuraka (Q; also sp. *curaca, kuraqka* [JVM: p. 192]): native elite; "local ethnic authority" [GP: p. 1085]; "representative of the local god" [HH: p. 84].

libra (S): a measure of weight equal to about 0.46 kg, for Peru and Mexico (HM: p. 79).

llaqta (Q; also sp. *llacta* [DGH: p. 207]): "town" [GP: p. 1087]; " 'Pueblo' [DGH: p. 207]. A town, a nucleated settlement . . ." [JVM: p. 192]; "town, city, fatherland, nation, country, community" [HH: p. 111].

marca (Q; also sp. *malka* [CP: p. 85]): "people [town], population" [CP: p. 85].

mascaypacha (Q): woven textile fringe worn as insignia of emperor's office.

mit'a (Q): "A period, one's turn . . . Prestations to one's ethnic group, one's lord and to the Inca state" [JVM: p. 192]; "period [season]; that which returns cyclically, and the turn in which to undertake something [task]" [GP: p. 1090].

mit'ayuq (Q): individual serving rotational labor service to the Inca state [Spurling 1992:118, fn. 177].

mitmaq (Q; pl. *mitmaqkuna*): "a settler from some other place; an Inka state colonist" [JH: p. 333]; "from *mit'iy*: to send; sent by one's ethnic group of origin to attend to outside interests" [GP: p. 1090].

montaña (S): upper, humid, forested environmental zone on eastern side of the Andes; source of fruit and wild biota.

orejón (S): long-ear; Inca nobility, distinguished by large earspools.

pachaka (Q; [GP: p. 1090], also sp. *pachak* [HH: p. 151]): unit of 100; often used to refer to census or sociopolitical unit ostensibly consisting of 100 households.

pachaka kuraka (Q): official at head of 100-household census unit.

panaqa (Q): royal dynastic descent group, or *ayllu*, founded by each ruler.

páramo (S): high rolling grassland of Ecuador and far northern Peru.

pichkachunka (Q, also sp. *pisqachunka* [GP: p. 1090]): unit of 50; often used to refer to census or sociopolitical unit ostensibly consisting of 50 households.

pichkachunka kamayuq (Q): official at head of 50-household census unit.

pichkapachaka (Q): unit of 500; often used to refer to census or sociopolitical unit ostensibly consisting of 500 households.

pichkapachaka kuraka (Q): official at head of 500-household census unit.

pichkawaranqa (Q): unit of 5,000; often used to refer to census or sociopolitical unit ostensibly consisting of 5,000 households.

pichkawaranqa kuraka (Q): official at head of 5,000-household census unit.

pirka (Q): rustic or fieldstone masonry.

pueblo (S): town, people.

puna (Q): high elevation environmental zone, generally characterized by rolling grasslands; natural habitat of camelids and principal zone for herding.

pururaucas (Q) ["Hidden Thieves"]: idols venerated by Incas as stones risen as warriors to aid defense of Cuzco against Chanka attack.

qhapaq ñan (Q; also sp. *capac ñan*): powerful road, i.e., imperial Inca highway [see GP: p. 1096].

qollana (Q): excellent; one of three divisions, *qollana-payan-kayaw*, found in Cuzco area sociopolitical organization.

qollqa (Q; also sp. *colca, qullqa* [GP: p. 1095], *qolqa* [HH: p. 187]): storehouse.

qompi (Q; also sp. *cumbi, qumpi* [GP: p. 1095]): fine cloth.

qoya (Q): queen, principal wife of ruler.

quechua (Q; also sp. *qheshwa, qheswa* [HH: p. 109]): temperate, mid-elevation environmental zone, found on eastern and western slopes of Andes, as well as in intermontane valleys; principal highland zone for maize-complex crops.

Quechua (Q): dominant language group in central Andean highlands; also, ethnic group that inhabited the northwest side of Lake Titicaca at the time of the Inca expansion.

relación (S): account, report.

runakhipu (Q): state officials responsible for census-taking.

runasimi (Q): human speech, i.e., Quechua.

saya (Q): a sociopolitical subdivision; "the upper or lower, the right or left moiety, in Andean dual organization" [JVM: p. 193].

selva alta (S): upper jungle.

selva baja (S): lower jungle.

señorío (S): a polity ruled by a native lord.

suni (Q): moderately high elevation environmental zone, above *quechua* and below *puna*; principal highland zone for tuber-complex crops.

suyu (Q): "territory, region" [HH: p. 242].

suyuyoc apu (Q): lord of a great political unit, sometimes specifically meaning half of the empire; *suyuyuq*: "administration of a subdivision" [GP: p. 1101].

tampu (Q, also sp. *tanpu* [GP: p. 1101]): "Inka state lodging on the road system" [JH: p. 333].

Tawantinsuyu: "the Inka empire; land of the four (*tawa*) parts or provinces (*suyu*)" [JH: p. 333].

tokoyrikoq (Q): independent Inca inspector who visited the provinces; "he who sees all" [Rowe 1946:264].

tokrikoq (Q; also sp. *toricoq* [JH: p. 333], *t'oqrikuq* [JVM: p. 193]): Inca provincial governor.

tumi (Q): ceremonial knife with a crescent-shaped head often used in sacrifices.

tupu (Q): "a measure of any kind, a league" [DHG: p. 347]; "agricultural measure" [CP: p. 1102]; "general measure" [CP: p. 136]; "measure (volume), measure of land" [HH: p. 253]. Not to be confused with an alternative meaning of *tupu* – "fastening pin" [HH: p. 253].

usnu (Q, also sp. *ushnu* [KJH: p. 334]): platform mound in a ceremonial complex or a drain into which libations were poured; "a centrally located ritual complex consisting of a drain with a stone, basin, and platform within Inka settlements" [JH: p. 334]; "ceremonial or administrative construction" [GP: p. 1103]; "a niche, usually in a wall, used for placing idols or other venerated or sacred objects" [HH: p. 274].

wak'a (Q; also sp. *huaca*, *waqa* [JH: p. 334]): shrine, sacred place, object, or power; "tutelary divinity, at the local level" [GP: p. 1104].

wamani (Q): "Incaic administrative district" [GP: p. 1104]; also, mountain peak spirit.

waranqa (Q): unit of 1,000; often used to refer to census or sociopolitical unit ostensibly consisting of 1,000 households.

waranqa kuraka (Q): official at head of 1,000-household census unit.

yana (Q; pl. *yanakuna*): "a servant, a young man in service [DGH: p. 363], from *yanapa*, reciprocal services given without accounts being kept . . ." [JVM: p. 194].

yunga (Q): low-elevation environmental zone, above the coastal plain on the west and the jungle on the east; principal zone for coca and fruits.

zeq'e (Q; also sp. *ceque*, *zeque*): "a radial line or path; a radial system of forty-one lines in Cuzco that integrated Inka kinship, cosmology, and calendrics" [JH: p. 334].

zinchi (Q; plural *zinchikuna*): valiant man, native elite or warlord, generally applied to pre-Inca era.

Notes

1 Introduction

1 Esp. Means 1928; Levillier 1940:207–486; Rowe 1985b:207–16; Porras Barrenechea 1986; Pärssinen 1992; Pease 1995; Hamilton 1996.
2 Segovia 1943; Molina 1988; Albornoz 1989; Cabello Valboa 1951; Murúa 1986.
3 Zárate 1862; Bibar 1966; Santillán 1968; Falcón 1946; Matienzo 1967; Xérez 1985; Acosta 1986; Avila: Salomon and Urioste 1991; Lizárraga 1909; Valdivia 1960.

2 The Land and its People

1 Witnesses made implausible and erratic claims about their own ages as well. For example, two noble witnesses claimed ages first of 120 and 132, and then of 86 and 86, in depositions presented a week apart in 1569 (Urton 1990:64).
2 Cobo 1979:252–3. There is a little evidence, however, that the Incas made some effort to keep track of the life spans or reigns of the most recent rulers. Two royal descendants of Pachakuti and Thupa Inka Yupanki, interviewed in Cuzco in 1570–2, consulted an illustrated wooden board and *khipu* (knot-records) to report that Pachakuti died at 100, Thupa Inka Yupanki at 58 or 60, and Wayna Qhapaq at 70. Pachakuti's age is pretty clearly a nicely rounded figure intended to mean that the empire's founder had lived to a grand old age. Other witnesses said that Thupa Inka Yupanki died young, between youth and old age, and old. Regarding Wayna Qhapaq, they said he died at about 60 or 70, very old, or with some grey hair, anywhere from two to ten years before the Spanish invasion (Toledo 1940b:92, 118, 140, 148, 157–8, 166, 173, 200, 202, 203).

3 The Incas before the Empire

1 In Betanzos's (1996:18) story, Yawar Waqaq received his name because he was born crying blood.

2   The Killke period was named after the ceramic style, first called Canchón, identified by Rowe (1944:60–2).

4   The History of the Empire: Narrative Visions

1   The Quipucamayos of Pacariqtambo averred that he subdued the entire altiplano through a mix of diplomacy and conquest, and then ventured northward to the Huánuco region of Peru's central highlands. They mentioned such regions as Paria, Pacajes, Carangas, Charkas, and Umasuyo (Callapiña et al. 1974 [1542/1608]:32–3). According to that account, Yawar Qhapaq had already vanquished Chucuito, home to the Lupaqa. Guaman Poma (1980 [1614]:/106[106]–/107[107], p. 87) also wrote that Wiraqocha Inka conquered through the central highlands of Peru and some lowlands, including the Chincha and Ica Valleys of the south Peruvian coast.

2   Despite such detailed versions of Wiraqocha Inka's exploits in the altiplano, Pärssinen (1992:82–4) points out that there appears to be no corroborative evidence for the king's adventures in the local documents from the region. Instead, the sources from the altiplano ascribe the conquests to armies operating during Pachakuti's and Thupa Inka Yupanki's reigns, which tends to support the notion of a very rapid imperial expansion, as Rowe originally suggested.

3   Not all accounts agreed with even these versions of the timing or importance of the Inca–Chanka conflicts described here. The purportedly earliest account by royal historians, the Pacariqtambo *khipu kamayuq*, did not even mention the Chankas by name nor describe an attack on Cuzco. They did state that Qhapaq Yupanki, the fifth ruler, conquered the Vilcas, Soras, and Aymaraes regions to the west of Cuzco (Callapiña 1974:31). Guaman Poma (1980:85) took the same position in his historical review. However, most modern scholars suggest that the Qhapaq Yupanki who conquered that region was actually a brother of Pachakuti, who commanded a major campaign through the central Peruvian sierra. The RGI documents from the region credit Pachakuti and Thupa Inka Yupanki with the conquests. Alternatively, Cobo first wrote that Inka Roq'a, the sixth ruler, had conquered the Chankas. He then amended his account to say that the Chankas had actually not really been conquered, but "had surrendered to the necessity of adapting to the times." It was actually Wiraqocha Inka who vanquished the Chankas after Yawar Waqaq fled Cuzco. Pachakuti nonetheless also had to subdue them during his reign, after pre-empting a rumored coup attempt by his brother Inka Urqon by having him secretly murdered (Cobo 1979:124–5, 127–8, 137).

4   The leader of the Chankas, named Uscovilca, was described as an idol or as the mummified corpse of the deceased Chanka lord in Sarmiento's (1960:231) account. Polo found the idol with Pachakuti's mummy (Rostworowski 1999:107).

5   Betanzos 1996 [1557]: ch. 17, pp. 74–9.

6   See, for example, Callapiña et al. 1974:31; Guaman Poma 1980:85; Cobo 1979:124–5, 127–8, 137.

7   Sarmiento and Cobo describe a early sortie led by Pachakuti and Inka
    Roq'a down the Urubamba Valley to Ollantaytambo and perhaps as far as
    Vilcabamba, about 200 km away (Ollantaytambo: Sarmiento 1960:239;
    Vilcabamba: Cobo 1979:135–7; see Rowe 1946:206; Saignes 1985:14–15;
    Pärssinen 1992:107–19). According to Betanzos (1996:85–91), that first
    venture took the Incas only as far as Xaquixaguana, in the Anta region west
    of Cuzco. They penetrated deeper on a later occasion when Pachakuti sent
    in a contingent after returning from wars to the west with the Soras, Lucanas,
    and Chankas. He continued that, after Pachakuti's first expedition, the Incas
    moved to annex lands south and west of Cuzco. Betanzos explained that
    Pachakuti first obtained obeisance from the Quechua, Omasayo, Aymaráes,
    Yanahuara, Chumbivilca, and Chanka. Following a sortie into Abancay, the
    army swung north to defeat the allied forces of the Soras, Rucanas, and
    unpacified Chankas.
    Other chroniclers and local documents reported variations on the same
    ventures. Witnesses from the Alca division of Chumbivilcas named Pachakuti
    as their conqueror, whereas the residents of Colquemarca in Chumbivilcas
    and (Rucanas) Antamarcas witnesses named Thupa Inka Yupanki. In another
    area, Toledan witnesses in Huamanga stated that Pachakuti had per-
    sonally conquered as far as the Soras lands. In contrast, another Toledan wit-
    ness, testifying in Xaquixaguana and professing himself to be Thupa Inka
    Yupanki's grandson, recounted that the campaign to Soras had actually been
    commanded by Pachakuti's brother Qhapaq Yupanki, not by the paramount
    himself (Alca: RGI 1:214; Colquemarca: RGI 1:220; Rucanas: RGI 1:230;
    Rucanas Antamarcas: RGI 1:241; Soras: Toledo 1940b:40, 44, 61–2).
    Sarmiento's chronicle appears to agree with the last version. The campaign
    to Soras complete, Pachakuti returned to Cuzco triumphant, while two
    other armies set out south to Cuntisuyu and east to Antisuyu, where they
    captured some highland and coca-producing lands and brought jungle cats
    and snakes back to Cuzco. The first contingent conquered as far as Arequipa,
    defeating the Collaguas, Canas, and Urocache (Canches). The other troops
    headed 40 leagues (i.e., ~200 km) into the montaña, where they took the
    coca-growing province of Caxarona (cf. Betanzos 1996:81–91; Cieza 1967:
    174,176).
8   *walkay*: to hang (Cerrón-Palomino 1976a:145).

5   The Politics of Blood in Cuzco

1   Betanzos (1996:106) wrote that this official was called "*Apo Ynga randi
    rimaric*, which means 'the lord who speaks in place of and in the name of
    the king'."
2   The ruler's mummy was sent to Lima on the orders of the Viceroy Cañete,
    along with those of Inka Roq'a, Wayna Qhapaq and four *qoya* (Hemming
    1970:298).
3   In 1532, Wayna Qhapaq's *panaqa* (*Tumipampa*, the 11th on the standard
    list) had still not yet been integrated into the formal structure even though
    the ruler had probably died in 1528. The delay may well have stemmed from

the unsettled political climate that prevailed during the fraternal war between Waskhar and Atawallpa.

4 Thus, Waskhar identified with *Qhapaq ayllu* and Atawallpa with *Hatun ayllu* through their mothers (Rostworowski 1983:173).

5 The mummy of Mama Oqllu, Thupa Inka Yupanki's wife, survived the devastation and was shipped to Lima in 1559 along with the mummies of several other kings and queens (see n. 2).

6 The Heartland of the Empire

1 Rostworowski (1999:50) conversely suggests that the name arose from the Quechua word *auca*, meaning soldier or enemy.

2 Regrettably, the early work that was done by various teams did not follow recording procedures that would meet modern standards. As a consequence, much that could have been learned archaeologically about the site has been put in doubt, at the very least (MacLean 1986).

7 Inca Ideology: Powers of the Sky and Earth, Past and Present

1 This section summarizes material from Bauer and Dearborn 1995, unless otherwise noted.

2 Zuidema (1982) has proposed a controversial third calendar, based on the movement of the moon with respect to fixed stars. The sidereal period of the moon is $27\frac{1}{3}$ days, and 12 sidereal months total 328 days. Zuidema has noted that Cobo's main list of shrines around Cuzco contains just 328 locations, and suggests that the Incas used a 37-day span when the Pleiades are too close to the sun to be seen easily to bring the lunar and solar calendars into annual coincidence. Although this calendar has met with some support, most scholars express considerable doubts about its existence (Sadowski 1989; Ziółkowski and Sadowski 1989; Bauer and Dearborn 1995:64–5). Two major objections to the calendar are (1) the chroniclers consistently refer to lunar calendars based on phases of the moon (synodic calendar), and (2) the 328-shrine list does not constitute Cobo's complete catalog, while other sources indicate that there were many additional shrines.

3 Between 1440 and 1570, 27 total or annular solar eclipses and about twice that many partial eclipses passed over lands within the Inca empire. A lunar eclipse would have been visible from one location almost every year (Bauer and Dearborn 1995:142).

4 Unless otherwise noted, this description of monthly ceremonies comes from Polo 1965a, b, c, d; Molina 1988; Cobo 1990; and Rowe's synthesis (1946:308–12).

5 Molina and Polo are generally considered to be the most likely authors of Cobo's source list. Bauer (1998:21) judges that the evidence weighs heavily in favor of Polo, while Rowe (1979a) and Hamilton (1990) conclude that there is insufficient evidence to assign authorship.

6 The description of the layout of the *zeq'e* system follows Bauer 1998, unless otherwise noted.

7 Zuidema 1977a; Aveni 1981; Bauer 1998:81.

8   Family, Community, and Class

1   Quechua: Santo Tomás 1951; González Holguín 1952; Aymara: Bertonio 1956; see also Rowe 1948.
2   Haggard and McLean 1941:77; Cobo said a *tupu* was 50 × 25 *brazas*, or about 90 × 45 m, which is about 0.4 ha; see also Polo 1916:70.

9   Militarism

1   See Hemming 1970:572–3 for a variety of estimates.
2   Betanzos (1996:144) wrote that Thupa Inka Yupanki took a personal guard of 5,000 soldiers on campaign to suppress a rebellion on the altiplano, consisting of 1,000 *orejones* from Cuzco and 4,000 others from the immediate vicinity. A similar figure of 5,000 is named for Waskhar's guard in his final sortie in the battle on the Apurimac (Betanzos 1996:223–4; Sarmiento 1960:269).
3   A rare exception was the support that Thupa Inka Yupanki was said to have received in his first efforts to take the Cañete stronghold of Guarco, but that aid evaporated in the face of the Incas' repeated failures (Cieza 1967:200–1).
4   During their assistance of the Spaniards in 1533, the Hatunxauxa and Lurinwanka provided 589 men, 437 women, 311 porters, and 110 servants, for a ratio of warriors to non-combatants of about 1:1.5. Between 1533 and 1548, 3,465 men, 1,915 women, and 7,131 porters were mobilized, for a ratio of 1:2.6 (Espinoza Soriano 1972; Murra 1975:252, insert; D'Altroy 1992:85). It is difficult to know in what ways the Spaniards' military needs may have distorted the ratio.
5   Sancho de la Hoz (1917:142–3) and Ruiz de Arce (1933:365) also reported that the Inca force of 15,000 initially retreated south in good order, down the Mantaro Valley from Hatun Xauxa, following Challcochima's first conflict with Pizarro's men in October 1533. A baggage train and assembly of women lagged some four leagues (~24 km) behind the main group, in which groups of women, porters, and other auxiliaries were protected by organized contingents of 100 effectives each. From the information available, it is not clear if the formation was standard for armies on the march or whether it was more strictly a defensive formation used in hostile territory or on ordered retreat. In any event, the pursuing cavalry easily broke up the formation and routed its personnel into the nearby hills, although they failed to cut them off from their retreat across the bridges farther south.

10   Provincial Rule

1   Cieza (1984 [1551]:223) mentioned 39 provinces, while Pedro Pizarro (1986 [1571]:221) named 33. Unfortunately, neither explained what he meant by the term and their lists are not remotely complete (see Hyslop 1990; Pärssinen 1992:294–301).
2   This summary largely follows Moore 1958:74–85, 165–74; see also Rowe 1946:271–2. Some chroniclers provided explicit lists of the acts that the Incas

considered illicit or punishable, but their accounts are often general or contradictory (e.g., Betanzos 1996:108–9; Murúa 1986:355–9; Guaman Poma 1980:159–66; Cobo 1979:203–7; Valera 1945). Of the modern studies of Inca law, Hermann Trimborn's (1925, 1937) and Sally Falk Moore's works provide treatments at the grand scale. Moore (1958) treats land tenure and taxes under the concept of law; the discussion here is reserved primarily for what she covers as criminal law. Trimborn sees a more systematic code than do Moore and I.

3   Among them were sodomy, fellatio, and miscegenation (e.g., Garcilaso 1966:162). The long history of non-procreative sex among north coastal peoples is visible in the graphic pottery dating to the Moche society (AD 100–700) and its successors. It is not clear from the available information if the acts were undertaken for pleasure, for ritual purposes, or both, or if some of the representations were purely mythical.

4   Cobo: i.e., 81 × 40.5 m = 3,280 sq m; @ 1.62 m = 1.0 fathom; Garcilaso: i.e., 1.5 × 1.59 acres/ha, or 0.94 ha.; see Rowe 1946:324.

5   Chiquitoy Viejo: Conrad 1977; Tambo Real: Hyslop 1984:42; Túcume: Heyerdahl et al. 1995.

6   Colcampata (Cuzco) and Collca or Cullca (Tumipampa), Huatanay and Huatana, Monaycuna and Monay, Pumacurco and Pumachupan (both Cuzco) and Pumapungo, Cachipamba and Cachipamba, Calixpuquio and Calyxpogyo, Guanacaure and Guanacuri (Arriaga 1965:24).

7   RGI 1; among the places mentioned are Monobamba, Uchubamba, Andamayo, and Comas, all well into the upper jungles.

11 Farmers, Herders, and Storehouses

1   30,000 households × 1.59 acre/*hanegada* (Haggard and McLean 1941:77).

2   Morris 1967, 1981; Mantaro: Browman 1970; Vilcaswaman: Cieza 1984 [1553]: ch. 89, p. 252; see LeVine 1992.

3   In a review of 287 documentary references to the subject, Murra (1980b:13, 25) found only 86 references to food. That figure is probably more a reflection of Spanish interest in exotica and armaments than anything else. Maize, with 29 citations, and *ch'arki*, with 12, were the most frequently listed foods.

4   e.g., at Huánuco Pampa, in the Upper Mantaro, the northern Calchaquí, La Quiaca, the Bolsón de Andalgalá, and the Lerma Valley.

12 Artisans and Artistry

1   Cobo 1979 [1653]: bk. II, ch. 24, p. 196.

2   See Berthelot 1986 for an overview of Inca mining.

3   I thank Melissa Hagstrum for making this point to me.

13 Invasion and Aftermath

1   This summary draws heavily from Hemming 1970:37–85; for eyewitness accounts, see Sancho de la Hoz 1917; Ruiz de Arce 1933; Mena 1937; Estete 1967; Xérez 1985.

Bibliography

Acosta, José de
1986. *Historia natural y moral de las Indias*. Historia 16, Madrid. (Originally written 1590.)

Acuto, Félix
1994. *La organización del almacenaje estatal: la ocupación inka en el sector norte del Valle Calchaquí y sus alrededores*. Licenciatura thesis, Facultad de Filosofía y Letras. Universidad de Buenos Aires, Buenos Aires.

Adamska, Anna, and Adam Michczński
1996. Towards Radiocarbon Chronology of the Inca State. *Andes. Boletín de la Misión Arqueológica Andina* 1:35–58.

Adorno, Rolena
1986. *Guaman Poma: Writing and Resistance in Colonial Peru*. University of Texas Press, Austin.

Agurto Calvo, Santiago
1980. *Cuzco – Traza urbana de la ciudad Inca*. Proyecto Per 39, UNESCO, Instituto Nacional de Cultura del Perú. Imprenta Offset Color S.R.L., Cuzco.
1987. *Estudios acerca de la construcción, arquitectura, y planeamiento incas*. Cámara Peruana de la Construcción, Lima.

Albarracín-Jordan, Juan, and James E. Mathews
1992. *Asentamientos prehispánicos del Valle de Tiwanaku*. Producciones CIMA, La Paz.

Albeck, María E.
1992–3. Areas agrícolas y densidad de ocupación prehispánica en la Quebrada de Humahuaca. *Avances en Arqueología* 2:56–77.

Albeck, María E., and M. Cristina Scattolin
1991. Cálculo fotogramétrico de superficies de cultivo en Coctaca y Rodero, Quebrada de Humahuaca. *Avances en Arqueología* 1:43–58.

Alberti, Giorgio, and Enrique Mayer, eds.
1974. *Reciprocidad e intercambio en los andes peruanos*. Instituto de Estudios Peruanos, Lima.

Albornoz, Cristóbal de
1989. Instrucción para descubrir todas las guacas del Piru y sus camayos y haziendas. In *Fábulas y mitos de los Incas*, edited by Henrique Urbano and

Pierre Duviols. Crónicas de America 48, pp. 161–98. Historia 16, Madrid. (Originally written 1582.)

Alcina Franch, José
1976. *Arqueología de Chinchero, 1.* Ministerio de Asuntos Exteriores, Madrid.
1978. Ingapirca: arquitectura y áreas de asentamiento. *Revista Española de Antropología Americana* 8:127–46.

Alcina Franch, José, Miguel Rivera, Jesus Galván, María Carmen García Palacios, Mercedes Guinea, Balbina Martínez-Caviró, Luis J. Ramos, and Tito Varela
1976. *Arqueología de Chinchero, 2. Cerámica y otros materiales.* Ministerio de Asuntos Exteriores, Madrid.

Alcock, Susan, Terence N. D'Altroy, Kathleen Morrison, and Carla Sinopoli, eds.
2001. *Empires: Perspectives from Archaeology and History.* Cambridge University Press, Cambridge.

Algaze, Guillermo
1993. *The Uruk World System.* University of Chicago Press, Chicago.

Alva, Walter, and Christopher B. Donnan
1994. *Royal Tombs of Sipán.* 2nd edn. Fowler Museum of Cultural History, University of California, Los Angeles.

Ambrosetti, Juan B.
1902. El sepulcro de La Paya últimamente descubierto en los valles Calchaquíes, Provincia de Salta. *Anales del Museo Nacional* 8:119–48.
1907–1908. *Exploraciones arqueológicas en la ciudad prehistórica de "La Paya" (Valle Calchaquí, Provincia de Salta).* 2 vols. Revista de la Universidad de Buenos Aires, Facultad de Filosofía y Letras, vol. 8 (Sección Antropología, 3). M. Biedmaé hijo, Buenos Aires.

Anders, Martha B.
1977. Sistema de depósitos en Pampa Grande. *Revista del Museo Nacional* 43:243–79.

Angles Vargas, Victor
1970. *P'isaq: Metrópoli inka.* Industrial Gráfica, Lima.
1972. *Machupijchu: Enigmática ciudad inka.* Industrial Gráfica, Lima.
1988. *Historia del Cusco incaico.* Industrial Gráfica, Lima.

Anónimo, Sitio del Cuzco
1934. Relación del sitio del Cuzco y principio de las guerras del Perú hasta la muerte de Diego de Almagro. In *Colección de libros y documentos inéditos para la historia del Perú,* edited by Carlos A. Romero and Horacio H. Urteaga, vol. 2. Sociedad de Bibliófolos Peruanos, Lima.

Arnold, Dean
1975. Ceramic Ecology of the Ayacucho Basin, Peru: Implications for Prehistory. *Current Anthropology* 16:183–205.
1985. *Ceramic Theory and Cultural Process.* Cambridge University Press, Cambridge.

Arriaga, Pablo José de
1968a. La extirpación de la idolatría del Pirú. In *Crónicas peruanas de interés indígena,* edited by Francisco Esteve Barba. Biblioteca de Autores Españoles

(continuación), vol. 209, pp. 191–275. Ediciones Atlas, Madrid. (Originally written 1621.)

Arriaga, Father Pablo Joseph de
1968b. *The Extirpation of Idolatry in Peru*. Translated by L. Clark Keatinge. University of Kentucky Press, Lexington. (Originally written 1621.)

Arriaga, Jesús
1965. *Apuntes de arqueología Cañar*. Universidad de Cuenca, Cuenca, Ecuador.

Ascher, Marcia, and Robert Ascher
1981. *Code of the Quipu*. University of Michigan Press, Ann Arbor.

Atienza, Lope de
1931. Compendio historial del estado de los indios del Perú. In *La religión del imperio de los Incas. Apéndice I*, edited by Jacinto Jijón y Caamaño, vol. 1, pp. 1–235. Escuela Tipográfica Salesiana, Quito. (Originally written 1575?)

Aveni, Anthony F.
1981. Horizon Astronomy in Incaic Cuzco. In *Archaeoastronomy in the Americas*, edited by Ray A. Williamson, pp. 305–18. Ballena Press, Los Altos, CA.
1982. *Archaeoastronomy in the New World: American Primitive Astronomy. Proceedings of an International Conference held at Oxford University, September 1981*. Cambridge University Press, Cambridge.

Bandelier, Adoph F.
1910. *The Islands of Titicaca and Coati*. Hispanic Society of America, New York.

Barfield, Thomas J.
2001. The Shadow Empires: Imperial State Formation along the Chinese–Nomad Frontier. In *Empires: Perspectives from Archaeology and History*, edited by Susan E. Alcock, Terence N. D'Altroy, Kathleen D. Morrison, and Carla M. Sinopoli, pp. 10–41. Cambridge University Press, Cambridge.

Barnes, Monica, and David Fleming
1989. Charles-Marie de la Condamine's Report on Ingapirca and the Development of Scientific Field Work in the Andes, 1735–1744. *Andean Past* 2:175–235.

Barnes, Monica, and Daniel Slive
1993. El Puma de Cuzco: ¿plano de la ciudad Ynga o noción europea? *Revista Andina* 11(1):79–102.

Bauden, Louis
1928. *L'empire socialiste des Inkas*. Institut d'Ethnologie, Paris.

Bauer, Brian S.
1991. Pacariqtambo and the Mythical Origins of the Inca. *Latin American Antiquity* 2:7–26.
1992a. *Avances en arqueología andina*. Translated by Javier Flores Espinoza. Archivos de Historia Andina, vol. 16. Centro de Estudios Regionales Andinos "Bartolomé de Las Casas," Cuzco.
1992b. Ritual Pathways of the Inca: An Analysis of the Collasuyu Ceques in Cuzco. *Latin American Antiquity* 3:183–205.

1992c. *The Development of the Inca State*. University of Texas Press, Austin.

1996. The Legitimization of the Inca State in Myth and Ritual. *American Anthropologist* 98(2):327–37.

1998. *The Sacred Landscape of the Inca: The Cusco Ceque System*. University of Texas Press, Austin.

1999. *The Early Ceramics of the Inca Heartland*. Fieldiana Anthropology, new series, no. 31. Field Museum of Natural History, Chicago.

Bauer, Brian S., and David S. P. Dearborn

1995. *Astronomy and Empire in the Ancient Andes*. University of Texas Press, Austin.

Bauer, Brian S., and Charles Stanish

1990. *Killke and Killke-Related Pottery from Cuzco, Peru, in the Field Museum of Natural History*. Fieldiana Anthropology, new series, no. 15. Field Museum of Natural History, Chicago.

Bengtsson, Lisbet

1998. *Prehistoric Stonework in the Peruvian Andes: A Case Study at Ollantaytambo*. Göteborg University, Dept. of Archaeology: Etnografiska museet, Göteborg.

Beorchia Nigris, Antonio

1985. *El enigma de los santuarios indígenas de alta montaña*. Centro de Investigaciones Arqueologicas de Alta Montaña, San Juan, Argentina.

Berberián, Eduardo E., and Rodolfo A. Raffino

1991. *Culturas indígenas de los Andes Meridionales*. Alhambra, Madrid.

Berthelot, Jean

1986. The Extraction of Precious Metals at the Time of the Inka. In *Anthropological History of Andean Polities*, edited by John V. Murra, Nathan Wachtel, and Jacques Revel, pp. 69–88. Cambridge University Press, Cambridge.

Bertonio, Ludovico

1956. *Vocabulario de la lengua aymara*. Facsimile edition, La Paz. (Originally written 1612.)

Betanzos, Juan de

1996. *Narrative of the Incas*. 1st edn., edited by Roland Hamilton and Dana Buchanan. University of Texas Press, Austin.

Bibar, Gerónimo de

1966. *Crónica y relación copiosa y verdadera de los reynos de Chile*, edited by Irving A. Leonard. Fondo Histórico y Bibliográfico José Toribio Medina, Santiago de Chile. (Originally written 1558.)

Bingham, Hiram

1913. In the Wonderland of Peru. The Work Accomplished by the Peruvian Expedition of 1912, under the Auspices of Yale University and the National Geographic Society. *National Geographic Magazine* 24(4):387–573.

1930. *Machu Picchu, a Citadel of the Incas: Report of the Explorations and Excavations made in 1911, 1912 and 1915 under the Auspices of Yale University and the National Geographic Society*. Yale University Press, New Haven.

Bird, Junius B., and John Hyslop
    1985. *The Preceramic Excavations at the Huaca Prieta, Chicama Valley, Peru.*
    New York, American Museum of Natural History.
Boman, Eric
    1908. *Antiquités de la Région Andine de la République Argentine et du Désert*
    D'Atacama. 2 vols. Imprimerie Nationale, Paris.
Borregán, Alonso
    1948. *Crónica de la conquista del Perú.* Publicaciones de la Escuela de Estu-
    dios Hispano-Americanos 46, Seville. (Originally written 1562–5.)
Bram, Joseph
    1941. *An Analysis of Inca Militarism.* American Ethnological Society, Mono-
    graph No. 4. New York.
Bray, Tamara L.
    1991. *The Effects of Inca Imperialism on the Northern Frontier.* University
    Microfilms, Ann Arbor.
    1993. Archaeological Survey in Northern Highland Ecuador: Inca Imperial-
    ism and the País Caranqui. *World Archaeology* 24(2):218–33.
Browman, David L.
    1970. *Early Peruvian Peasants: The Culture History of a Central Highlands*
    Valley. Unpublished Ph.D. Dissertation, Department of Anthropology,
    Harvard University, Cambridge, MA.
Brown, David O.
    1991. *Administration and Settlement Planning in the Provinces of the Inka*
    Empire: A Perspective from the Inka Provincial Capital of Pumpu on the
    Junín Plain in the Central Highlands of Peru. Unpublished Ph.D. Disserta-
    tion, Department of Anthropology, University of Texas at Austin. Univer-
    sity Microfilms, Ann Arbor.
Brown, P. F.
    1987. Economy, Ecology and Population: Recent Changes in Peruvian Aymara
    Land Use Patterns. In *Arid Land Use Strategies and Risk Management in the*
    Andes, edited by David Browman, pp. 99–120. Westview Press, Boulder, CO.
Brumfiel, Elizabeth
    1987. Elite and Utilitarian Crafts in the Aztec State. In *Specialization,*
    Exchange, and Complex Societies, edited by Elizabeth Brumfiel and Timothy
    K. Earle, pp. 102–18. Cambridge University Press, Cambridge.
Brush, Steven B.
    1976. Man's Use of an Andean Ecosystem. *Human Ecology* 4(2):147–66.
    1977. *Mountain, Field and Family: The Economy and Human Ecology of an*
    Andean Valley. University of Pennsylvania Press, Philadelphia.
Burchard, Roderick E.
    1974. Coca y trueque de alimentos. In *Reciprocidad e Intercambio en los*
    Andes Peruanos, edited by Giorgio Alberti and Alberto Meyers, pp. 209–51.
    Instituto de Estudios Peruanos, Lima.
Burger, Richard L.
    1992. *Chavin and the Origins of Andean Civilization.* 1st pbk. edn., with color
    plates. Thames and Hudson, London.

Bürgi, Peter
1990. *El Control Inka de la Zona Interandina del Centro-Sur Andino: El Ejemplo del Valle de Torata, Dpto. de Moquegua.* University of Chicago, Chicago.
1993. *The Inka Empire's Expansion into the Coastal Sierran Region West of Lake Titicaca.* Unpublished Ph.D. Dissertation, Department of Anthropology, University of Chicago.

Burling, Robbins
1974. *The Passage of Power: Studies in Political Succession.* Academic Press, New York.

Cabello Valboa, Miguel
1951. *Miscelánea antártica: una historia del Perú antiguo.* Universidad Nacional Mayor de San Marcos. Instituto de Etnología y Arqueología, Lima.

Calderari, Milena
1991. Estilos cerámicos incaicos de La Paya. In *Actas del XI Congreso Nacional de Arqueología Chilena,* vol. 2, pp. 151–64. Museo Nacional de Historia Natural, Sociedad Chilena de Arqueología, Santiago.

Callapiña, Supno y Otros Quipucamayos
1974. *Relación de los Quipucamayos,* edited by Juan José Vega. Biblioteca Universitaria, Lima.

Camino, Alejandro
1989. Trueque, correrías e intercambios entre los quechuas andinos y los piro y machiguenga de la montaña peruana. In *Organización económica en los Andes,* edited by Javier Medina. Hisbol, La Paz.

Carbajal, Pedro de
1965. Descripción fecha de la Provincia de Vilcas Guaman. In *Relaciones Geográficas de Indias I.* Biblioteca de Autores Españoles (continuación), vol. 183, pp. 205–19. Ediciones Atlas, Madrid. (Originally written 1586.)

Carrasco, Pedro
1982. The Political Economy of the Aztec and Inca States. In *The Inca and Aztec States 1400–1800: Anthropology and History,* edited by George A. Collier, Renato I. Rosaldo, and John D. Wirth, pp. 23–40. Academic Press, New York.

Carrión Cachot, Rebeca
1955. El culto al agua en el antiguo Perú. *Revista del Museo Nacional* 2(2):50–140.

Castillo B., Luis Jaime, and Christopher B. Donnan
1994. La ocupación Moche de San José de Moro, Jequetepeque. In *Moche: Propuestas y Perspectivas,* edited by Santiago Uceda C. and Elías Mujica B. Travaux de L'Institut Français d'Études Andines, vol. 79, Lima.

Castro, Cristóbal de, and Diego de Ortega Morejón
1974. Relación y declaración del modo que este valle de Chincha y sus comarcanos se governaven antes que oviese Ingas y despues q(ue) los vuo hasta q(ue) los Cristianos entraron en esta tierra. *Historia y Cultura* 8:91–104. (Originally written 1558.)

Centro de Estudios Regionales Andinos Bartolomé de Las Casas/Gobierno Regional Inka
1991. *Compendio cartográfico de la región Inka.*

Cerrón-Palomino, Rodolfo
1976a. *Diccionario Quechua Junín-Huanca*. Instituto de Estudios Peruanos, Lima.
1976b. *Gramática Quechua Junín-Huanca*. Instituto de Estudios Peruanos, Lima.

Ceruti, María Constanza
1997. *Arqueología de alta montaña*. Salta, Argentina.
1999. *Cumbres sagradas del noroeste argentino: avances en arqueología de alta montaña y etnoarqueología de santuarios de altura andinos*. 1st edn. Eudeba, Buenos Aires.

Céspedes Paz, Ricardo
1982. La Arqueología del area de Pocona. *Cuadernos de Investigación, Serie Arqueología* 1:89–99.

Chase-Dunn, Christopher, and Thomas D. Hall, eds.
1991. *Core/Periphery Relations in Precapitalist Worlds*. Westview Press, Boulder, CO.

Chávez Ballón, Manuel
1970. Ciudades incas: Cuzco, capital del imperio. *Wayka* 3:1–15.

Cieza de León, Pedro de
1967. *El Señorío de los Incas; 2a. parte de la Crónica del Perú*. Instituto de Estudios Peruanos, Lima. (Originally written 1551.)
1984. *Crónica del Perú: primera parte*. Fondo Editorial de la Pontificia Universidad Católica del Perú: Academia Nacional de la Historia, Lima. (Originally published 1553.)
1987. *Crónica del Perú: tercera parte*. Fondo Editorial de la Pontificia Universidad Católica del Perú: Academia Nacional de la Historia, Lima. (Originally written 1551.)

Classen, Constance
1993. *Inca Cosmology and the Human Body*. University of Utah Press, Salt Lake City.

Cobo, Bernabé
1956. *Obras*. 2 vols. Biblioteca de Autores Españoles (continuación), vol. 91–92. Ediciones Atlas, Madrid.
1979. *History of the Inca Empire: An Account of the Indians' Customs and their Origin, Together with a Treatise on Inca Legends, History, and Social Institutions*. Translated by Roland Hamilton. University of Texas Press, Austin.
1990. *Inca Religion and Customs*. 1st edn., edited by Roland Hamilton. University of Texas Press, Austin.

Conrad, Geoffrey W.
1977. Chiquitoy Viejo: An Inca Administrative Center in the Chicama Valley, Peru. *Journal of Field Archaeology* 4(1):1–18.

Conrad, Geoffrey W., and Arthur Demarest
1984. *Religion and Empire*. Cambridge University Press, Cambridge.

Cook, Noble David
1981. *Demographic Collapse: Indian Peru, 1520–1620*. Cambridge University Press, Cambridge.

Cornejo Guerrero, Miguel A.
  2000. *An Inka Province: Pachacamac and the Ischma Nation*. Ph.D. Dissertation, Department of Archaeology and Anthropology, Australian National University, Canberra.
Costin, Cathy L.
  1986. *From Chiefdom to Empire State: Ceramic Economy among the Prehispanic Wanka of Highland Peru*. Unpublished Ph.D. Dissertation, Department of Anthropology, University of California. University Microfilms, Ann Arbor.
  1993. Textiles, Women, and Political Economy in Late Prehispanic Peru. *Research in Economic Anthropology* 14:3–28.
  2001. Production and Exchange of Ceramics. In *Empire and Domestic Economy*, by Terence N. D'Altroy, Christine A. Hastorf, and Associates, pp. 203–42. Kluwer Academic/Plenum Press, New York.
Costin, Cathy L., and Timothy K. Earle
  1989. Status Distinction and Legitimation of Power as Reflected in Changing Patterns of Consumption in Late Prehispanic Peru. *American Antiquity* 54: 691–714.
Costin, Cathy L., Timothy K. Earle, Bruce Owen, and Glenn S. Russell
  1989. Impact of Inka Conquest on Local Technology in the Upper Mantaro Valley, Peru. In *What's New?: A Closer Look at the Process of Innovation*, edited by Sander E. van der Leeuw and Robin Torrance. One World Archaeology Series, vol. 14, pp. 107–39. Unwin and Allen, London.
D'Altroy, Terence N.
  1987. Transitions in Power: Centralization of Wanka Political Organization under Inka Rule. *Ethnohistory* 34:78–102.
  1992. *Provincial Power in the Inka Empire*. Smithsonian, Washington, D.C.
  1994a. Factionalism and Political Development in the Central Andes. In *Factional Competition and Political Development in the New World*, edited by Elizabeth Brumfiel and John Fox, pp. 171–87. Cambridge University Press, Cambridge.
  1994b. Public and Private Economy in the Inka Empire. In *The Economic Anthropology of the State*, edited by Elizabeth Brumfiel. Society for Economic Anthropology Monograph 11, pp. 171–222. University Press of America, Lanham, MD.
D'Altroy, Terence N., and Ronald A. Bishop
  1990. The Provincial Organization of Inka Ceramic Production. *American Antiquity* 55:120–38.
D'Altroy, Terence N., and Timothy K. Earle
  1985. Staple Finance, Wealth Finance, and Storage in the Inka Political Economy (with Comment and Reply). *Current Anthropology* 25:187–206.
D'Altroy, Terence N., and Christine A. Hastorf
  1984. The Distribution and Contents of Inca State Storehouses in the Xauxa Region of Peru. *American Antiquity* 49:334–49.
D'Altroy, Terence N., and Verónica I. Williams
  1998. *Final Report: Provisioning the Inka Economy in Kollasuyu*. Grant from the National Science Foundation (SBR-97-07962) to analyze Inka-era ceramics through Neutron Activation Analysis. Washington, D.C.

D'Altroy, Terence N., Verónica I. Williams, and Ana María Lorandi
    In press. The Inkas in the Southern Lands. In *Variations in the Expression of Inka Power*, edited by Richard Burger, Craig Morris, and Ramiro Matos Mendieta. Dumbarton Oaks, Washington, D.C.
D'Altroy, Terence N., Ana María Lorandi, Verónica I. Williams, Christine A. Hastorf, Elizabeth DeMarrais, Milena Calderari, and Melissa Hagstrum
    2000. Inka Imperial Rule in the Valle Calchaquí, Argentina. *Journal of Field Archaeology* 27:1–26.
D'Altroy, Terence N., Christine A. Hastorf, and Associates
    2001. *Empire and Domestic Economy*. Kluwer Academic / Plenum Press, New York.
Davies, Nigel
    1995. *The Incas*. University Press of Colorado, Niwot, CO.
Dearborn, David S. P., and Katharina J. Schreiber
    1986. Here Comes the Sun: The Cuzco-Machu Picchu Connection. *Archaeoastronomy* 9:15–37.
    1989. Houses of the Rising Sun. In *Time and Calendars in the Inca Empire*, edited by Mariusz S. Ziółkowski and Robert M. Sadowski, pp. 49–74. British Archaeological Reports, International Series, no. 479, Oxford.
Dearborn, David S. P., Katharina J. Schreiber, and Raymond E. White
    1987. Intimachay, a December Solstice Observatory. *American Antiquity* 52: 346–52.
Dearborn, David S. P., and Raymond E. White
    1983. The "Torreón" at Machu Picchu as an Observatory. *Archaeoastronomy* 5:S37–S49.
Demarest, Arthur Andrew
    1981. *Viracocha: The Nature and Antiquity of the Andean High God*. Harvard University, Peabody Museum of Archaeology and Ethnology, Monograph No. 6. Cambridge, MA.
DeMarrais, Elizabeth
    1997. *Materialization, Ideology, and Power: The Development of Centralized Authority among the Pre-Hispanic Polities of the Valle Calchaquí, Argentina*. Unpublished Ph.D. Dissertation, Department of Anthropology, University of California, Los Angeles. University Microfilms, Ann Arbor.
DeMarrais, Elizabeth, Luis Jaime Castillo, and Timothy Earle
    1996. Ideology, Materialization, and Power Strategies. *Current Anthropology* 37(1):15–86.
Deustua, José
    1978. Acceso a recursos en Yanque-Collaguas 1591: Una experiencia estadística. In *Etnohistoria y Antropología Andina*, compiled by Marcia Koth de Paredes and A. Castelli, pp. 41–51. Museo Nacional de Historia, Lima.
Diaz, Henry F., and V. Markgraf, eds.
    1992. *El Niño: Historical and Paleoclimatic Aspects of the Southern Oscillation*. Cambridge University Press, New York.
Diez de San Miguel, Garci
    1964. *Visita hecha a la Provincia de Chucuito por Garci Diez de San Miguel en el año 1567*, edited by Waldemar Espinoza Soriano. Casa de la Cultura del Perú, Lima.

Dillehay, Tom D.
   1975. Tawantinsuyu Integration of the Chillon Valley, Peru: A Case of Inca
      Geo-Political Mastery. *Journal of Field Archaeology* 4(4):397–405.
Dillehay, Tom D., and Américo Gordon
   1988. La actividad prehispánica de los Incas y su influencia en la Araucania.
      In *La Frontera del Estado Inca*, edited by Tom D. Dillehay and Patricia J.
      Netherly. Proceedings, 45 Congreso Internacional de Americanistas, Bogotá,
      Colombia, 1985, pp. 215–34. British Archaeological Reports, International
      Series, no. 442. Oxford.
Dillehay, Tom D., and Patricia J. Netherly, eds.
   1988. *La Frontera del Estado Inca*. British Archaeological Reports, Interna-
      tional Series, no. 442. Oxford.
Donkin, R. A.
   1979. *Agricultural Terracing in the New World*. Viking Fund Publications in
      Anthropology, 56. Wenner-Gren Foundation for Anthropological Research,
      University of Arizona Press, Tucson.
Donnan, Christopher B., ed.
   1986. *Early Ceremonial Architecture in the Andes*. Dumbarton Oaks,
      Washington, D.C.
Doyle, Michael W.
   1986. *Empires*. Cornell University Press, Ithaca.
Dunbar Temple, Ella
   1942. Los caciques Apoalaya. *Revista del Museo Nacional* 11:147–78.
Duviols, Pierre
   1976a. La capacocha: mecanismo y función del sacrificio humano, su proyec-
      ción, su papel en la política integracionista y en la economía redistributive
      del Tawantinsuyu. *Allpanchis Phuturinqa* 9:11–57.
   1976b. "Punchao," Idolo mayor del Coricancha. Historia y typología.
      Antropología Andina 1–2:156–83.
   1977. Los nombres quechua de Viracocha, supuesto "Dios Creador" de los
      evangelizadores. *Allpanchis Phuturinqa* 10:153–64.
   1979a. Datacion, paternité et idéologique de la >Declaración de los Quipuca-
      mayos a Vaca de Castro<. In *Les cultures ibériques en devenir, essais publiés
      en hommage à la mémoire de Marcel Bataillon (1895–1977)*, pp. 583–91.
      La Fondation Singer-Polignac, Paris.
   1979b. La dinastía de los Incas: ¿monarquía o diarquía? Argumentos huerís-
      ticos a favor de una tesis estructuralista. *Journal de la Société des Ameri-
      canistes* 64:67–83.
   1980. La guerra entre el Cuzco y los chanka: ¿Historia o mito? *Revista de la
      Universidad Complutense* 28(117):363–72.
Dwyer, Edward B.
   1971. *The Early Inca Occupation of the Valley of Cuzco, Peru*. Unpublished
      Ph.D. Dissertation, Department of Anthropology, University of California,
      Berkeley.
Earle, Timothy K.
   1994. Wealth Finance in the Inka Empire: Evidence from the Calchaquí Valley,
      Argentina. *American Antiquity* 59(3):443–60.

Earle, Timothy K., and Terence N. D'Altroy
1982. Storage Facilities and State Finance in the Upper Mantaro Valley, Peru. In *Contexts for Prehistoric Exchange*, edited by Jonathan E. Ericson and Timothy K. Earle, pp. 265–90. Academic Press, New York.
1989. The Political Economy of the Inka Empire: The Archaeology of Power and Finance. In *Archaeological Thought in America*, edited by Carl C. Lamberg-Karlovsky, pp. 183–204. Cambridge University Press, Cambridge.
Earle, Timothy K., Terence N. D'Altroy, Christine A. Hastorf, Catherine J. Scott, Cathy L. Costin, Glenn S. Russell, and Elsie Sandefur
1987. *Archaeological Field Research in the Upper Mantaro, Peru, 1982–1983: Investigations of Inka Expansion and Exchange.* Institute of Archaeology, University of California, Monograph 28. Los Angeles.
Eaton, George F.
1916. *The Collection of Osteological Material from Machu Picchu.* Memoir No. 5, Connecticut Academy of Arts and Sciences.
Eisenstadt, Shmuel
1963. *The Political Systems of Empires.* Free Press, Glencoe, IL.
Ekholm, Kasja, and Jonathan Friedman
1979. Capital Imperialism and Exploitation in Ancient World Systems. In *Power and Propaganda*, edited by Mogens T. Larsen. Mesopotamia 7, pp. 41–58. Akademisk Forlag, Copenhagen.
Engels, Donald W.
1978. *Alexander the Great and the Logistics of the Macedonian Army.* University of California Press, Berkeley and Los Angeles.
Erickson, Clark L.
1993. The Social Organization of Prehispanic Raised Field Agriculture in the Lake Titicaca Basin. In *Economic Aspects of Water Management in the Prehispanic New World*, edited by Vernon L. Scarborough and Barry L. Isaac. Research in Economic Anthropology, Supplement 7, pp. 369–426. JAI Press, Greenwich, CT.
Espinoza Soriano, Waldemar
1963. La guaranga y la reducción de Huancayo: Tres documentos inéditos de 1571 para la etnohistoria del Perú. *Revista del Museo Nacional* 32:8–80.
1964. El curacazgo de Conchucos y la visita de 1543. *Bulletin de L'Institut Français d'Études Andines* 3(1):9–31.
1969. *Lurinhuaila de Huacjra: Un ayllu y un curacazgo huanca.* Casa de Cultura, Lima.
1970. Los mitmas yungas de Collique en Cajamarca, siglos XV, XVI, y XVII. *Revista del Museo Nacional* 36:9–57.
1972. Los Huancas, aliados de la conquista: Tres informaciones inéditas sobre la participación indígena en la conquista del Perú, 1558–1560–1561. *Anales Científicos de la Universidad del Centro del Perú* 1:3–407.
1973. Las colonias de mitmas múltiples en Abancay, siglos XV y XVI. *Revista del Museo Nacional* 39:225–99.
1974. Los señoríos étnicos del valle de Condebamba y provincia de Cajabamba. Etnohistoria de las huarangas de llucho y mitmas. Siglos XV–

XX. *Anales Científicos de la Universidad Nacional del Centro del Perú* 3: 1–376.

1975. Los mitmas huayacuntu en Quito o guarniciones para la represión armada, siglos XV y XVI. *Revista del Museo Nacional* 41:351–94.

1976. Los mitmas de Nasca en Ocoña, Vitor y Camaná. *Bulletin de L'Institut Français d'Études Andines* 5(1–2):85–95.

1977. Los cuatro suyos del Cuzco (siglo XV y XVI). *Bulletin de l'Institut Français d'Études Andines* 6(3–4):109–22. Lima.

1980. Acerca de la historia militar inca. *Allpanchis Phuturinqa* 14(16):171–86.

1983. Los mitmas plateros de Ishma en le país de los Ayamarca, siglos XV–XIX. *Boletín de Lima* 30(5):38–52.

1984. Los mitmas salineros de Tarma, Chinchacocha y Pasco. Siglos XX a.C.–XX d.C. *Allpanchis Phuturinqa* 24:183–250.

1987a. *Artesanos, transacciones, monedas y formas de pago en el mundo andino. Siglos XV y XVI.* Banco Central de la Reserva del Perú, Lima.

1987b. Migraciones internas en el Reino Colla: Tejedores, Plumeros, y Alfareros del Estado Imperial Inca. *Chungará* 19:243–89.

Espinoza Soriano, Waldemar, ed.
1978. *Los modos de producción en el imperio de los Incas.* Editorial Mantaro-Gratifal, Lima.

Estete, Miguel de
1967. *La relación del viaje que hizo el señor Capitán Hernando Pizarro por mandado del señor Gobernador, su hermano, desde el pueblo de Caxamalca a Pachacamac y de allí a Jauja*, edited by Concepción Bravo, pp. 130–48. Historia 16, Madrid. (Originally written 1532–3.)

Falcón, Francisco
1946. Representación hecha por el Licenciado Falcón en concilio provincial sobre los daños y molestias que se hacen a los indios. In *Los Pequeños Grandes Libros de Historia Americana*, edited by Francisco A. Loayza. Series 1, vol. 10, pp. 121–64. D. Miranda, Lima. (Originally written 1567.)

Farrington, Ian S.
1974. Irrigation and Settlement Pattern: Preliminary Research Results from the North Coast of Peru. In *Irrigation's Impact on Society*, edited by T. E. Downing and M. Gibson. Anthropological Papers, no. 25, pp. 83–94. University of Arizona.

1983. Prehistoric Intensive Agriculture: Preliminary Notes on River Canalization in the Sacred Valley of the Incas. In *Drained Field Agriculture in Central and South America*, edited by John Darch. British Archaeological Reports, International Series, no. 189, pp. 221–35. Oxford.

1984. Medidas de tierra en el Valle de Yucay, Cusco. *Gaceta Arqueológica Andina* 11:10–11.

1992. Ritual Geography, Settlement Patterns and the Characterization of the Provinces of the Inka Heartland. *World Archaeology* 23:368–85.

1995. The Mummy, Estate, and Palace of Inka Huayna Capac at Quispeguanca. *Tawantinsuyu* 1:55–65.

Farrington, Ian S., and Rodolfo Raffino
1996. Moso suyukunapa tariqnin; Nuevos hallazgos en el Tawantinsuyu. Inka news from around the empire. *Tawantinsuyu* 2:73–7.

Fejos, Paul
1944. *Archaeological Exploration in the Cordillera Vilcabamba, Southeastern Peru*. Viking Fund, Publications in Anthropology, no. 3. New York.

Figuencia Pinos, Rolando
1995. *Coyuctor, un recinto sagrado*. (Cañar?), Editorial Casa de la Cultura Núcleo del Cañar.

Flannery, Kent V., Joyce Marcus, and Robert G. Reynolds
1989. *The Flocks of the Wamani: A Study of Llama Herders on the Punas of Ayacucho, Peru*. Academic Press, San Diego.

Flores Ochoa, Jorge A.
1977. *Pastores de Puna, uywamichiq punarunakuna*. 1st edn., vol. 5. Instituto de Estudios Peruanos, Lima.
1978. Organization social y complementaridad económica en los Andes centrales. In *Actes de XLII Congrès International des Américanistes*, vol. 4, pp. 9–38. Paris.

Flores Ochoa, Jorge A. and P. Paz Florez
1984. El cultivo en Qocha en la Puna sur Andina. In *Contribuciones a los estudios de los Andes Centrales*, edited by Shozo Masuda, pp. 59–100. University of Tokyo Press, Tokyo.

Fock, Nils
1961. Inka Imperialism in Northwest Argentina, and Chaco Burial Forms. *Folk* 3:67–90.

Fonseca Martel, Cesar
1974. Modalidades de la minka. In *Reciprocidad e Intercambio en los Andes Peruanos*, edited by Giorgio Alberti and Alberto Meyers, pp. 89–109. Instituto de Estudios Peruanos, Lima.

Fresco, Antonio
1984. Excavaciones en Ingapirca (Ecuador): 1978–1982. *Revista Española de Antropología Americana* 14:85–101.

Gade, Daniel W.
1977. Llama, alpaca y vicuña: ficción y realidad. In *Pastores de Puna, uywamichiq punarunakuna*, edited by Jorge Flores Ochoa, pp. 113–20. Instituto de Estudios Peruanos, Lima.

Garcilaso de la Vega, El Inca
1966. *Royal Commentaries of the Incas and General History of Peru*, translated by Harold V. Livermore. University of Texas Press, Austin. (Originally written 1609.)

Gareis, Iris
1991. Especialistas religiosos Andinos en la epoca de los Incas y baja la Dominacion Española. *Revista del Museo de Arqueología* 2:85–103.

Garnsey, Peter, and Richard Saller
1987. *The Roman Empire*. University of California Press, Berkeley.

Gasparini, Graziano, and Luise Margolies
1980. *Inca Architecture*. Translated by Patricia J. Lyon. Indiana University Press, Bloomington.

Gibaja Oviedo, Arminda

1984. Excavaciones en Ollantaytambo, Cusco. *Gaceta Arqueológica Andina* 3(9):4–5.

Glave Testino, Luis Miguel, and María Isabel Remy

1983. *Estructura agraria y vida rural en una región andina: Ollantaytambo entre los siglos XVI–XIX*. Centro de Estudios Rurales Andinos "Bartolomé de las Casas," Cuzco.

González, Alberto R.

1979. Pre-Columbian Metallurgy of Northwest Argentina. In *Pre-Columbian Metallurgy of South America*, edited by Elizabeth Benson, pp. 133–202. Dumbarton Oaks, Washington, D.C.

1982. Las "provincias" inca del antiguo Tucuman. *Revista del Museo Nacional* 46:317–80.

1983. Inca Settlement Patterns in a Marginal Province of the Empire: Sociocultural Implications. In *Prehistoric Settlement Patterns: Essays in Honor of Gordon R. Willey*, edited by Evon Z. Vogt and Richard M. Leventhal, pp. 337–60. Harvard University, Cambridge, MA.

González, Alberto R., and Pío Pablo Díaz

1992. La Casa Morada. *Estudios de Arqueología* 5:9–54.

González, Alberto Rex, and Victor Núñez Regueiro

1958–1959. Apuntes preliminares sobre la arqueología de Campo de Pucará y alrededores (Dpto. de Andalgalá, Pcia. de Catamarca). *Anales de Arqueología y Etnología* 14–15:115–62.

González Carré, Enrique, Jorge Cosmopolis A., and Jorge Lévano P.

1981. *La ciudad inca de Vilcashuaman*. Universidad Nacional de San Cristóbal de Huamanga, Ayacucho, Peru.

González Corrales, José A.

1984. Arquitectura y cerámica Killke del Cusco. *Revista del Museo e Instituto de Arqueología* 25:37–46. Universidad Nacional de San Antonio Abad, Cuzco.

González Holguín, Diego

1952. *Vocabulario de la lengua general de todo el Perú, llamada lengua Qquichua o del Inca*. New edn. Imprenta Santa María, Lima. (Originally written 1608.)

Gorbak, Celina, Mirtha Lischetti, and Carmen Paula Munoz

1962. Batallas rituales del Chiaraje y del Tocto de la provincia de Kanas (Cuzco, Peru). *Revista del Museo Nacional* 31:245–304.

Gordon, Robert B., and John W. Rutledge

1984. Bismuth Bronzes from Machu Picchu, Peru. *Science* 223:585–6.

Gose, Peter

1993. Segmentary State Formation and the Ritual Control of Water under the Incas. *Comparative Studies in Society and History* 35(3):480–514.

1996a. Oracles, Divine Kingship, and Political Representation in the Inka State. *Ethnohistory* 43(1):1–32.

1996b. The Past is a Lower Moiety: Diarchy, History, and Divine Kingship in the Inka Empire. *History and Anthropology* 9(4):383–414.

Grosboll, Sue
1993. . . . And He Said in the Time of the Ynga, They Paid Tribute and Served the Ynga. In *Provincial Inca: Archaeological and Ethnohistorical Assessment of the Impact of the Inca State*, edited by Michael Malpass, pp. 44–76. University of Iowa Press, Iowa.

Guaman Poma de Ayala, Felipe
1936. *Bueva corónica y buen gobierno*. Travaux et Mémoires de l'Institut d'Ethnologie 22. Paris.
1980. *El primer nueva corónica y buen gobierno*. 1st edn., edited by John V. Murra, Rolena Adorno, and Jorge Urioste. Siglo Veintiuno, Mexico, D.F.

Guevara Avila, Hugo, and Luis Guzman Palomino
1992. *El ocaso del Imperio de los Incas*. Talleres Gráficos del Centro de Elaboración de Material Educativo de la Universidad Nacional de Educación, Lima.

Guibovich, Pedro
1996. An Inka State Ritual: The Capac Hucha. (MS.)

Guillén Guillén, Edmundo
1994. *La guerra de la reconquista inka*. R. A. Ediciones, Lima.

Guzmán Ladrón de Guevara, Carlos
1959. Algunos establecimientos incas en la sierra central. Hoyas del Mantaro y del Pampas. In *Actas Y Trabajos del II Congreso Nacional de Historia del Perú: Epoca Prehispánica*, vol. 1, pp. 243–53, Lima.

Gyarmati, János
1997. *Cochabamba Archaeological Project, Field Report 1997.*

Gyarmati, János, and András Varga
1999. *The Chacaras of War: An Inka State in the Cochabamba Valley, Bolivia*. Trans. Magdalena Seleanu. Museum of Ethnography, Budapest.

Haggard, J. Villasana, and Malcolm D. McLean
1941. *Handbook for Translators of Spanish Historical Documents*. Semco Color Press, Oklahoma City.

Hamilton, Roland
1990. Introduction: Father Cobo and the Incas. In *Inca Religions and Customs*, translated and edited by Roland Hamilton. University of Texas Press, Austin.
1996. Introduction. In *Narrative of the Incas*, edited by Roland Hamilton and Dana Buchanan, pp. ix–xiv. University of Texas Press, Austin.

Hampe, M. T.
1982. Las momias de los Incas en Lima. *Revista del Museo Nacional* 46: 405–18.

Harris, Olivia
1978. El parentesco y la economía vertical en el ayllu Laymi (norte de Potosí). *Avances* no. 1.

Harth-Terré, Emilio
1964. El pueblo de Huánuco Viejo. *Arquitecto Peruano* 320(21):1–20.

Hassig, Ross
1985. *Trade, Tribute, and Transportation: The Sixteenth-Century Political Economy of the Valley of Mexico*. University of Oklahoma Press, Norman.

1988. *Aztec Warfare: Imperial Expansion and Political Control.* University of Oklahoma Press, Norman.

Hastorf, Christine A.

1990. The Effect of the Inka State on Sausa Agricultural Production and Crop Consumption. *American Antiquity* 55:262–90.

1992. *Agriculture and the Onset of Political Inequality before the Inka.* Cambridge University Press, Cambridge.

Hastorf, Christine A., and Michael DeNiro

1985. Reconstruction of Prehistoric Plant Production and Cooking Practices by a New Isotopic Method. *Nature* 315:489–91.

Hastorf, Christine, and Timothy K. Earle

1985. Intensive Agriculture and the Geography of Political Change in the Upper Mantaro Region of Central Peru. In *Prehistoric Intensive Agriculture in the Tropics,* edited by Ian Farrington. British Archaeological Reports, International Series, no. 232, pp. 569–95. Oxford.

Heffernan, Kenneth J.

1989. *Limatambo in Late Prehistory: Landscape Archaeology and Documentary Images of Inca Presence in the Periphery of Cuzco.* Unpublished Ph.D. Dissertation, Department of Anthropology, Australian National University, Canberra.

1995. Paullu, Tocto Usica and Chilche in the Royal Lands of Limatambo and Quispeguanca. *Tawantinsuyu* 1:66–85.

1996. *Limatambo: Archaeology, History, and the Regional Societies of Inca Cusco.* Tempus Reparatum, Oxford. British Archaeological Reports International Series, no. 644.

Helmer, Marie

1955–6. "La visitación de los Yndios Chupachos." Inka et encomendero 1549. *Travaux de L'Institut Français d'Études Andines* 5:3–50. (Originally written 1549.)

Hemming, John

1970. *The Conquest of the Incas.* Macmillan, London.

Hemming, John, and Edward Ranney

1992. *Monuments of the Inca.* University of New Mexico Press, Albuquerque.

Herrera y Tordesillas, Antonio de

1946. *Historia general de los hechos de los Castellanos en las Islas y Tierra Firme del Mar Océano.* 10 vols. Editorial Guaranía, Buenos Aires.

1952. *Historia general de los hechos de los Castellanos en las Islas y Tierra Firme del Mar Océano,* vol. 10. Década Quinta, Madrid.

Heyerdahl, Thor, Daniel H. Sandweiss, and Alfredo Narváez

1995. *Pyramids of Túcume: The Quest for Peru's Forgotten City.* Thames and Hudson, New York.

Higueras-Hare, Alvaro

1996. *Prehispanic Settlement and Land Use in Cochabamba, Bolivia.* Unpublished Ph.D. Dissertation, Department of Anthropology, University of Pittsburgh. University Microfilms, Ann Arbor.

Hollowell, Lee
  1987. *Study of Precision Cutting and Fitting of Stone in Pre-historic Andean Walls and Re-assessment of the Fortaleza at Ollantaytambo, Peru.* National Geographic Society, Report no. 2832. Washington, D.C.

Hornberger, Esteban, and Nancy H. Hornberger
  1983. *Diccionario tri-lingüe, quechua de Cusco: quechua, English, castellano.* 2nd edn. Qoya Raymi, La Paz.

Hosler, Diane, Heather Lechtman, and Olaf Holm
  1990. *Axe-Monies and their Relatives.* Studies in Pre-Columbian Art and Archaeology, no. 30. Dumbarton Oaks, Washington, D.C.

Howe, Ellen, and Ulrich Petersen
  1994. Silver and Lead in the Late Prehistory of the Mantaro Valley, Peru. In *Archaeometry of Pre-Columbian Sites and Artifacts: Proceedings of a Symposium Organized by the UCLA Institute of Archaeology and the Getty Conservation Institute*, edited by D. A. Scott and P. Meyers, pp. 183–98. Getty Conservation Institute, Malibu.

Hoyos, María de, and Verónica I. Williams
  1994. Un patrón de asentamiento estatal para propósitos especiales. Resumenes. Actas y Memorias del XI Congreso Nacional de Arqueología Argentina. *Revista del Museo de Historia Natural de San Rafael* I:196–9.

Huaycochea Nuñez de la Torre, Flor de María
  1994. *Qolqas.* Bancos de Reserva Andinos, Cuzco.

Huidobro Bellido, José
  1992. Influencia Tiwanaku en el Kusko. *Pumapunku* 3:9–29.

Hyslop, John
  1979. El area Lupaqa bajo del dominio incaico, un reconocimiento arqueológico. *Histórica* 3(1):53–81.
  1984. *The Inka Road System.* Academic Press, New York.
  1985. *Inkawasi: The New Cuzco.* British Archaeological Reports, International Series, no. 234. Oxford.
  1988. Las fronteras estatales extremas del Tawantinsuyu. In *La Frontera del Estado Inca*, edited by Tom D. Dillehay and Patricia J. Netherly. Proceedings, 45 Congreso Internacional de Americanistas, Bogotá, Colombia, 1985, pp. 35–57. British Archaeological Reports, International Series, no. 442. Oxford.
  1990. *Inka Settlement Planning.* University of Texas Press, Austin.
  1993. Factors Influencing the Transmission and Distribution of Inka Cultural Materials throughout Tawantinsuyu. In *Latin American Horizons*, edited by Don S. Rice, pp. 337–56. Dumbarton Oaks, Washington, D.C.

Idrovo Urigüen, Jaime
  1984. *Prospection archéologique de la vallée de Cuenca – Ecuador.* Ph.D. Dissertation, Université de Paris I, Panteon Sorbonne, Paris.
  1988. Tomebamba: primera fase de conquista incaica en los Andes septentrionales: los Cañaris y la conquista incasica del austro ecuatoriano. In *La Frontera del Estado Inca*, edited by Tom D. Dillehay and Patricia J. Netherly. Proceedings, 45 Congreso Internacional de Americanistas, Bogotá, Colombia, 1985, pp. 87–104. British Archaeological Reports, International Series, no. 442. Oxford.

Isbell, Billie Jean
    1978. *To Defend Ourselves: Ecology and Ritual in an Andean Village*. Institute of Latin American Studies, University of Texas, Austin.
Julien, Catherine J.
    1982. Inca Decimal Administration in the Lake Titicaca Region. In *The Inca and Aztec States 1400–1800: Anthropology and History*, edited by George A. Collier, Renato I. Rosaldo, and John D. Wirth, pp. 119–51. Academic Press, New York.
    1983. *Hatunqolla: A View of Inca Rule from the Lake Titicaca Region*. Publications in Anthropology, vol. 15. University of California Press, Berkeley.
    1987. The Uru Tribute Category: Ethnic Boundaries and Empire in the Andes. *Proceedings of the American Philosophical Society* 131(1):53–91.
    1988. How Inca Decimal Administration Worked. *Ethnohistory* 35:257–79.
    1992. *Condesuyo: The Political Division of Territory under Inca and Spanish Rule*. BAS, vol. 19. Bonner Amerikanistische Studien, Bonn.
    1993. Finding a Fit: Archaeology and Ethnohistory of the Incas. In *Provincial Inca: Archaeological and Ethnohistorical Assessment of the Impact of the Inca State*, edited by Michael Malpass, pp. 177–233. University of Iowa Press, Iowa City.
Julien, Daniel G.
    1993. Late Pre-Inkaic Ethnic Groups in Highland Peru: An Archaeological-Ethnohistorical Model of the Political Geography of the Cajamarca Region. *Latin American Antiquity* 4(3):246–73.
Katz, Friedrich
    1972. *The Ancient American Civilizations*. Praeger, New York.
Kendall, Ann
    1974. Architecture and Planning at the Inca Sites in the Cusichaca Area. *Baessler Archiv, n.F* 22:73–137.
    1976. Descripción e inventario de las formas arquitectónicas inca. Patrones de distribución e inferencias cronológicas. *Revista del Museo Nacional* 42:13–96.
    1985. *Aspects of Inca Architecture – Description, Function, and Chronology*. 2 vols. British Archaeological Reports, International Series, no. 242. Oxford.
    1988. Inca Planning north of Cuzco between Anta and Machu Picchu and along the Urubamba Valley. In *Recent Studies in Pre-Columbian Archaeology*, edited by Nicholas J. Saunders and Olivier de Montmollin. British Archaeological Reports, International Series, no. 421(ii), pp. 457–88. Oxford.
    1989. *Everyday Life of the Incas*. Dorset Press, New York.
    1994. *Proyecto Arqueológico Cusichaca, Cusco. Investigaciones arqueológicas y de rehabilitación agrícola*, vol. 1. Southern Peru Copper Corporation, Lima.
    1996. An Archaeological Perspective for Late Intermediate Period Inca Development in the Cuzco Region. *Structure, Knowledge, and Representation in the Andes* 24(1&2):121–56.
Kendall, Ann, Rob Early, and Bill Sillar
    1992. Report on Archaeological Field Season Investigating Early Inca Architecture at Juchuy Coscco (Q'aqya Qhawana) and Warq'ana, Province of

Calca, Dept. of Cuzco, Peru. In *Ancient America: Contributions to New World Archaeology*, edited by Nicholas J. Saunders, pp. 189–255. Oxbow Books, Oxford.

Kirchoff, Paul

1949. The Social and Political Organization of the Andean Peoples. In *Handbook of South American Indians: The Comparative Ethnology of South American Indians*, edited by Julian Steward. Bulletin 143, vol. 5, pp. 293–311. Bureau of American Ethnology, Washington, D.C.

Kolata, Alan L.

1991. The Technology and Organization of Agricultural Production in the Tiwanaku State. *Latin American Antiquity* 2:99–125.

1993. *The Tiwanaku: Portrait of an Andean Civilization*. Blackwell, Cambridge, MA.

Kosok, Paul

1965. *Life, Land, and Water in Ancient Peru*. Long Island University Press, New York.

Krapovickas, Pedro

1974. Un taller de lapidario en el Pucará de Tilcara. *Runa* 9 (pts. 1 and 2):137–51. (Originally written 1958–9.)

1981–2. Hallazgos incaicos en Tilcara y Yacoraite (una reinterpretación). *Relaciones de la Sociedad Argentina de Antropología* 14 (Part 1: La arquitectura):67–80.

Kroeber, Alfred L.

1930. *Archaeological Exploration in Peru, Part II: The Northern Coast*. Field Museum of Natural History, Anthropology Memoirs, vol. 2. Chicago.

La Lone, Darrell E.

1982. The Inca as a Nonmarket Economy: Supply on Command versus Supply and Demand. In *Contexts for Prehistoric Exchange*, edited by Jonathan E. Ericson and Timothy K. Earle, pp. 291–316. Academic Press, New York.

1994. An Andean World-System: Production Transformations under the Inka Empire. In *The Economic Anthropology of the State*, edited by Elizabeth Brumfiel. Society for Economic Anthropology Monograph 11, pp. 17–41. University Press of America, Lanham, MD.

La Lone, Mary B.

1985. *Indian Land Tenure in Southern Cuzco: From Inca to Colonial Patterns*. Unpublished Ph.D. Dissertation, Department of Anthropology, University of California, Los Angeles. University Microfilms, Ann Arbor.

La Lone, Mary B., and Darrell E. La Lone

1987. The Inka State in the Southern Highlands: State Administrative and Production Enclaves. *Ethnohistory* 34:47–62.

Las Casas, Bartolomé de

1958. *Apologética historia*. Biblioteca de Autores Españoles (continuación), vol. 105. Ediciones Atlas, Madrid.

Laurencich-Minelli, Laura

1998. Una contribución a la etnohistoria del Perú. El documento "Historia et Rudimenta Linguae Piruanorum". *Tawantinsuyu* 5:103–12.

Lechtman, Heather
1984. Andean Value Systems and the Development of Prehistoric Metallurgy. *Technology and Culture* 25:1–36.

Lee, Vincent R.
1989. *Chanasuyu: The Ruins of Inca Vilcabamba*. Sixpac Manco Publications, Wilson, WY.
1990. *The Building of Sacsayhuaman, and Other Papers*. Sixpac Manco Publications, Wilson, WY.
2000. *Forgotten Vilcabamba*. Sixpac Manco Publications, Wilson, WY.

Levillier, Roberto, ed.
1940. *Don Francisco de Toledo, supremo organizador del Peru: Su vida, su obra [1515–1582]*, 3 vols. Espasa-Calpe, Buenos Aires.

LeVine, Terry Y.
1985. *Inka Administration in the Central Highlands: A Comparative Study*. Unpublished Ph.D. Dissertation, Institute of Archaeology, University of California, Los Angeles. University Microfilms, Ann Arbor.
1987. Inka Labor Service at the Regional Level: The Functional Reality. *Ethnohistory* 34:14–46.

LeVine, Terry Y., ed.
1992. *Inka Storage Systems*. University of Oklahoma Press, Norman.

Lizárraga, Reginaldo de
1909. *Descripción breve de toda la tierra del Perú, Tucumán, Río de Plata y Chile*. Historiadores de Indias, vol. 2. Nueva Biblioteca de Autores Españoles, edited by M. Serrano y Sanz, vol. 15, pp. 485–690. Bailly Bailliére e hijos, Madrid. (Originally written 1605.)

Locke, Leland L.
1923. *The Ancient Quipu or Peruvian Knot Record*. The American Museum of Natural History, New York.

Lorandi, Ana María
1984. Soñocamayoc: Los olleros del Inka en los centros manufactureros del Tucumán. *Revista del Museo de la Plata, Sección Antropología* 7(62):303–27.
1988. Los Diaguitas y el Tawantinsuyu: Una hipótesis de conflicto. In *La Frontera del Estado Inca*, edited by Tom D. Dillehay and Patricia J. Netherly. Proceedings, 45 Congreso Internacional de Americanistas, Bogotá, Colombia, 1985, pp. 235–59. British Archaeological Reports, International Series, no. 442. Oxford.
1991. Evidencias en torno a los mitmaqkuna incaicos en el N.O. Argentino. *Anthropologica* 9:213–36. Lima, Pontificia Universidad Católica del Perú.

Lorandi, Ana María, and Roxana Boixadós
1987–8. Etnohistoria de los valles calchaquíes en los siglos XVI y XVII. *Runa* 17–18:263–420.

Lorandi, Ana María, María Beatriz Cremonte, and Verónica Williams
1992. Identification étnica de los mitmakuna instalados en el establecimiento incaico Potrero-Chaquiago. *Actas del XI Congreso Nacional de Arqueología Chilena* 11:195–200.

Lothrop, Samuel Kirkland
   1938. *Inca Treasure as Depicted by Spanish Historians*, vol. 2. The Southwest Museum, Los Angeles.
Lounsbury, Floyd G.
   1986. Some Aspects of the Inka Kinship System. In *Anthropological History of Andean Polities*, edited by John V. Murra, Nathan Wachtel, and Jacques Revel, pp. 121–36. Cambridge University Press, Cambridge.
Luteyn, James L., and Steven P. Churchill
   2000. Vegetation of the Tropical Andes. In *Imperfect Balance: Pre-Columbian Human Ecosystems*, edited by David Lentz, pp. 281–310. Columbia University Press, New York.
Luttwak, Edward N.
   1976. *The Grand Strategy of the Roman Empire from the First Century AD to the Third*. Johns Hopkins University Press, Baltimore.
MacCormack, Sabine
   1991. *Religion in the Andes: Vision and Imagination in Early Colonial Peru*. Princeton University Press, Princeton, NJ.
MacLean, Margaret G.
   1986. *Sacred Land, Sacred Water: Inca Landscape Planning in the Cuzco Area*. Unpublished Ph.D. Dissertation, Department of Anthropology, University of California, Berkeley. University Microfilms, Ann Arbor.
Malpass, Michael A.
   1996. *Daily Life in the Inca Empire*. Greenwood Press, Westport, CT.
Malpass, Michael, ed.
   1993. *Provincial Inca: Archaeological and Ethnohistorical Assessment of the Impact of the Inca State*. University of Iowa Press, Iowa City.
Mann, Michael
   1986. *The Sources of Social Power*. Cambridge University Press, Cambridge.
Mannheim, Bruce
   1991. *The Language of the Inka since the European Invasion*. University of Texas Press, Austin.
Marcus, Joyce, and Jorge E. Silva
   1988. The Chillón Valley "Coca Lands": Archaeological Background and Ecological Context. In *Conflicts over Coca Fields in XVIth-Century Perú*, by María Rostworowski de Diez Canseco, pp. 1–32. Memoirs of the Museum of Anthropology, University of Michigan, No. 21. Ann Arbor.
Mariño de Lobera, Pedro
   1960. *Crónica del reyno de Chile*. Biblioteca de Autores Españoles (continuación), vol. 131, pp. 227–562. Ediciones Atlas, Madrid. (Originally written 1580.)
Masuda, Shozo, Izumi Shimada, and Craig Morris, eds.
   1985. *Andean Ecology and Civilization*. University of Tokyo Press, Tokyo.
Matienzo, Juan de
   1967. *Gobierno del Perú*, edited by Guillermo Lohmann Villena, Travaux de l'Institut Français d'Études Andines, vol. 11. Lima. (Originally written 1567.)

Matos Mendieta, Ramiro
1994. *Pumpu: Centro Administrativo Inka de la Puna de Junín.* Editorial Horizonte, Lima.

McEwan, Colin, and María Isabel Silva
1989. Que fueron a hacer los Incas en la costa central del Ecuador? *Proceedings of the 46th International Congress of Americanists*, pp. 163–85. British Archaeological Reports International Series, no. 503, Oxford.

McEwan, Colin, and Maarten van de Guchte
1992. Ancestral Time and Sacred Space in Inca State Ritual. In *The Ancient Americas: Art from Sacred Landscapes*, edited by Richard F. Townsend, pp. 359–73. The Art Institute of Chicago, Chicago.

Means, Philip A.
1928. Biblioteca Andina. *Transactions of the Connecticut Academy of Arts and Sciences* 29:271–525.

Mena, Cristóbal de (El Anónimo Sevillano)
1937. La conquista del Perú. In *Las relaciones primitivas de la conquista del Perú, Cuadernos de historia*, edited by Raúl Porras Barrenechea. Los cronistas de la conquista, no. 1, vol. 2, pp. 79–101. Les Presses Modernes, Paris. (Originally written 1534.)

Menzel, Dorothy
1959. The Inca Conquest of the South Coast of Peru. *Southwestern Journal of Anthropology* 15:125–42.

Métraux, Alfred
1969. *The History of the Incas.* Schocken Books, New York.

Miller, George R., and Anne L. Gill
1990. Zooarchaeology at Pirincay, a Formative Period Site in Highland Ecuador. *Journal of Field Archaeology* 17(1):49–68.

Miranda, Christóbal de
1925. *Relación de los corregimientos y otras oficios que se proveen en los reynos e provincias del Pirú, en el distrito e gobernación del visorrey dellos,* edited by Roberto Levillier. Imprento de Juan Pueyo, Madrid. (Originally written 1583.)

Mitchell, William
1980. Local Ecology and the State: Implications of Contemporary Quechua Land Use for the Inca Sequence of Agricultural Work. In *Beyond the Myths of Culture: Essays in Cultural Materialism*, edited by Eric B. Ross, pp. 139–54. Academic Press, New York.

Mitchell, William P., and David Guillet, eds.
1994. *Irrigation at High Altitudes: The Social Organization of Water Control Systems in the Andes.* American Anthropological Association, Washington, D.C.

Molina, Cristóbal de (el Cuzqueño)
1988. Relación de la Fábulas y Ritos de la Incas. In *Fábulas y ritos de los Incas*, edited by Henrique Urbano and Pierre Duviols, pp. 47–134. Historia 16, Madrid. (Originally written 1575.)

Montesinos, Fernando
1920. *Memoriales antiguas historiales del Perú.* Translated and edited by Philip A. Means. Hakluyt Society, London.

Moore, Sally F.
1958. *Power and Property in Inca Peru*. Greenwood Press, Westport, CT.
Moorehead, Elizabeth L.
1978. Highland Inca Architecture in Adobe. *Ñawpa Pacha* 16:65–94.
Morris, Craig
1967. *Storage in Tawantinsuyu*. Unpublished Ph.D. Dissertation, Department of Anthropology, University of Chicago. University Microfilms, Ann Arbor.
1972. State Settlements in Tawantinsuyu: A Strategy of Compulsory Urbanism. In *Contemporary Archaeology*, edited by Mark P. Leone, pp. 393–401. Southern Illinois University Press, Carbondale.
1974. Reconstructing Patterns of Nonagricultural Production in the Inca Economy: Archaeology and Documents in Instituted Analysis. In *Reconstructing Complex Societies*, edited by Carol Moore. Supplement to Bulletin of the American Schools of Oriental Research, vol. 20, pp. 49–68. Chicago.
1978. The Archeological Study of Andean Exchange Systems. In *Social Archeology: Beyond Subsistence and Dating*, edited by Charles L. Redman, Mary Jane Berman, Edward V. Curtin, William T. Langhorne, Jr., Nina M. Versaggi, and Jeffrey C. Wanser, pp. 303–27. Academic Press, New York.
1981. Tecnología y organización inca del almacenamiento de víveres en la sierra. In *Runakunap Kawsayninkupaq Rurasqankuna: La tecnología en el mundo andino*, edited by Heather Lechtman and Ana María Soldi, pp. 327–75. UNAM, Mexico City.
1982. The Infrastructure of Inka Control in the Peruvian Central Highlands. In *The Inca and Aztec States 1400–1800: Anthropology and History*, edited by George A. Collier, Renato I. Rosaldo, and John D. Wirth, pp. 153–71. Academic Press, New York.
1988. Mas allá de las fronteras de Chincha. In *La Frontera del Estado Inca*, edited by Tom D. Dillehay and Patricia J. Netherly. Proceedings, 45 Congreso Internacional de Americanistas, Bogotá, Colombia, 1985, pp. 131–40. British Archaeological Reports, International Series, no. 442. Oxford.
1990. Arquitectura y estructura del espacio en Huánuco Pampa. *Cuadernos Instituto Nacional de Antropología* 12:27–45.
1991. Signs of Division, Symbols of Unity: Art in the Inka Empire. In *Circa 1492: Art in the Age of Exploration*, edited by Jay A. Levenson, pp. 521–8. National Gallery of Art and Yale University Press, Washington D.C., New Haven, and London.
1992. Foreword. In *Inka Storage Systems*, edited by Terry Y. LeVine, pp. ix–xiii. University of Oklahoma Press, Norman.
1995. Symbols to Power: Styles and Media in the Inka State. In *Style, Society, and Person: Archaeological and Ethnological Perspectives*, edited by Christopher Carr and Jill E. Neitzel, pp. 419–33. Plenum Press, New York.
1998. Inka Strategies of Incorporation and Governance. In *Archaic States*, edited by Gary M. Feinman and Joyce Marcus, pp. 293–309. School of American Research Press, Santa Fe.
Morris, Craig, and Donald E. Thompson
1985. *Huánuco Pampa: An Inca City and Its Hinterland*. Thames and Hudson, London.

Moseley, Michael E.
1983. The Good Old Days Were Better: Agrarian Collapse and Tectonics. *American Anthropologist* 85:773–99.
1992. *Incas and Their Ancestors: Archaeology of Peru*. Thames and Hudson, New York.

Moseley, Michael E., and Kent C. Day, eds.
1982. *Chan Chan: Andean Desert City*. University of New Mexico Press, Albuquerque.

Moseley, Michael Edward, and Alana Cordy-Collins
1990. *The Northern Dynasties: Kingship and Statecraft in Chimor: A Symposium at Dumbarton Oaks, 12th and 13th October 1985*. Dumbarton Oaks Research Library and Collection, Washington, D.C.

Moseley, Michael E., D. Wagner, and James B. Richardson III
1992. Space Shuttle Imagery of Recent Catastrophic Climate Change along the Arid Andean Coast. In *Paleoshorelines and Prehistory: An Investigation of Method*, edited by L. L. Johnson, pp. 215–35. CRC Press, Boca Raton, LA.

Mulvany de Peñaloza, Eleanora
1986. Nuevas evidencias de la ocupación incaica en el valle de Lerma. *Runa* 16:59–84.

Mulvany de Peñaloza, Eleanora, and Silvia Soria
1998. Sitios y caminos en los bosques serranos de los Andes meridionales. *Tawantinsuyu* 5:120–6.

Mumford, Jeremy
1998. The Taki Onqoy and the Andean Nation: Sources and Interpretations. *Latin American Research Review* 33(1):150–65.

Murra, John V.
1958. On Inca Political Structure. *Proceedings of the Annual Spring Meeting of the American Ethnological Society*, pp. 30–41. University of Washington, Seattle.
1960. Rite and Crop in the Inca State. In *Culture in History*, edited by Stanley Diamond, pp. 393–407. Columbia University Press, New York.
1962. Cloth and its Functions in the Inca State. *American Anthropologist* 64:710–28.
1965. Herds and Herders in the Inca State. In *Man, Culture, and Animals*, edited by Anthony Leeds and Andrew P. Vayda, pp. 185–215. American Association for the Advancement of Science, Publication no. 78. Washington, D.C.
1966. New Data on Retainer and Servile Populations in Tawantinsuyu. In *XXXVI Congreso Internacional de Americanistas, Spain 1964*, vol. 2, pp. 35–45. Seville.
1968. An Aymara Kingdom in 1567. *Ethnohistory* 15:115–51.
1972. El "control vertical" de un máximo de pisos ecológicos en la economía de las sociedades andinas. In *Visita de la Provincia de León de Huánuco en 1562, Iñigo Ortiz de Zúñiga, visitador*, edited by John V. Murra, vol. 2, pp. 427–76. Universidad Nacional Hermilio Valdizán, Huánuco, Peru.
1975. *Formaciones económicas y políticas del mundo andino*. Instituto de Estudios Peruanos, Lima.

1978. Los olleros del Inka: Hacia una historia y arqueología del Qollasuyu. In *Historia, Problema, y Promesa: Homenaje a Jorge Basadre*, edited by F. Miro Quesada, Franklin Pease G. Y., and Daniel Sobrevilla, pp. 415–23. Pontificia Universidad Católica del Perú, Lima.

1980a. Derechos a las tierras en el Tawantinsuyu. *Revista de la Universidad Complutense* 28(117):273–87.

1980b. *The Economic Organization of the Inka State*. JAI Press, Greenwich, CT. (Doctoral dissertation originally written 1956.)

1982. The Mit'a Obligations of Ethnic Groups to the Inka State. In *The Inca and Aztec States 1400–1800: Anthropology and History*, edited by George Collier, Renato Rosaldo, and John Wirth, pp. 237–62. Academic Press, New York.

1986. The Expansion of the Inka State: Armies, War, and Rebellions. In *Anthropological History of Andean Polities*, edited by John V. Murra, Nathan Wachtel, and Jacques Revel, pp. 49–58. Cambridge University Press, Cambridge.

Murúa, Fray Martín

1962. *Historia general del Perú, origen y descendencia de los Inca*. Bibliotheca Americana Vetus, Madrid. (Originally written 1590–1600.)

1986. *Historia general del Perú*, edited by Manuel Ballesteros. Historia 16, Madrid. (Originally written *ca.* 1605.)

Netherly, Patricia J.

1978. *Local Level Lords on the North Coast of Peru*. Unpublished Ph.D. Dissertation, Department of Anthropology, Cornell University. University Microfilms, Ann Arbor.

1984. The Management of Late Andean Irrigation Systems on the North Coast of Peru. *American Antiquity* 49(2):227–54.

Nielsen, Axel

1996. Demografía y cambio social en Quebrada de Humahuaca (Jujuy, Argentina) 700–1535 d.C. *Relaciones de la Sociedad Argentina de Antropología* 21:307–85.

Niemeyer F., Hans, and Virgilio Schiappacasse F.

1988. Patrones de asentamiento incaicos en el Norte Grande de Chile. In *La Frontera del Estado Inca*, edited by Tom D. Dillehay and Patricia J. Netherly. Proceedings, 45 Congreso Internacional de Americanistas, Bogotá, Colombia, 1985, pp. 141–80. British Archaeological Reports, International Series, no. 442. Oxford.

Niles, Susan A.

1980. Pumamarca: A Late Intermediate Period Site near Ollantaytambo. *Ñawpa Pacha* 18:49–62.

1987. *Callachaca: Style and Status in an Inca Community*. University of Iowa Press, Iowa City.

1999. *The Shape of Inca History: Narrative and Architecture in an Andean Empire*. University of Iowa Press, Iowa City.

Nordenskiöld, Erland von

1924. *Forschungen und Abenteuer in Südamerica*. Strecker und Schröder, Stuttgart.

Noticia del Perú
1918. El descubrimiento y la conquista del Perú; relación inédita de Miguel de Estete. La publica con una introducción y notas Carlos M. Larrea. *Boletín de la Sociedad Ecuatoriana de Estudios Históricas Americanos* 1(3):300–50.

Núñez, Lautaro
1986. The Evolution of a Valley: Population and Resources of Tarapacá over a Millennium. In *Anthropological History of Andean Polities*, edited by John V. Murra, Nathan Wachtel, and Jacques Revel, pp. 23–34. Cambridge University Press, Cambridge.

Oberem, Udo
1968. Die Berfestung Quitoloma im Nördlichen Hochland Ecuadors. *Baessler Archiv, n.F.* 16:331–54.

1980. *Festungsanlagen im Andengebiet. Allgemeine und Vergleichende Archäologie – Beiträge*, vol. 2, pp. 487–503. Deutsches Archäologes Institut, Bonn.

Oberem, Udo, and Roswith Hartmann
1976. Indios Cañaris de la Sierra Sur del Ecuador. In *El Cuzco del Siglo XVI*, pp. 373–90. Seminar für Völderkunde, Universität Bonn, Bonn.

Olaverría, Miguel de
1852. Informe de Don Miguel de Olaverría sobre el Reyno de Chile, sus Indios y sus guerras. In *Documentos sobre la Historia la Estadística y la Geografía de Chile, Historia física y política de Chile según documentos*, edited by Claude Gay, vol. 2, pp. 13–54. E. Thunot, Paris. (Originally written 1594.)

Orlove, Benjamin S., John H. Chiang, and Mark A. Cane
2000. Forecasting Andean Rainfall and Crop Yield from the Influence of El Niño on Pleiades Visibility. *Nature* 403:68–71.

Ortiz de Zúñiga, Iñigo
1967. *Visita de la Provincia de León de Huánuco en 1562, Iñigo Ortiz de Zúñiga, visitador*, edited by John V. Murra, vol. 1. Universidad Nacional Hermilio Valdizán, Huánuco, Peru. (Originally written 1562.)

1972. *Visita de la Provincia de León de Huánuco en 1562, Iñigo Ortiz de Zúñiga, visitador*, edited by John V. Murra, vol. 2. Universidad Nacional Hermilio Valdizán, Huánuco, Peru. (Originally written 1562.)

Ortloff, Charles R.
1993. Chimu Hydraulics Technology and Statecraft on the North Coast of Peru, AD 1000–1470. In *Economic Aspects of Water Management in the Prehispanic New World*, edited by Vernon L. Scarborough and Barry L. Isaac. Research in Economic Anthropology, Supplement 7, pp. 327–67. JAI Press, Greenwich, CT.

Ortloff, Charles R., and Alan Kolata
1989. Hydraulic Analysis of Tiwanaku Aqueduct Structures at Lukurmata and Pajchiri, Bolivia. *Journal of Archaeological Science* 16:513–35.

1993. Climate and Collapse: Agro-Ecological Perspectives on the Decline of the Tiwanaku State. *Journal of Archaeological Science* 20(2):195–221.

Owen, Bruce
2001. The Economy of Metal and Shell Wealth Goods. In *Empire and Domes-*

tic Economy, by Terence N. D'Altroy, Christine A. Hastorf, and Associates, pp. 265–95. Kluwer Academic/Plenum Press, New York.

Owen, Bruce D., and Marilyn A. Norconk

1987. Appendix I: Analysis of the Human Burials, 1977–1983 Field Seasons: Demographic Profiles and Burial Practices. In *Archaeological Field Research in the Upper Mantaro, Peru, 1982–1983*, edited by Timothy K. Earle et al. Monograph 28, pp. 107–23. Institute of Archaeology, University of California, Los Angeles.

Pachacuti Yamqui Salcamayhua, Joan de Santa Cruz

1968. *Relación de antigüedades deste Reyno del Perú*. Biblioteca de Autores Españoles (continuación), vol. 209, pp. 279–319. Ediciones Atlas, Madrid. (Originally written 1613.)

1993. *Relación de antigüedades deste Reyno del Perú*. Estudio Etnohistórico y Lingüístico de Pierre Duviols and César Itier. Travaux de l'Institut Français d'Études Andines, vol. 74. Lima. (Originally written 1613.)

Parsons, Jeffrey R.

1998. A Regional Perspective on the Inka Impact in the Sierra Central, Perú. *Tawantinsuyu* 5:153–9.

Parsons, Jeffrey R., and Charles M. Hastings

1988. The Late Intermediate Period. In *Peruvian Prehistory*, edited by Richard W. Keatinge, pp. 190–229. Cambridge University Press, Cambridge.

Parsons, Jeffrey R., Charles M. Hastings, and Ramiro Matos Mendieta

1998. Rebuilding the State in Highlands Peru: Herder–Cultivator Interaction during the Late Intermediate Period in the Tarama-Chinchaycocha Region. *Latin American Antiquity* 8(4):317–41.

2000. *Prehispanic Settlement Patterns in the Upper Mantaro and Tarma Drainages, Junín, Peru*. University of Michigan, Museum of Anthropology, Memoir, no. 34, Parts 1 and 2. Ann Arbor.

Pärssinen, Martti

1992. *Tawantinsuyu: The Inca State and its Political Organization*. Societas Historica Finlandiae, Helsinki.

Pärssinen, Martti, and Ari Siiriäinen

1997. Inca-Style Ceramics and their Chronological Relationship to the Inca Expansion in the Southern Lake Titicaca Area (Bolivia). *Latin American Antiquity* 8:255–71.

Pease G. Y., Franklin

1973. *El Dios creador andino*. Mosca Azul Editores, Lima.

1978. *Del Tawantinsuyu a la historia del Perú*. Instituto de Estudios Peruanos, Lima.

1982. The Formation of Tawantinsuyu: Mechanisms of Colonization and Relationship with Ethnic Groups. In *The Inca and Aztec States 1400–1800: Anthropology and History*, edited by George A. Collier, Renato I. Rosaldo, and John D. Wirth, pp. 173–98. Academic Press, New York.

1991. *Los Incas*. Pontificia Universidad Católica del Perú, Fondo Editorial, Lima.

1995. *Las Crónicas y los Andes*. Pontificia Universidad Católica del Perú, Lima.

Pease G. Y., Franklin, ed.

1977. *Collaguas I*. Pontificia Universidad Católica del Perú, Fondo Editorial, Lima.

Pizarro, Hernando

1959. Carta a Oidores de Santo Domingo, Panama. In *La historia general y natural de la Indias [1550]*, by Gonzalo Fernández de Oviedo y Valdés. Biblioteca de Autores Españoles (continuación), vol. 121, pp. 84–90. Ediciones Atlas, Madrid. (Originally written 1533.)

Pizarro, Pedro

1986. *Relación del descubrimiento y conquista de los reinos del Perú*. 2nd edn., edited by Guillermo Lohmann Villena. Pontificia Universidad Católica del Perú, Fondo Editorial, Lima. (Originally written 1571.)

Planella, María Teresa, and Rubén Stehberg

1994. Etnohistoria y arqueología en el estudio de la fortaleza indigena de Cerro Grande de la Compañia. *Revista Chungará* 26(1):65–78.

Planella, María Teresa, Rubén Stehberg, Blanca Tagle, Hans Niemeyer, and Carmen del Río

1991. La fortaleza indígena del Cerro Grande de la Compañía (Valle del Cachapoal) y su relación con el proceso expansivo meridional incaico. In *Actas del XII Congreso Nacional de Arqueología Chilena*, pp. 403–21, Temuco, Chile.

Plaza Schuller, Fernando

1976. *La incursión inca en el septentrión andino ecuatoriano*. Serie Arqueología, vol. 2. Instituto Otavaleño de Antropología, Otavalo, Ecuador.

1980. *El Complejo de fortalezas de Pambamarca*. Serie Arqueología, no. 3. Instituto Otavaleño de Antropología, Otavalo.

Polo de Ondegardo, Juan

1916. Relación de los fundamentos acerca del notable daño que resulta de no guardar a los indios sus fueros. In *Colección de Libros y Documentos Referentes a la Historia del Perú*, edited by Horacio H. Urteaga, vol. 3, pp. 45–188. Sanmartí, Lima. (Originally written 1571.)

1917. La Relación del linaje de los Incas y cómo extendieron ellos sus conquistas. In *Colección de Libros y Documentos Referentes a la Historia del Perú*, edited by Horacio H. Urteaga, vol. 4, pp. 45–94. Sanmartí, Lima. (Originally written 1567.)

1940. Informe del Licenciado Juan Polo de Ondegardo al Licenciado Briviesca de Muñatones sobre la perpetuidad de las encomiendas en el Perú. *Revista Histórica* 13:128–96. (Originally written 1561.)

1965a. On the Errors and Superstitions of the Indians, Taken from the Treatise and Investigation done by Licentiate Polo. In *Information Concerning the Religion and Government of the Incas*, translated by A. Brunel, John Murra, and Sidney Muirden, pp. 1–53. Human Relations Area Files, New Haven, CT.

1965b. A Report on the Basic Principles Explaining the Serious Harm which Follows when the Traditional Rights of the Indians are not Respected. In *Information Concerning the Religion and Government of the Incas*, translated by A. Brunel, John Murra, and Sidney Muirden, pp. 53–196. Human Relations Area Files, New Haven, CT.

1965c. Instruction against the Ceremonies and Rites that the Indians Practice in Conformance with the Stage of their Infidelity. In *Information Concerning the Religion and Government of the Incas*, translated by A. Brunel, John Murra, and Sidney Muirden, pp. 196–208. Human Relations Area Files, New Haven, CT.

1965d. Superstitions of the Indians, taken from the Second Provincial Council of Lima. In *Information Concerning the Religion and Government of the Incas*, translated by A. Brunel, John Murra, and Sidney Muirden (Appendix B), pp. 209–11. Human Relations Area Files, New Haven, CT. (Originally written 1567.)

Ponsonby, Arthur
1929. *Falsehood in War-Time*. Dutton and Company, New York.

Porras Barrenechea, Raúl
1986. *Los cronistas del Perú*. Biblioteca Clásicos del Perú, no. 2. Banco de Crédito del Perú, Lima.

Protzen, Jean-Pierre
1980. Inca Stonemasonry. *Scientific American* 254(2):94–103.
1982. Inca Quarrying and Stonecutting. *Ñawpa Pacha* 21:183–219.
1993. *Inca Architecture and Construction at Ollantaytambo*. Oxford University Press, Oxford.

Pulgar Vidal, Javier
1987. *Geografía del Perú*. 9th edn. Editorial Inca, Lima.

Raffino, Rodolfo
1983. *Los Inkas del Kollasuyu*. 2nd edn. Ramos Americana Editora, La Plata, Argentina.
1993. *Inka. Arqueología, historia, y urbanismo del altiplano andino*. Corregidor, Buenos Aires.

Ramírez, Susan E.
1982. Retainers of the Lords or Merchants: A Case of Mistaken Identity? In *El Hombre y su Ambiente en los Andes Centrales*, edited by Luis Millones and Hiroyasu Tomoeda. Senri Ethnological Studies, vol. 10, pp. 123–36. National Museum of Ethnology, Osaka.
1990. The Inca Conquest of the North Coast: A Historian's View. In *The Northern Dynasties: Kingship and Statecraft in Chimor*, edited by Michael E. Moseley and Alana Cordy-Collins, pp. 507–37. Dumbarton Oaks, Washington, D.C.
1996. *The World Upside Down: Cross-Cultural Contact and Conflict in Sixteenth-Century Peru*. Stanford University Press, Stanford.

Ramos Gavilán, Alonso
1976. *Historia de Nuestra Senora de Copacabana*. 2nd edn. Academia Boliviana de la Historia, La Paz. (Originally written 1621.)

Randall, Robert
1982. Qoyllur Rit'i, an Inca Fiesta of the Pleiades: Reflections on Time and Space in the Andean World. *Bulletin de l'Institut Français d'Études Andines* 11(1–2):37–81.

Rappaport, Roy A.
1971. The Sacred in Human Evolution. *Annual Review of Ecology and Systematics* 2:23–44.

Rawls, Joseph
1979. *An Analysis of Prehispanic Andean Warfare.* Unpublished Ph.D. Dissertation, Department of Anthropology, University of California, Los Angeles. University Microfilms, Ann Arbor.

Raymondi, Antonio
1874–1879. *El Perú – Historia de la Geografía del Perú.* 3 vols. Imprenta del Estado, Lima.

Regal Matienzo, Alberto
1936. *Los caminos del Inca en el antiguo Perú.* Sanmartí, Lima.
1972. *Los puentes del Inca en el antiguo Perú.* Imprenta Gráfica Industrial, Lima.

Reinhard, Johan
1985. Sacred Mountains: An Ethno-archaeological Study of High Andean Ruins. *Mountain Research and Development* 5(4):299–317.
1992. An Archaeological Investigation of Inca Ceremonial Platforms on the Volcano Copiapo, Central Chile. In *Ancient America: Contributions to New World Archaeology*, edited by Nicholas J. Saunders, pp. 145–72. Oxbow Monographs, no. 24. Oxford.
1993. Llullaillaco: An Investigation of the World's Highest Archaeological Site. *Latin American Indian Literatures Journal* 9(1):31–65.
1998. *Discovering the Inca Ice Maiden: My Adventures on Ampato.* National Geographic Society, Washington, D.C.
1999. Frozen in Time. *National Geographic Magazine* 196(5):36–55.

Reinhard, Johan, and Stephen Alvarez
1996. Peru's Ice Maidens: Unwrapping the Secrets. *National Geographic* 189(6):62–81.

Relaciones Geográficas de Indias (RGI)
1965. 3 vols. Biblioteca de Autores Españoles (continuación), vols. 183–5. Ediciones Atlas, Madrid. (Originally written 1557–86.)

Renard-Casevitz, F. M., Thierry Saignes, and A. C. Taylor
1986. *L'Inca, L'Espagnol, et les Sauvages.* Editions Recherche sur les Civilisations, Synthèse no. 21, Paris.

Rivera, Miguel
1976. La cerámica inca de Chinchero. In *Arqueología de Chinchero, 2. Cerámica y otros materiales.* José Alcina Franch et al. Memorias de la Misión Científica Española en Hispanoamerica, vol. 3, pp. 27–90. Ministerio de Asuntos Exteriores, Madrid.

Roman y Zamora, Jerónimo
1897. *Repúblicas de Indias, idolatrías y gobierno en México y Perú antes de la conquista*, vols. 1–2. Colección de Libros Raros o Curiosos que Tratan de América, vols. 14–15. V. Suárez, Madrid.

Rostworowski de Diez Canseco, María
1953. *Pachacutec Inca Yupanqui.* Editorial Torres Aguirre, Lima.
1960a. Succession, Coöption to Kingship, and Royal Incest among the Inca. *Southwestern Journal of Anthropology* 16:417–26.
1960b. *Pesos y medidas en el Perú pre-hispánico.* Imprenta Minerva, Lima.
1961. *Curacas y sucesiones costa norte.* Imprenta Minerva, Miraflores, Peru.

1962. Nuevos datos sobre tenencia de tierras reales en el incario. *Revista del Museo Nacional* 31:130–59.

1963. Dos manuscritos inéditos con datos sobre Manco II, tierras personales de los Incas y mitimaes. *Nueva Corónica* 1:223–39.

1966. Las tierras reales y su mano de obra en el Tahuantinsuyu. In *XXXVI Congreso Internacional de Americanistas, Spain 1964*, vol. 2, pp. 31–4. Seville.

1970a. El repartimiento de doña Beatriz Coya, en el valle de Yucay. *Historia y Cultura* 4:153–268.

1970b. Mercaderes del valle de Chincha en la época prehispánica: Un documento y unos comentarios. *Revista Española de Antropología Americana* 5:135–78.

1977. *Etnía y Sociedad Costa Peruana prehispánica*. Instituto de Estudios Peruanos, Lima.

1983. *Estructuras andinas del poder*. Instituto de Estudios Peruanos, Lima.

1989. *Costa peruana prehispánica*. Instituto de Estudios Andinos, Lima.

1990 (1988). *Conflicts over Coca Fields in XVIth-Century Peru*. University of Michigan, Museum of Anthropology, Memoirs, vol. 21. Ann Arbor.

1999. *History of the Inca Realm*. Translated by Harry B. Iceland. Cambridge University Press, Cambridge.

Rowe, Ann P.

1978. Technical Features of Inca Tapestry Tunics. *Textile Museum Journal* 17:5–28.

1997. Inca Weaving and Costume. *Textile Museum Journal* 34–5:5–54.

Rowe, John H.

1944. *An Introduction to the Archaeology of Cuzco*. Peabody Museum of American Archaeology and Ethnology, Papers, vol. 27, no. 2. Cambridge, MA.

1946. Inca Culture at the Time of the Spanish Conquest. In *Handbook of South American Indians*, edited by Julian Steward. Bulletin 143, vol. 2, pp. 183–330. Bureau of American Ethnology, Washington, D.C.

1948. The Kingdom of Chimor. *Acta Americana* 6:26–59.

1957. The Incas under Spanish Colonial Institutions. *The Hispanic American Historical Review* 37(2):155–99.

1958. The Age Grades of the Inca Census. In *Miscellanea Paul Rivet Octogenario Dicata II. XXXI Congreso Internacional de Americanistas*, pp. 499–522. Universidad Nacional Autónoma de México, Mexico.

1960. The Origins of Creator Worship among the Incas. In *Culture in History*, edited by Stanley Diamond, pp. 408–29. Columbia University Press, New York.

1967. What Kind of a Settlement was Inca Cuzco? *Ñawpa Pacha* 5:59–77.

1979a. An Account of the Shrines of Ancient Cuzco. *Ñawpa Pacha* 17:2–80.

1979b. Foreword. In *History of the Inca Empire*, edited by Roland Hamilton, pp. ix–xi. University of Texas Press, Austin.

1979c. Standardization in Inca Tapestry Tunics. In *The Junius B. Bird Pre-Columbian Textile Conference*, edited by Ann P. Rowe, Elizabeth P. Benson, and Anne-Louise Schaffer, pp. 239–64. The Textile Museum, Dumbarton Oaks, Washington, D.C.

1982. Inca Policies and Institutions Relating to the Cultural Unification of the Empire. In *The Inca and Aztec States 1400–1800: Anthropology and History*, edited by George A. Collier, Renato I. Rosaldo, and John D. Wirth, pp. 93–118. Academic Press, New York.

1985a. La constitución inca del Cuzco. *Histórica* 9(1):35–73.

1985b. Probanza de los Incas nietos de conquistadores. *Histórica* 9:193–245.

1990a. Foreword. In *Inca Religion and Customs*, edited by Roland Hamilton, pp. vii–ix. University of Texas Press, Austin.

1990b. Machu Picchu a la luz de documentos de siglo XVI. *Histórica* 14(1):139–54.

1991. Los monumentos perdidos de la plaza mayor del Cuzco incaico. *Saqsaywaman* 3:81–109.

1997. Las tierras reales de los incas. In *Arqueología, Antropología, e Historia en los Andes*, edited by Rafael Varón Gabai and Javier Flores Espinoza, pp. 277–87. Instituto de Estudios Peruanos, Lima.

Rowlands, Michael J., Mogens T. Larsen, and Kristian Kristiansen, eds.
1987. *Centre and Periphery in the Ancient World*. Cambridge University Press, Cambridge.

Ruiz de Arce, Juan
1933. Relación de servicios en Indias . . . *Boletín de la Real Academia de Historia* 102:327–84. (Originally written *ca.* 1545.)

Russell, Glenn S.
1988. *The Effect of Inka Administrative Policy on the Domestic Economy of the Wanka, Peru: The Production and Use of Stone Tools*. Ph.D. Dissertation, Department of Anthropology, University of California, Los Angeles.

Sadowski, Robert M.
1989. The Sky above the Incas: An Abridged Astronomical Calendar for the 16th Century. In *Time and Calendars in the Inca Empire*, edited by Mariusz S. Ziółkowski and Robert M. Sadowski, pp. 75–106. British Archaeological Reports, International Series, no. 479. Oxford.

Sahlins, Marshall David
1981. *Historical Metaphors and Mythical Realities: Structure in the Early History of the Sandwich Islands Kingdom*. University of Michigan Press, Ann Arbor.

Saignes, Thierry
1985. *Los Andes orientales: historia de un olvido*. Instituto Francés de Estudios Andinos and Centro de Estudios de la Realidad Económica y Social, Cochabamba, Bolivia.

Sallnow, Michael J.
1987. *Pilgrims of the Andes: Regional Cults in Cusco*. Smithsonian Institution Press, Washington, D.C.

Salomon, Frank
1986. *Native Lords of Quito in the Age of the Incas*. Cambridge University Press, Cambridge.

1987. A North Andean Status Trader Complex under Inka Rule. *Ethnohistory* 34(1):63–77.

1991. Introduction. In *The Huarochirí Manuscript: A Testament of Ancient and Colonial Andean Religion*, edited by Frank L. Salomon and Jorge Urioste. University of Texas Press, Austin.

Salomon, Frank, and Jorge Urioste, eds.
1991. *The Huarochirí Manuscript: A Testament of Ancient and Colonial Andean Religion (Often Attributed to Francisco de Avila)*. University of Texas Press, Austin.

Sámano-Xérez
1937. *Relación*. Cuadernos de Historia del Perú, edited by Raúl Porras Barrenechea, Paris.

Sancho de la Hoz, Pedro
1917. Relación. In *[1532–1533] Colección de Libros y Documentos Referentes a la Historia del Perú*, edited by Horacio H. Urteaga, vol. 5, pp. 122–202. Sanmartí, Lima. (Originally written 1532–3.)

Sandefur, Elsie
1988. *Andean Zooarchaeology: Animal Use and the Inka Conquest of the Upper Mantaro Valley*. Unpublished Ph.D. Dissertation, Institute of Archaeology, University of California, Los Angeles. University Microfilms, Ann Arbor.

Sandweiss, Daniel
1992. *The Archaeology of Chincha Fishermen: Specialization and Status in Inka Peru*. Carnegie Museum of Natural History, Bulletin no. 29. Pittsburgh.

Santillán, Hernando de
1968. *Relación del orígen, descendencia, política y gobierno de los incas*. Biblioteca de Autores Españoles (continuación), vol. 209, pp. 97–149. Ediciones Atlas, Madrid. (Originally written 1563.)

Santo Tomás, Fray Domingo de
1951. *Lexicón, o vocabulario de la lengua general del Perú*. Facsimile edition by Raúl Porras Barranechea, Lima. (Originally written 1560.)

Sarmiento de Gamboa, Pedro
1960. *Historia de los Incas*. Biblioteca de Autores Españoles (continuación), vol. 135, pp. 193–297. Ediciones Atlas, Madrid. (Originally written 1572.)

Scattolin, María Cristina, and Verónica Williams
1992. Actividades minero-metalúrgicas prehispánicas en el noroeste argentino: nuevas evidencias y su significación. *Bulletin de L'Institut Français D'Études Andines* 21(1):59–87.

Schaedel, Richard P.
1978. Early State of the Incas. In *The Early State*, edited by Henri M. Claessen and Peter Skalnik, pp. 289–320. Mouton, The Hague.

Schjellerup, Inge
1997. *Incas and Spaniards in the Conquest of the Chachapoyas: Archaeological and Ethnohistorical Research in the North-Eastern Andes of Peru*. Gothenberg University, Dept. of Archaeology, Series B. Gothenberg Archaeological Theses, no. 7. Gothenberg.

Schobinger, Juan
1995. *Anconcagua. Un enterratoria incaico a 5.300 metros de altura*. Inca Editorial, Mendoza, Argentina.

Schobinger, Juan, et al.
1966. La "momia" del Cerro el Toro. *Suplemento al tomo 21 de Anales de Arqueología y Etnología.*

Schreiber, Katharina J.
1987. Conquest and Consolidation: A Comparison of the Wari and Inka Occupations of a Highland Peruvian Valley. *American Antiquity* 52:266–84.
1992. *Wari Imperialism in Middle Horizon Peru.* Anthropological Papers No. 87, Museum of Anthropology, University of Michigan, Ann Arbor.

Sciscento, Margaret Mary
1990. *Imperialism in the High Andes: Inka and Wari Involvement in the Chuquibamba Valley, Peru.* Unpublished Ph.D. Dissertation, Department of Anthropology, University of California, Santa Barbara. University Microfilms, Ann Arbor.

Segovia, Bartolomé de
1943. Relación de muchas cosas acaecidas en el Peru . . . In *Los Pequeños Grandes Libros de Historia Americana,* ser. 1 [incorrectly attributed to Cristóbal de Molina (el Almagrista)], vol. 4, pp. 1–78 [first document]. Librería e Imprenta D. Miranda, Lima. (Originally written 1553.)
1968. Relación de muchas cosas acaecidas en el Peru . . . In *Crónicas peruanas de interés indígena* [often attributed to Cristóbal de Molina (el Almagrista)]. Biblioteca de Autores Españoles vol. 209. Ediciones Atlas, Madrid. (Originally written 1553.)

Seltzer, Geoffrey O., and Christine A. Hastorf
1990. Climatic Change and its Effect on Prehispanic Agriculture in the Central Peruvian Andes. *Journal of Field Archaeology* 17:397–414.

Sherbondy, Jeanette E.
1992. Water Ideology in Inca Ethnogenesis. In *Andean Cosmologies Through Time,* edited by Robert V. H. Dover, Katharine E. Seibold, and John H. McDowell, pp. 46–66. Indiana University Press, Bloomington.
1994. Water and Power: The Role of Irrigation Districts in the Transition from Inca to Spanish Cuzco. In *Irrigation at High Altitudes: The Social Organization of Water Control Systems in the Andes,* edited by William P. Mitchell and David Guillet. Society for Latin American Anthropology Publication Series, vol. 12, pp. 69–97. American Anthropological Association, Washington, D.C.

Shimada, Izumi
1994. *Pampa Grande and the Mochica Culture.* 1st edn. University of Texas Press, Austin.

Silva, Osvaldo
1986. Los promaucaes y la frontera meridional incaica en Chile. In *Cuadernos de Historia 6,* Santiago, Chile.

Silva Sifuentes, Jorge
1995. *El Imperio de los Incas.* Fondo Editorial de Cofide, Lima.

Silverblatt, Irene
1978. Andean Women in the Inca Empire. *Feminist Studies* 4(3):37–61.
1987. *Moon, Sun, Witches: Gender Ideologies and Class in Inca and Colonial Peru.* Princeton University Press, Princeton, NJ.

Sinopoli, Carla M.
   1994. The Archaeology of Empires. *Annual Review of Anthropology* 23:159–80.
Smith, Michael
   1996. *The Aztecs*. Blackwell, New York.
Snead, James
   1992. Imperial Infrastructure and the Inka State Storage System. In *Inka Storage Systems*, edited by Terry Y. LeVine, pp. 62–106. University of Oklahoma Press. Norman.
Spalding, Karen
   1985. *Huarochirí*. Stanford University Press, Stanford.
Spurling, Geoffrey E.
   1982. Inka militarism. (MS.)
   1992. *The Organization of Craft Production in the Inka State: The Potters and Weavers of Milliraya*. Unpublished Ph.D. Dissertation, Department of Anthropology, Cornell University. University Microfilms, Ann Arbor.
Squier, Ephraim George
   1877. *Peru: Incidents of Travel and Exploration in the Land of the Incas*. Macmillan, London.
Stanish, Charles
   1997. Nonmarket Imperialism in the Prehispanic Americas: The Inka Occupation of the Titicaca Basin. *Latin American Antiquity* 8:195–216.
Stanish, Charles, and Lee Steadman
   1994. *Archaeological Research at the Site of Tumatumani, Juli, Peru*. Fieldiana Anthropology, no. 23. The Field Museum of Natural History, Chicago.
Stehberg, Rubén
   1976. *La Fortaleza de Chena y su relación con la ocupación incaica de Chile Central*. Museo Nacional de Historia Natural, Publicación Ocasional, no. 23. Santiago, Chile.
Stehberg, Rubén, and Nazareno Carvajal
   1988. Road System of the Incas in the South Part of their Tawantinsuyu Empire. *National Geographic Research* 4(1):74–87.
Stein, Gil J.
   2000. *Rethinking World-Systems*. University of Arizona Press, Tucson.
Stern, Steven
   1982. *Peru's Indian Peoples and the Challenge of Spanish Conquest*. University of Wisconsin Press, Madison.
Strube Erdmann, León
   1963. *Vialidad Imperial de los Incas*. Serie Histórica no. 33. Instituto de Estudios Americanistas, Facultad de Filosofía y Humanidades, Universidad Nacional de Córdoba, Córdoba, Argentina.
Thomas, R. Brooke
   1973. *Human Adaptation to a High Andean Energy Flow System*. Department of Anthropology, Pennsylvania State University, Occasional Papers in Anthropology, no. 7. University Park.

Thompson, Donald E.

1967. Investigaciones arqueológicas en las aldeas chupachu de Ichu y Auquimarka. In *Visita de la Provincia de León de Huánuco en 1562, Iñigo Ortiz de Zúñiga, visitador*, edited by John V. Murra, vol. 1, pp. 357–62. Universidad Nacional Hermilio Valdizán, Huánuco, Peru.

Thompson, Donald E., and John V. Murra

1966. The Inca Bridges in the Huánuco Region. *American Antiquity* 31:632–9.

Titu Cusi Yupanqui, Inca Diego de Castro

1916. Relación de la conquista del Perú y hechos del Inca Manco II; Instrucción para el muy Ille. Señor Ldo. Lope Garciá de Castro, Gouernador que fue destos rreynos del Pirú. *Colección de Libros y Documentos Referentes a la Historia del Perú*, edited by Horacio H. Urteaga, ser. 1, vol. 2. Sanmartí, Lima. (Originally written 1570.)

Toledo, Francisco de

1940a. Información hecha por orden de Don Francisco de Toledo en su visita de las Provincias del Perú, en la que declaran indios ancianos sobre el derecho de los cicaciques y sobre el gobierno que tenían aquellos pueblos antes que los Incas los conquistasen. In *Don Francisco de Toledo, supremo organizador del Peru: Su vida, su obra [1515–1582]*, edited by Roberto Levillier, vol. 2, pp. 14–37. Espasa-Calpe, Buenos Aires. (Originally written 1570.)

1940b. Información hecha en el Cuzco por orden del Virrey Toledo, con respuestas al mismo interrogatorio utilizado en las cuatro informaciones anteriores. Anadese un auto del año 1563 del Conde de Nieva, en el cual otorga ese Virrey investidura a un cacique en la misma forma en que antes la daban los incas a los curacas. In *Don Francisco de Toledo, supremo organizador del Peru: Su vida, su obra [1515–1582]*, edited by Roberto Levillier, vol. 2, pp. 65–98. Espasa-Calpe, Buenos Aires. (Originally written 1571.)

Tomka, Steven A.

1987. Resource Ownership and Utilization Patterns among the Yanque-Collaguas as Manifested in the Visita de Yanque-Collaguas, 1591. *Andean Perspective Newsletter* 5:15–24.

1994. *Quinua and Camelids on the Bolivian Altiplano: An Ethnoarchaeological Approach to Agro-Pastoral Subsistence with an Emphasis on Agro-Pastoral Transhumance*. Unpublished Ph.D. Dissertation, Department of Anthropology, University of Texas, Austin. University Microfilms, Ann Arbor.

Torero, Alfredo

1964. Los dialectos quechuas. *Anales Científicos* 2:446–78.

1974. *El quechua y la historia social andina*. Universidad Ricardo Palma, Lima.

Tosi, Joseph A., Jr.

1960. *Zonas de vida natural en el Perú: Memoria explicativa sobre el mapa ecológico del Perú*. Instituto Interamericano de Ciencias Agrícolas de la OEA, Zona Andina, Boletín Técnico no. 5. Lima.

Trimborn, Hermann

1925. Straftat und Sühne in Alt-Peru. *Zeitschrift für Ethnologie* 57:194–240.

1937. Der Rechtsbruch in den Hochkuturen Amerikas. *Zeitschrift für vergleichende Rechtswissenschaft* 51:8–129.

Troll, Carl
  1968. The cordilleras of the Tropical Americas. In *Geo-ecology of the Mountainous Regions of the Tropical Americas*, edited by Carl Troll. Proceedings of the UNESCO Mexico Symposium, 1966, pp. 13–56. Ferd. Dümmlers Verlag, Bonn.
Truhan, Deborah L.
  1997. Demografía y etnicidad: Los Cañaris del Corregimiento de Cuenca, siglos XVI–XVII. Paper delivered at the 49th International Congress of Americanists, Quito.
Trujillo, Diego de
  1967/1985. *Relación del descubrimiento del reino del Peru* . . . , edited by Concepción Bravo, pp. 191–206. Historia 16, Madrid. (Originally written 1571.)
Ubbelohde-Doering, Heinrich
  1967. *On the Royal Highway of the Inca.* Translated by Margaret Brown. Praeger, New York.
Uhle, Max
  1903. *Pachacamac – Report of the William Pepper, M.D., LL.D., Peruvian Expedition of 1896.* Department of Archaeology, University of Pennsylvania, Philadelphia.
  1909. La esfero de influencias del país de los incas. *Revista Histórica* 4:5–40.
  1917. Fortalezas incaicas: Incallacta – Machupichu. *Revista Chilena de Historia y Geografía* 21:154–70.
  1923. *Las Ruinas de Tombebamba.* Imprenta Julio Sáenz Rebolledo, Quito.
Urton, Gary
  1981. *At the Crossroads of the Earth and the Sky: An Andean Cosmology.* University of Texas Press, Austin.
  1990. *The History of a Myth: Pacariqtambo and the Origin of the Inkas.* University of Texas Press, Austin.
  1995. A New Twist in an Old Yarn: Variation in Knot Directionality in the Inka Khipus. *Baessler-Archiv n.F. Band* 42:271–305.
  1997. *The Social Life of Numbers.* University of Texas Press, Austin.
  1999. *Inca Myths.* 1st University of Texas Press edn. University of Texas Press, Austin.
  2001. A calendrical and demographic tomb text from northern Peru. *Latin American Antiquity* 12:127–47.
Vaca de Castro Cavellero, Cristobal
  1908. Ordenanzas de tambos. *Revista Histórica* 3:427–92. (Originally written 1543.)
Valcárcel, Carlos Daniel
  1987. *Historia de la educación inkaica.* Editorial Educativa INIDE, Lima.
Valcárcel, Luis E.
  1934–5. Sajsawaman Redescubierto. 3 parts. *Revista del Museo Nacional* 3(1–2):3–36.
Valdivia, Pedro de
  1960. *Carta al Emperador Carlos V.* Biblioteca de Autores Españoles (continuación), vol. 131, pp. 3–74. Ediciones Atlas, Madrid.

Valencia Z., A.
   1982. Complejo arqueológico de Yucay. In *Arqueología de Cuzco*, edited by
   I. Oberti R., pp. 65–80. Ediciones Instituto Nacional de Cultural, Cuzco.
Valera, Blas
   1945. La Historia de los Incas. In *Las Costumbres Antiguas de los Incas*, edited
   by Francisco de Loyaza. Pequeños Grandes Libros de Historia Americana,
   ser. 1, vol. 8, Lima. (Originally written *ca.* 1585–90.)
Vallis, G. K.
   1986. El Niño: A Chaotic Dynamical System? *Science* 232:243–5.
Valverde, María Ramírez
   1970. Visita a Pocona. *Historia y Cultura* 4:269–308. (Originally written 1557.)
Van Buren, Mary
   1996. Rethinking the Vertical Archipelago: Ethnicity, Exchange, and History
   in the South Central Andes. *American Anthropologist* 98(2):338–51.
Van Creveld, Martin L.
   1977. *Supplying War: Logistics from Wallenstein to Patton.* 1st paperback
   edn. Cambridge University Press, New York.
Van de Guchte, Maarten J. D.
   1990. *"Carving the World": Inca Monumental Sculpture and Landscape.*
   Unpublished Ph.D. Dissertation, Department of Anthropology, University of
   Illinois at Urbana-Champaign. University Microfilms, Ann Arbor.
Varón Gabai, Rafael, and Javier Flores Espinoza, eds.
   1997. *Arqueología, antropología e historia en los Andes: Homenaje a María
   Rostworowski.* IEP/Banco Central de Reserva del Peru, Lima.
Villanueva Urteaga, H.
   1971. Documentos sobre Yucay, siglo XVI. *Revista del Archivo Histórico de
   Cuzco* 13:1–148.
Villanueva Urteaga, Horacio, and Jeanette Sherbondy
   1979. *Cuzco: aguas y poder*, vol. 1. Centro de Estudios Rurales Andinos Bar-
   tolomé de Las Casas, Cuzco.
Wachtel, Nathan
   1977. *The Vision of the Vanquished.* Translated by Ben Reynolds and Sian
   Reynolds. Barnes and Noble, New York.
   1982. The Mitimas of the Cochabamba Valley: The Colonization Policy of
   Huayna Capac. In *The Inca and Aztec States 1400–1800: Anthropology and
   History*, edited by George A. Collier, Renato I. Rosaldo, and John D. Wirth,
   pp. 199–235. Academic Press, New York.
   1986. Men of the Water: The Uru Problem (Sixteenth and Seventeenth
   Centuries). In *Anthropological History of Andean Polities*, edited by John
   V. Murra, Nathan Wachtel, and Jacques Revel, pp. 283–310. Cambridge
   University Press, Cambridge.
Wallerstein, Immanuel
   1974. *The Modern World-System I.* Academic Press, New York.
Wedin, Åke
   1965. *El sistema decimal en el imporio incaico; estudio sobre estructura
   política, división territorial y población.* Instituto Ibero-American Gotem-
   burgo, Gothenberg, Sweden.

West, Terry L.
1981. Llama Caravans of the Andes. *Natural History* 90(12):62–73.

Wicander, Reed, and James S. Monroe
1989. *Historical Geology: Evolution of the Earth and Life through Time.* West Publishing Co., St. Paul.

Wiener, Charles
1880. *Pérou et Bolivie.* Librairie Hachette, Paris.

Williams, Verónica I.
1983. Evidencia de actividad textil en el establecimiento incaico Potrero Chaquiago (Provincia de Catamarca). *Relaciones de la Sociedad Argentina de Antropología* 15:49–59.
1996. *La ocupación inka en la región central de Catamarca (República Argentina).* Ph. D. Dissertation, Facultad de Ciencias Naturales. La Plata, Universidad Nacional de La Plata.

Williams, Verónica I., and Ana María Lorandi
1986. *Evidencias funcionales de un establecimiento incaico en el noroeste argentino.* Comechingonia, Vol. Homenaje al 450 Congreso Internacional de Americanistas (Bogotá), Córdoba.

Windley, B. F.
1995. *The Evolving Continents.* 3rd edn. Wiley, New York.

Winterhalder, Bruce
1994. The Ecological Basis of Water Management in the Central Andes: Rainfall and Temperature in Southern Peru. In *Irrigation at High Altitudes: The Social Organization of Water Control Systems in the Andes,* edited by William P. Mitchell and David Guillet. Society for Latin American Anthropology Publication Series 12, pp. 21–67. American Anthropological Association, Washington, D.C.

Wolf, Eric R.
1982. *Europe and the People without History.* University of California Press, Berkeley and Los Angeles.

World Weather Records 1951–60
1966. *South America, Central America, West Indies, and Caribbean and Bermuda,* vol. 3. United States Department of Commerce, Environmental Science Service Administration, Environmental Data Services. U.S. Government Printing Office, Washington, D.C.

Xérez, Francisco de
1985. *Verdadera Relación de la Conquista del Perú y Provincia del Cuzco llamada la Nueva Castilla,* edited by Concepcion Bravo. Historia 16, Madrid. (Originally written 1534.)

Zárate, Augustín de
1862. *Historia del descubrimiento y conquista de la Provincia del Perú.* Biblioteca de Autores Españoles (continuación), vol. 26, pp. 459–574. Ediciones Atlas, Madrid. (Originally written 1555.)

Ziółkowski, Mariusz S.
1996. *La guerra de los wawqi: los objetivos y los mecanismos de la rivalidad dentro de la élite inka, siglos XV–XVI.* Ediciones Abya-Yala, Quito-Ecuador.

Ziółkowski, Mariusz S., and Robert M. Sadowski, eds.

> 1989. *Time and Calendars in the Inca Empire*. British Archaeological Reports, International Series, no. 479. Oxford.

Zuidema, R. Tom

> 1964. *The Ceque System of Cuzco*. Translated by Eva M. Hooykaas. International Archives of Ethnography, Supplement to vol. 50. E. J. Brill, Leiden, Netherlands.

> 1977a. The Inca Calendar. In *Native American Astronomy*, edited by Anthony F. Aveni, pp. 219–59. University of Texas Press, Austin.

> 1977b. The Inca Kinship System: A New Theoretical View. In *Andean Kinship and Marriage*, edited by Ralph Bolton and Enrique Mayer, pp. 240–81. American Anthropological Association Special Publication, no. 7, Washington, D.C.

> 1982. Myth and History in Ancient Peru. In *The Logic of Culture*, edited by I. Rossi, pp. 150–75. Bergin, South Hadley, MA.

> 1983. Hierarchy and Space in Incaic Social Organization. *Ethnohistory* 30:49–75.

> 1990. *Inca Civilization in Cuzco*. Translated by Jean-Jacques Decoster. University of Texas Press, Austin.

> 1991. Guaman Poma and the Art of Empire: Toward an Iconography of Inca Royal Dress. In *Transatlantic Encounters: Europeans and Andeans in the Sixteenth Century*, edited by K. J. Andrien and Rolena Adorno, pp. 151–275. University of California Press, Berkeley.

Zuidema, R. Tom, and D. Poole

> 1982. Los límites de los cuatro suyus incaicos en el Cuzco. *Bulletin de L'Institut Français d'Études Andines* 11(1–2):83–9.

Index

Page numbers in *italic* refer to illustrations.